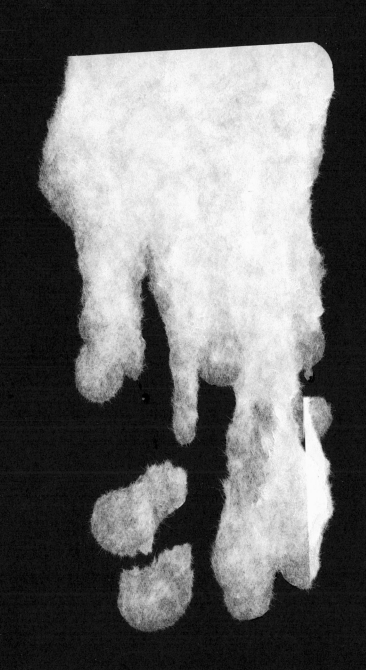

LEWIS CARROLL'S
SYMBOLIC LOGIC

Charles Lutwidge Dodgson, a self-portrait. Dodgson was born on January 27, 1832, and died on January 14, 1898. The logician who as Lewis Carroll wrote *Alice's Adventures in Wonderland* was also an avid amateur photographer, specializing in portraiture. This print was made from the original five-by-six-inch glass negative in the Gernsheim Collection. The negative has the inventory number 2439 in Dodgson's handwriting on it. (Gernsheim Collection, Humanities Research Center, University of Texas, Austin)

LEWIS CARROLL'S

SYMBOLIC LOGIC

SYMBOLIC LOGIC
by Lewis Carroll

Part I, Elementary, 1896. Fifth Edition.
Part II, Advanced, never previously published.

Together with Letters from Lewis Carroll to eminent nineteenth-century Logicians and to his "logical sister," and eight versions of the Barber-Shop Paradox.

Edited, with annotations and an introduction, by
WILLIAM WARREN BARTLEY, III

Clarkson N. Potter, Inc., Publishers, New York

DISTRIBUTED BY CROWN PUBLISHERS, INC.

Library of Congress Cataloging in Publication Data

Dodgson, Charles Lutwidge, 1832–1898.
    Lewis Carroll's Symbolic logic.

    1. Logic, Symbolic and mathematical. I. Title.
II. Title: Symbolic logic.
BC135.D67 1977   511'.3   76-20589
ISBN 0-517-52383-3

Dedicated
to the Memory
of Aristotle

Note to the Reader
From the Editor
and Publisher

A few of the author's examples, which refer in preposterous ways to certain minority groups, may strike some readers as offensive. These examples were always intended to appear absurd. The logician W. E. Johnson, a contemporary of Lewis Carroll, described Carroll's method as that of selecting "propositions which are obviously false." There is nonetheless no doubt that were the author alive today he would have chosen different examples. For he was sensitive to points of taste and went to some lengths to avoid giving offence and to censure those who did. For the editor or publisher to have removed these examples now, however, would have been to do violence to a work that we wished to publish in its original form. We trust that readers encountering offensive statements—whether they be offensive to minorities or offensive to majorities—may place them in their historical setting.

CONTENTS

Editor's Introduction 3

Editor's Acknowledgements 37

Editor's Bibliography 39

Part One

Elementary

Introduction to Learners 51

Preface to Fourth Edition 55

BOOK I THINGS AND THEIR ATTRIBUTES 59

Chapter I 〰 Introductory 59

Things 59
Attributes 59
Adjuncts 59

Chapter II 〰 Classification 60

Classification 60
Class 60
Peculiar Attributes 60
Genus 60
Species 60
Differentia 60
Real and **Unreal**, or **Imaginary**, Classes 60

Individual   61
A Class regarded as a single Thing   61

Chapter III ⚓ Division   61

[§1] *Introductory*   61

Division   61
Codivisional Classes   62

[§2] *Dichotomy*   62

Dichotomy   62
Arbitrary limits of Classes   62
Subdivision of Classes   63

Chapter IV ⚓ Names   63

Name   63
Real and **Unreal** Names   64
Three ways of expressing a Name   64
Two senses in which a plural Name may be used   64

Chapter V ⚓ Definitions   65

Definition   65
Examples worked as models   65

BOOK II PROPOSITIONS   67

Chapter I ⚓ Propositions Generally   67

[§1] *Introductory*   67

Technical meaning of "some"   67
Proposition   67
Normal form of a Proposition   67
Subject, Predicate, and **Terms**   67

[§2] *Normal form of a Proposition*   68

Its four parts:
  (1) **Sign of Quantity**   68
  (2) Name of Subject   68

  (3) **Copula**   68
  (4) Name of Predicate   68

[§3] *Various kinds of Propositions*   68

 Three kinds of Propositions:
  (1) Begins with "Some."   Called a **Particular** Proposition: also a
   Proposition **in I**   68
  (2) Begins with "No."   Called a **Universal Negative** Proposition:
   also a Proposition **in E**   68
  (3) Begins with "All."   Called a **Universal Affirmative** Proposition: also a Proposition **in A**   68
 A Proposition, whose Subject is an Individual, is to be regarded as
 Universal   68
 Two kinds of Propositions: Propositions of Existence, and Propositions
 of Relation   69

Chapter II ✵ Propositions of Existence   69
 Proposition of Existence   69

Chapter III ✵ Propositions of Relation   70

[§1] *Introductory*   70

 Proposition of Relation   70
 Universe of Discourse, or **Univ.**   70

[§2] *Reduction of a Proposition of Relation to Normal form*   71

 Rules   71
 Examples worked   71

[§3] *A Proposition of Relation, beginning with "All," is a Double Proposition*   74

 Its equivalence to *two* Propositions   75

[§4] *What is implied, in a Proposition of Relation, as to the Reality of its
Terms?*   76

 Propositions beginning with "Some"   76
 Propositions beginning with "No"   76
 Propositions beginning with "All"   76

[§5] *Translation of a Proposition of Relation into one or more Propositions
of Existence*   76

 Rules   77
 Examples worked   77

BOOK III THE BILITERAL DIAGRAM   79

Chapter I 𝔛 Symbols and Cells   79

The Diagram assigned to a certain Set of Things, viz. our Univ.   79
Univ. divided into the x-Class and the x'-Class   79
The North and South Halves assigned to these two Classes   79
The x-Class subdivided into the xy-Class and the xy'-Class   80
The North-West and North-East Cells assigned to these two Classes   80
The x'-Class similarly divided   80
The South-West and South-East Cells similarly assigned   80
The West and East Halves have thus been assigned to the y-Class and
    the y'-Class   80
Table I. Adjuncts of Classes, and Compartments, or Cells, assigned
    to them   81

Chapter II 𝔛 Counters   82

Meaning of a Red Counter placed in a Cell   82
Meaning of a Red Counter placed on a Partition   82
American phrase **sitting on the fence**   82
Meaning of a Grey Counter placed in a Cell   82

Chapter III 𝔛 Representation of Propositions   82

[§1] *Introductory*   82

The word "Things" to be henceforwards omitted   82
Uniliteral Proposition   83
Biliteral Proposition   83
Proposition **in terms of** certain Letters   83

[§2] *Representation of Propositions of Existence*   83

The Proposition "Some x exist"   83
Three other similar Propositions   83
The Proposition "No x exist"   83
Three other similar Propositions   84
The Proposition "Some xy exist"   84
Three other similar Propositions   84
The Proposition "No xy exist"   84
Three other similar Propositions   84
The Proposition "No x exist" is *Double*, and is equivalent to the two
    Propositions "No xy exist" and "No xy' exist"   85

[§3] *Representation of Propositions of Relation*   85

The Proposition "Some x are y"   85

Three other similar Propositions 85

The Proposition "Some y are x" 85

Three other similar Propositions 86

Trio of equivalent Propositions, viz.
 Some xy exist $=$ Some x are y $=$ Some y are x 86

Converse Propositions, and **Conversion** 86

Three other similar Trios 86

The Proposition "No x are y" 86

Three other similar Propositions 87

The Proposition "No y are x" 87

Three other similar Propositions 87

Trio of equivalent Propositions, viz.
 No xy exist $=$ No x are y $=$ No y are x 87

Three other similar Trios 88

The Proposition "All x are y" 88

The Proposition "All x are y" is *Double*, and is equivalent to the two Propositions "Some x are y" and "No x are y'" 88

Tables II, III. Representation of Propositions of Existence and Relation 88

Seven other similar Propositions 89

Chapter IV ⚜ Interpretation of Biliteral Diagram, When Marked with Counters 90

Interpretation of ⊡ 90

And of three other similar arrangements 90

Interpretation of ◻ 91

And of three other similar arrangements 91

Interpretation of ⊡ 91

And of three other similar arrangements 91

Interpretation of ⊙⊙ 91

And of three other similar arrangements 91

Interpretation of ○○ 91

And of three other similar arrangements 91

Interpretation of ⊙○ 91

And of seven other similar arrangements 92

BOOK IV THE TRILITERAL DIAGRAM   93

Chapter I ⚜ Symbols and Cells   93

Change of Biliteral into Triliteral Diagram   93
The *xy*-Class subdivided into the *xym*-Class and the *xym'*-Class   93
The Inner and Outer Cells of the North-West Quarter assigned to
    these Classes   94
The *xy'*-Class, the *x'y*-Class, and the *x'y'*-Class similarly subdivided   94
The Inner and Outer Cells of the North-East, the South-West, and the
    South-East Quarters similarly assigned   94
The Inner Square and the Outer Border have thus been assigned to
    the *m*-Class and the *m'*-Class   94
Rules for finding readily the Compartment, or Cell, assigned to any
    given Attribute or Attributes   94
Table IV. Attributes of Classes, and Compartments, or Cells,
    assigned to them   95

Chapter II ⚜ Representation of Propositions in Terms of *x* and *m*, or of *y* and *m*   96

[§1] *Representation of Propositions of Existence in terms of* x *and* m, *or of* y *and* m   96

The Proposition "Some *xm* exist"   96
Seven other similar Propositions   96
The Proposition "No *xm* exist"   96
Seven other similar Propositions   96

[§2] *Representation of Propositions of Relation in terms of* x *and* m, *or of* y *and* m   97

The Pair of Converse Propositions
    Some *x* are *m* = Some *m* are *x*   97
Seven other similar Pairs   97
The Pair of Converse Propositions
    No *x* are *m* = No *m* are *x*   97
Seven other similar Pairs   97
The Proposition "All *x* are *m*"   97
Fifteen other similar Propositions   97
Tables V, VI, VII, VIII. Representation of Propositions in terms of
    x and *m*, or of *y* and *m*   98

Chapter III ⚔ Representation of Two Propositions of Relation, One in Terms of *x* and *m*, and the Other in Terms of *y* and *m*, on the Same Diagram 102

The Digits I and O to be used instead of Red and Grey Counters 102
Rules 102
Examples worked 102

Chapter IV ⚔ Interpretation, in Terms of *x* and *y*, of Triliteral Diagram, When Marked with Counters or Digits 104

Rules 104
Examples worked 105

BOOK V SYLLOGISMS 107

Chapter I ⚔ Introductory 107

Syllogism 107
Premisses 107
Conclusion 107
Eliminands 107
Retinends 107
Consequent 107
The Symbol ∴ 107
Specimen-Syllogisms 108

Chapter II ⚔ Problems in Syllogisms 109

[§1] *Introductory* 109

Concrete and **Abstract** Propositions 109
Method of translating a Proposition from concrete into abstract form 109
Two forms of Problems 109

[§2] *Given a Pair of Propositions of Relation, which contain between them a Pair of codivisional Classes, and which are proposed as Premisses: to ascertain what Conclusion, if any, is consequent from them* 110

Rules 110
Examples worked fully 110
The same worked briefly, as models 113

[§3] *Given a Trio of Propositions of Relation, of which every two contain a Pair of codivisional Classes, and which are proposed as a Syllogism: to ascertain whether the proposed Conclusion is consequent from the proposed Premisses, and, if so, whether it is complete*   115

    Rules   115
    Examples worked briefly, as models   115

BOOK VI   THE METHOD OF SUBSCRIPTS   119

Chapter I Introductory   119

    Meaning of x_1, xy_1, &c.   119
    Entity   119
    Meaning of x_0, xy_0, &c.   119
    Nullity   119
    The Symbols † and ℙ   119
    Like and **Unlike** Signs   120

Chapter II Representation of Propositions
of Relation   120

    The Pair of Converse Propositions
      Some x are y = Some y are x 120
    Three other similar Pairs   120
    The Pair of Converse Propositions
      No x are y = No y are x 120
    Three other similar Pairs   120
    The Proposition "All x are y"   121
    The Proposition "All x are y" is *Double*, and is equivalent to the two
      Propositions "Some x exist" and "No x are y'"   121
    Seven other similar Propositions   121
    Rule for translating: "All x are y" from abstract into subscript form, and
      vice versa   121

Chapter III Syllogisms   122

[§1] *Representation of Syllogisms*   122

    Rules   122

[§2] *Formulæ for solving Problems in Syllogisms* 122

Three Formulæ worked out:

Fig. I. $xm_0 \dagger ym'_0 \parallel xy_0$, its two Variants ($\alpha$) and ($\beta$) 124

Fig. II. $xm_0 \dagger ym_1 \parallel x'y_1$ 124

Fig. III. $xm_0 \dagger ym_0 \dagger m_1 \parallel x'y'_1$ 125

Table IX. Formulæ and Rules 126

Examples worked briefly, as models 126

Notes 128

[§3] *Fallacies* 129

Fallacy 129

Method of finding Forms of Fallacies 129

Forms best stated in *words* 130

Three Forms of Fallacies:

(1) Fallacy of Like Eliminands not asserted to exist 130

(2) Fallacy of Unlike Eliminands with an Entity-Premiss 130

(3) Fallacy of two Entity-Premisses 131

[§4] *Method of proceeding with a given Pair of Propositions* 131

Rules 131

BOOK VII SORITESES 133

Chapter I ⚔ Introductory 133

Sorites 133

Premisses 133

Partial Conclusion 133

Complete Conclusion (or **Conclusion**) 133

Eliminands 133

Retinends 133

Consequent 133

The Symbol ∴ 133

Specimen-Soriteses 134

Chapter II ⚔ Problems in Soriteses 135

[§1] *Introductory* 135

Form of Problem 135

Two Methods of Solution 135

[§2] *Solution by Method of Separate Syllogisms* 135

Rules 135

Example worked 135

[§3] *Solution by Method of Underscoring*   138

    Underscoring   138
    Subscripts to be omitted   138
    Example worked fully   138
    Example worked briefly, as model   139
    Seventeen Examination-Papers   140

BOOK VIII EXAMPLES, ANSWERS, AND SOLUTIONS

BOOK VIII EXAMPLES, ANSWERS, AND SOLUTIONS   143

Chapter I ⚔ Examples   143

[§1] *Propositions of Relation, to be reduced to normal form*   143

[§2] *Pairs of Abstract Propositions, one in terms of* x *and* m, *and the other in terms of* y *and* m, *to be represented on the same Triliteral Diagram*   144

[§3] *Marked Triliteral Diagrams, to be interpreted in terms of* x *and* y   145

[§4] *Pairs of Abstract Propositions, proposed as Premisses: Conclusions to be found*   146

[§5] *Pairs of Concrete Propositions, proposed as Premisses: Conclusions to be found*   147

[§6] *Trios of Abstract Propositions, proposed as Syllogisms: to be examined* 153

[§7] *Trios of Concrete Propositions, proposed as Syllogisms: to be examined* 154

[§8] *Sets of Abstract Propositions, proposed as Premisses for Soriteses: Conclusions to be found*   158

[§9] *Sets of Concrete Propositions, proposed as Premisses for Soriteses: Conclusions to be found*   160

Chapter II ⚔ Answers   176

    Answers to
      §1   176
      §2   177
      §3   178
      §4   179
      §5   180
      §§6, 7   183
      §§8, 9   185

Chapter III ⚡ Solutions 187

[§1] *Propositions of Relation reduced to normal form* 187

Solutions for §1 187

[§2] *Method of Diagrams* 191

Solutions for
§4 Nos. 1–12 191
§5 Nos. 1–12 192
§6 Nos. 1–10 195
§7 Nos. 1–6 197

[§3] *Method of Subscripts* 199

Solutions for
§4 199
§5 Nos. 13–24 202
§5 Nos. 1–12 and 25–101 204
§6 207
§7 208
§8 216
§9 219

Part Two

Advanced

BOOK IX SOME ACCOUNT OF
PARTS II AND III 229

BOOK X INTRODUCTORY 231

Chapter I ⚡ Introductory 231

Chapter II ⚡ The Existential Import of Propositions 232

Letter from Lewis Carroll to T. Fowler, November 13, 1885 238

Chapter III ⚘ The Use of "Is-not"
(or "Are-not") as a Copula   238

Chapter IV ⚘ The Theory that Two Negative
Premisses Prove Nothing   240

Chapter V ⚘ Euler's Method of Diagrams   240

Chapter VI ⚘ Venn's Method of Diagrams   242

Chapter VII ⚘ My Method of Diagrams   244

Chapter VIII ⚘ Solution of a Syllogism by
Various Methods   246

    (1) Solution by ordinary Method   246
    (2) Symbolic Representation   247
    (3) Solution by Euler's Method of Diagrams   247
    (4) Solution by Venn's Method of Diagrams   249
    (5) Solution by my Method of Diagrams   249
    (6) Solution by my Method of Subscripts   249

Chapter IX ⚘ My Method of Treating Syllogisms
and Sorites   250

Notes to Book X   251

BOOK XI SYMBOLS, LOGICAL CHARTS   255

Chapter I ⚘ Logical Symbols   255

Chapter II ⚘ Figures or Forms   257
    Fig. I   258
    Fig. Iα 258
    Fig. Iβ 258
    Fig. II   258
    Fig. III   258
    Fig. IV   258
    Fig. V   259
    Fig. VI   260

Chapter III ⚘ Fallacies   260

Chapter IV ❧ Logical Charts 263

Logical Chart I 264
Logical Chart II 265
Logical Chart III 266
Logical Chart IV 267
Logical Chart V 268
Interpretation of Charts I–V 269
Interpretation of Chart VI 269
Logical Chart VI 270
Logical Chart VI* 271
Logical Chart VI** 272
Interpretation of Chart VII 273
Logical Chart VII 273
Illustrations from Carroll's Workbook of Logical Charts 275

BOOK XII THE METHOD OF TREES 279

Chapter I ❧ Introductory 279

Chapter II ❧ Sorites-Problems with Biliteral Premisses 280

Chapter III ❧ Sorites-Problems with Triliteral and Multiliteral Premisses 285

Tree 1 290
Tree 2 295
Tree 3 299
Tree 4 303
Letter from Carroll to John Cook Wilson, November 6, 1896 305
Tree 5 312

The Method of Trees: Appendix 318

BOOK XIII SOME PROBLEMS TO BE SOLVED BY THE METHODS OF PART II 321

Chapter I ❧ Introductory 321

Chapter II ⚔ Problems in Sequences   322

Tree for Problem One   322
Commentary on the Tree for Problem One   323
Tree for Problem Three   323
Addendum: Excerpts from the Eighth and Ninth Papers on Logic   323

Chapter III ⚔ The Problem of the School-Boys   326

Some answers to the Problem of the School-Boys   327
Tree I   328
Tree II   330
Tree III   331

Chapter IV ⚔ The Pork-Chop Problem   331

Version I   331
Version II   333
Solution to the Pork-Chop Problem   334
Pork-Chop Problem Dictionary   334
Pork-Chop Problem in Subscript Form   335
Pork-Chop Problem Register   335
Carroll's Letters to John Cook Wilson on the Pork-Chop Problem
  I.   November 12, 1896   336
  II. November 1, 1896   336
  III. November 12, 1896   337

Chapter V ⚔ Froggy's Problem   338

Dictionary for Froggy's Problem   342

Chapter VI ⚔ The Members of Parliament Problem   343

The Solution to the Members of Parliament Problem
  The Problem in Abstract Form   344
Carroll's Letters to John Cook Wilson concerning the Members of
Parliament Problem
  I.   October 29, 1896   345
  II. Undated, probably October 30, 1896   345
  III. November 3, 1896   346
Carroll's Letters to his sister Miss Louisa Dodgson concerning the
Members of Parliament Problem
  I.   November 16, 1896   346
  II. November 18, 1896
      Louisa Dodgson's Attempt to Solve the M.P. Problem   349

Chapter VII ❦ The Problem of Six Friends and their Wives   350

Version I   350
Version II   351

Chapter VIII ❦ The Problem of the Five Liars The Salt and Mustard Problem   352

The Problem of the Five Liars
  Version I   353
  Version II   354
Carroll's Letters to John Cook Wilson concerning the Five Liars and
Salt and Mustard Problems
    I.   October 25, 1896   355
   II.   October 28, 1896   356
  III. November 2, 1896   358
  IV. November 16, 1896   360
   V.   December 18, 1896   361

Chapter IX ❦ The Great-Grandson Problem   362

Solution to the Great-Grandson Problem
Carroll's Letters to John Cook Wilson about this Problem
    I. February 16, 1897   363
   II. May 17, 1897   363

Chapter X ❦ The Jack Sprat Problem   364

Carroll's letter to his sister, Miss Louisa Dodgson, of September 28,
1896, on the Jack Sprat Problem   365
An answer to the Jack Sprat Problem   372

Chapter XI ❦ The Library Problem   373

Carroll's Letters to John Cook Wilson relevant to the Library Problem
    I.   November 4, 1896   374
   II.   November 11, 1896   375
  III. November 18, 1896   376
  IV. November 26, 1896   376

Chapter XII ❦ The Pigs and Balloons Problem   378

Chapter XIII ❦ The Problem of Grocers on Bicycles   381

Chapter XIV 🕱 The Pets Problem   382

Chapter XV 🕱 The Winds and Windows Problem   382

BOOK XIV SOME FURTHER PROBLEMS TO
BE SOLVED BY THE METHODS OF PART II 385

Problems and Exercises 1–83   386

BOOK XXI LOGICAL PUZZLES   423

Chapter I 🕱 Introductory   423

Chapter II 🕱 Classical Puzzles   425

  1. Introductory   425
  2. Pseudomenos   425
  3. Crocodilus   425
  4. Antistrephon   426
  5. Achilles   426
  6. Raw Meat   426

Chapter III 🕱 Other Puzzles   427

  1. About Less   427
  2. Men Tall and Numerous   427
  3. The Socialist Orator and the Irish Mob 427
  4. Death at Any Moment   427
  5. The Small Girl and Her Sympathetic Friend 427
  6. A Notice at the Seaside   428
  7. On the Way to the Barber-Shop   428
  8. What the Tortoise Said to Achilles   431

Chapter IV 🕱 Solutions of Classical Puzzles   434

  1. Introductory   434
  2. Pseudomenos   434
  3. Crocodilus   436
  4. Antistrephon   438
  5. Achilles   438
  6. Raw Meat   439

Chapter V ⚔ Solutions of Other Puzzles 440

1. About Less 440
2. Men Tall and Numerous 440
3. The Socialist Orator and the Irish Mob 441
4. Death at Any Moment 441
7. On the Way to the Barber-Shop 442
   Letter to J. Welton on the Barber-Shop 443

Appendix A [to Book XXI] 444

Editor's Note on Carroll's Barber-Shop Paradox 444

Appendix B [to Book XXI]. Versions of the Barber-Shop Paradox 449

I. A Disputed Point in Logic. April 1894 451
II. A Disputed Point in Logic: A Concrete Example. April 11, 1894 453
III. A Disputed Point in Logic: A Concrete Example. April 16, 1894 453
IV. A Disputed Point in Logic. May 1, 1894 454
V. A Theorem in Logic. June 1894 455
VI. A Logical Paradox. July 1894 456
   Note 459
VII. A Logical Puzzle. September 1894 460

Appendix C [to Book XXI] 466

Editor's Note on Carroll's "What the Tortoise Said to Achilles" 466
Exchange of Correspondence between Carroll and G. F. Stout 471
Letter from Carroll to John Cook Wilson, December 14, 1896 475

BOOK XXII SOLUTIONS TO PROBLEMS SET BY OTHER WRITERS 477

Chapter I ⚔ Problems 477

Taken from the works of George Boole, Augustus DeMorgan, W. B. Grove, W. Stanley Jevons, John Neville Keynes, John Venn, and the Members of the Johns Hopkins University 477

Illustration from Carroll's Workbook, showing how he worked out some of the problems given 486

LEWIS CARROLL'S
SYMBOLIC LOGIC

SYMBOLIC LOGIC

Editor's Introduction, Acknowledgements, and Bibliography

"For a *complete* logical argument," Arthur began with admirable solemnity, "we need two prim Misses——"

"Of course!" she interrupted. "I remember that word now. And they produce——?"

"A Delusion," said Arthur.

"Ye—es?" she said dubiously. "I don't seem to remember that so well. But what is the *whole* argument called?"

"A Sillygism."

—From *Sylvie and Bruno* (p. 259)

Editor's Introduction

During the 1880s and 1890s, when Lewis Carroll (The Rev. C. L. Dodgson) was completing his last stories for children—*Sylvie and Bruno* and *Sylvie and Bruno Concluded*—he was also composing one of the most brilliantly eccentric logic textbooks ever written: a work in three parts, or volumes, titled simply *Symbolic Logic*.

Part I, published in 1896, is still read by most students of logic, and is widely quoted in modern logic textbooks. But Part II, on which Carroll was working when he died in January 1898, vanished without trace some seventy-six years ago. Many logicians have doubted that it ever existed, or have supposed either that Carroll never got to it or that, if he did get to it, he did not get far.

I have during the past eighteen years been able to locate the missing manuscript and galley proofs for Part II. Although not complete, it is longer and more important than Part I. In the pages that follow this material is published for the first time, together with a new, fifth edition of Part I.

This missing work is a contribution to literature as well as logic. The author of *Alice in Wonderland* and *Through the Looking-Glass*, the inventor of the Cheshire Cat, the White Rabbit, and the Gryphon, continued to create fabulous beasts as he grew older, and these wandered back and forth from *Sylvie and Bruno* to *Symbolic Logic*. There are famous crocodiles and frogs in *Sylvie and Bruno*. And in *Symbolic Logic* we find a moving logical paradox about a hungry crocodile and a delectable baby, as well as learning more about Froggy's character. Also brought to life in the pages of *Symbolic Logic* are the Small Girl and her Sympathetic Friend, Achilles and the Tortoise, the Crocodile and the Liar, the Three Barbers, the Five Liars, the pork-chop-eating Logician and Gambler. A few of these

characters are familiar, but most are brand new, and they sharpen their
wits on one another, and on us, in the pages that follow.

Symbolic logic was of course hardly the first among Lewis Carroll's
many interests. He was by profession, and under his real name, Charles
Lutwidge Dodgson, a geometer and Oxford don who lectured on mathematics. His first and glorious second string was, as Lewis Carroll, to
create *Alice in Wonderland* and *Through the Looking-Glass.* Logic was
probably not even Carroll's *second* second string. It has been written,
and may be true, that his "main interest in life was photography";
certainly he was among the most distinguished Victorian portrait
photographers, and among Victorian photographers of children he was
without peer.[1]

Yet his logic was his last, and in his own estimation, his most important
second string. *Symbolic Logic,* Part I, was published in February 1896.
By September 28 of that year, Carroll reported to his "mathematical
sister" Loui (Miss Louisa Dodgson) that he had abandoned his manuscript on "religious difficulties." That subject, he wrote to her, "is one
that hundreds of living men could do, if they would only try, *much* better
than I could, whereas there is no living man who could (or at any rate
who would take the trouble to) arrange & finish, & publish, the 2nd
Part of the Logic.... I am working at it, day & night."

He was still working at it on his deathbed in January 1898, and as we
know from his diaries and correspondence and from the testimony of his
nephew,[2] part of the work had been set in galley proof and was circulating
among friends and adversaries, such as John Cook Wilson, Professor of
Logic at Oxford.

Yet after his death, manuscript and galley proof vanished. Throughout
the years of posthumous fame that descended upon Lewis Carroll and his
family and their descendants like a whirlwind, through the years around
the centenary celebration of his birth in 1932—when bits of manuscript
and letters from him soared to record prices in the auctioning rooms—
not a whisper was heard of the missing work on logic. By 1955 it was as if
it had never existed: When the fourth edition of *Symbolic Logic,* Part I,

---

[1] See Helmut Gernsheim, *Lewis Carroll: Photographer,* revised edition (New York:
Dover Publications, 1969). The Gernsheim Collection of Lewis Carroll's
photographs is now housed in the Humanities Research Center of the University
of Texas, Austin.
[2] Stuart Dodgson Collingwood, *The Life and Letters of Lewis Carroll (Rev. C. L.
Dodgson)* (London: T. Fisher Unwin, 1898), p. 345.

was reprinted in America, its publisher remarked in his prefatory note that Part II had apparently not reached printing.

Lewis Carroll had anticipated that his work in logic might not survive his death, and he had taken careful steps to forestall this possibility. In a remarkable letter to his publisher, Frederick O. Macmillan (dated February 4, 1893), Carroll wrote: "I have been at the book for 20 years or more, & have a mass of M.S. on hand, but I doubt if any one, but myself, would understand it enough to get it through the Press. So if, at my decease, it were still M.S., it would all be wasted labour. What I want to do is, to get it all into type, & arranged: then it could be utilised even if I did not live to complete it. I could do this in the course of the next 3 or 4 months; & then I should want to publish Part I only, & keep Parts II & III standing in type for a year or more, as it would need a great deal of revision, & correction, for which I should submit copies, in slip, to all my friends. Could this be managed?"

Some such arrangement was managed. And much of Carroll's projected work did reach printing. The larger part of it has been in Oxford the whole time. I discovered one book (that is, one chapter) of *Symbolic Logic*, Part II, some eighteen years ago, at Christ Church, Oxford, Carroll's college. After a decade of searching, I found in New York City, in the winter of 1969, three more books set in galley proof. In 1972 and 1973 I came upon more workbooks, manuscripts, and typesetting for Part II in Princeton and in Texas. A detailed account of my search, and of these findings, is given below.

From these surviving galleys, scraps of manuscript, uninterpreted diagrams, and correspondence, I have prepared this edition of both parts of *Symbolic Logic*.

Carroll published his works on logic under his pseudonym, "Lewis Carroll." Like *Alice in Wonderland, Through the Looking-Glass, Sylvie and Bruno, The Hunting of the Snark*, and *The Game of Logic*, Carroll's *Symbolic Logic* was addressed to a wide general audience and, quite explicitly, to children. His use of a pseudonym for his books and articles on logic as well as the works for children has nothing to do with arrested psychological development or a "split personality," but with practical considerations of money and privacy, two respectable and conscious Victorian concerns. Of his works that could be considered mathematical in character, *The Game of Logic* (1886) and *Symbolic Logic* were the only ones popularly addressed, and their author obviously stood a much better chance to win popular attention to logic—and the sales that he sought—by publishing them under his famous pseudonym than he did by publishing them as the Rev. C. L. Dodgson, M.A.

The idea that logic was not only proper but appealing to children was no mere whimsy of Carroll's. The great American philosopher and logician, Charles Sanders Peirce, also advocated the teaching of logic and logic graphs to children. "The aid that the system of graphs thus affords to the process of logical analysis, by virtue of its own analytical purity, is surprisingly great," Peirce writes. "Taught to boys and girls before grammar, to the point of thorough familiarisation, it would aid them through all their lives."[3] A similar inspiration underlies the approach to the teaching of mathematics found in the several pedagogical movements that go under the title, "The New Math," all of which make extensive use of elementary symbolic logic, logical diagrams, and logical algebra.

Any child of moderate intelligence, and any general reader, may turn at once to Carroll's own text. Contrary to what is occasionally written, Carroll's work in logic is not, and was not intended as, any sort of "intelligence test." Any person capable of doing arithmetic can read and understand the greater part of this work.

The remainder of this introduction is not addressed to child readers, but is intended for the variegated collection of persons who will be interested in this text for one reason or another: the Lewis Carroll enthusiast, collector, or bibliographer; persons interested in missing manuscripts and scholarly detective work; those who like to work out logical puzzles; and perhaps most important, general readers with some interest in philosophical questions who are willing to learn something about logic and its history by studying an odd, long-lost textbook by one of the most appealing eccentric geniuses of the Victorian period.

Had I not believed that such wider interest and importance attached to this text, I should not have spent on it the time foreseen both by Carroll —who doubted that anyone else would ever trouble to arrange and publish the second part of his work—and by his nephew Collingwood, who accurately noted that "it will be exceedingly difficult for any one else to take up the thread of the argument, even if any one could be found willing to give the great amount of time and trouble which would be needed."[4]

---

[3] C. S. Peirce, *Collected Papers*, vol. IV, p. 516, section 619 (Cambridge, Mass.: Harvard University Press, 1933).
[4] Collingwood, *The Life and Letters of Lewis Carroll*, p. 345.

Before turning to Carroll's text, I shall give a brief account of (1) how Part II was discovered, and the condition of the text from which this edition was prepared; (2) the revolutions in logic that took place in the nineteenth and early twentieth centuries, in order better to place Carroll's work in its context; and (3) Carroll's specific contributions to logic. These matters are treated in turn in the next three sections of this introduction.

–II–

> They sought it with thimbles,
>   they sought it with care;
> They pursued it with forks and hope;
> They threatened its life with a railway-share;
> They charmed it with smiles and soap.
>   *—The Hunting of the Snark*

I became interested in the papers of Lewis Carroll in the spring of 1959, when I was living in London and writing about scientific explanation. As I pored over the literature on this topic, analysing essays by W. V. Quine, Gilbert Ryle, and other philosophers, I repeatedly encountered references to Lewis Carroll's essay in the philosophical journal *Mind* about Achilles and the Tortoise.[5]   After comparing Carroll's original essay with these contemporary discussions I found that no sense could be made of scientific explanation in such terms.   So I hit upon the idea of checking Carroll's papers in Oxford to see whether they contained background material either to explain Carroll's position or to confirm, as I suspected might be the case, that Ryle and others were misinterpreting Carroll.[6] When in those days I went to Oxford, I stayed as a guest of the late Michael Foster, Student of Christ Church, who kindly made arrangements for me in the Christ Church Library.   So on my next visit I spent several days in the library reading Carroll's papers.   This was in April 1959.

The Carroll remains in Christ Church are not extensive and consist in good part of bequests by T. Vere Bayne and William Warner, both Students of Christ Church during Carroll's time.   Among the material

---

[5] Reprinted in Book XXI.
[6] The results of this work on scientific explanation were published in W. W. Bartley, III, "Achilles, the Tortoise and Explanation in Science and in History," *British Journal for the Philosophy of Science*, 13, no. 49 (1962), pp. 15–33.   See also this volume, Book XXI, Appendix C.

Thomas Vere Bayne (1829–1908), Carroll's childhood friend and lifelong associate at Christ Church, Oxford. Many of the papers concerning Carroll at Christ Church derive from the Bayne Collection. (National Portrait Gallery, London)

so preserved I found only one discussion of Achilles and the Tortoise, and this was contained in a set of nine galley proofs marked "Logic Part II" containing the text of what appears in this edition as Book XXI, "Logical Puzzles." I knew that Carroll had published only one part of *Symbolic*

Logic during his lifetime, and was immediately aware of the possible significance of my find. My first assumption, however, was that these galley pages must be well known. Here I was wrong: None of the existing catalogues, handbooks, and checklists of Lewis Carroll papers, which I consulted then and in the weeks following in the British Museum and in other libraries, made any mention of them. By the middle of May I had written to inquire of most of the collections of Carrolliana—among others, to the Harvard and Princeton libraries, and to the Henry E. Huntington Library in Pasadena. I also wrote to Carroll's printers, Oxford University Press and Messrs. Richard Clay, as well as to his publisher, Macmillan and Company, Ltd. I also inquired of several private collectors about the remainder of Part II. My investigations yielded only negative results. No collector or collection appeared to have the missing proofs; and two points of information discouraged further search. The first was that most of Carroll's papers had been burned in Oxford shortly after his death; the second, that the archives of his publisher, Messrs. Macmillan, had been destroyed during the Second World War in the blitz.

The latter information turned out to be false, as I learned only many years later. But the first information was correct. As Carroll's biographer Roger Lancelyn Green explains, "Lewis Carroll's importance in the world of literature was not recognised for some time after his death.... When Dodgson died, his rooms at Christ Church were needed immediately for another don: however carefully his family sorted the multitudinous papers in those rooms, still it was inevitable (however much we may regret it now) that many cartloads were taken out and burnt.... The family had no ancestral mansion in which to store several dozen chests of papers of doubtful value: naturally, nearly everything was destroyed or disposed of in the sale—which consisted mainly of books and effects.... In the course of time, Dodgson's possessions were scattered among members of the family, some of them were forgotten, and only during the last few decades, and particularly at the time of the centenary celebrations in 1932, did the next generation begin to look for their uncle's miscellaneous literary remains."[7]

Thus discouraged, I turned my attention away from the Carroll papers. Not until the spring of 1965 did I get back on their track again. At luncheon one day in La Jolla, California, I was introduced to Warren

---

[7] Roger Lancelyn Green (Ed.), *The Diaries of Lewis Carroll*, 2 Volumes (Oxford: Oxford University Press, 1954), Preface, pp. xii and xiii, Vol. I.

Weaver, among many other things a distinguished collector of Carrolliana and the chief student of his mathematical writings. I had corresponded with Weaver in 1959, but this time he was able to give me a new lead. I learned from him that Brig. General Sir Harold Hartley had acquired a wastebasket full of effects from Carroll's desk at the time of his death, and that this contained some mathematical papers. Of course I wanted to see these, and in the course of the next several years I made three wild goose chases across the Atlantic to try to see them. Alas, when I finally learned their contents, it was to find that the collection contained nothing of Lewis Carroll's work on logic.

But ventures like this helped at least to keep my interest alive, and finally, in the winter of 1968–69, I decided to have one more try at writing to Carroll researchers and collectors about the logic. This time I was in luck. In January 1969, Morton N. Cohen, Professor of English at the Graduate Center of the City University of New York, included in his detailed reply to my letter a description of some photocopies of galley proofs for *Symbolic Logic* in his possession.[8] I flew to New York City soon after and had the exhilarating experience, in Cohen's apartment in Greenwich Village, of reading for the first time three of the books (that is, chapters) presented below. Had Cohen not recognised this important material, this work could hardly have been published. I am much in his debt, as are all admirers of Lewis Carroll.

A few months later, in his library at All Souls College, Oxford, John Sparrow permitted me to examine the originals from which Cohen's photocopies had been made. They had been preserved with the papers of John Cook Wilson, which Sparrow had received from the late A. S. L. Farquharson, who had edited Wilson's posthumous papers. Wilson had in turn got the galley proofs in the mail from Carroll himself on November 6, 1896, and had apparently forgotten to return them. It is thus due to a series of lucky accidents that this work has survived and can now finally be published.

In the light of these finds, a great deal of correspondence and manuscript material by Carroll that had previously been uninterpretable became comprehensible. I had to go to the Harvard, Princeton, Huntington, and other libraries, to check their Carroll archives again. My most important additional finds were made in 1972, at Princeton, where I found the logic diagrams reproduced in Book XI. I also found

---

[8] Cohen has, together with Roger Lancelyn Green, edited a definitive edition of Carroll's correspondence.

there an old workbook of Carroll's, containing about sixty pages of mathematical and logical jottings that had seemed undecipherable to those who had examined them previously.   I was able to make sense of a large part of the workbook.   Much of it is simply Carroll's working out of answers to the problems he presents in Book XXII of *Symbolic Logic*. Later, in 1973, I examined another preparatory workbook for *Symbolic Logic* in the Warren Weaver Collection at the Humanities Research Center of the University of Texas.

Since September 1971, when I reported my discoveries at the Fourth International Congress for Logic, Methodology, and Philosophy of Science, in Bucharest, the existence of this material has become public knowledge, and I have described something of its character in the *Scientific American* and the *Times Literary Supplement*.

I make this brief report of my search because I have often been urged to do so and because it says so much about the character of research since the introduction of the jet aeroplane.   It also has a wonderland quality about it, although the very well-organised Victorian gentleman who composed both the present work on logic and *Alice in Wonderland* could hardly in his wildest flights of fancy have supposed that some seventy years after his death a mad American would ride around on a flying machine from San Francisco and Vienna to London, New York, New Jersey, and Texas to read notebooks and galley pages that must have been carefully ordered and inventoried in the 1890s, and all quite readily available then on Carroll's own worktable in Oxford.

I now turn from my account of the search for the material to discuss the condition of the work and to explain how I have put it together.

First, as to Part I, I have thought it appropriate to call this a new, fifth edition.   I have not altered the content of the body of the fourth edition, but I have eliminated the original Appendix.   It had been intended by Carroll to give the reader some sample of "what was coming," and overlapped with material in Part II; so I have distributed its contents into the remains of Part II as sensibly as I could.   I have reinserted the famous story about Queen Victoria, which Carroll inserted in the second edition and dropped in the fourth.   I also took this opportunity to publish the answers to several of the exercises in Part I that do not appear in the fourth edition but which Carroll had worked out in material preserved at Christ Church and in the Huntington Library.   I have also corrected obvious printing errors.   It was Carroll's own intention to publish a fifth edition: he had announced this in his letters to his publisher Frederick O. Macmillan (dated April 14, 1897, and August 9, 1897), and he was working on such an edition shortly before his death.

As to Part II, a rather longer description is in order. Although it can, as presented here, be read in a *fairly* continuous way, the reader should remember that it is a fragment. A complete and continuous text in all likelihood never existed. Carroll's method of working was to set up in type, as they were completed, various parts and chapters of *Symbolic Logic*, regardless of their final arrangement. Thus he writes in his *Diary* entry for January 23, 1893: "Working at Logic. I [am] thinking of getting most of the book into type, & getting friends to criticise it." Again, in his *Diary* entry for November 19, 1894, he writes: "Received from Clay [his printers] remainder of MS. for examples, & proofs. Shall now begin putting all into type, regardless of order, for Parts I, II, III." All material known by me to have been intended by Carroll for Part II is included here. Of course some additional material may have been written, and if we are fortunate, it may still exist and perhaps will turn up one day.

Part I had concluded with Book VIII. Of the surviving material for Part II, four books set up in galley proof in fairly finished form survive. These are, according to the numbering adopted for this edition, Books XII, XIV, XXI, and XXII. Four additional books presented here have been arranged by me out of material designated by Carroll for Part II but not sorted out and classified into books. This material appears in Books IX, X, XI, and XIII, and is, with the exception of Book XI, almost entirely in Carroll's own words.

A few pages of rough and unfinished manuscript designated for Book XV and Book XIX also survive at Christ Church. This material overlaps with material published here in finished form in Books VI and XXI, and appears to be no more than preliminary worksheets prepared in the 1880s. I have seen no point to reproducing it.

A book by book account of the background and arrangement of the second part follows.

Books IX and X. These are drawn from Carroll's Appendix to Part I, being given there as "a taste of what is coming." About a half-dozen words have been changed to harmonise the text with the rest of the work, but the sense has not been altered.

Book XI. The charts and other information and content of this book are entirely Carroll's. The prose commentary connecting the information and charts is the editor's. The material in this book is drawn from the Morris L. Parrish Collection, Princeton University Library; the Warren Weaver Collection, Humanities Research Center, University of Texas, Austin; and the Library of Christ Church, Oxford.

Book XII. This book is entirely in Carroll's own words, being drawn from a set of galley proofs preserved by John Cook Wilson, now in the collection of Mr. John Sparrow, All Souls College, Oxford. I have corrected obvious misprints, here as elsewhere, since the surviving galley proofs are virtually uncorrected.

Book XIII. This book too is entirely in Carroll's own words. But it has been arranged by the editor, drawing from a variety of sources indicated in the annotations. Part of the book appears in the Appendix to Part I, fourth edition.

Book XIV. This book is taken from the set of galley proofs in the Sparrow Collection.

Book XXI. This book is taken from the set of galley proofs in the Library of Christ Church, Oxford.

Book XXII. This book is taken from the set of galley proofs in the Sparrow Collection.

The numbering of the books is in part Carroll's, in part the editor's. Books XXI and XXII are numbered by Carroll in galley proof, and his numbering is retained here. No numbers were designated by Carroll for the two other books that reached galley proof. Hence I numbered these in a way that perhaps makes some sense and provides some continuity. Had Carroll lived to complete the work, the numbering might well have been different. I could of course have spread out the material in Books IX through XIV in such a way as to make the gap that now appears—no material is designated for Books XV through XX—unapparent to the casual reader. But to do so would have been irresponsible; and to leave a gap will perhaps drive home that *some material must be missing.* Carroll was usually careful to provide, in a rather methodical way, explicit directions as to how to attack each of his problems. Yet a number of the problems given in Part II, most especially those in the final book, Book

XXII, cannot be solved by means of the rules given up to that point in the surviving material. As it stands Book XXII consists of only one chapter. Possibly Carroll intended to provide not only solutions but also a method of solution for each of these problems in further chapters to Book XXII. But it seems more likely that a general treatment of advanced method would have preceded Book XXI, to be used in dealing with the problems given in Books XXI and XXII.

Any reader who finds himself unable to cope with one or another of the problems in Book XXII will find methods of solution given in the textbooks that Carroll lists at the beginning of that book; frequently the authors cited also give their own solutions. Carroll would have wished to demonstrate the superiority of *his* methods in dealing with problems developed by other writers.

I have in addition inserted a number of letters from Carroll to other persons, particularly to John Cook Wilson and to Carroll's sister, Miss Louisa Dodgson, dealing with logical matters and attempting solutions to the problems presented in the text. Many readers will find these letters particularly fascinating. Letter writing of this sort was essential to Carroll in the composition of his logical work. In his autobiography, written many years after Carroll's death, the Bishop of Peterborough reminisced on his days at Christ Church as follows: "In later life [Carroll] chose logic as the special subject of his study, and then he would constantly send his servant across to Strong [Thomas Banks Strong, Bishop of Oxford] with hard questions carefully written down for him to answer. Strong at first took these questions seriously, and set himself to give reasoned answers to them; but he soon discovered, on the receipt of an answer from Dodgson with hardly a moment's delay, that he was being used, not by a tireless seeker after truth, but by a very determined and skilful games player, who had worked out all possible solutions, and was prepared to play a game of logic chopping till the skies fell."[9]

The description just given is far from the truth, yet it suggests how Carroll must have appeared to his Oxford contemporaries, and how little his work was understood by those among whom he lived. He has been described as a "loner" in logic. The only logician with whom he was in regular contact was John Cook Wilson, and Wilson—despite the intensity of their correspondence—provided little stimulation. Wilson bitterly opposed symbolic and mathematical logic, and later marvelled that

---

[9] Claude M. Blagden (Bishop of Peterborough, 1927–1949), *Well Remembered* (London: Hodder and Stoughton, 1953).

Bertrand Russell, whose work he described as "contemptible stuff," could find a publisher.

In addition to letters, I have inserted a number of editor's appendices, and have given variant versions of problems presented in the text. Presented here for the first time are all eight versions of the famous Barber-Shop Paradox, several of which have never previously been published, and most of which are unknown to the general public.

As editor I take responsibility for these additions, which are meant to throw light on the text that would have been provided by Carroll's own commentary had he survived to complete the work.

Professional logicians will wish to note that the publisher's copy-editor, who prepared the book for the typesetters, altered Carroll's original use of quotation marks ("inverted commas") to conform to contemporary American typesetting conventions. One result is that names are frequently indicated by italics rather than by quotation marks. Since Carroll's own approach to naming and to the use of quotation marks is neither fully self-consistent nor in conformity with the practice of contemporary logicians, I have seen no point in insisting that the book be reset to reflect Carroll's original conventions. This would have greatly increased the cost of the book to the reader. In any case, Carroll's meaning remains clear.

–III–

The history of logic is conventionally divided into three main periods:[10] traditional or Aristotelian logic, beginning with Aristotle in the fourth century B.C.; Boolean or algebraic logic, beginning with the work of George Boole in England in 1847 and extending through the end of the nineteenth century; and mathematical logic, or logistics, which dates technically from the appearance of Gottlob Frege's *Bregriffschrift* in 1879, but for all practical purposes began in the first decade of the twentieth century, when Bertrand Russell brought Frege's neglected work to public notice.

This tripartite division neglects many developments in the history of logic: the different forms of ancient and medieval logic, the sixteenth-century critique of Peter Ramus, seventeenth-century Port-Royal logic in

---

[10] Such a division is adopted, for example, by Jørgen Jørgensen in his study in three volumes, *A Treatise of Formal Logic* (Copenhagen, 1931).

France, the eccentric but highly influential work of Sir William Hamilton in the first half of the nineteenth century. It also passes over the many separate and sharply distinguished episodes in twentieth-century logic, and completely neglects important developments in logical theory made by the Arabs, or in India or China. For our purposes, however, the conventional division is helpful and serves to put Lewis Carroll's work in its proper context.

Aristotelian logic remained dominant in England well into the nineteenth century, and since the eighteenth century it had been taught in England in the archaic mnemonic form given to it by Henry Aldrich in his *Artis Logicae Compendium* of 1691. By the beginning of the nineteenth century it had fallen on hard times, so that Lord Dudley, writing to Bishop Copleston in 1841, spoke of the "general neglect and contempt of logic."[11] This sort of logic got a final burst of life from the textbook and encyclopedia articles of Archbishop Whately (1826), but gradually gave way, after 1847, to algebraic logic.

Aristotelian logic, which is thought by some writers to have developed in the Athenian Agora as part of the education of lawyers and politicians, had at its origins a practical aim: to sort out valid from invalid arguments. Since Aristotle, logicians have tried to formulate those rules underlying arguments which, when followed, will ensure that only true conclusions are drawn from true premisses. These are called the "rules of valid argument"; and an argument is valid when and only when no counterexample exists. A counterexample is produced when, by following the rules suggested, one may reason from a set of true premisses to a false conclusion. The point is to avoid such invalid arguments and any rules of inference that permit them.

Take the following argument, which can be handled within Aristotelian logic:

> All men are mortal;
> All Greeks are men.
> ∴ All Greeks are mortal.

This is, in Aristotelian logic, a valid syllogistic inference in the first *figure*, and in the *mood AAA*. The figure is determined by the position of the middle term ("men" in this example) and the mood depends on the kinds of statements involved. In this example only statements in *A*, that

---

[11] Richard Whately, *Elements of Logic*, 9th edition (Boston: James Munroe, 1860) p. xvi.

is, statements beginning with "All" are involved. The mood *AAA* indicates that the two premisses and the conclusion are each individually statements in *A*. The rule of inference involved in our example goes like this:

$$\text{All } M \text{ are } X;$$
$$\underline{\text{All } G \text{ are } M.}$$
$$\therefore \text{ All } G \text{ are } X.$$

Any argument of this *form*, no matter what one substitutes for *M*, *X*, and *G*, will be valid.

There were either fifteen or nineteen or twenty-four such valid forms of inference codified by medieval Aristotelian logicians, each of which is fully specified by its moods and figure. (The adoption of one codification as opposed to another depends chiefly on whether one permits universal statements—those in *A*—to have existential import, that is, to imply the existence of their subjects.)

The difficulty, which had been known for centuries, is that many arguments exist that are intuitively valid yet for which *valid rules of inference* cannot be formulated within the framework of Aristotelian logic. The history of Aristotelian logic is largely that of successive attempts to reconstruct the syllogism or extend it to cover new forms of inference. Unfortunately this cannot be done. Take the following example:

Rebecca is the mother of Jacob;
Jacob is the father of Joseph;
The mother of the father is the paternal grandmother.
_____

∴ Rebecca is the paternal grandmother of Joseph.

This argument is easily formulated in the *language* of Aristotelian logic, the language of "categorical propositions," as follows:

$$\text{All } A \text{ are } B;$$
$$\text{All } C \text{ are } D;$$
$$\underline{\text{All } E \text{ are } F.}$$
$$\therefore \text{ All } A \text{ are } G.$$

Yet once formulated in this way, it is impossible to state a valid rule of inference exhibiting the *form* of this *obviously valid* argument. Phrases like "mother of Jacob," once *fused* into a single term (*B*), cannot be separated out again. Here one may easily make substitutions for the letters *A* through *G* that will produce a counterexample.

In brief, the logical structure of the language of categorical propositions, of the syllogism, is too weak to exhibit the way in which the predicate "mother of Jacob" contains the subject of the second premiss and a part of the subject of the third premiss. Neither syllogism nor sorites, nor the other apparatus of Aristotelian logic, can handle such arguments.

Within the structure of the modern logic of relations, as taught in contemporary logic textbooks, it is easy to exhibit the valid rule of inference followed in this example. This rule of inference is

From three premisses of the form

$$Mxy$$
$$Fyz$$
$$M'F = T$$

A conclusion may be drawn of the form Txz.

Or to put the matter in the quantifiers favoured by contemporary school logic:

From three premisses of the form

$$Mab$$
$$Fbc$$
$$(x)(y)(z)[Mxy \cdot Fyz \supset Txz]$$

A conclusion may be drawn of the form Tac.

Here x, y, and z stand in the first formulation (and a, b, and c in the second formulation) for the proper names of individuals (in our example, Rebecca, Jacob, and Joseph), and M, F, and T stand for relations between such individuals: in this example, "mother of," "father of," and "paternal grandmother of." Our rule of inference states that any conclusion of the logical form Txz is unconditionally deducible from a set of statements of the forms Mxy and Fyz and $M'F = T$.

This is just one example of a valid rule of inference that cannot be expressed, let alone formalized, in the figures and moods of traditional Aristotelian logic but that can be fully formalized in the wider logical structure afforded by modern logic.

The example comes from contemporary logic of the third period. But the breakthrough from Aristotelian logic to a wider logical structure came in 1847, when two books published in England marked a new era in the history of logic: George Boole's *The Mathematical Analysis of Logic* and Augustus DeMorgan's *Formal Logic*. For the remainder of the nineteenth century, Boolean algebraic logic dominated logical work, teaching, and research, except in Oxford, where it got comparatively little attention.

Lewis Carroll's academic career coincides almost exactly with the breakdown of Aristotelian logic and the flowering of Boolean algebraic logic. Born in Daresbury, Cheshire, in 1832 (and christened Charles Lutwidge Dodgson), Carroll went up to Oxford as an undergraduate in 1851, was elected Student (Fellow) of Christ Church in 1852, and remained there, a teacher of mathematics, for the rest of his life. His own work is a contribution to the algebra of logic, the techniques it introduces being in the main developments and modifications of those of Boole and of Venn. As Carroll jotted in his *Diary* in 1884: "In these last few days I have been working at a Logical Algebra and seem to be getting to a simpler notation than Boole's."

The period spanned by Carroll's life was then crucial for the development of logic, and marks its growth from a stagnant discipline in which almost no work was being done to one of intensely active investigation. Statistics of publication alone confirm the change in logic's status. In the period from 1798 to 1837 only four works in logic were published. Between 1838 and 1847 none were published. The decade of 1848 to 1857 saw three works published; the next decade saw eight; between 1868 and 1877 thirty-one works appeared. And in the next decade, 1878–1887, no less than one hundred logical treatises were presented to the public—among them the great works of John Neville Keynes and John Venn, and Lewis Carroll's own *Game of Logic*.[12]

In his own pioneering work, Boole had attempted to show how it was possible by the aid of a system of mathematical signs closely related to school algebra to deduce the conclusions of all the traditional modes of reasoning (for example, the moods of the syllogism, the sorites, the disjunctive syllogism), and *in addition* a vast number of other conclusions and arguments that could not be handled by Aristotelian logic. After Boole, the syllogism's importance was said to have been exaggerated: The syllogism was seen as a restricted form of class-inclusion inference—not wrong, but highly inadequate.[13]

---

[12] See E. W. Beth, "Hundred Years of Symbolic Logic," in *Dialectica*, I (November 1947), pp. 331–32, and Alonzo Church's bibliographies in *The Journal of Symbolic Logic*, 1936, 1938, and subsequent volumes on a continuing basis.

[13] See Martin Gardner's good discussion of Aristotelian logic in *Logic Machines, Diagrams and Boolean Algebra* (New York: Dover Publications, 1968).

Charles Lutwidge Dodgson (Lewis Carroll) as a young man. This photograph of Dodgson holding his camera lens was made by O. G. Rejlander. (Gernsheim Collection, Humanities Research Center, University of Texas, Austin)

With this extension beyond traditional logic also came simplification of what remained within the powers of traditional logic. An example is found in the present work, particularly the first part, in which Carroll disposes of traditional syllogisms and sorites with three simple rules. "As to Syllogisms," he wrote, "I find that their nineteen forms, with about a score of others which [textbooks] have ignored, can all be arranged under *three* forms, each with a very simple Rule of its own." Aristotelian logic as a whole, he exclaims, constitutes "an almost useless machine, for practical purposes, many of the Conclusions being incomplete, and many quite legitimate forms being ignored."

The *revolutionary* character of the transition from traditional to Boolean logic is not apparent from the extension and development of the theory of valid inference alone. Although Boole and his successors never rejected the syllogism, but saw it merely as a restricted form of inference, they did emphatically reject the *claims* that had been made for the syllogism, and herein lies the revolutionary act. Archbishop Whately had written: "For Logic, which is, as it were, the Grammar of Reasoning, does not bring forward the regular Syllogism as a *distinct mode of argumentation*, designed to be *substituted* for any other mode; but as the form to which *all* correct reasoning may be ultimately reduced."[14] The syllogism was, prior to Boole, the *paradigm* of correct reasoning. For the Aristotelians, reducibility to syllogistic form was, to quote Whately again, "a *test* to try the validity of any argument."[15] John Stuart Mill, in his own famous work of logic (1843), defended the Aristotelian position on this essential point. In his chapter "Of Ratiocination or Syllogism," after listing the ordinary forms of syllogism, he comments, "All valid ratiocination, all reasoning by which from general propositions previously admitted, other propositions, equally or less general, are inferred, may be exhibited in some of the above forms." He goes on, "We are therefore at liberty, in conformity with the general opinion of logicians, to consider the two elementary forms of the first figure as the universal types of all correct ratiocination."

Boole and his successors in the second period emphatically rejected the claim that all valid reasoning may be reduced to syllogistic form.

The nature of the revolution in practice can be seen by comparing the character of the exercises in the logical textbooks of the successive periods. In the 119 examples given as exercises in the second Appendix to Whately's

---

[14] Whately, *Elements of Logic*, p. 13.
[15] Whately, *Elements of Logic*, p. 14. My italics.

Elements of Logic, the assignment is as follows: In those examples that are already apparent syllogisms, validity is to be tested by various specified means; in those of the examples that are *not,* as given, in syllogistic form, the assignment is to attempt to reduce them to that form. This type of exercise vanishes from post-Boolean logic.

It is generally true that scientific revolutions tend to produce a shift in the problems, and kinds of problems, available and deemed suitable for scrutiny in textbooks. These revolutions also tend to produce a shift in the criteria that determine what counts either as an admissible problem or as a legitimate solution.

To understand the new kind of exercise that was assiduously invented for new textbooks, we need to discover what Booleans considered to be the chief problem of logic. For traditional logicians, such as Whately and Mill, the chief problem had been to reduce all available forms of reasoning to the syllogism. For the post-Booleans, a different task was in hand. The new problem was identified by Boole. "Boole," so Jevons later wrote, "first put forth the problem of Logical Science in its complete generality: *Given certain logical premises or conditions, to determine the description of any class of objects under those conditions.*" John Neville Keynes puts a similar point: "The great majority of direct problems involving complex propositions may be brought under the general form, *Given any number of universal propositions involving any number of terms, to determine what is all the information that they jointly afford with regard to any given term or combination of terms.* If the student turns to Boole, Jevons, or Venn, he will find that this problem is treated by them as the central problem of symbolic logic."[16]

The "algebraic" character of this formulation of the central problem of logic will be obvious to any mathematician and can easily be conveyed to the nonspecialist. Take any particular term whatever—*A, B, C,* and so on—that occurs once or more in a set of propositions. The new problem is to determine the total amount of combined information about the given term contained in the whole set of propositions. Most problems and exercises for students given by Boole, Jevons, Venn, DeMorgan, and other logicians working in the algebraic period in logic, follow this prescription, as do the problems contained in the present text by Lewis Carroll.

Even Carroll's famous Barber-Shop Paradox, which—in all its eight

---

[16] See W. Stanley Jevons, *Philosophical Transactions* (London: Plenum Publishers, 1870), and *The Principles of Science* (London: Macmillan, 1874), Chapter 6. See also John Neville Keynes, *Studies and Exercises in Formal Logic,* 1906 edition (London: Macmillan), p. 506. See the editor's Appendix A to Book XXI.

versions—occupies a featured place in Book XXI, is of this character. Two rules govern the movements of the three barbers, Allen, Brown, and Carr, in and out of their shop:

(1) When Carr goes out, then if Allen goes out, Brown stays in.
(2) When Allen goes out, Brown goes out.

The problem set is to determine what information these two rules provide concerning the possible movements of Carr.   We learn in Book XXI that John Cook Wilson claimed that under these conditions Carr could never leave the shop, whereas Carroll claimed that Carr *could* leave the shop. Cook Wilson did not understand Boolean algebra; and more recent commentators on this "paradox," although they do, to be sure, know Boolean algebra, appear to forget the original algebraic context in which the example was put forward.   Otherwise they would hardly have given the problem the particular kind of attention that they have.

Here is another example of the same sort of problem, which Carroll presents in Book XXII, and which had previously been treated by Keynes and by the American logician, Mrs. Christine Ladd-Franklin, a student of Charles Sanders Peirce:

Six children, *A*, *B*, *C*, *D*, *E*, *F*, are required to obey the following rules:

(1) On Monday and Tuesday no four can go out;
(2) On Thursday, Friday, and Saturday, no three can stay in;
(3) On Tuesday, Wednesday, and Saturday, if *B* and *C* are together (i.e., if both go out, or both stay in), then *A*, *B*, *E*, and *F* must be together;
(4) On Monday and Saturday, *B* cannot go out, unless either *D* stays in or *A*, *C*, and *E* stay in.

A and *B* are first to decide what they will do; and *C* makes his decision before the other three.   Find:

(1) When *C* must go out,
(2) When he must stay in,
(3) When he may do as he pleases.

In the case of the Six Children, as in the case of the Barber-Shop, we have to determine what total information is conveyed about *C*—or Carr—when all the premises and other information are combined according to algebraic procedure.   These problems being entirely representative of the kind of problem presented during the second period of logic, and also entirely apparent exemplifications of "the central problem of symbolic logic" as seen by Boole and his successors, it is evident how much the exercises of the logical textbooks of this, or any other, period reveal about the logical theory of the period. Practice demonstrates theory, and vice versa.

We now have sufficient information to contrast algebraic and contemporary mathematical logic. Whereas logicians agree that the difference between traditional Aristotelian logic and contemporary logic is of a revolutionary character, they are often unaware of the truly revolutionary difference between Boolean logic and contemporary logic. John Passmore expresses the prevailing opinion when he writes, "From Boole, modern formal logic has a continuous history."[17] Although contemporary logic has absorbed and incorporated Boolean algebra, it has rejected all characterisations of the nature and aim of logic published during the second period; and this introduces an important, and widely ignored, discontinuity. The problems and exercises of contemporary logic are quite different from those of the Boolean logicians, including Carroll.

Delightful evidence for this claim is at hand in Carroll's text. The algebraic-type problem that attracted his interest, and which entered logic after Boole, was beautifully adapted to his literary genius. The majority of his problems list a set of premises from which it is required that the reader draw the correct and complete conclusion. Logic as presented by Carroll is no aid towards the foundations of mathematics but a kind of instructional aid, of obvious pedagogical utility, for detectives. It is almost as if Sherlock Holmes had commissioned Carroll to aid in the education of poor Dr. Watson. The remarkable problems that Carroll created, of which the Barber-Shop Paradox is only one example, resemble situation comedies and mystery settings more than they do the investigations of contemporary logicians. There is in them a large dose of Conan Doyle and Wilkie Collins, arousing suspense, goading the reader on to search out the villainous "superfluous" premiss, and to figure out, often as not by the most murderous process, the correct—and usually unexpected—conclusion.

The Schoolboy Problem, which is set out in full in Book XIII, is a splendid example. It begins: "All the boys, in a certain School, sit together in one large room every evening. They are of no less than five nationalities—English, Scotch, Welsh, Irish, and German. One of the Monitors (who is a great reader of Wilkie Collins' novels) is very observant, and takes MS. notes of almost everything that happens, with the view of

---

[17] John Passmore, *A Hundred Years of Philosophy* (London: Duckworth, 1957), p. 127.

being a good sensational witness, in case any conspiracy to commit a murder should be on foot." There follow twelve premisses which show the schoolboys in various activities. At the end Carroll writes, "Here the MS. breaks off suddenly. The Problem is to complete the sentence [the consequent of the final premiss], if possible."

The solution to this problem is "elementary, my dear Watson," yet contemporary mathematical logicians are not ordinarily trained to solve— let alone create—such problems. Over the past ten years, in three universities in Britain and America, I have in vain asked logicians of high distinction to solve this problem.[18] Even when I gave them Carroll's own solution and asked them to test the argument for correctness, they still tended to scamper off like white rabbits, even though the latter was a task for which their training had prepared them. Occasionally they would counterattack, and demand an explanation of my "antiquarian interest."

The point is that contemporary logicians—unlike Carroll, Jevons, Keynes, or Venn—are preoccupied with questions having to do with the foundations of mathematics, consistency proofs, proof construction, axiomatisation, decision procedures, and the limitations of all these. The questions set for students in the textbooks that they write rarely require the deduction of a conclusion from a set of premisses. Rather, both premisses and conclusion are given, and the student is asked to examine the argument as a whole for validity, usually by means of a consistency test similar to the kind Carroll uses in Book XII. The radical problem shift involved in the transition from late nineteenth-century logic to twentieth-century logic is thus reflected in the practice of logicians even at the most elementary level of introductory textbooks.

Although this has meant, or at least has been accompanied by, immense progress in the foundations of mathematics, it is not an entirely fortunate development for philosophy. For although an understanding of what has happened in mathematical logic is essential to the contemporary philosopher, most philosophical problems require, for their solution, the kinds of deductive and analytical skills for which Carroll, Jevons, Venn, and their contemporaries invented their puzzles, and do *not* require the metamathematical theory and techniques of contemporary logic.

It is of course often claimed that the theory and techniques of mathe-

---

[18] As this book was going to press, two friends, Professor Thomas Settle, of the University of Guelph, and my colleague Professor Norman Buder, provided me with correct deductions. Their proofs were individually very different, and neither would have satisfied Lewis Carroll. But they did get Carroll's answer.

matical logic are essential to the solution of traditional philosophical problems—that, indeed, the traditional philosophical problems can be *dissolved* by methods of language analysis similar to those used by mathematical logicians in dealing with logical paradoxes. But these claims, based on a false analogy dependent on the presence of self-reference, have all foundered.[19]

The case is an interesting one. Many twentieth-century philosophers supposed that techniques rather like those developed by Russell and others for isolating meaningless from meaningful, nonwell-formed from well-formed, utterances could be extended *beyond* formal logic to the traditional problems of philosophy. It was supposed that the ancient problems of metaphysics, like the *logical* paradoxes, could be made to disappear through the development of canons of meaningfulness and well-formed utterance; that, indeed, these hoary metaphysical theories had arisen in the first place only because of the absence of techniques of linguistic and logical analysis for ascertaining meaninglessness. This project was, however, doomed to failure. For the self-reference that is to be found in the logical antinomies is *simply absent* from most traditional philosophical problems. Since the failure of this project was not foreseen, the story of much twentieth-century philosophy is that of an attempt to dissolve traditional metaphysics through the systematic application of a false parallel: the assumption that philosophical problems were generated, and could be avoided, in a way parallel to that in which logical paradoxes were generated and resolved.

The importance given to mathematical logic in the current philosophy curriculum, both undergraduate and graduate, needs to be reexamined in the light of this failure. At present the situation is exceptionally curious: Although contemporary philosophers are given a specialised education in mathematical logic, their ordinary work in philosophy is littered with elementary logical mistakes. Non sequiturs abound. One philosopher, for instance, once argued that what is known as the hypothetico-deductive theory of science must be wrong on the grounds that if laws cannot be deduced from observation statements, then observation statements cannot be deduced from laws.[20] Even worse, another contemporary philosopher

---

[19] For a discussion of this matter see W. W. Bartley, III, *Wittgenstein* (New York: Lippincott, 1973; and London: Quartet Books, 1974), pp. 7of. and pp. 42f. See also Sir Karl Popper: *The Logic of Scientific Discovery* (New York: Harper and Row, 1968), p. 17.

[20] See S. E. Toulmin, *Introduction to the Philosophy of Science* (London: Hutchinson, 1953), pp. 40–41 and 84–85.

has argued from the fact that some statements *logically entail* other statements without utilising general laws, to the conclusion that some statements can *explain* certain other statements without the use of general laws.[21] These are the sorts of mistakes that nineteenth-century education in logical algebra works to prevent, whereas education in mathematical logic is largely irrelevant in their prevention. More important examples can be given. One can hardly believe, for instance, that the controversy over the role of probability theory in the evaluation of scientific hypotheses could have continued so long—from 1934 to the present day—had the proponents of probability evaluation had a more adequate grounding in logical algebra. The suggestions made here are worth separate examination, and bear on the present work in suggesting its relevance despite the Victorian dress that it wears.

It is interesting that the nature of development from the Boolean to the contemporary period, and the discontinuity between the two periods, should now be blurred. The explanation for this may be surprisingly simple. Although the contribution of Boole and DeMorgan to the understanding of logic was nothing short of revolutionary, the change of perspective accompanying so radical a scientific revolution is hardly accomplished in a day. Almost always essential to the success of a scientific revolution is the institutionalisation of its doctrines in *textbooks*. But algebraic logic never quite reached the textbook stage. The ground for the proper reception of Boole's work was not adequately prepared, and it took the two generations following him to work out rough spots in his work and to standardise Boolean algebra. By that time the second period had given way to the third, that of mathematical logic. And the latter is not simply an outgrowth of either traditional or algebraic logic; problems in the foundations of mathematics of much broader than algebraic character provided an independent source for its development.

The lack of a standard textbook for algebraic logic may explain in part why it is little understood or studied, and why its existence as a distinct period in the history of logic is sometimes unnoticed. Writing of the state of logic when Russell entered the field, one eminent philosopher of science, Hans Reichenbach, said of the ideas of the logical algebraists that they "had not yet acquired any significant publicity; they were more or less the private property of a group of mathematicians."[22] Of course

---

[21] See Alan Donagan, "Explanation in History," *Mind*, N.S. 66, (1957).
[22] Hans Reichenbach, "Bertrand Russell's Logic," in P. A. Schilpp (Ed.), *The Philosophy of Bertrand Russell* (New York: Harper Torchbook, 1963), p. 24.

there were textbooks of a sort during this period: those, for instance, of
Venn, Keynes, and Jevons.   But these works were, as is often the case
just after the birth of a new science, at one and the same time textbooks
and works of advanced research.   Venn, Keynes, and Jevons did intend
to instruct the public and provide texts for the study of logic to rival the
standard Aristotelian works, such as Archbishop Whately's *Elements of
Logic*.   But these early textbooks in logical algebra were polemical works,
addressed to Aristotelians and to one another, as well as works of research,
trying to work out and to come to agreement on issues left unresolved by
Boole and DeMorgan.   Venn, Keynes, and Jevons did advanced research
and did some popularising on the side.   Whereas Carroll was chiefly
popularising, and happened to toss off, casually as it were, insights of
genius.   Carroll's work was the first attempt to popularise algebraic
logic—and it was also the last.   After 1903, with the publication of
Bertrand Russell's *The Principles of Mathematics*, teaching and research in
logic were permanently and radically altered.

In sum, the alteration made in the transition to the third period was
such that Boolean logic, unlike Aristotelian logic, was not rejected.
Almost all its techniques were accepted and incorporated into the new
mathematical logic that was developed by Whitehead and Russell.   Wise
after the event, contemporary logicians now emphasise a *continuity* in
development of technique and theory from Boole through Russell, ignoring
the fact that the Boolean conception of the character of logic and its chief
problems is abandoned after Russell's work.

–IV–

In suggesting that there has been a misleading emphasis on continuity in
logic from the second to the third period, I do not deny that continuity
exists, or that it is important.   One may even consider Lewis Carroll's
contributions to symbolic logic in terms of such an assumed continuity.
Although his work in logic is overshadowed by the advances of the decade
following his death, and by the flowering of mathematical logic in the last
half century, various connections may be drawn between his work and
contemporary logic.   Indeed, Part II of *Symbolic Logic* reveals Carroll as
a more interesting technical innovator than had hitherto been supposed,
as well as an unrivalled propounder of problems, puzzles, and paradoxes.

Enough is said in the previous section to prevent the reader from
supposing that Carroll ought to be regarded, as Frege and Peano rightly

are, a precursor of Whitehead and Russell, or one of the fathers of contemporary mathematical logic. Quite the contrary, it is the merit of Carroll's peculiar and eccentric work that it brings home, in a way that Venn's with its more conventional academic style does not, the dramatic difference between pre-Russellian logical algebra and post-Russellian logistics. As one reads these heavily italicized and chatty pages, one can even *hear* Lewis Carroll teaching logic, step by step, to Oxford high-school girls, as well as to the "child friends" who came to his rooms for tea and to play the game of logic.

An assessment of Carroll's work needs to distinguish between his technical contributions and his "ornamental presentations" and examples, and past writers have easily been able to do this on the basis of *Symbolic Logic*, Part I, alone.

As a technical contribution Part I was quite interesting but not innovative in a major way. Carroll's modification of the rather cumbersome Boolean notation, and his use of boxes rather than circles for the pictorial representation of the relationship among classes, easily earned him a place, although not a prominent one, in the history of logic. By contrast, Carroll's examples and exercises manifested genius. Here he has no rivals. As in his famous treatment of such "paradoxes" as the Barber-Shop and Achilles and the Tortoise, his logical insights merged with his literary genius. He focused with particular clarity on baffling problems connected with hypothetical statements whose issues contemporary logicians still contest. Riddles about hypothetical or conditional statements, counterfactual and otherwise, turn up even in some of his children's stories. In *Sylvie and Bruno* (1889) we read: "'I can assure you,' [the Professor] said earnestly, 'that *provided the bath was made*, I used it every morning. I certainly *ordered* it—*that* I am clear about—my only doubt is, whether the man ever finished making it.'"[23]

The high quality of this part of Carroll's work led some logicians, such as Russell, and some historians of mathematics, such as Eric Temple Bell, to give Carroll's work the highest praise. Bell, for example, wrote that Carroll "had in him the stuff of a great mathematical logician," and that "As a mathematical logician, he was far ahead of his British contemporaries."[24]

The surviving fragments of Part II of *Symbolic Logic* confirm and strengthen this opinion. Even on the technical level, one finds in Part II what

---

[23] Lewis Carroll, *Sylvie and Bruno* (London: Macmillan, 1889), p. 28.
[24] Quoted from Bell in Florence Becker Lennon, *The Life of Lewis Carroll*, third revised edition (New York: Dover Publications, 1972), p. 335.

one might expect of a first-class logician working just seven years before
Russell published *The Principles of Mathematics*. At a time when his
Oxford contemporaries were in part still tied to Aristotelian doctrines, in
part flirting with psychologistic logic under the influence of F. H. Bradley
and Oxford idealism, Carroll was remarkably free of both influences.
Although an Oxford man, he was closer in his approach to logical theory
and practice to his contemporaries at Cambridge, such as Venn, Neville
Keynes, and Johnson

Carroll seems not only to have been influenced by such men, but to
have been in contact with Cambridge mathematics and logic from an
early date.   Although the origin of his interest in logic is sometimes put as
late as 1885,[25] it is now known that he was at work on logic before this.
In one letter to his publishers, Messrs. Macmillan, dated February 1, 1893,
Carroll reports that he had been working on his book on logic since the
early 1870s.   Both Carroll's interest in syllogistic argument, its uses and
limitations, and his concern with the programme of teaching and examining in mathematics at Cambridge are evident in his *Euclid and His Modern
Rivals* (1879), particularly in Carroll's appendices from Todhunter and
DeMorgan wherein the Cambridge system is explicitly discussed.   During
this time, and throughout most of the nineteenth century and until the
end of the First World War, Cambridge was at the center of logical
innovation and development.   Boole, Professor of Mathematics at Cork,
Ireland, published his work at Cambridge.   DeMorgan, Professor of
Mathematics at University College, London, had been educated at
Cambridge.   Venn, W. E. Johnson, and Keynes were Cambridge men,
as were Whitehead and Russell.   Carroll's *Symbolic Logic* was the only
logical work of any importance whatever to be produced at Oxford.
Years later Cambridge returned the compliment.   In 1932 R. B. Braithwaite, the Cambridge logician, wrote, "In Cambridge it is now *de rigueur*
for economists as well as logicians to pretend to derive their inspiration
from Lewis Carroll."

Thus the claim sometimes heard that Carroll was unaware of the
work of contemporaries is false.[26]   He had mastered Venn's 1881 version
of Boole's logical algebra, as well as the famous logical diagrams of both
Euler and Venn.   Through Venn's work he was also aware, if only at
second hand, of developments on the continent.   He had studied the
famous Johns Hopkins *Studies in Logic* of 1883, edited by Charles Sanders

---

[25] *Lewis Carroll: 1832–1932* (New York: Columbia University Press, 1932).
[26] See Lennon, *Life of Lewis Carroll*, p. 335.

Peirce, and thus knew the work of Allan Marquand, O. H. Mitchell, Mrs. Christine Ladd-Franklin, B. I. Gilman, and Peirce himself in America. The sale of Carroll's library and effects in 1898 included, in addition to a copy of Keynes's *Studies and Exercises in Formal Logic* (1894 edition), inscribed to "Rev. C. L. Dodgson, with the author's kind regards," numerous other works in logic, including copies of R. H. Lotze's work (English translation of 1884), and works in logic by J. Gilbert, DeMorgan, Bernard Bosanquet, Venn, Bradley, J. S. Mill, Sir William Hamilton, William Whewell, Jevons, Boole, and others. Some of these works presumably influenced his own writing; others he needed to consult in order to deal with his Oxford adversaries, such as John Cook Wilson, who had studied with Lotze at Göttingen.

Whatever his antecedents, then, Carroll's basic techniques and problems were similar to those of his *Cambridge* contemporaries. Had he been able to send his servant with messages and problems to Venn and Johnson at Cambridge, instead of having to rely on Strong and Cook Wilson at Oxford, the stamp of these Cambridge associations might have been even more apparent.

These connections notwithstanding, one finds in Carroll's Part II a number of things that in themselves are not so terribly surprising but that do go beyond the practice of his Cambridge contemporaries and that one is surprised to find in Carroll in view of what was hitherto known about his logical work. As early as 1894 he had, for example, applied "truth tables" to the solution of logical problems. The application of truth tables did not come into general use until the twenties, and their invention is frequently ascribed in the current ahistorical way to Jan Łucasiewicz and Ludwig Wittgenstein. The method was known to Boole, Frege, Peirce, and to other nineteenth-century logicians too.

Even more interesting, we find that between 1894 and 1896 Carroll developed a "Method of Trees" to determine the validity of what were, by the standards of his English contemporaries, highly complicated arguments. This provided, in effect, a mechanical test of validity through a *reductio ad absurdum* argument for a large part of the logic of terms. The idea was to test whether a conclusion followed from particular premises by hypothetically assuming it to be false and then conjoining it to the premises. If the result was inconsistent, then the premises did indeed imply the conclusion; otherwise, not. In the course of the consistency test, one's argument often branches and subbranches away from the original root, thus creating the kind of "tree effect" that one sees, for instance, in family trees. Thus the two names Carroll himself used for his approach: the "Method of Trees" and the "Genealogical Method." Carroll's procedure bears a striking resemblance to the trees employed with increasing popularity by contemporary logicians according to a method of "Semantic Tableaux" published in 1955 by the Dutch logician E. W. Beth. The basic ideas are identical. The tree method pioneered by Beth was developed by a number of logicians in the late fifties—including Kurt Schütte (1956) and Stig Kanger (1957)—and is now available to the elementary student in Richard C. Jeffrey's *Formal Logic: Its Scope and Limits*.[27]

These attainments on Carroll's part—despite serious defects with regard to comprehensiveness and rigour—testify to his stature as a symbolic logician. No contemporary logician, of course, would choose to work according to Carroll's cumbersome method rather than according to Beth's. The point is that despite the poverty of his technical apparatus, Carroll was able to develop the basic idea at all.

Other parts of Carroll's work are also remarkably contemporary in spirit. Particularly intriguing is his brief discussion of the liar paradoxes and of the problem of self-reference: "If a man says 'I am telling a lie,' and speaks truly, he *is* telling a lie, and therefore speaks falsely: but if he speaks falsely, he is *not* telling a lie, and therefore speaks truly." This is Carroll's rendering of the "simplest form" of the famous "Liar Paradox," an ancient difficulty of the highest significance, related repeatedly in the writings of the logicians of antiquity, and even in the *New Testament*. In recent years some logicians have tended to dismiss the Liar Paradox out of hand, declaring—perhaps after an all-too-hasty reading of the work of Alfred Tarski—that the paradox arises from permitting *self-reference*, from permitting sentences to refer to their own truth and falsity. In his famous paper on "The Concept of Truth in Formalized Languages" (1931), Tarski argues that no consistent language can contain the means for speaking of the meaning or the truth of its own expressions. When a language does permit self-reference, it is, then, not surprising that it should lead to inconsistency and paradox.

In a delightfully refreshing way, Carroll takes up this suggestion, considers it seriously, and then rejects it—all in the space of a few lines.

---

[27] Richard C. Jeffrey, *Formal Logic: Its Scope and Limits* (New York: McGraw-Hill, 1967). See also Stig Kanger, *Provability in Logic* (Stockholm: Almqvist and Wiksell, 1957), and Kurt Schütte, "Ein System des Verknüpfenden Schliessens," *Archiv für mathematische Logik und Grundlagenforschung*, Heft 2/2–4, 1956. Beth himself allowed that traditional logic made use of semantic tableaux but added, correctly, that "nowadays such devices are more systematically applied and more thoroughly analysed."

"The best way out of the difficulty [of the Liar]," Carroll suggests, "seems to be to raise the question whether the Proposition 'I am telling a lie' can reasonably be supposed to refer to *itself* as its own subject matter." He reflects that "I am telling a lie" may indeed not be permitted to refer to itself, "since its doing so would lead to an absurdity." But Carroll goes on at once to stress that self-reference in and by itself is not objectionable, remarking that a man's statement that "I am telling the truth" leads to no absurdity.

The fact of the matter seems to be that *some* self-referential statements do indeed engender paradox:

> The sentence in this box is false.

Whereas other self-referential statements cause no difficulty:

> The sentence in this box is true.

This recondite point Carroll got just right—at least at first. One distinguished logician summed up the situation thus: If some particular sorts of self-reference were disallowed, "we would lose virtually all of the most interesting fields in contemporary studies in the philosophical foundations of mathematics. The fundamental theorems of set theory and of recursion theory would disappear, and mathematicians and logicians the world over would be out of business."[28]

Although Carroll got this point right in his first approach to the problem, Cook Wilson's arguments later caused him, wrongly, to back down; and he got into an interesting muddle (see Book XIII, Chapter 8). Frequently Carroll was unable to follow through some of his most interesting flashes of insight. Braithwaite stated this difficulty when he wrote, "Lewis Carroll was ploughing deeper than he knew. His mind was permeated by an admirable logic which he was unable to bring to full consciousness and explicit criticism. And it is this unconscious logic which is, I feel, the main reason for the supreme excellence of those unique works of genius, the two Alice books, and of what excellence there is in the two *Sylvie and Bruno*'s and in the poems. Nearly all Carroll's jokes are jokes either in pure or in applied logic. And this is one of the reasons why the books make such an appeal to children."[29]

On one point, which has been exaggerated by commentators on Part I

---

[28] Alan Ross Anderson, "St. Paul's Epistle to Titus," in Robert L. Martin (Ed.), *The Paradox of the Liar* (New Haven: Yale University Press, 1970).
[29] R. B. Braithwaite, "Lewis Carroll as Logician," *The Mathematical Gazette*, 16 (July 1932), pp. 174–78.

of *Symbolic Logic* out of proportion to its significance at the time, Carroll was regrettably conservative. He stuck to the Aristotelian doctrine, which is closer to ordinary usage, that categorical propositions in "Form A"—that is, "all" propositions such as "All men are mortal"—have what is called "existential import." That is, they imply the existence of their subjects—in this case that there are some men. Thus in our example, "All men are mortal" is equivalent to *two* statements: "No men are not mortal" and "Some men are mortal." Since every "All" statement contains a "Some" statement, all "All" statements assert the real existence of their subjects.

This point happens to be important since the power of modern mathematical logic rests in part on a certain symmetry that is destroyed by the doctrine of existential import. It was due to such considerations, among others, that logicians in the mid-nineteenth century, led by Boole and Venn, had begun to deny that "All" statements have existential import. Today the Boolean interpretation is almost universally accepted by mathematical logicians, although it was challenged by a distinguished American logician as recently as 1964.[30] The issue here, as Carroll well understood, is not the truth or falsity of the doctrine but a question of convenience. Prior to Russell's work, which united logic and mathematics in a way never dreamt of by Carroll, it was not hard to underestimate the obstacle that the doctrine posed to the development of mathematical logic.

One can, however, *interpret* Carroll's decision techniques and his formalism in such a way that one gets Boolean rather than Aristotelian (or Carrollian) results. Take as an example "All xy are z." Carroll would render this in subscript notation as $xy_1z'_0$. If one takes the subscript 1 to indicate the assertion of existence, as does Carroll, difficulties arise. But one may read it as no more than a kind of pointer demarcating subject (xy) from predicate (z). Then one may read the statement equally easily as "No xy are not-z" or "All xy are z." And these last two expressions contemporary logicians *do* take to be equivalent. The construction just suggested differs from Carroll's and would if adopted lead to some different results.

---

[30] Richard B. Angell, "The Boolean Interpretation Is Wrong," in Irving M. Copi and James A. Gould (Eds.), *Readings on Logic*, second edition (New York: Macmillan, 1972). Boole's own teaching is not identical to what is now called the "Boolean" interpretation. See Boole's works or A. N. Prior, "Categoricals and Hypotheticals in George Boole and His Successors," *Australasian Journal of Philosophy*, vol. 27, 1949, p. 175.

Nonetheless, some evidence suggests that this very question of notation provided part of Carroll's motivation in hanging onto the doctrine of existential import; for Carroll had in his notation no other way to demarcate subject from predicate. It is curious that a minor problem in notation should determine a decision of theoretical importance, yet an undated fragment of a letter to Cook Wilson from Carroll supports just this suggestion. In it Carroll complains that the expression ABC'_0 provides no indication of which letter or letters are intended as subject, which as predicate. He reminds Wilson that the expression may be written in six different ways in the subject-predicate form that Wilson had requested: "AB is C"; "A not-C is not-B"; "B not-C is not-A"; "A is not $(B$ not-$C)$"; "B is not $(A$ not-$C)$"; and "Not-C is not AB." Since these are universal statements in A, it is interesting that Carroll allows them as possible renderings of ABC'_0 even though no existential import is indicated. Apparently he was reconsidering his views on existential import, and we find in his *Diary* entry for 8 August 1896 this note: "I find I must rewrite, in *Symbolic Logic*, the section on Propositions in A." Moreover, when writing his section (Book II, Chapter III) on "What is Implied, in a Proposition of Relation, as to the Reality of its Terms?" Carroll sternly warns, "Note that the rules, here laid down, are *arbitrary*, and *only apply to Part I of my Symbolic Logic*." Possibly he intended at some point in Part II to drop the existential interpretation of propositions in A. There is also the point that in Part II substitution letters sometimes denote propositions rather than terms; in which cases the question of existential import does not arise.

However these questions of interpretation and modification may be, it is nonetheless clear that in the main Carroll held to the doctrine of existential import.

So far we have spoken mainly of techniques and technical assumptions. Some readers of Part I have urged that its main interest lies in its examples and problems. Such readers, considering that Part II is even more heavily weighted to examples, may be tempted to say the same of it. One may without underestimating the technical contributions contained in both parts of the work agree to this estimate. This emphasis on exercises was deliberate. Carroll had, in the appendix to his *Euclid and His Modern Rivals*, quoted with approval Todhunter's defence of the English, and particularly Cambridge, system of mathematical examinations: "English mathematicians...are unrivalled for their ingenuity and fertility in the construction and solution of problems....In the important mathematical examinations which are conducted at Cambridge the rapid and correct solution of problems is of paramount value, so that any teacher who can develop that power in his pupils will need no other evidence of the merits of his system.

"Let an inquirer carefully collect the mathematical examination papers issued throughout England in a single year, including those proposed at the Universities and the Colleges, and those set at the Military Examinations, the Civil Service Examinations, and the so-called Local Examinations. I say then, without fear of contradiction, that the original problems and examples contained in these papers will for interest, variety, and ingenuity surpass any similar set that could be found in any country of the world. Then any person practically conversant with teaching and examining can judge whether the teaching is likely to be the worst where the examining is the most excellent."[31]

However readers may judge Carroll's last work as a whole, they must agree, to use Todhunter's expression, that "the original problems and examples. . .will for interest, variety, and ingenuity surpass any similar set that could be found." These examples will interest both amateur and specialist readers more than anything else. For over seventy years logicians have been quietly stealing for their own textbooks and classes the eccentric problems that Carroll set in the first part of *Symbolic Logic*. They have, however, had a rather easy time of it: for Carroll provided answers to his exercises at the end of Part I. In Part II we get over one hundred new exercises and problems. Carroll's own answers to a few of these can be garnered from his correspondence with Cook Wilson and with his sister Louisa Dodgson—on whom he inflicted the problems mercilessly. Most of the exercises, however, including one with fifty delicious premisses, await our own consideration and conclusions. No solutions are given in the surviving text. Could Carroll but watch us, he would *chortle* with delight.

W.W.B.

Piedmont Pines
Montclair-Oakland
California

---

[31] Quote by C. L. Dodgson from Isaac Todhunter's "The Conflict of Studies" in Appendix I to Dodgson, *Euclid and His Modern Rivals* (London: Macmillan, 1879).

Editor's Acknowledgements

The editor wishes to express his deepest thanks to the family of the late Charles Lutwidge Dodgson and to the executors of his estate for permission to publish unpublished material.

For help in locating the missing manuscript of *Symbolic Logic*, the editor is grateful above all to Professor Morton Cohen, whose help and advice at all times in the preparation of this manuscript have been invaluable.

For permission to use unpublished material in their several collections, the editor is obliged to the Henry E. Huntington Library, Pasadena, the British Museum Library, the Guildford Muniment Room, the library and governing body of Christ Church, Oxford, the Harcourt Amory Collection of Harvard University, the Morris L. Parrish Collection of Victorian Novelists in the Princeton University Library, the Humanities Research Center of the University of Texas, Philip H. and A. S. W. Rosenbach Foundation Museum, Philadelphia, Professor Morton Cohen of the City University of New York, Mr. John Sparrow of All Souls College, Oxford, and The National Portrait Gallery, London.

For research support the editor is indebted to the United States Educational Commission in the United Kingdom, the American Council of Learned Societies, and the Research Committees of the University of California, the University of Pittsburgh, and the California State University.

For assistance in arrangements, permissions, and such like the editor is indebted to Michael Horniman, Philip D. Jacques, John Sparrow, and the governing body of Christ Church, Oxford.

For help in preliminary reports and publications connected with the book the editor is indebted to Arthur Crook, Dennis Flanagan, Daniel Halpern, David Popoff, and Patrick Suppes.

For advice at various stages in investigation and preparation of the manuscript, the editor acknowledges the help of the following persons: Professor Joseph Agassi, the late Professor Alan Ross. Anderson, Miss G. M. A. Beck, Dr. James Bohan, Professor R. B. Braithwaite, Professor Norman Buder, Professor Arthur W. Burks, Mr. L. Jonathan Cohen,

Miss Enid Dance, Dr. David Farmer, Mr. T. M. Farmiloe, the late Michael Foster, Mr. Martin Gardner, Professor Peter Geach, Mr. Roger Lancelyn Green, Professor Jean G. Harrell, Mr. Tyrus G. Harmsen, Air Marshal Sir Christopher Hartley, Brig.-Gen. Sir Harold Hartley, the late W. G. Hiscock, Mr. Stephen Kresge, Mrs. Florence Becker Lennon, Professor Edward MacKinnon, Mr. J. F. A. Mason, Professor Gerald J. Massey, Professor Eugene D. Mayers, Dr. Margaret O'Sullivan, Miss Janice Pargh, Professor Sir Karl Popper, Mr. Clarkson N. Potter, Mr. W. Prime, Professor Nicholas Rescher, Mr. Vivian Ridler, Mr. Roger E. Stoddard, Mr. Alexander D. Wainwright, Dr. Warren Weaver, Mr. H. J. R. Wing, and Professor Elizabeth Wolgast.

The editor wants to record a particular debt and thanks to Professor T. W. Settle, who read every word of this large and complicated manuscript with the greatest care and made detailed and important suggestions for its improvement. Almost every part of the manuscript has been improved as a result of his suggestions.

None of the persons named is in any way responsible for the errors that may remain in this work, for which the editor takes full responsibility.

For their help and care in typing and preparation of the manuscript the editor is grateful to Rita Goldhor, Donna McKernan, Jeannette Rothman, and Debra Switzer. Miss Lisbeth Duncan is gratefully thanked for her illustration.

The editor thanks the reference staffs of the libraries of the University of California, Berkeley, and of the California State University, Hayward, as well as those of the San Francisco Public Library and the Berkeley-Oakland Library Service System for day-to-day help in locating references, books, and journals.

It is a particular pleasure for the editor to thank the hundreds of students of elementary logic whom it has been his pleasure to instruct during the past several years in the delights and intricacies of Lewis Carroll's logic.

W.W.B.

Hayward
California

Editor's Bibliography

Included in this bibliography are works cited or consulted in the preparation of the introduction and the text, as well as some general works which the reader may find helpful for further study in logic and its history, or for a better understanding of Lewis Carroll.

Joseph Agassi. *Towards an Historiography of Science.* The Hague: Mouton, 1963.

Joseph Agassi. "Variations on the Liar's Paradox," *Studia Logica*, 15 (1964), pp. 237–38.

Peter Alexander. "Logic and the Humour of Lewis Carroll," *Proceedings of the Leeds Philosophical and Literary Society*, 6 (May 1951), pp. 551–66.

Alan Ross Anderson. "St. Paul's Epistle to Titus," in Robert L. Martin (Ed.), *The Paradox of the Liar*, New Haven: Yale University Press, 1970.

Alan Ross Anderson and Nuel D. Belnap, Jr. "A Proof of the Löwenheim-Skolem Theorem (Abstract)," *Journal of Symbolic Logic*, 24 (1959), pp. 285–86.

W. W. Bartley, III. "Achilles, the Tortoise, and Explanation in Science and History," *British Journal for the Philosophy of Science*, 13 (1962), pp. 15–33.

W. W. Bartley, III. "Lewis Carroll as a Logician," *Times Literary Supplement* (London), June 15, 1973.

W. W. Bartley, III. "Lewis Carroll's Lost Book on Logic," *Scientific American*, July 1972, pp. 38–46.

W. W. Bartley, III. "Lewis Carroll's Unpublished Work in Symbolic Logic," *Abstracts of the 4th International Congress for Logic, Methodology and Philosophy of Science*, Bucharest, 1971, p. 416.

W. W. Bartley, III. "Through the Logical Microscope on the Far Side of the Looking-Glass: Lewis Carroll's Logical Problems," *Antaeus*, Spring-Summer 1974, pp. 400–407.

W. W. Bartley, III. *Wittgenstein.* New York: Lippincott, 1973; and London: Quartet Books, 1974.

Evert W. Beth. *Formal Methods.* Dordrecht, Holland: D. Reidel, 1962.

Evert W. Beth. "Hundred Years of Symbolic Logic: A Retrospect on the Occasion of the Boole-DeMorgan Centenary," *Dialectica*, I (November 1947), pp. 331–46.

Duncan Black. "Discovery of Lewis Carroll Documents," in *Notes and Queries*, February 1953.

Duncan Black. *The Theory of Committees and Elections.* Cambridge: Cambridge University Press, 1958.

Claude M. Blagden. *Well Remembered.* London: Hodder and Stoughton, 1953.

I. M. Bochenski. *A History of Formal Logic.* Notre Dame: University of Notre Dame Press, 1961.

George Boole. *The Mathematical Analysis of Logic.* Cambridge: Macmillan, 1847.

George Boole. *An Investigation of the Laws of Thought.* New York: Dover Publications, 1958.

R. B. Braithwaite. "Lewis Carroll as Logician," *The Mathematical Gazette,* 16 (July 1932), pp. 174–78.

Arthur W. Burks and Irving M. Copi. "Lewis Carroll's Barber Shop Paradox," *Mind,* N.S. 59, pp. 219–22.

Lewis Carroll (The Rev. C. L. Dodgson). *Alice in Wonderland.* London: Macmillan, 1865.

Lewis Carroll. *The Hunting of the Snark, An Agony in Eight Fits.* London: Macmillan, 1876.

Lewis Carroll. *Sylvie and Bruno.* London: Macmillan, 1889.

Lewis Carroll. *Sylvie and Bruno Concluded.* London: Macmillan, 1893.

Lewis Carroll. *Symbolic Logic and the Game of Logic.* New York: Dover Publications, 1958.

Lewis Carroll. *Through the Looking-Glass, and What Alice Found There.* London: Macmillan, 1871.

Catalogue of the Furniture, Personal Effects, and the Interesting and Valuable Library of Books. The Property of the late Rev. C. L. Dodgson, M.A., Ch. Ch. Oxford, more widely known as "Lewis Carroll," etc. Oxford: Hall and Son, 1898.

Morton N. Cohen. "Lewis Carroll's 'Black Art,'" in Colin Ford (Ed.), *Lewis Carroll at Christ Church.* London: National Portrait Gallery, 1974.

Morton N. Cohen and Roger Lancelyn Green. *The Letters of Lewis Carroll.* London: Macmillan, 1976.

Morton N. Cohen and Roger Lancelyn Green. "The Search for Lewis Carroll's Letters," *Manuscripts,* 20 (Spring 1968), pp. 4–15.

Stuart Dodgson Collingwood. *The Life and Letters of Lewis Carroll.* London: T. Fisher Unwin, 1898.

Stuart Dodgson Collingwood (Ed.). *The Unknown Lewis Carroll* (reprint of *The Lewis Carroll Picture Book*). New York: Dover Publications, 1961.

Irving M. Copi and James Gould. *Readings on Logic* (2nd ed.). New York: Macmillan, 1972.

Augustus DeMorgan. *A Budget of Paradoxes.* London: Longmans, Green, 1872.

Augustus DeMorgan. *Formal Logic.* London: Taylor and Walton, 1847.

Sophia Elizabeth DeMorgan. *Memoir of Augustus DeMorgan.* London: Longmans, Green, 1882.

The Diaries of Lewis Carroll. (Original in the British Museum, copy at the Guildford Museum. A large portion of this is published as *The Diaries of Lewis Carroll,* edited and supplemented by Roger Lancelyn Green, in two volumes.) London: Cassell, 1953.

Charles Lutwidge Dodgson. *Curiosa Mathematica. Part I.: A New Theory of Parallels* (3rd. ed.). London: Macmillan, 1890.

Charles Lutwidge Dodgson. *Euclid and His Modern Rivals.* London: Macmillan, 1879.

Alan Donagan. "Explanation in History," *Mind,* N.S. 66 (April 1957), pp. 145–64.

D. P. Eperson. "Lewis Carroll—Mathematician," *Mathematical Gazette*, 17 (May 1933), pp. 92–100.

Gottlob Frege. *The Basic Laws of Arithmetic*. Berkeley: University of California Press, 1964.

Gottlob Frege. *Conceptual Notation*. Oxford: Oxford University Press, 1972.

Gottlob Frege. *Foundations of Arithmetic*. Oxford: Blackwell, 1950.

Martin Gardner (Ed.). *The Annotated Alice*. New York: Clarkson N. Potter, 1960.

Martin Gardner. Column in *Scientific American*, March 1960, pp. 172–76.

Martin Gardner. *Logic Machines, Diagrams and Boolean Algebra*. New York: Dover Publications, 1968.

Peter Geach. "Symbolic Logic" (Letter to the Editor), *Times Literary Supplement* (London), December 26, 1968.

Helmut Gernsheim. *Lewis Carroll: Photographer* (Rev. ed.). New York: Dover Publications, 1969.

Roger Lancelyn Green. *Lewis Carroll*. London: Bodley Head, 1960.

Roger Lancelyn Green. *The Lewis Carroll Handbook*. Oxford: Oxford University Press, 1962.

Derek Hudson. *Lewis Carroll*. London: Constable, 1954.

Jabberwocky: The Journal of the Lewis Carroll Society, London.

Richard Jeffrey. *Formal Logic: Its Scope and Limits*. New York: McGraw-Hill, 1967.

W. Stanley Jevons. *Elementary Lessons in Logic*. New York: Macmillan, 1914.

W. Stanley Jevons. *The Principles of Science*. London: Macmillan, 1874.

W. Stanley Jevons. *Studies in Deductive Logic*. London: Macmillan, 1884.

W. E. Johnson. "Hypotheticals in a Context," *Mind*, N.S. 4 (1895), pp. 143–44.

W. E. Johnson. "A Logical Paradox," *Mind*, N.S. 3 (1894), p. 583.

E. E. C. Jones. "Lewis Carroll's Logical Paradox," *Mind*, N.S. 190, pp. 146–48.

E. E. C. Jones. "Lewis Carroll's Logical Paradox," *Mind*, N.S. 190, pp. 576–78.

Jørgen Jørgensen. *A Treatise of Formal Logic*. Copenhagen: Levin & Munksgaard, 1931.

Stig Kanger. *Provability in Logic*. Stockholm: Almqvist and Wiksell, 1957.

John Neville Keynes. *Studies and Exercises in Formal Logic*. London: Macmillan, 1906 (and earlier editions).

William Kneale. "Universality and Necessity," *British Journal for the Philosophy of Science*, August 1961, pp. 89–102.

William and Martha Kneale. *The Development of Logic*. Oxford: Oxford University Press, 1962.

Thomas S. Kuhn. *The Structure of Scientific Revolutions*. Chicago: University of Chicago Press, 1962.

Florence Becker Lennon. *The Life of Lewis Carroll*. New York: Dover Publications, 1972.

C. I. Lewis. *A Survey of Symbolic Logic*. New York: Dover Publications, 1960.

Lewis Carroll: 1832–1932. New York: Columbia University Press, 1932.

Falconer Madan (Ed.). *The Lewis Carroll Centenary in London 1932*. London: Bumpus, 1932.

R. L. Martin (Ed.). *The Paradox of the Liar*. New Haven: Yale University Press, 1970.

John Stuart Mill. *A System of Logic*. London: J. W. Parker, 1843.

Charles Sanders Peirce (Ed.). *Studies in Logic by Members of the Johns Hopkins University*. Boston: Little, Brown, 1883.

Sir Karl Popper. *The Logic of Scientific Discovery*. London: Hutchinson, 1959.

Sir Karl Popper. "New Foundations for Logic," *Mind*, 56 (July 1947).

Arthur N. Prior. "Categoricals and Hypotheticals in George Boole and His Successors," *Australasian Journal of Philosophy*, 27 (1949), pp. 171–96.

Hans Reichenbach. "Bertrand Russell's Logic," in P. A. Schilpp (Ed.), *The Philosophy of Bertrand Russell*. New York: Harper Torchbook, 1963.

Bertrand Russell. *Introduction to Mathematical Philosophy*. London: Allen and Unwin, 1919.

Bertrand Russell. *The Principles of Mathematics*. London: Allen and Unwin, 1903.

Kurt Schütte. "Ein System des Verknüpfenden Schliessens," *Archiv für mathematische Logik und Grundlagenforschung*, Heft 2/2–4, 1956.

Tom Settle. "The Switches Paradox: Which Switch?," *Philosophy and Phenomenological Research*, 33 (1973), pp. 421–28.

Alfred Sidgwick. "Hypotheticals in a Context," *Mind*, N.S. 4 (1895), p. 143.

Alfred Sidgwick. "A Logical Paradox," *Mind*, N.S. 3 (1894), p. 582.

Patricia Meyer Spacks. "Logic and Language in 'Through the Looking Glass,'" *Etc: A Review of General Semantics*, 18 (April 1961), pp. 91–100.

Thomas Banks Strong. "Lewis Carroll," *Cornhill Magazine*, March 1898, pp. 303–10.

S. E. Toulmin. *Introduction to the Philosophy of Science*. London: Hutchinson, 1953 (pp. 40–41 and 84–85).

Rev. W. Tuckwell. *Reminiscences of Oxford*, 1900 (pp. 161–62).

John Venn. *Symbolic Logic*. London: Macmillan, 1894.

Warren Weaver. "Lewis Carroll: Mathematician," *Scientific American*, April 1956, pp. 116–28.

Warren Weaver. "The Mathematical Manuscripts of Charles Lutwidge Dodgson (Lewis Carroll) in the Morris L. Parrish Collection," *Manuscript Book*, Princeton University Library.

Warren Weaver. "The Mathematical Manuscripts of Lewis Carroll," *Princeton University Library Chronicle*, 16 (Autumn 1954).

Warren Weaver. "The Mathematical Manuscripts of Lewis Carroll," *Proceedings of the American Philosophical Society* (October 1954), pp. 377–81.

Warren Weaver. "The Parrish Collection of Carrolliana," *Princeton University Library Chronicle*, 17 (Winter 1956).

Richard Whately. *Elements of Logic*. Boston and Cambridge: James Munroe, 1860.

Sidney Herbert Williams and Falconer Madan. *Handbook of the Literature of the Rev. C. L. Dodgson (Lewis Carroll)*. Oxford: Oxford University Press, 1931.

John Cook Wilson (signed "W."). "Lewis Carroll's Logical Paradox," *Mind*, N.S. 190, pp. 292–93.

John Cook Wilson. *Statement and Inference*. (Ed.) A. S. L. Farquharson. Oxford: Oxford University Press, 1926.

SYMBOLIC LOGIC

Part One
Elementary

A Fascinating
Mental Recreation
for the Young

BY LEWIS CARROLL

with Annotations
by the Editor

A Syllogism worked out.

That story of yours, about your once meeting the sea=serpent, always sets me off yawning;
I never yawn, unless when I'm listening to something totally devoid of interest.

The Premisses, separately.

The Premisses, combined.

The Conclusion.

That story of yours, about your once meeting the sea=serpent, is totally devoid of interest.

This end-page illustrates the derivation of a conclusion from two premisses using Carroll's method of diagrams. (From *Symbolic Logic,* fourth edition of Part I)

29 Bedford Street,
Covent Garden,
August, 1895.

Dear Madam, or Sir,

Any one, who has to superintend the education of young people (say between 12 and 20 years of age), must have realised the importance of supplying them with healthy mental recreations, to occupy times when both brain and muscles have done their fair share of work for the day. The best possible resource, no doubt, is *reading*; and a taste for reading is quite the most valuable acquirement you can give to your pupil. But *variety* is essential, and many a boy or girl is glad to exchange the merely *passive* enjoyment of reading a book for something which will employ the *hands* as well as the *eyes*, and which will call out some form of mental *activity*. Under this heading may be reckoned such occupations as drawing, painting, &c.: also (what many young people keenly enjoy) the guessing of puzzles, which generally involves a certain amount of *handiwork*. And all games and puzzles (excepting of course *whist*) allow, and even encourage, *talking*—which in itself is one of the best and healthiest of mental recreations. Also many of them (and this is a most valuable property) will only yield the *full* enjoyment, that is to be got out of them, in return for a certain amount of *painstaking*. The chess-player, who has learned the true meaning of *"whatsoever thy hand findeth to do, do it with thy might,"* and who gives his full attention to the game, and tries to find the *best* solution for the problems that arise in it, will get *ten* times the enjoyment received by the languid, indolent player, who moves the pieces almost at random, and takes no interest whatever in winning or losing.

I claim, for Symbolic Logic, a very high place among recreations that have the nature of games or puzzles; and I believe that any one, who will really *try* to understand it, will find it more interesting and more absorbing than most of the games or puzzles yet invented. The reading of the *book* about it is a *very* small part of the business: the *real* occupation and the *real* enjoyment come when the reader has gained the power of solving for himself the fascinating *problems* of the Science. And this power is far

45

sooner, and far more easily, acquired in *Symbolic Logic* than it is in the Science as taught in the ordinary text-books.

The occupation, of solving such problems, furnishes keen and inexhaustible enjoyment, even for the *solitary* student.   But a still greater amount of pleasure may be obtained, when two or three students, of tolerably equal powers, agree to work it *together*.   It adds enormously to one's interest in such problems, to be able to *talk* them over with another: and the help it gives, in getting one's own ideas *clear* on the subject, is simply invaluable.

Symbolic Logic has one *unique* feature, as compared with games and puzzles, which entitles it, I hold, to rank above them all.   The accomplished backgammon player has received, no doubt, a great deal of enjoyment, well worth the winning, in the process of making himself a good player; but, when that object is attained, it is of no *further* use to him, except for the one purpose of playing more games, and winning more victories, and possibly becoming the Champion-player for his town or county.   Now the accomplished *Logician* has not only enjoyed himself, all the time he was working up to that position, fully as much as the Champion-player has done; but he finds himself, when that position is won, the holder of an "Open Sesame!" to an inexhaustible treasure-house of varied interests.   He may apply his skill to any and every subject of human thought; in every one of them it will help him to get *clear* ideas, to make *orderly* arrangement of his knowledge, and more important than all, to detect and unravel the *fallacies* he will meet with in every subject he may interest himself in.

Among the popular ones, about Logic there are *three* special ideas which have prevented its receiving anything like the attention which it deserves.

One is, that it is much too hard for average intellects; that only the exceptionally gifted can make anything of it; and that it is *quite* beyond the reach of children.

Another is that even those, who *do* succeed in mastering its principles, find it hopelessly dry and uninteresting.

These two charges seem to dispose of its claim to be regarded as a *Recreation*.   And if, abandoning this claim, it demands our attention as a *Science*, it must of course offer us something of practical *use*, to repay us for the trouble of studying it.   And here comes in the *third* of these popular ideas, viz., that its results are absolutely and entirely *useless*.

The first two objections may fairly be urged, I think, against *Formal Logic*.   Some of the text-books of this Science might almost have been composed with the benevolent intention of furnishing, for the eager minds of children, the *hardest* work that could be devised—giving the *maximum* of fatigue with the *minimum* of result. As compared with *Symbolic* Logic, it is much as if a schoolmaster were to close his cricket-ground, and erect a *treadmill* for his boys instead!

Think of some complicated algebraical problem, which, if worked out with x, y, z, would require the construction of several intricate simultaneous equations, ending in an affected quadratic. Then imagine the misery of having to solve it in *words* only, and being forbidden the use of *symbols*. This will give you a very fair idea of the difference, in solving a Syllogism or Sorites, between the use of *Symbolic* Logic, and of *Formal* Logic as taught in the ordinary text-books.

As to the *first* popular idea—that Logic is much too hard for ordinary folk, and specially for children, I can only say that I have taught the method of Symbolic Logic to *many* children, with entire success. They learn it easily, and take *real* interest in it. High-School girls take to it readily. I have had classes of such girls, and also of the *mistresses*, who are of course yet more interesting pupils to deal with. When your little boys, or little girls, can solve *Syllogisms*, I fancy they will be much more eager to have fresh *Pairs of Premisses* supplied them, than any *riddles* you can offer them!

As to Symbolic Logic being *dry*, I can only say, *try* it! I have amused myself with various scientific pursuits for some forty years, and have found none to rival it for sustained and entrancing attractiveness.

As to its being *useless*, I think I have already said enough.

This is, I believe, the very first attempt (with the exception of my own little book, *The Game of Logic*, published in 1886, a very incomplete performance) that has been made to *popularise* this fascinating subject. It has cost me *years* of hard work: but if it should prove, as I hope it may, to be of *real* service to the young, and to be taken up, in High Schools and in private families, as a valuable addition to their stock of healthful mental recreations, such a result would more than repay ten times the labour that I have expended on it.

Your obedient servant,
LEWIS CARROLL

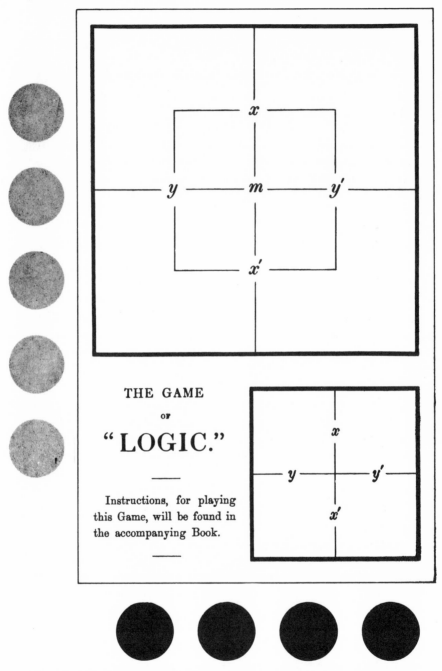

The original editions of *Symbolic Logic,* Part I, provided the reader with a playing-board and counters, as reproduced here. (From *Symbolic Logic,* fourth edition of Part I)

Advertisement

An envelope, containing two blank Diagrams (Biliteral and Triliteral) and 9 Counters (4 Red and 5 Grey), may be had, from Messrs. Macmillan, for 3*d.*, by post 4*d.*

I shall be grateful to any Reader of this book who will point out any mistakes or misprints he may happen to notice in it, or any passage which he thinks is not clearly expressed.

I have a quantity of MS. in hand for Parts II and III, and hope to be able—should life, and health, and opportunity, be granted to me, to publish them in the course of the next few years. Their contents will be as follows:

Part II. Advanced

Further investigations in the subjects of Part I. Propositions of other forms (such as "Not-all *x* are *y*"). Triliteral and Multiliteral Propositions (such as "All *abc* are *de*"). Hypotheticals. Dilemmas. Paradoxes* &c. &c.

Part III. Transcendental

Analysis of a Proposition into its Elements. Numerical and Geometrical Problems. The Theory of Inference. The Construction of Problems. And many other *Curiosa Logica*.

P. S.

I take this opportunity of giving what publicity I can to my contradiction of a silly story, which has been going the round of the papers, about my having presented certain books to Her Majesty the Queen. It is so constantly repeated, and is such absolute fiction, that I think it worthwhile to state, once for all, that it is utterly false in every particular: nothing even resembling it has ever occurred.†

* The word "Paradoxes" was dropped after the third edition, perhaps owing to Carroll's recasting of the Liar Problem (for which see Book XIII, Chapter VIII).

† This Postscript appears in the Second Edition of *Symbolic Logic* alone. The story was that Queen Victoria, after reading *Alice in Wonderland*, had expressed her desire to receive the author's next work—whereupon he sent her *The Condensation of Determinants*.

INTRODUCTION

To Learners

The Learner, who wishes to try the question *fairly* whether this little book does, or does not, supply the materials for a most interesting mental recreation, is *earnestly* advised to adopt the following Rules:

(1) Begin at the *beginning*, and do not allow yourself to gratify a mere idle curiosity by dipping into the book, here and there. This would very likely lead to your throwing it aside, with the remark "This is *much* too hard for me!," and thus losing the chance of adding a very *large* item to your stock of mental delights. This Rule (of not *dipping*) is very *desirable* with *other* kinds of books—such as novels, for instance, where you may easily spoil much of the enjoyment you would otherwise get from the story, by dipping into it further on, so that what the author meant to be a pleasant surprise comes to you as a matter of course. Some people, I know, make a practice of looking into Vol. III first, just to see how the story ends: and perhaps it *is* as well just to know that all ends *happily*—that the much-persecuted lovers *do* marry after all, that he is proved to be quite innocent of the murder, that the wicked cousin is completely foiled in his plot and gets the punishment he deserves, and that the rich uncle in India (*Qu.* Why in *India*? *Ans.* Because, somehow, uncles never *can* get rich anywhere else) dies at exactly the right moment—before taking the trouble to read Vol. I. This, I say, is *just* permissible with a *novel*, where Vol. III has a *meaning*, even for those who have not read the earlier part of the story; but, with a *scientific* book, it is sheer insanity: you will find the latter part *hopelessly* unintelligible, if you read it before reaching it in regular course.

51

(2) Don't begin any fresh Chapter, or Section, until you are certain that you *thoroughly* understand the whole book *up to that point*, and that you have worked, correctly, most if not all of the examples which have been set.   So long as you are conscious that all the land you have passed through is absolutely *conquered*, and that you are leaving no unsolved difficulties *behind* you, which will be sure to turn up again later on, your triumphal progress will be easy and delightful.   Otherwise, you will find your state of puzzlement gets worse and worse as you proceed, till you give up the whole thing in utter disgust.

(3) When you come to any passage you don't understand, *read it again*: if you *still* don't understand it, *read it again*: if you fail, even after *three* readings, very likely your brain is getting a little tired.   In that case, put the book away, and take to other occupations, and next day, when you come to it fresh, you will very likely find that it is *quite* easy.

(4) If possible, find some genial friend, who will read the book along with you, and will talk over the difficulties with you.   *Talking* is a wonderful smoother-over of difficulties.   When *I* come upon anything— in Logic or in any other hard subject—that entirely puzzles me, I find it a capital plan to talk it over, *aloud*, even when I am all alone.   One can explain things so *clearly* to one's self!   And then, you know, one is so *patient* with one's self: one *never* gets irritated at one's own stupidity!

If, dear Reader, you will faithfully observe these Rules, and so give my little book a really *fair* trial, I promise you, most confidently, that you will find Symbolic Logic to be one of the most, if not *the* most, fascinating of mental recreations!   In this First Part, I have carefully avoided all difficulties which seemed to me to be beyond the grasp of an intelligent child of (say) twelve or fourteen years of age.   I have myself taught most of its contents, *viva voce*, to *many* children, and have found them take a real intelligent interest in the subject.   For those, who succeed in mastering Part I, and who begin, like Oliver, "asking for more," I hope to provide, in Part II, some *tolerably* hard nuts to crack—nuts that will require all the nut-crackers they happen to possess!

Mental recreation is a thing that we all of us need for our mental health; and you may get much healthy enjoyment, no doubt, from Games, such as Back-gammon, Chess, and the new Game "Halma."   But, after all, when you have made yourself a first-rate player at any one of these Games, you have nothing real to *show* for it, as a *result*!   You enjoyed the Game, and the victory, no doubt, *at the time*: but you have no *result* that you can treasure up and get real *good* out of.   And, all the while, you have been leaving unexplored a perfect *mine* of wealth.   Once master the machinery of Symbolic Logic, and you have a mental occupation always at hand, of absorbing interest, and one that will be of real *use* to you in *any* subject you may take up. It will give you clearness of thought—the ability to *see your way* through a puzzle—the habit of arranging your ideas in an orderly and get-at-able form—and, more valuable than all, the power to detect *fallacies*, and to tear to pieces the flimsy illogical arguments, which you will so continually encounter in books, in newspapers, in speeches, and even in sermons, and which so easily delude those who have never taken the trouble to master this fascinating Art. *Try it.* That is all I ask of you!

L.C.

29, Bedford Street, Strand
   February 21, 1896.

PREFACE
TO FOURTH
EDITION[1]

The chief alterations, since the First Edition, have been made in the Chapter on "Classification" and the Book on "Propositions." The chief additions have been the questions on words and phrases, added to the Examination-Papers at p. 140, and the Notes inserted at p. 128.

In Book I, Chapter II, I have adopted a new definition of "Classification," which enables me to regard the whole Universe as a "Class," and thus to dispense with the very awkward phrase "a Set of Things."

In the Chapter on "Propositions of Existence" I have adopted a new "normal form," in which the Class, whose existence is affirmed or denied, is regarded as the *Predicate*, instead of the *Subject*, of the Proposition, thus evading a very subtle difficulty which besets the other form. These subtle difficulties seem to lie at the root of every Tree of Knowledge, and they are *far* more hopeless to grapple with than any that occur in its higher branches. For example, the difficulties of the Forty-Seventh Proposition of Euclid are mere child's play compared with the mental torture endured in the effort to think out the essential nature of a straight Line. And, in the present work, the difficulties of the "Five Liars" Problem, at p. 352,

---

[1] Carroll did not write essentially new prefaces to the successive editions of *Symbolic Logic*, but incorporated and elaborated on his earlier remarks, as well as introducing corrections and new material. Thus only the preface to the fourth edition is reproduced here.

are "trifles, light as air," compared with the bewildering question "What is a Thing?"

In the Chapter on "Propositions of Relation" I have inserted a new Section, containing the proof that a Proposition, beginning with "All," is a *Double* Proposition (a fact that is quite independent of the arbitrary rule, laid down in the next Section, that such a Proposition is to be understood as implying the actual *existence* of its Subject). This proof was given, in the earlier editions, incidentally, in the course of the discussion of the Biliteral Diagram: but its *proper* place, in this treatise, is where I have now introduced it.

In the Sorites-Examples, I have made a good many verbal alterations, in order to evade a difficulty, which I fear will have perplexed some of the Readers of the first three Editions. Some of the Premisses were so worded that their Terms were *not* Specieses of the Univ. named in the Dictionary, but of a larger Class, of which the Univ. was only a portion. In all such cases, it was intended that the Reader should perceive that what was asserted of the larger Class was thereby asserted of the Univ., and should ignore, as superfluous, all that it asserted of its *other* portion. Thus, in Ex. 15, the Univ. was stated to be "ducks in this village," and the third Premiss was "Mrs. Bond has no gray ducks," i.e. "No gray ducks are ducks belonging to Mrs. Bond." Here the Terms are *not* Specieses of the Univ., but of the larger Class "ducks," of which the Univ. is only a portion: and it was intended that the Reader should perceive that what is here asserted of "ducks" is thereby asserted of "ducks in this village," and should treat this Premiss as if it were "Mrs. Bond has no gray ducks in this village," and should ignore, as superfluous, what it asserts as to the *other* portion of the Class "ducks," viz. "Mrs. Bond has no gray ducks *out* of this village."

I have also given a new version of the Problem of the "Five Liars." My object, in doing so, is to escape the subtle and mysterious difficulties which beset all attempts at regarding a Proposition as being its own Subject, or a Set of Propositions as being Subjects for one another. It is, certainly, a most bewildering and unsatisfactory theory: one cannot help feeling that there is a great lack of *substance* in all this shadowy host—that, as the procession of phantoms glides before us, there is not *one* that we can pounce upon, and say "*Here* is a Proposition that *must* be either true or false!"—that it is but a Barmecide Feast, to which we have been bidden—and that its prototype is to be found in that mythical island, whose inhabitants "earned a precarious living by taking in each others' washing"! By simply translating "telling two Truths" into "taking *both* of two condiments (salt and mustard)," "telling two Lies" into "taking *neither* of them," and "telling a Truth and a Lie (order not specified)" into "taking only *one* condiment (it is not specified *which*)," I have escaped all those metaphysical puzzles, and have produced a Problem which, when translated into a Set of symbolized Premisses, furnishes the very same *Data* as were furnished by the Problem of the "Five Liars."

The coined words, introduced in previous editions, such as "Eliminands" and "Retinends," perhaps hardly need any apology: they were indispensable to my system: but the new plural, here used for the first time, viz. "Soriteses," will, I fear, be condemned as "bad English," unless I say a word in its defence. We have *three* singular nouns, in English, of plural *form*, "series," "species," and "Sorites": in all three, the awkwardness, of using the same word for both singular and plural, must often have been felt: this has been remedied, in the case of "series" by coining the plural "serieses," which has already found its way into the dictionaries: so I am no rash innovator, but am merely "following suit," in using the new plural "Soriteses."

In conclusion, let me point out that even those, who are obliged to study *Formal* Logic, with a view to being able to answer Examination-Papers in that subject, will find the study of *Symbolic* Logic most helpful for this purpose, in throwing light upon many of the obscurities with which Formal Logic abounds, and in furnishing a delightfully easy method of *testing* the results arrived at by the cumbrous processes which Formal Logic enforces upon its votaries.

This is, I believe, the very first attempt (with the exception of my own little book, *The Game of Logic*, published in 1886, a very incomplete performance) that has been made to *popularise* this fascinating subject. It has cost me *years* of hard work: but if it should prove, as I hope it may, to be of *real* service to the young, and to be taken up, in High Schools and in private families, as a valuable addition to their stock of healthful mental recreations, such a result would more than repay ten times the labour that I have expended on it.

L.C.

29 Bedford Street, Strand.
Christmas, 1896

BOOK I
THINGS AND THEIR
ATTRIBUTES

Chapter I 🌿 Introductory

The Universe contains **Things**.

[For example, "I," "London," "roses," "redness," "old English books," "the letter which I received yesterday."]

Things have **Attributes**.

[For example, "large," "red," "old," "which I received yesterday."]

One Thing may have many Attributes; and one Attribute may belong to many Things.

[Thus, the Thing "a rose" may have the Attributes "red," "scented," "full-blown," &c.; and the Attribute "red" may belong to the Things "a rose," "a brick," "a ribbon," &c.]

Any Attribute, or any Set of Attributes, may be called an **Adjunct**.

[This word is introduced in order to avoid the constant repetition of the phrase "Attribute or Set of Attributes."

Thus, we may say that a rose has the Attribute "red" (or the Adjunct "red," whichever we prefer); or we may say that it has the Adjunct "red, scented and full-blown."]

59

Chapter II ❧ Classification

"Classification," or the formation of Classes, is a Mental Process, in which we imagine that we have put together, in a group, certain Things. Such a group is called a **Class**.

This Process may be performed in three different ways, as follows:

(1) We may imagine that we have put together all Things. The Class so formed (i.e. the Class "Things") contains the whole Universe.

(2) We may think of the Class "Things," and may imagine that we have picked out from it all the Things which possess a certain Adjunct *not* possessed by the whole Class. This Adjunct is said to be **peculiar** to the Class so formed. In this case, the Class "Things" is called a **Genus** with regard to the Class so formed: the Class, so formed, is called a **Species** of the Class "Things": and its peculiar Adjunct is called its **Differentia**.

As this Process is entirely *Mental*, we can perform it whether there *is*, or *is not*, an *existing* Thing which possesses that Adjunct. If there *is*, the Class is said to be **Real**; if *not*, it is said to be **Unreal**, or **Imaginary**.

[For example, we may imagine that we have picked out, from the Class "Things," all the Things which possess the Adjunct "material, artificial, consisting of houses and streets"; and we may thus form the Real Class "towns." Here we may regard "Things" as a *Genus*, "Towns" as a *Species* of Things, and "material, artificial, consisting of houses and streets" as its *Differentia*.

Again, we may imagine that we have picked out all the Things which possess the Adjunct "weighing a ton, easily lifted by a baby"; and we may thus form the *Imaginary* Class "Things that weigh a ton and are easily lifted by a baby."]

(3) We may think of a certain Class, *not* the Class "Things," and may imagine that we have picked out from it all the Members of it which possess a certain Adjunct *not* possessed by the whole Class. This Adjunct is said to be **peculiar** to the smaller Class so formed. In this case, the Class thought of is called a **Genus** with regard to the smaller Class picked out from it: the smaller Class is called a **Species** of the larger: and its peculiar Adjunct is called its **Differentia**.

[For example, we may think of the Class "towns," and imagine that we have picked out from it all the towns which possess the Attribute "lit with gas"; and we may thus form the Real Class "towns lit with gas."

Here we may regard "Towns" as a *Genus*, "Towns lit with gas" as a *Species* of Towns, and "lit with gas" as its *Differentia*.

If, in the above example, we were to alter "lit with gas" into "paved with gold," we should get the *Imaginary* Class "towns paved with gold."]

A Class, containing only *one* Member, is called an **Individual**.

[For example, the Class "towns having four million inhabitants," which Class contains only *one* Member, viz. "London."]

Hence, any single Thing, which we can name so as to distinguish it from all other Things, may be regarded as a one-Member Class.

[Thus "London" may be regarded as the one-Member Class, picked out from the Class "towns," which has, as its Differentia, "having four million inhabitants."]

A Class, containing two or more Members, is sometimes regarded as *one single Thing*. When so regarded, it may possess an Adjunct which is *not* possessed by any Member of it taken separately.

[Thus, the Class "The soldiers of the Tenth Regiment," when regarded as *one single Thing*, may possess the Attribute "formed in square," which is *not* possessed by any Member of it taken separately.]

Chapter III ❧ Division

[§1] **Introductory**

"Division" is a Mental Process, in which we think of a certain Class of Things, and imagine that we have divided it into two or more smaller Classes.

[Thus, we might think of the Class "books," and imagine that we had divided it into the two smaller Classes "bound books" and "unbound books," or into the three Classes, "books priced at less than a shilling," "shilling-books," "books priced at more than a shilling," or into the twenty-six Classes, "books whose names begin with *A*," "books whose names begin with *B*," &c.]

A Class, that has been obtained by a certain Division, is said to be "codivisional" with every Class obtained by that Division.

[Thus, the Class "bound books" is codivisional with each of the two Classes, "bound books" and "unbound books."

Similarly, the Battle of Waterloo may be said to have been "contemporary" with every event that happened in 1815.]

Hence a Class, obtained by Division, is codivisional with itself.

[Thus, the Class "bound books" is codivisional with itself.

Similarly, the Battle of Waterloo may be said to have been "contemporary" with itself.]

[§2] Dichotomy

If we think of a certain Class, and imagine that we have picked out from it a certain smaller Class, it is evident that the *Remainder* of the large Class does *not* possess the Differentia of that smaller Class. Hence it may be regarded as *another* smaller Class, whose Differentia may be formed, from that of the Class first picked out, by prefixing the word "not"; and we may imagine that we have *divided* the Class first thought of into *two* smaller Classes, whose Differentiæ are *contradictory*. This kind of Division is called **Dichotomy**.

[For example, we may divide "books" into the two Classes whose Differentiæ are "old" and "not-old."]

In performing this Process, we may sometimes find that the Attributes we have chosen are used so loosely, in ordinary conversation, that it is not easy to decide *which* of the Things belong to the one Class and *which* to the other. In such a case, it would be necessary to lay down some arbitrary *rule*, as to *where* the one Class should end and the other begin.

[Thus, in dividing "books" into "old" and "not-old," we may say "Let all books printed before A.D. 1801, be regarded as 'old,' and all others as 'not-old.'"]

Henceforwards let it be understood that, if a Class of Things be divided into two Classes, whose Differentiæ have contrary meanings, each Differentia is to be regarded as equivalent to the other with the word "not" prefixed.

[Thus, if "books" be divided into "old" and "new," the Attribute "old" is to be regarded as equivalent to "not-new," and the Attribute "new" as equivalent to "not-old."]

After dividing a Class, by the Process of *Dichotomy*, into two smaller Classes, we may sub-divide each of these into two still smaller Classes; and this Process may be repeated over and over again, the number of Classes being doubled at each repetition.

[For example, we may divide "books" into "old" and "new" (i.e. "*not*-old"): we may then sub-divide each of these into "English" and "foreign" (i.e. "*not*-English"), thus getting *four* Classes, viz.

(1) old English;
(2) old foreign;
(3) new English;
(4) new foreign.

If we had begun by dividing into "English" and "foreign," and had then sub-divided into "old" and "new," the four Classes would have been

(1) English old;
(2) English new;
(3) foreign old;
(4) foreign new.

The Reader will easily see that these are the very same four Classes which we had before.]

Chapter IV ❧ Names

The word "Thing," which conveys the idea of a Thing, *without* any idea of an Adjunct, represents *any* single Thing.　Any other word (or phrase), which conveys the idea of a Thing, *with* the idea of an Adjunct represents *any* Thing which possesses that Adjunct; i.e., it represents any Member of the Class to which that Adjunct is *peculiar*.

Such a word (or phrase) is called a **Name**; and, if there be an existing Thing which it represents, it is said to be a Name of that Thing.

[For example, the words "Thing," "Treasure," "Town," and the phrases "valuable Thing," "material artificial Thing consisting of houses and streets," "Town lit with gas," "Town paved with gold," "old English Book."]

Just as a Class is said to be *Real*, or *Unreal*, according as there *is*, or *is not*, an existing Thing in it, so also a Name is said to be *Real*, or *Unreal*, according as there *is*, or *is not*, an existing Thing represented by it.

[Thus, "Town lit with gas" is a *Real* Name: "Town paved with gold" is an *Unreal* Name.]

Every Name is either a Substantive only, or else a phrase consisting of a Substantive and one or more Adjectives (or phrases used as Adjectives).

Every Name, except "Thing," may usually be expressed in three different forms:

(a) The Substantive "Thing," and one or more Adjectives (or phrases used as Adjectives) conveying the ideas of the Attributes;

(b) A Substantive, conveying the idea of a Thing with the ideas of *some* of the Attributes, and one or more Adjectives (or phrases used as Adjectives) conveying the ideas of the *other* Attributes;

(c) A Substantive conveying the idea of a Thing with the ideas of *all* the Attributes.

[Thus, the phrase "material living Thing, belonging to the Animal Kingdom, having two hands and two feet" is a Name expressed in Form (a).

If we choose to roll up together the Substantive "Thing" and the Adjectives "material, living, belonging to the Animal Kingdom," so as to make the new Substantive "Animal," we get the phrase "Animal having two hands and two feet," which is a Name (representing the same Thing as before) expressed in Form (b).

And, if we choose to roll up the whole phrase into one word, so as to make the new Substantive "Man," we get a Name (still representing the very same Thing) expressed in Form (c).]

A Name, whose Substantive is in the *plural* number, may be used to represent either

(1) Members of a Class, *regarded as separate Things*; or

(2) a whole Class, *regarded as one single Thing*.

[Thus, when I say "Some soldiers of the Tenth Regiment are tall," or "The soldiers of the Tenth Regiment are brave," I am using the Name "soldiers of the Tenth Regiment" in the *first* sense; and it is just the same as if I were to point to each of them *separately*, and to say "*This* soldier of the Tenth Regiment is tall," "*That* soldier of the Tenth Regiment is tall," and so on.

But, when I say "The soldiers of the Tenth Regiment are formed in square," I am using the phrase in the *second* sense; and it is just the same as if I were to say "The *Tenth Regiment* is formed in square."]

Chapter V 🐦 Definitions

It is evident that every Member of a *Species* is *also* a Member of the *Genus* out of which that Species has been picked, and that it possesses the *Differentia* of that Species. Hence it may be represented by a Name consisting of two parts, one being a Name representing any Member of the *Genus*, and the other being the *Differentia* of that Species. Such a Name is called a **Definition** of any Member of that Species, and to give it such a Name is to **define** it.

[Thus, we may define a "Treasure" as a "valuable Thing." In this case we regard "Things" as the *Genus*, and "valuable" as the *Differentia*.]

The following Examples, of this Process, may be taken as models for working others.

[Note that, in each Definition, the Substantive, representing a Member (or Members) of the *Genus*, is printed in Capitals.]

1. Define "a Treasure."
   Ans. "A valuable THING."
2. Define "Treasures."
   Ans. "Valuable THINGS."
3. Define "a Town."
   Ans. "A material artificial THING, consisting of houses and streets."
4. Define "Men."
   Ans. "Material, living THINGS, belonging to the Animal Kingdom, having two hands and two feet";
      or else
   "ANIMALS having two hands and two feet."

5. Define "London."

Ans. "The material artificial THING, which consists of houses and streets, and has four million inhabitants";

or else

"The TOWN which has four million inhabitants."

[Note that we here use the article "the" instead of "a," because we happen to know that there is only *one* such Thing.

The Reader can set himself any number of Examples of this Process, by simply choosing the Name of any common Thing (such as "house," "tree," "knife"), making a Definition for it, and then testing his answer by referring to any English Dictionary.]

BOOK II
PROPOSITIONS

Chapter I 🌿 Propositions Generally

Note that the word "some" is to be regarded, henceforward, as meaning "one or more."

The word "Proposition," as used in ordinary conversation, may be applied to *any* word, or phrase, which conveys any information whatever.

[Thus the words "yes" and "no" are Propositions in the ordinary sense of the word; and so are the phrases "you owe me five farthings" and "I don't!"

Such words as "oh!" or "never!", and such phrases as "fetch me that book!" "which book do you mean?" do not seem, at first sight, to convey any *information*; but they can easily be turned into equivalent forms which do so, viz. "I am surprised," "I will never consent to it," "I order you to fetch me that book," "I want to know which book you mean."]

But a **Proposition**, as used in this First Part of *Symbolic Logic*, has a peculiar form, which may be called its **Normal form**; and if any Proposition, which we wish to use in an argument, is not in normal form, we must reduce it to such a form, before we can use it.

A **Proposition**, when in normal form, asserts, as to certain two Classes, which are called its **Subject** and **Predicate**, either

(1) that *some* Members of its Subject are Members of its Predicate; or

67

(2) that *no* Members of its Subject are Members of its Predicate; or

(3) that *all* Members of its Subject are Members of its Predicate.

The Subject and the Predicate of a Proposition are called its **Terms**.

Two Propositions, which convey the *same* information, are said to be **equivalent**.

[Thus, the two Propositions, "I see John" and "John is seen by me," are equivalent.]

[§2] Normal form of a Proposition

A Proposition, in normal form, consists of four parts, viz.

(1) The word "some," or "no," or "all." (This word, which tells us *how many* Members of the Subject are also Members of the Predicate, is called the **Sign of Quantity**.)

(2) Name of Subject.

(3) The verb "are" (or "is"). (This is called the **Copula**.)

(4) Name of Predicate.

[§3] Various kinds of Propositions

A Proposition, that begins with "Some," is said to be **Particular**. It is also called "a Proposition **in I**."

[Note, that it is called "Particular," because it refers to a *part* only of the Subject.]

A Proposition, that begins with "No," is said to be **Universal Negative**. It is also called "a Proposition **in E**."

A Proposition, that begins with "All," is said to be **Universal Affirmative**. It is also called "a Proposition **in A**."

[Note, that they are called "Universal," because they refer to the *whole* of the Subject.]

A Proposition, whose Subject is an *Individual*, is to be regarded as *Universal*.

[Let us take, as an example, the Proposition "John is not well." This of course implies that there is an *Individual*, to whom the speaker refers when he mentions "John," and whom the listener *knows* to be referred to.]

Hence the Class "men referred to by the speaker when he mentions 'John'" is a one-Member Class, and the Proposition is equivalent to "*All* the men, who are referred to by the speaker when he mentions 'John,' are not well."]

Propositions are of two kinds, "Propositions of Existence" and "Propositions of Relation."

These shall be discussed separately.

Chapter II ❧ Propositions of Existence

A **Proposition of Existence**, when in normal form, has, for its *Subject*, the Class "existing Things."

Its Sign of Quantity is "Some" or "No."

[Note that, though its Sign of Quantity tells us *how many* existing Things are Members of its Predicate, it does *not* tell us the *exact* number: in fact, it only deals with *two* numbers, which are, in ascending order, o and 1 or more.]

It is called "a Proposition of Existence" because its effect is to assert the *Reality* (i.e. the real *existence*), or else the *Imaginariness*, of its Predicate.

[Thus, the Proposition "Some existing Things are honest men" asserts that the Class "honest men" is *Real*.

This is the *normal* form; but it may also be expressed in any one of the following forms:

(1) Honest men exist;
(2) Some honest men exist;
(3) The Class "honest men" exists;
(4) There are honest men;
(5) There are some honest men.

Similarly, the Proposition "No existing Things are men 50 feet high" asserts that the Class "men 50 feet high" is *Imaginary*.

This is the *normal* form; but it may also be expressed in any one of the following forms:

(1) Men 50 feet high do not exist;
(2) No men 50 feet high exist;

(3) The Class "men 50 feet high" does not exist;
(4) There are not any men 50 feet high;
(5) There are no men 50 feet high.]

Chapter III 🜨 Propositions of Relation

[§1] Introductory

A **Proposition of Relation**, of the kind to be here discussed, has, for its Terms, two Specieses of the same Genus, such that each of the two Names conveys the idea of some Attribute *not* conveyed by the other.

[Thus, the Proposition "Some merchants are misers" is of the right kind, since "merchants" and "misers" are Specieses of the same Genus "men"; and since the Name "merchants" conveys the idea of the Attribute "mercantile," and the name "misers" the idea of the Attribute "miserly," each of which ideas is *not* conveyed by the other Name.

But the Proposition "Some dogs are setters" is *not* of the right kind, since, although it is true that "dogs" and "setters" are Specieses of the same Genus "animals," it is *not* true that the Name "dogs" conveys the idea of any Attribute not conveyed by the Name "setters." Such Propositions will be discussed in Part II.][1]

The Genus, of which the two Terms are Specieses, is called the **Universe of Discourse**, or (more briefly) the **Univ.**

The Sign of Quantity is "Some" or "No" or "All."

[Note that, though its Sign of Quantity tells us *how many* Members of its Subject are *also* Members of its Predicate, it does not tell us the *exact* number: in fact, it only deals with *three* numbers, which are, in ascending order, 0, 1 or more, the total number of Members of the Subject.]

It is called "a Proposition of Relation" because its effect is to assert that a certain *relationship* exists between its Terms.

---

[1] Carroll's discussion of such propositions does not survive in the remnants of part II published here.

[§2] **Reduction of a Proposition of Relation to Normal form**

The Rules, for doing this, are as follows:

(1) Ascertain what is the *Subject* (i.e., ascertain what Class we are *talking about*);

(2) If the verb, governed by the Subject, is *not* the verb "are" (or "is"), substitute for it a phrase beginning with "are" (or "is");

(3) Ascertain what is the *Predicate* (i.e., ascertain what Class it is, which is asserted to contain *some*, or *none*, or *all*, of the Members of the Subject);

(4) If the Name of each *Term* is *completely expressed* (i.e. if it contains a Substantive), there is no need to determine the Univ.; but, if either Name is *incompletely expressed*, and contains *Attributes* only, it is then necessary to determine a Univ., in order to insert its Name as the Substantive.

(5) Ascertain the *Sign of Quantity*;

(6) Arrange in the following order:

> Sign of Quantity,
> Subject,
> Copula,
> Predicate.

[Let us work a few Examples, to illustrate these Rules.

(1)

Some apples are not ripe.

(1) The Subject is "apples."

(2) The Verb is "are."

(3) The Predicate is "not-ripe. ..." (As no Substantive is expressed, and we have not yet settled what the Univ. is to be, we are forced to leave a blank.)

(4) Let Univ. be "fruit."

(5) The Sign of Quantity is "some."

(6) The Proposition now becomes

> Some | apples | are | not-ripe fruit.

(2)

None of my speculations have brought me as much as 5 per cent.

(1) The Subject is "my speculations."

(2) The Verb is "have brought," for which we substitute the phrase "are...that have brought."

(3) The Predicate is "... that have brought &c."

(4) Let Univ. be "transactions."

(5) The Sign of Quantity is "none of."

(6) The Proposition now becomes

None of | my speculations | are | transactions that have brought me
as much as 5 per cent.

(3)

None but the brave deserve the fair.

To begin with, we note that the phrase "none but the brave" is equivalent
to "no *not*-brave."

(1) The Subject has for its *Attribute* "not-brave." But no *Substantive*
is supplied. So we express the Subject as "not-brave...."

(2) The Verb is "deserve," for which we substitute the phrase
"are deserving of."

(3) The Predicate is "... deserving of the fair."

(4) Let Univ. be "persons."

(5) The Sign of Quantity is "no."

(6) The Proposition now becomes

No | not-brave persons | are | persons deserving of the fair.

(4)

A lame puppy would not say "thank you" if you offered to lend it
a skipping-rope.

(1) The Subject is evidently "lame puppies," and all the rest of the
sentence must somehow be packed into the Predicate.

(2) The Verb is "would not say," &c., for which we may substitute
the phrase "are not grateful for."

(3) The Predicate may be expressed as "... not grateful for the loan
of a skipping rope."

(4) Let Univ. be "puppies."

(5) The Sign of Quantity is "all."

(6) The Proposition now becomes

All | lame puppies | are | puppies not grateful for the loan of a
skipping-rope.

(5)

No one takes in the *Times*, unless he is well-educated.

(1) The Subject is evidently persons who are not well-educated
("no *one*" evidently means "no *person*").

(2) The Verb is "takes in," for which we may substitute the phrase
"are persons taking in."

(3) The Predicate is "persons taking in the *Times*."

(4) Let Univ. be "persons."

(5) The Sign of Quantity is "no."
(6) The Proposition now becomes

No | persons who are not well-educated | are | persons taking in the *Times*.

(6)

My carriage will meet you at the station.

(1) The Subject is "my carriage." This, being an *Individual*, is equivalent to the Class "my carriages." (Note that this Class contains only *one* Member.)
(2) The Verb is "will meet," for which we may substitute the phrase "are ... that will meet."
(3) The Predicate is "... that will meet you at the station."
(4) Let Univ. be "things."
(5) The Sign of Quantity is "all."
(6) The Proposition now becomes

All | my carriages | are | things that will meet you at the station.

(7)

Happy is the man who does not know what "toothache" means!

(1) The Subject is evidently "the man &c." (Note that in this sentence, the *Predicate* comes first.) At first sight, the Subject seems to be an *Individual*; but on further consideration, we see that the article "the" does *not* imply that there is only *one* such man. Hence the phrase "the man who" is equivalent to "all men who."
(2) The Verb is "are."
(3) The Predicate is "happy...."
(4) Let Univ. be "men."
(5) The Sign of Quantity is "all."
(6) The Proposition now becomes

All | men who do not know what "toothache" means | are | happy men.

(8)

Some farmers always grumble at the weather, whatever it may be.

(1) The Subject is "farmers."
(2) The Verb is "grumble," for which we substitute the phrase "are ... who grumble."
(3) The Predicate is "... who always grumble &c."
(4) Let Univ. be "persons."
(5) The Sign of Quantity is "some."
(6) The Proposition now becomes

Some | farmers | are | persons who always grumble at the weather, whatever it may be.

(9)

No lambs are accustomed to smoke cigars.

(1) The Subject is "lambs."
(2) The Verb is "are."
(3) The Predicate is ". . . accustomed &c."
(4) Let Univ. be "animals."
(5) The Sign of Quantity is "no."
(6) The Proposition now becomes

No | lambs | are | animals accustomed to smoke cigars.

(10)

I ca'n't understand examples that are not arranged in regular order,
like those I am used to.

(1) The Subject is "examples that," &c.
(2) The Verb is "I ca'n't understand," which we must alter, so as to
have "examples," instead of "I," as the nominative case. It may
be expressed as "are not understood by me."
(3) The Predicate is ". . . not understood by me."
(4) Let Univ. be "examples."
(5) The Sign of Quantity is "all."
(6) The Proposition now becomes

All | examples that are not arranged in regular order like those
I am used to | are | examples not understood by me.**]**

[§3] A Proposition of Relation, beginning with "All," is a Double Proposition

A Proposition of Relation, beginning with "All," asserts (as we already
know) that "*All* Members of the Subject are Members of the Predicate."
This evidently contains, as a *part* of what it tell us, the smaller Proposition
"*Some* Members of the Subject are Members of the Predicate."

[Thus, the Proposition "*All* bankers are rich men" evidently contains the
smaller Proposition "*Some* bankers are rich men."]

The question now arises "What is the *rest* of the information which this
Proposition gives us?"

In order to answer this question, let us begin with the smaller Proposition, "*Some* Members of the Subject are Members of the Predicate," and
suppose that this is *all* we have been told; and let us proceed to inquire
what *else* we need to be told, in order to know that "*All* Members of the
Subject are Members of the Predicate."

[Thus, we may suppose that the Proposition "*Some* bankers are rich men"
is all the information we possess; and we may proceed to inquire what
other Proposition needs to be added to it, in order to make up the entire
Proposition "*All* bankers are rich men."]

Let us also suppose that the Univ. (i.e. the Genus, of which both the
Subject and the Predicate are Specieses) has been divided (by the Process
of *Dichotomy*) into two smaller Classes, viz.

    (1) the Predicate;
    (2) the Class whose Differentia is *contradictory* to that of the Predicate.

[Thus, we may suppose that the Genus "men," (of which both "bankers"
and "rich men" are Specieses) has been divided into the two smaller
Classes, "rich men," "poor men."]

Now we know that *every* Member of the Subject is (as shown at p. 65) a
Member of the Univ.   Hence *every* Member of the Subject is either in
Class (1) or else in Class (2).

[Thus, we know that *every* banker is a Member of the Genus "men."
Hence, *every* banker is either in the Class "rich men," or else in the Class
"poor men."]

Also we have been told that, in the case we are discussing, *some* Members
of the Subject are in Class (1).   What *else* do we need to be told, in order
to know that *all* of them are there?   Evidently we need to be told that
none of them are in Class (2); i.e. that *none* of them are Members of the
Class whose Differentia is *contradictory* to that of the Predicate.

[Thus, we may suppose we have been told that *some* bankers are in the
Class "rich men."   What *else* do we need to be told, in order to know that
all of them are there?   Evidently we need to be told that *none* of them
are in the Class "*poor* men."]

Hence a Proposition of Relation, beginning with "All," is a *Double*
Proposition, and is **equivalent** to (i.e. gives the same information as) the
two Propositions

    (1) *Some* Members of the Subject are Members of the Predicate;
    (2) *No* Members of the Subject are Members of the Class whose
        Differentia is *contradictory* to that of the Predicate.

[Thus, the Proposition "*All* bankers are rich men" is *Double* Proposition,
and is equivalent to the *two* Propositions
    (1) "*Some* bankers are rich men";
    (2) "*No* bankers are *poor* men."]

[§4] **What is implied, in a Proposition of Relation, as to the Reality of its Terms?**

Note that the rules, here laid down, are *arbitrary*, and only apply to Part I of my *Symbolic Logic*.

A Proposition of Relation, beginning with "Some," is henceforward to be understood as asserting that there are *some existing Things*, which, being Members of the Subject, are also Members of the Predicate; i.e. that *some existing Things* are Members of *both* Terms at once. Hence it is to be understood as implying that *each* Term, taken by itself, is *Real*.

[Thus, the Proposition "Some rich men are invalids" is to be understood as asserting that *some existing Things* are "rich invalids." Hence it implies that *each* of the two Classes, "rich men" and "invalids," taken by itself, is *Real*.]

A Proposition of Relation, beginning with "No," is henceforward to be understood as asserting that there are *no existing Things* which, being Members of the Subject, are also Members of the Predicate; i.e. that *no existing Things* are Members of *both* Terms at once. But this implies nothing as to the *Reality* of either Term taken by itself.

[Thus, the Proposition "No mermaids are milliners" is to be understood as asserting that *no existing Things* are "mermaid-milliners." But this implies nothing as to the *Reality*, or the *Unreality*, of either of the two Classes, "mermaids" and "milliners," taken by itself. In this case as it happens, the Subject is *Imaginary*, and the Predicate *Real*.]

A Proposition of Relation, beginning with "All," contains (see §3) a similar Proposition beginning with "Some." Hence it is to be understood as implying that *each* Term, taken by itself, is *Real*.

[Thus, the Proposition "All hyænas are savage animals" contains the Proposition "Some hyænas are savage animals." Hence it implies that *each* of the two Classes, "hyænas" and "savage animals," taken by itself, is *Real*.]

[§5] **Translation of a Proposition of Relation into one or more Propositions of Existence**

We have seen that a Proposition of Relation, beginning with "Some," asserts that *some existing Things*, being Members of its Subject, are *also*

Members of its Predicate. Hence, it asserts that some existing Things are Members of *both*; i.e., it asserts that some existing Things are Members of the Class of Things which have *all* the Attributes of the Subject and the Predicate.

Hence, to translate it into a Proposition of Existence, we take "existing Things" as the new *Subject*, and Things, which have *all* the Attributes of the Subject and the Predicate, as the new Predicate.

Similarly for a Proposition of Relation beginning with "No."

A Proposition of Relation, beginning with "All," is (as shown in §3) equivalent to *two* Propositions, one beginning with "Some" and the other with "No," each of which we now know how to translate.

[Let us work a few examples, to illustrate these Rules.

(1)

Some apples are not ripe.

Here we arrange thus:

Some	*Sign of Quantity.*
existing Things	*Subject.*
are	*Copula.*
not-ripe apples	*Predicate.*

or thus:

Some | existing Things | are | not-ripe apples.

(2)

Some farmers always grumble at the weather, whatever it may be.

Here we arrange thus:

Some | existing Things | are | farmers who always grumble at the weather, whatever it may be.

(3)

No lambs are accustomed to smoke cigars.

Here we arrange thus:

No | existing Things | are | lambs accustomed to smoke cigars.

(4)

None of my speculations have brought me as much as 5 per cent.

Here we arrange thus:

No | existing Things | are | speculations of mine, which have brought me as much as 5 per cent.

(5)

None but the brave deserve the fair.

Here we note, to begin with, that the phrase "none but the brave" is equivalent to "no not-brave men." We then arrange thus:

No | existing Things | are | not-brave men deserving of the fair.

(6)

All bankers are rich men.

This is equivalent to the two Propositions "Some bankers are rich men" and "No bankers are poor men."

Here we arrange thus:

Some | existing Things | are | rich bankers;

and

No | existing Things | are | poor bankers.]

[Work Examples §1, 1–4 (p. 143)]

BOOK III
THE BILITERAL
DIAGRAM

xy	xy'
$x'y$	$x'y'$

Chapter I ❧ Symbols and Cells

First, let us suppose that the above Diagram is an enclosure assigned to a certain Class of Things, which we have selected as our "Universe of Discourse," or, more briefly, as our "Univ."

[For example, we might say "Let Univ. be 'books'"; and we might imagine the Diagram to be a large table, assigned to all "books."]

[The Reader is strongly advised, in reading this Chapter, *not* to refer to the above Diagram, but to draw a large one for himself, *without any letters*, and to have it by him while he reads, and keep his finger on that particular *part* of it, about which he is reading.]

Secondly, let us suppose that we have selected a certain Adjunct, which we may call x, and have divided the large Class, to which we have assigned the whole Diagram, into the two smaller Classes whose Differentiæ are x and not-x (which we may call x'), and that we have assigned the *North* Half of the Diagram to the one (which we may call "the Class of x-Things," or "the x-Class"), and the *South* Half to the other (which we may call "the Class of x'-Things," or "the x'-Class").

[For example, we might say "Let x mean 'old,' so that x' will mean 'new,'" and we might suppose that we had divided books into the two

79

Classes whose Differentiæ are "old" and "new," and had assigned the
North Half of the table to "*old* books" and the *South* Half to "*new* books."

Thirdly, let us suppose that we have selected another Adjunct, which we
may call y, and have subdivided the x-Class into the two Classes whose
Differentiæ are y and y', and that we have assigned the North-*West* Cell
to the one (which we may call "the xy-Class"), and the North-*East* Cell
to the other (which we may call "the xy'-Class").

[For example, we might say "Let y mean 'English,' so that y' will mean
'foreign,'" and we might suppose that we had subdivided "old books"
into the two Classes whose Differentiæ are "English" and "foreign," and
had assigned the North-*West* Cell to "old *English* books," and the
North-*East* Cell to "old *foreign* books."]

Fourthly, let us suppose that we have subdivided the x'-Class in the same
manner, and have assigned the South-*West* Cell to the $x'y$-Class, and the
South-*East* Cell to the $x'y'$-Class.

[For example, we might suppose that we had subdivided "new books"
into the two Classes "new *English* books" and "new *foreign* books," and
had assigned the South-*West* Cell to the one, and the South-*East* Cell to
the other.]

It is evident that, if we had begun by dividing for y and y', and had then
subdivided for x and x', we should have got the *same* four Classes. Hence
we see that we have assigned the *West* Half to the y-Class, and the *East*
Half to the y'-Class.

[Thus, in the above Example, we should find that we had assigned the
West Half of the table to "*English* books" and the *East* Half to "*foreign*
books."

We have, in fact, assigned the four Quarters of the
table to four different Classes of books, as here shown.]

old English books	old foreign books
new English books	new foreign books

The Reader should carefully remember that, in such a phrase as "the
x-Things," the word "Things" means that particular *kind* of Things, to
which the whole Diagram has been assigned.

[Thus, if we say "Let Univ. be 'books,'" we mean that we have assigned
the whole Diagram to "books." In that case, if we took x to mean
"old," the phrase "the x-Things" would mean "the old books."]

The Reader should not go on to the next Chapter until he is *quite familiar* with the *blank* Diagram I have advised him to draw.

He ought to be able to name, *instantly*, the *Adjunct* assigned to any Compartment named in the right-hand column of the following Table.

Also he ought to be able to name, *instantly*, the *Compartment* assigned to any Adjunct named in the left-hand column.

To make sure of this, he had better put the book into the hands of some genial friend, while he himself has nothing but the blank Diagram, and get that genial friend to question him on this Table, *dodging* about as much as possible. The Questions and Answers should be something like this:

TABLE I

Adjuncts of Classes	Compartments, or Cells, assigned to them
x	North Half
x'	South Half
y	West Half
y'	East Half
xy	North-West Cell
xy'	North-East Cell
$x'y$	South-West Cell
$x'y'$	South-East Cell

Q. Adjunct for West Half?

A. y.

Q. Compartment for xy'?

A. North-East Cell.

Q. Adjunct for South-West Cell?

A. $x'y$.

&c., &c.

After a little practice, he will find himself able to do without the blank Diagram, and will be able to see it *mentally* ("in my mind's eye, Horatio!") while answering the questions of his genial friend. When *this* result has been reached, he may safely go on to the next Chapter.

Chapter II ⚜ Counters

Let us agree that a *Red* Counter, placed within a Cell, shall mean "This Cell is *occupied*" (i.e., "There is at least *one* Thing in it").

Let us also agree that a *Red* Counter, placed on the partition between two Cells, shall mean "The Compartment, made up of these two Cells, is *occupied*; but it is not known *whereabouts*, in it, its occupants are." Hence it may be understood to mean "At least *one* of these two Cells is occupied: possibly *both* are."

Our ingenious American cousins have invented a phrase to describe the condition of a man who has not yet made up his mind *which* of two political parties he will join: such a man is said to be **sitting on the fence.** This phrase exactly describes the condition of the Red Counter.

Let us also agree that a *Grey* Counter, placed within a Cell, shall mean "This Cell is *empty*" (i.e., "There is *nothing* in it").

[The Reader had better provide himself with four Red Counters and five Grey ones.]

Chapter III ⚜ Representation of Propositions

[§1] **Introductory**

Henceforwards, in stating such Propositions as "Some *x*-Things exist" or "No *x*-Things are *y*-Things," I shall omit the word "Things," which the Reader can supply for himself, and shall write them as "Some *x* exist" or "No *x* are *y*."

[Note that the word "Things" is here used with a special meaning, as explained at p. 24.]

A Proposition, containing only *one* of the Letters used as Symbols for Attributes, is said to be **Uniliteral**.

[For example, "Some *x* exist," "No *y′* exist," &c.]

A Proposition, containing *two* Letters, is said to be **Biliteral**.

[For example, "Some *xy′* exist," "No *x′* are *y*," &c.]

A Proposition is said to be **in terms of** the Letters it contains, whether with or without accents.

[Thus, "Some *xy′* exist," "No *x′* are *y*," &c., are said to be *in terms of x* and *y*.]

[§2] **Representation of Propositions of Existence**

Let us take, first, the Proposition "Some *x* exist."

[Note that this Proposition is (as explained at p. 69) equivalent to "Some existing Things are *x*-Things."]

This tells us that there is at least *one* Thing in the North Half; that is, that the North Half is *occupied*.   And this we can evidently represent by placing a *Red* Counter (here represented by a *dotted* circle) on the partition which divides the North Half.

[In the "books" example, this Proposition would be "Some old books exist."]

Similarly we may represent the three similar Propositions "Some *x′* exist," "Some *y* exist," and "Some *y′* exist."

[The Reader should make out all these for himself.
In the "books" example, these Propositions would be "Some new books exist," &c.]

Let us take, next, the Proposition "No *x* exist."

This tells us that there is *nothing* in the North Half; that is, that the North Half is *empty*; that is, that the North-West Cell and the North-East Cell are both of them *empty*.   And this we can represent by placing *two Grey* Counters in the North Half, one in each Cell.

[The Reader may perhaps think that it would be enough to place a *Grey* Counter on the partition in the North Half, and that, just as a *Red* Counter, so placed, would mean "This Half is *occupied*," so a *Grey* one would mean "This Half is *empty*."

This, however, would be a mistake. We have seen that a *Red* Counter, so placed, would mean "At least *one* of these two Cells is occupied: possibly *both* are." Hence a *Grey* one would merely mean "At least *one* of these two Cells is empty: possibly *both* are." But what we have to represent is that both Cells are *certainly* empty: and this can only be done by placing a *Grey* Counter in *each* of them.

In the "books" example, this Proposition would be "No old books exist."]

Similarly we may represent the three similar Propositions "No *x'* exist," "No *y* exist," and "No *y'* exist."

[The Reader should make out all these for himself.

In the "books" example, these three Propositions would be "No new books exist," &c.]

Let us take, next, the Proposition "Some *xy* exist."

This tells us that there is at least *one* Thing in the North-West Cell; that is, that the North-West Cell is *occupied*. And this we can represent by placing a *Red* Counter in it.

[In the "books" example, this Proposition would be "Some old English books exist."]

Similarly we may represent the three similar Propositions "Some *xy'* exist," "Some *x'y* exist," and "Some *x'y'* exist."

[The Reader should make out all these for himself.

In the "books" example, these three Propositions would be "Some old foreign books exist," &c.]

Let us take, next, the Proposition "No *xy* exist."

This tells us that there is *nothing* in the North-West Cell; that is, that the North-West Cell is *empty*. And this we can represent by placing a *Grey* Counter in it.

[In the "books" example, this Proposition would be "No old English books exist."]

Similarly we may represent the three similar Propositions "No *xy'* exist," "No *x'y* exist," and "No *x'y'* exist."

[The Reader should make out all these for himself.

In the "books" example, these three Propositions would be "No old foreign books exist," &c.]

We have seen that the Proposition "No *x* exist" may be represented by placing *two Grey* Counters in the North Half, one in each Cell.

We have also seen that these two *Grey* Counters, taken *separately*, represent the two Propositions "No *xy* exist" and "No *xy′* exist."

Hence we see that the Proposition "No *x* exist" is a *Double* Proposition, and is equivalent to the *two* Propositions "No *xy* exist" and "No *xy′* exist."

[In the "books" example, this Proposition would be "No old books exist."
Hence this is a *Double* Proposition, and is equivalent to the *two*
Propositions "No old *English* books exist" and "No old *foreign* books exist."]

[§3] Representation of Propositions of Relation

Let us take, first, the Proposition "Some *x* are *y*."

This tell us that at least *one* Thing, in the *North* Half, is also in the *West* Half. Hence it must be in the space *common* to them, that is, in the *North-West Cell*. Hence the North-West Cell is *occupied*. And this we can represent by placing a *Red* Counter in it.

[Note that the *Subject* of the Proposition settles which *Half* we are to use;
and that the *Predicate* settles in which *portion* of it we are to place the Red
Counter.
In the "books" example, this Proposition would be "Some old books
are English."]

Similarly we may represent the three similar Propositions "Some *x* are *y′*," "Some *x′* are *y*," and "Some *x′* are *y′*."

[The Reader should make out all these for himself.
In the "books" example, these three Propositions would be "Some old
books are foreign," &c.]

Let us take, next, the Proposition "Some *y* are *x*."

This tells us that at least *one* Thing, in the *West* Half, is also in the *North* Half. Hence it must be in the space *common* to them, that is, in the *North-West Cell*. Hence the North-West Cell is *occupied*. And this we can represent by placing a *Red* Counter in it.

[In the "books" example, this Proposition would be "Some English books
are old."]

Similarly we may represent the three similar Propositions "Some y are x'," "Some y' are x," and "Some y' are x'."

> [The Reader should make out all these for himself.
> In the "books" example, these three Propositions would be "Some English books are new," &c.]

We see that this *one* Diagram has now served to represent no less than *three* Propositions, viz.

(1) Some xy exist;

(2) Some x are y;

(3) Some y are x.

Hence these three Propositions are equivalent.

> [In the "books" example, these Propositions would be
> (1) Some old English books exist;
> (2) Some old books are English;
> (3) Some English books are old.]

The two equivalent Propositions, "Some x are y" and "Some y are x," are said to be **Converse** to each other; and the Process, of changing one into the other, is called **Converting**, or **Conversion**.

> [For example, if we were told to convert the Proposition
>
> Some apples are not ripe,
>
> we should first choose our Univ. (say "fruit"), and then complete the Proposition, by supplying the Substantive "fruit" in the Predicate, so that it would be
>
> Some apples are not-ripe fruit;
>
> and we should then convert it by interchanging its Terms, so that it would be
>
> Some not-ripe fruit are apples.]

Similarly we may represent the three similar Trios of equivalent Propositions; the whole Set of *four* Trios being as follows:

(1) Some xy exist = Some x are y = Some y are x.

(2) Some xy' exist = Some x are y' = Some y' are x.

(3) Some $x'y$ exist = Some x' are y = Some y are x'.

(4) Some $x'y'$ exist = Some x' are y' = Some y' are x'.

Let us take, next, the Proposition "No x are y."

This tells us that no Thing, in the *North* Half, is also in the *West* Half.   Hence there is *nothing* in the space *common* to them, that is, in the *North-West Cell*.   Hence the North-West Cell is *empty*. And this we can represent by placing a *Grey* Counter in it.

[In the "books" example, this Proposition would be "No old books are English."]

Similarly we may represent the three similar Propositions "No *x* are *y′*," "No *x′* are *y*," and "No *x′* are *y′*."

[The Reader should make out all these for himself.
   In the "books" example, these three Propositions would be "No old books are foreign," &c.]

Let us take, next, the Proposition "No *y* are *x*."

This tells us that no Thing, in the *West* Half, is also in the *North* Half.   Hence there is *nothing* in the space *common* to them, that is, in the *North-West Cell*.   That is, the North-West Cell is *empty*. And this we can represent by placing a *Grey* Counter in it.

[In the "books" example, this Proposition would be "No English books are old."]

Similarly we can represent the three similar Propositions "No *y* are *x′*," "No *y′* are *x*," and "No *y′* are *x′*."

[The Reader should make out all these for himself.
   In the "books" example, these three Propositions would be "No English books are new," &c.]

We see that this *one* Diagram has now served to represent no less than *three* Propositions, viz.

(1) No *xy* exist;
(2) No *x* are *y*;
(3) No *y* are *x*.

Hence these three Propositions are equivalent.

[In the "books" example, these Propositions would be
   (1) No old English books exist;
   (2) No old books are English;
   (3) No English books are old.]

The two equivalent Propositions, "No x are y" and "No y are x," are said to be "Converse" to each other.

[For example, if we were told to convert the Proposition

No porcupines are talkative,

we should first choose our Univ. (say "animals"), and then complete the Proposition, by supplying the Substantive "animals" in the Predicate, so that it would be

No porcupines are talkative animals,

and we should then convert it, by interchanging its Terms, so that it would be

No talkative animals are porcupines.]

Similarly we may represent the three similar Trios of equivalent Propositions; the whole Set of *four* Trios being as follows:

(1) No xy exist = No x are y = No y are x.
(2) No xy' exist = No x are y' = No y' are x.
(3) No $x'y$ exist = No x' are y = No y are x'.
(4) No $x'y'$ exist = No x' are y' = No y' are x'.

Let us take, next, the Proposition "All x are y."

We know (see p. 74) that this is a *Double* Proposition, and equivalent to the *two* Propositions "Some x are y" and "No x are y'," each of which we already know how to represent.

[Note that the *Subject* of the given Proposition settles which *Half* we are to use; and that its *Predicate* settles in which *portion* of that Half we are to place the Red Counter.]

TABLE II

Some x exist	⊙	No x exist	○ ○
Some x' exist	⊙	No x' exist	○ ○
Some y exist	⊙	No y exist	○ / ○
Some y' exist	⊙	No y' exist	○ / ○

Similarly we may represent the seven similar Propositions

All x are y', All y are x',
All x' are y, All y' are x,
All x' are y', All y' are x'.
All y are x,

TABLE III

Proposition	Diagram	Proposition	Diagram
Some xy exist = Some x are y = Some y are x	(⊙ in top-left)	All x are y	(⊙ top-left, ○ top-right)
Some xy' exist = Some x are y' = Some y' are x	(⊙ in top-right)	All x are y'	(○ top-left, ⊙ top-right)
Some $x'y$ exist = Some x' are y = Some y are x'	(⊙ in bottom-left)	All x' are y	(⊙ bottom-left, ○ bottom-right)
Some $x'y'$ exist = Some x' are y' = Some y' are x'	(⊙ in bottom-right)	All x' are y'	(○ bottom-left, ⊙ bottom-right)
No xy exist = No x are y = No y are x	(○ in top-left)	All y are x	(⊙ top-left, ○ bottom-left)
No xy' exist = No x are y' = No y' are x	(○ in top-right)	All y are x'	(○ top-right, ⊙ bottom-right)
No $x'y$ exist = No x' are y = No y are x'	(○ in bottom-left)	All y' are x	(⊙ top-right, ○ bottom-right)
No $x'y'$ exist = No x' are y' = No y' are x'	(○ in bottom-right)	All y' are x'	(○ top-left, ⊙ bottom-left)
Some x are y, and some are y'	(⊙ top-left, ⊙ top-right)	Some y are x, and some are x'	(⊙ top-left, ⊙ bottom-left)
Some x' are y, and some are y'	(⊙ bottom-left, ⊙ bottom-right)	Some y' are x, and some are x'	(⊙ top-right, ⊙ bottom-right)

Let us take, lastly, the Double Proposition "Some *x* are *y* and some are *y*′," each part of which we already know how to represent.

Similarly we may represent the three similar Propositions,

Some *x*′ are *y* and some are *y*′,
Some *y* are *x* and some are *x*′,
Some *y*′ are *x* and some are *x*′.

The Reader should now get his genial friend to question him, severely, on these two Tables. The *Inquisitor* should have the Tables before him: but the *Victim* should have nothing but a blank Diagram, and the Counters with which he is to represent the various Propositions named by his friend, e.g. "Some *y* exist," "No *y*′ are *x*," "All *x* are *y*," &c. &c.

Chapter IV ❧ Interpretation of Biliteral Diagram, When Marked with Counters

The Diagram is supposed to be set before us, with certain Counters placed upon it; and the problem is to find out what Proposition, or Propositions, the Counters represent.

As the process is simply the reverse of that discussed in the previous Chapter, we can avail ourselves of the results there obtained, as far as they go.

First, let us suppose that we find a *Red* Counter placed in the North-West Cell.

We know that this represents each of the Trio of equivalent Propositions

Some *xy* exist = Some *x* are *y* = Some *y* are *x*.

Similarly we may interpret a *Red* Counter, when placed in the North-East, or South-West, or South-East Cell.

Next, let us suppose that we find a *Grey* Counter placed in the North-West Cell.

We know that this represents each of the Trio of equivalent Propositions

No xy exist = No x are y = No y are x.

Similarly we may interpret a *Grey* Counter, when placed in the North-East, or South-West, or South-East Cell.

Next, let us suppose that we find a *Red* Counter placed on the partition which divides the North Half.

We know that this represents the Proposition "Some x exist."

Similarly we may interpret a *Red* Counter, when placed on the partition which divides the South, or West, or East Half.

Next, let us suppose that we find *two Red* Counters placed in the North Half, one in each Cell.

We know that this represents the *Double* Proposition "Some x are y and some are y'."

Similarly we may interpret *two Red* Counters, when placed in the South, or West, or East Half.

Next, let us suppose that we find *two Grey* Counters placed in the North Half, one in each Cell.

We know that this represents the Proposition "No x exist."

Similarly we may interpret *two Grey* Counters, when placed in the South, or West, or East Half.

Lastly, let us suppose that we find a *Red* and a *Grey* Counter placed in the North Half, the *Red* in the North-*West* Cell, and the *Grey* in the North-*East* Cell.

We know that this represents the Proposition "All x are y."

[Note that the *Half*, occupied by the two Counters, settles what is to be the *Subject* of the Proposition, and that the *Cell*, occupied by the *Red* Counter, settles what is to be its *Predicate*.]

Similarly we may interpret a *Red* and a *Grey* Counter, when placed in any one of the seven similar positions:

Red in North-East, Grey in North-West;
Red in South-West, Grey in South-East;
Red in South-East, Grey in South-West;
Red in North-West, Grey in South-West;
Red in South-West, Grey in North-West;
Red in North-East, Grey in South-East;
Red in South-East, Grey in North-East.

Once more the genial friend must be appealed to, and requested to examine the Reader on Tables II and III, and to make him not only *represent* Propositions, but also *interpret* Diagrams when marked with Counters.

The Questions and Answers should be like this:

Q. Represent "No x' are y'."
A. Grey Counter in South-East Cell.
Q. Interpret Red Counter on East partition.
A. "Some y' exist."
Q. Represent "All y' are x."
A. Red in North-East Cell; Grey in South-East Cell.
Q. Interpret Grey Counter in South-West Cell.
A. No $x'y$ exist = No x' are y = No y are x'.
&c., &c.

At first the Examinee will need to have the Board and Counters before him; but he will soon learn to dispense with these, and to answer with his eyes shut, or gazing into vacancy.

[Work Examples §1, 5–8 (p. 143).]

BOOK IV
THE TRILITERAL
DIAGRAM

xy	xy'
$x'y$	$x'y'$

xy m'			xy' m'
	xy m	xy' m	
	$x'y$ m	$x'y'$ m	
$x'y$ m'			$x'y'$ m'

Chapter I ⚘ Symbols and Cells

First, let us suppose that the above *left*-hand Diagram is the Biliteral Diagram that we have been using in Book III, and that we change it into a *Triliteral* Diagram by drawing an *Inner Square*, so as to divide each of its four Cells into two portions, thus making eight Cells altogether. The *right*-hand Diagram shows the result.

> [The Reader is strongly advised, in reading this Chapter, *not* to refer to the above Diagrams, but to make a large copy of the right-hand one for himself, *without any letters*, and to have it by him while he reads, and keep his finger on that particular *part* of it, about which he is reading.]

Secondly, let us suppose that we have selected a certain Adjunct, which we may call *m*, and have subdivided the *xy*-Class into the two Classes whose Differentiæ are *m* and *m'*, and that we have assigned the North-West *Inner* Cell to the one (which we may call "the Class of *xym*-Things," or "the *xym*-Class"), and the North-West *Outer* Cell to the other (which we may call "the Class of *xym'*-Things," or "the *xym'*-Class").

> [Thus, in the "books" example, we might say "Let *m* mean 'bound,' so that *m'* will mean 'unbound,'" and we might suppose that we had

93

subdivided the Class "old English books" into the two Classes, "old English bound books" and "old English unbound books," and had assigned the North-West *Inner* Cell to the one, and the North-West *Outer* Cell to the other.]

Thirdly, let us suppose that we have subdivided the xy'-Class, the $x'y$-Class, and $x'y'$-Class in the same manner, and have, in each case, assigned the *Inner* Cell to the Class possessing the Attribute m, and the *Outer* Cell to the Class possessing the Attribute m'.

[Thus, in the "books" example, we might suppose that we had subdivided the "new English books" into the two Classes, "new English bound books" and "new English unbound books," and had assigned the South-West *Inner* Cell to the one, and the South-West *Outer* Cell to the other.]

It is evident that we have now assigned the *Inner Square* to the m-Class, and the *Outer Border* to the m'-Class.

[Thus, in the "books" example, we have assigned the *Inner Square* to "bound books" and the *Outer Border* to "unbound books."]

When the Reader has made himself familiar with this Diagram, he ought to be able to find, in a moment, the Compartment assigned to a particular *pair* of Attributes, or the Cell assigned to a particular *trio* of Attributes. The following Rules will help him in doing this:

(1) Arrange the Attributes in the order x, y, m.
(2) Take the *first* of them and find the Compartment assigned to it.
(3) Then take the *second*, and find what *portion* of that Compartment is assigned to it.
(4) Treat the *third*, if there is one, in the same way.

[For example, suppose we have to find the Compartment assigned to ym. We say to ourselves "y has the *West* Half; and m has the *Inner* portion of that West Half."

Again, suppose we have to find the Cell assigned to $x'ym'$. We say to ourselves "x' has the *South* Half; y has the *West* portion of that *South* Half, i.e. has the *South-West Quarter*; and m' has the *Outer* portion of that South-West Quarter."]

The Reader should now get his genial friend to question him on the Table given on the next page, in the style of the following specimen-Dialogue.

Q. Adjunct for South Half, Inner Portion?
A. $x'm$.

Q. Compartment for m'?

A. The Outer Border.

Q. Adjunct for North-East Quarter, Outer Portion?

A. $xy'm'$.

Q. Compartment for ym?

A. West Half, Inner Portion.

Q. Adjunct for South Half?

A. x'.

Q. Compartment for $x'y'm$?

A. South-East Quarter, Inner Portion.

&c., &c.

TABLE IV

Adjuncts of Classes	*Compartments, or Cells, assigned to them*
x	North Half
x'	South Half
y	West Half
y'	East Half
m	Inner Square
m'	Outer Border
xy	North-West Quarter
xy'	North-East Quarter
$x'y$	South-West Quarter
$x'y'$	South-East Quarter
xm	North Half, Inner Portion
xm'	North Half, Outer Portion
$x'm$	South Half, Inner Portion
$x'm'$	South Half, Outer Portion
ym	West Half, Inner Portion
ym'	West Half, Outer Portion
$y'm$	East Half, Inner Portion
$y'm'$	East Half, Outer Portion
xym	North-West Quarter, Inner Portion
xym'	North-West Quarter, Outer Portion
$xy'm$	North-East Quarter, Inner Portion
$xy'm'$	North-East Quarter, Outer Portion
$x'ym$	South-West Quarter, Inner Portion
$x'ym'$	South-West Quarter, Outer Portion
$x'y'm$	South-East Quarter, Inner Portion
$x'y'm'$	South-East Quarter, Outer Portion

Chapter II ❧ Representation of Propositions in Terms of x and m, or of y and m

Representation of Propositions of Existence in terms of x and m, or of y and m

Let us take, first, the Proposition "Some xm exist."

[Note that the *full* meaning of this Proposition is (as explained at p. 76) "Some existing Things are xm-Things."]

This tells us that there is at least *one* Thing in the Inner portion of the North Half; that is, that this Compartment is *occupied*. And this we can evidently represent by placing a *Red* Counter on the partition which divides it.

[In the "books" example, this Proposition would mean "Some old bound books exist" (or "There are some old bound books").]

Similarly we may represent the seven similar Propositions,

Some xm' exist,
Some $x'm$ exist,
Some $x'm'$ exist,
Some ym exist,
Some ym' exist,
Some $y'm$ exist,
Some $y'm'$ exist.

Let us take, next, the Proposition "No xm exist."

This tells us that there is *nothing* in the Inner portion of the North Half; that is, that this Compartment is *empty*. And this we can represent by placing *two Grey* Counters in it, one in each Cell.

Similarly we may represent the seven similar Propositions, in terms of x and m, or of y and m, viz. "No xm' exist," "No $x'm$ exist," &c.

These sixteen Propositions of Existence are the only ones that we shall have to represent on this Diagram.

[§2] **Representation of Propositions of Relation in terms of x and m, or of y and m**

Let us take, first, the Pair of Converse Propositions

    Some x are m = Some m are x.

We know that each of these is equivalent to the Proposition of Existence "Some xm exist," which we already know how to represent.

Similarly for the seven similar Pairs, in terms of x and m, or of y and m.

Let us take, next, the Pair of Converse Propositions

    No x are m = No m are x.

We know that each of these is equivalent to the Proposition of Existence "No xm exist," which we already know how to represent.

Similarly for the seven similar Pairs, in terms of x and m, or of y and m.

Let us take, next, the Proposition "All x are m."

We know (see p. 75) that this is a *Double* Proposition, and equivalent to the *two* Propositions "Some x are m" and "No x are m'," each of which we already know how to represent.

Similarly for the fifteen similar Propositions, in terms of x and m, or of y and m.

These thirty-two Propositions of Relation are the only ones that we shall have to represent on this Diagram.

The Reader should now get his genial friend to question him on the following four Tables.

The Victim should have nothing before him but a blank Triliteral Diagram, a Red Counter, and two Grey ones, with which he is to represent the various Propositions named by the Inquisitor, e.g. "No y' are m," "Some xm' exist," &c., &c.

TABLE V

Some *xm* exist = Some *x* are *m* = Some *m* are *x*	
No *xm* exist = No *x* are *m* = No *m* are *x*	
Some *xm'* exist = Some *x* are *m'* = Some *m'* are *x*	
No *xm'* exist = No *x* are *m'* = No *m'* are *x*	
Some *x'm* exist = Some *x'* are *m* = Some *m* are *x'*	
No *x'm* exist = No *x'* are *m* = No *m* are *x'*	
Some *x'm'* exist = Some *x'* are *m'* = Some *m'* are *x'*	
No *x'm'* exist = No *x'* are *m'* = No *m'* are *x'*	

TABLE VI

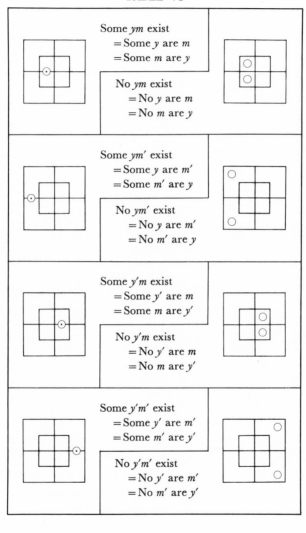

Some *ym* exist
= Some *y* are *m*
= Some *m* are *y*

No *ym* exist
= No *y* are *m*
= No *m* are *y*

Some *ym'* exist
= Some *y* are *m'*
= Some *m'* are *y*

No *ym'* exist
= No *y* are *m'*
= No *m'* are *y*

Some *y'm* exist
= Some *y'* are *m*
= Some *m* are *y'*

No *y'm* exist
= No *y'* are *m*
= No *m* are *y'*

Some *y'm'* exist
= Some *y'* are *m'*
= Some *m'* are *y'*

No *y'm'* exist
= No *y'* are *m'*
= No *m'* are *y'*

TABLE VII

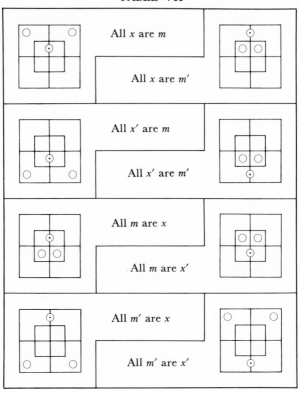

TABLE VIII

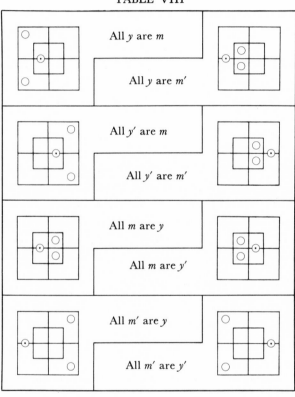

Chapter III ❧ Representation of Two Propositions of Relation, One in Terms of x and m, and the Other in Terms of y and m, on the Same Diagram

The Reader had better now begin to draw little Diagrams for himself, and to mark them with the Digits I and O instead of using the Board and Counters: he may put a I to represent a *Red* Counter (this may be interpreted to mean "There is at least *one* Thing here"), and a O to represent a *Grey* Counter (this may be interpreted to mean "There is *nothing* here").

The Pair of Propositions, that we shall have to represent, will always be, one in terms of x and m, and the other in terms of y and m.

When we have to represent a Proposition beginning with "All," we break it up into the *two* Propositions to which it is equivalent.

When we have to represent, on the same Diagram, Propositions, of which some begin with "Some" and others with "No," we represent the *negative* ones *first*. This will sometimes save us from having to put a I "on a fence" and afterwards having to shift it into a Cell.

[Let us work a few examples.

(1)

No x are m';
No y' are m.

Let us first represent "No x are m'." This gives us Diagram (a).

Then, representing "No y' are m" on the same Diagram, we get Diagram (b).

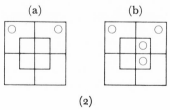

(a)   (b)

(2)

Some m are x;
No m are y.

If, neglecting the Rule, we were to begin with "Some m are x," we should get Diagram (a).

And if we were then to take "No *m* are *y*," which tells us that the Inner North-West Cell is *empty*, we should be obliged to take the I off the fence (as it no longer has the choice of *two* Cells), and to put it into the Inner North-East Cell, as in Diagram (c).

This trouble may be saved by beginning with "No *m* are *y*," as in Diagram (b).

And *now*, when we take "Some *m* are *x*," there is no fence to sit on! The I has to go, at once, into the North-East Cell, as in Diagram (c).

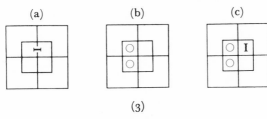

(3)

No *x'* are *m'*;
All *m* are *y*.

Here we begin by breaking up the Second into the two Propositions to which it is equivalent.   Thus we have *three* Propositions to represent, viz.

(1) No *x'* are *m'*;
(2) Some *m* are *y*;
(3) No *m* are *y'*.

These we will take in the order 1, 3, 2.

First we take No. (1), viz. "No *x'* are *m'*."   This gives us Diagram (a). Adding to this, No. (3), viz. "No *m* are *y'*," we get Diagram (b).

This time the I, representing No. (2), viz. "Some *m* are *y*," *has* to sit on the fence, as there is no O to order it off!   This gives us Diagram (c).

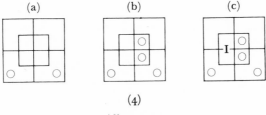

(4)

All *m* are *x*;
All *y* are *m*.

Here we break up *both* Propositions, and thus get *four* to represent, viz.

(1) Some *m* are *x*;
(2) No *m* are *x'*;
(3) Some *y* are *m*;
(4) No *y* are *m'*.

These we will take in the order 2, 4, 1, 3.

First we take No. (2), viz. "No *m* are *x'*." This gives us Diagram (a).

To this we add No. (4), viz. "No *y* are *m'*," and thus get Diagram (b).

If we were to add to this No. (1), viz. "Some *m* are *x*," we should have to put the I on a fence: so let us try No. (3) instead, viz. "Some *y* are *m*." This gives us Diagram (c).

And now there is no need to trouble about No. (1), as it would not add anything to our information to put a I on the fence. The Diagram *already* tells us that "Some *m* are *x*."]

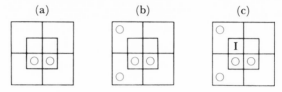

(a) (b) (c)

[Work Examples §1, 9–12 (p. 143); §2, 1–20 (p. 144).]

Chapter IV ❦ Interpretation, in Terms of *x* and *y*, of Triliteral Diagram, When Marked with Counters or Digits

The problem before us is, given a marked Triliteral Diagram, to ascertain *what* Propositions of Relation, in terms of *x* and *y*, are represented on it.

The best plan, for a *beginner*, is to draw a *Biliteral* Diagram alongside of it, and to transfer, from the one to the other, all the information he can. He can then read off, from the Biliteral Diagram, the required Propositions. After a little practice, he will be able to dispense with the Biliteral Diagram, and to read off the result from the Triliteral Diagram itself.

To *transfer* the information, observe the following Rules:

(1) Examine the North-West Quarter of the Triliteral Diagram.

(2) If it contains a I, in *either* Cell, it is certainly *occupied*, and you may mark the North-West Quarter of the Biliteral Diagram with a I.

(3) If it contains *two* O's, one in *each* Cell, it is certainly *empty*, and you may mark the North-West Quarter of the Biliteral Diagram with a O.

(4) Deal in the same way with the North-East, the South-West, and the South-East Quarter.

[Let us take, as examples, the results of the four Examples worked in the previous Chapters.

(1)

In the North-West Quarter, only *one* of the two Cells is marked as *empty*: so we do not know whether the North-West Quarter of the Biliteral Diagram is *occupied* or *empty*: so we cannot mark it.

In the North-East Quarter, we find *two* O's: so *this* Quarter is certainly *empty*; and we mark it so on the Biliteral Diagram.

In the South-West Quarter, we have no information *at all*.

In the South-East Quarter, we have not enough to use.

We may read off the result as "No *x* are *y'*," or "No *y'* are *x*," whichever we prefer.

(2)

In the North-West Quarter, we have not enough information to use.

In the North-East Quarter, we find a I. This shows us that
it is *occupied*: so we may mark the North-East Quarter on the
Biliteral Diagram with a I.

In the South-West Quarter, we have not enough information to use.

In the South-East Quarter, we have none at all.

We may read off the result as "Some *x* are *y'*," or "Some *y'* are *x*," whichever we prefer.

(3)

In the North-West Quarter, we have *no* information. (The I, sitting on the fence, is of no use to us until we know on *which* side he means to jump down!)

In the North-East Quarter, we have not enough information to use. Neither have we in the South-West Quarter.

The South-East Quarter is the only one that yields enough information to use.   It is certainly *empty*: so we mark it as such on the Biliteral Diagram.

We may read off the result as "No *x′* are *y′*," or "No *y′* are *x′*," whichever we prefer.

(4)

The North-West Quarter is *occupied*, in spite of the O in the Outer Cell.   So we mark it with a I on the Biliteral Diagram.

The North-East Quarter yields no information.

The South-West Quarter is certainly *empty*.   So we mark it as such on the Biliteral Diagram.

The South-East Quarter does not yield enough information to use. We read off the result as "All *y* are *x*."]

[Review Tables V, VI (pp. 98, 99).   Work Examples §1, 13–16 (p. 144); §2, 21–32 (p. 144); §3, 1–20 (p. 145).]

BOOK V
SYLLOGISMS

Chapter I ❦ Introductory

When a Trio of Biliteral Propositions of Relation is such that

(1) All their six Terms are Species of the same Genus,
(2) Every two of them contain between them a Pair of codivisional Classes,
(3) The three Propositions are so related that, if the first two were true, the third would be true,

the Trio is called a **Syllogism**; the Genus, of which each of the six Terms is a Species, is called its **Universe of Discourse**, or, more briefly, its **Univ.**; the first two Propositions are called its **Premisses**, and the third its **Conclusion**; also the Pair of codivisional Terms in the Premisses are called its **Eliminands**, and the other two its **Retinends**.

The Conclusion of a Syllogism is said to be **consequent** from its Premisses: hence it is usual to prefix to it the word "Therefore" (or the Symbol ∴).

[Note that the Eliminands are so called because they are *eliminated*, and do not appear in the Conclusion; and that the Retinends are so called because they are *retained*, and *do* appear in the Conclusion.

Note also that the question, whether the Conclusion is or is not *consequent* from the Premisses, is not affected by the *actual* truth or falsity of any of the Trio, but depends entirely on their *relationship to each other*.

107

As a specimen-Syllogism, let us take the Trio

No *x*-Things are *m*-Things;
No *y*-Things are *m'*-Things.
No *x*-Things are *y*-Things.

which we may write, as explained at p. 82, thus:

No *x* are *m*;
No *y* are *m'*.
No *x* are *y*.

Here the first and second contain the Pair of codivisional Classes *m* and *m'*; the first and third contain the Pair *x* and *x*; and the second and third contain the Pair *y* and *y*.

Also the three Propositions are (as we shall see hereafter) so related that, if the first two were true, the third would also be true.

Hence the Trio is a *Syllogism*; the two Propositions, "No *x* are *m*" and "No *y* are *m'*," are its *Premisses*; the Proposition "No *x* are *y*" is its *Conclusion*; the Terms *m* and *m'* are its *Eliminands*; and the Terms *x* and *y* are its *Retinends*.

Hence we may write it thus:

No *x* are *m*;
No *y* are *m'*.
∴ No *x* are *y*.

As a second specimen, let us take the Trio

All cats understand French;
Some chickens are cats.
Some chickens understand French.

These, put into normal form, are

All cats are creatures understanding French;
Some chickens are cats.
Some chickens are creatures understanding French.

Here all the six Terms are Species of the Genus "creatures."

Also the first and second Propositions contain the Pair of codivisional Classes "cats" and "cats"; the first and third contain the Pair "creatures understanding French" and "creatures understanding French"; and the second and third contain the Pair "chickens" and "chickens."

Also the three Propositions are (as we shall see at p. 114) so related that, if the first two were true, the third would be true. (The first two are, as it happens, *not* strictly true in *our* planet. But there is nothing to hinder them from being true in some *other* planet, say *Mars* or *Jupiter*—in which case the third would *also* be true in that planet, and its inhabitants would probably engage chickens as nursery-governesses. They would thus secure a singular *contingent* privilege, unknown in England, namely, that they would be able, at any time when provisions ran short, to utilise the nursery-governess for the nursery-dinner!)

Hence the Trio is a *Syllogism*; the Genus "creatures" is its 'Univ.'; the two Propositions, "All cats understand French" and "Some chickens are cats," are its *Premisses*; the Proposition "Some chickens understand French" is its *Conclusion*; the Terms "cats" and "cats" are its *Eliminands*; and the Terms, "creatures understanding French" and "chickens," are its *Retinends*.

Hence we may write it thus:

All cats understand French;
Some chickens are cats.
∴ Some chickens understand French.]

Chapter II ⚔ Problems in Syllogisms

[§1] **Introductory**

When the Terms of a Proposition are represented by *words*, it is said to be **concrete**; when by *letters*, **abstract.**

To translate a Proposition from concrete into abstract form, we fix on a Univ., and regard each Term as a *Species* of it, and we choose a letter to represent its *Differentia*.

[For example, suppose we wish to translate "Some soldiers are brave" into abstract form. We may take "men" as Univ., and regard "soldiers" and "brave men" as *Species* of the *Genus* "men"; and we may choose x to represent the peculiar Attribute (say "military") of "soldiers," and y to represent "brave." Then the Proposition may be written "Some military men are brave men"; i.e. "Some x-men are y-men"; i.e. (omitting "men," as explained at p. 82) "Some x are y."

In practice, we should merely say "Let Univ. be "men," x = soldiers, y = brave," and at once translate "Some soldiers are brave" into "Some x are y."]

The Problems we shall have to solve are of two kinds, viz.

(1) Given a Pair of Propositions of Relation, which contain between them a pair of codivisional Classes, and which are proposed as Premisses: to ascertain what Conclusion, if any, is consequent from them.

(2) Given a Trio of Propositions of Relation, of which every two contain a pair of codivisional Classes, and which are proposed as a Syllogism: to ascertain whether the proposed Conclusion is consequent from the proposed Premisses, and, if so, whether it is *complete*.

These Problems we will discuss separately.

[§2] Given a Pair of Propositions of Relation, which contain between them a pair of codivisional Classes, and which are proposed as Premisses: to ascertain what Conclusion, if any, is consequent from them

The Rules, for doing this, are as follows:

(1) Determine the Universe of Discourse.

(2) Construct a Dictionary, making m and m (or m and m') represent the pair of codivisional Classes, and x (or x') and y (or y') the other two.

(3) Translate the proposed Premisses into abstract form.

(4) Represent them, together, on a Triliteral Diagram.

(5) Ascertain what Proposition, if any, in terms of x and y, is *also* represented on it.

(6) Translate this into concrete form.

It is evident that, if the proposed Premisses were true, this other Proposition would *also* be true. Hence it is a *Conclusion* consequent from the proposed Premisses.

[Let us work some examples.

(1)

No son of mine is dishonest;
People always treat an honest man with respect.

Taking "men" as Univ., we may write these as follows:

No sons of mine are dishonest men;
All honest men are men treated with respect.

We can now construct our Dictionary, viz. m = honest; x = sons of mine; y = treated with respect.

(Note that the expression "x = sons of mine" is an abbreviated form of "x = the Differentia of 'sons of mine,' when regarded as a Species of 'men.'")

The next thing is to translate the proposed Premisses into abstract form, as follows:

No *x* are *m'*;

All *m* are *y*.

Next, by the process described at p. 102, we represent these on a Triliteral Diagram, thus:

Next, by the process described at p. 105, we transfer to a Biliteral Diagram all the information we can.

The result we can read either as "No *x* are *y'*" or as "No *y'* are *x*," whichever we prefer. So we refer to our Dictionary, to see which will look best; and we choose

No *x* are *y'*,

which, translated into concrete form, is

No son of mine ever fails to be treated with respect.

(2)

All cats understand French;

Some chickens are cats.

Taking "creatures" as Univ., we write these as follows:

All cats are creatures understanding French;

Some chickens are cats.

We can now construct our Dictionary, viz. *m* = cats; *x* = understanding French; *y* = chickens.

The proposed Premisses, translated into abstract form, are

All *m* are *x*;

Some *y* are *m*.

In order to represent these on a Triliteral Diagram, we break up the first into the two Propositions to which it is equivalent, and thus get the *three* Propositions

(1) Some *m* are *x*;

(2) No *m* are *x'*;

(3) Some *y* are *m*.

The Rule, given at p. 102, would make us take these in the order 2, 1, 3.

This, however, would produce the result

So it would be better to take them in the order 2, 3, 1.
Nos. (2) and (3) give us the result here shown; and now
we need not trouble about No. (1), as the Proposition
"Some *m* are *x*" is *already* represented on the Diagram.

Transferring our information to a Biliteral Diagram, we get

This result we can read either as "Some *x* are *y*" or "Some *y* are *x*."
After consulting our Dictionary, we choose

Some *y* are *x*,

which, translated into concrete form, is

Some chickens understand French.

(3)

All diligent students are successful;
All ignorant students are unsuccessful.

Let Univ. be "students"; *m* = successful; *x* = diligent; *y* = ignorant.
These Premisses, in abstract form, are

All *x* are *m*;
All *y* are *m*′.

These, broken up, give us the four Propositions

(1) Some *x* are *m*;
(2) No *x* are *m*′;
(3) Some *y* are *m*′;
(4) No *y* are *m*."

which we take in the order 2, 4, 1, 3.

Representing these on a Triliteral Diagram, we get

And this information, transferred to a Biliteral Diagram, is

Here we get *two* Conclusions, viz.:

All *x* are *y*′;
All *y* are *x*′.

And these, translated into concrete form, are

All diligent students are (not-ignorant, i.e.) learned;
All ignorant students are (not-diligent, i.e.) idle.

(See p. 63.)

(4)

Of the prisoners who were put on their trial at the last Assizes,
all, against whom the verdict "guilty" was returned, were
sentenced to imprisonment;
Some, who were sentenced to imprisonment, were also
sentenced to hard labour.

Let Univ. be "the prisoners who were put on their trial at the last
Assizes"; m = who were sentenced to imprisonment; x = against whom
the verdict "guilty" was returned; y = who were sentenced to hard labour.
The Premisses, translated into abstract form, are

All x are m;
Some m are y.

Breaking up the first, we get the three

(1) Some x are m;
(2) No x are m';
(3) Some m are y.

Representing these, in the order 2, 1, 3, on a Triliteral
Diagram, we get

Here we get no Conclusion at all.
You would very likely have guessed, if you had seen *only* the Premisses,
that the Conclusion would be

Some, against whom the verdict "guilty" was returned, were
sentenced to hard labour.

But this Conclusion is not even *true*, with regard to the Assizes I have here
invented.
"Not *true*!" you exclaim. "Then who *were* they, who were sentenced
to imprisonment and were also sentenced to hard labour? They *must*
have had the verdict 'guilty' returned against them, or how could they
be sentenced?"
Well, it happened like *this*, you see. They were three ruffians, who
had committed highway-robbery. When they were put on their trial,
they *pleaded* "guilty." So no *verdict* was returned at all; and they were
sentenced at once.]

I will now work out, in their briefest form, as models for the Reader to
imitate in working examples, the above four concrete Problems.

(1) [see p. 110]

No son of mine is dishonest;
People always treat an honest man with respect.

Univ. "men"; m = honest; x = my sons; y = treated with respect.

No x are m';
All m are y.

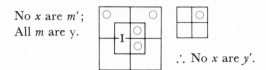

∴ No x are y'.

i.e. "No son of mine ever fails to be treated with respect."

(2) [see p. 111]

All cats understand French;
Some chickens are cats.

Univ. "creatures"; m = cats; x = understanding French; y = chickens.

All m are x;
Some y are m.

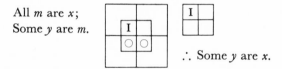

∴ Some y are x.

i.e. "Some chickens understand French."

(3) [see p. 112]

All diligent students are successful;
All ignorant students are unsuccessful.

Univ. "students"; m = successful; x = diligent; y = ignorant.

All x are m;
All y are m'.

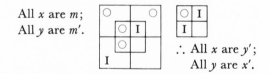

∴ All x are y';
All y are x'.

i.e. "All diligent students are learned; and all ignorant students are idle."

(4) [see p. 113]

Of the prisoners who were put on their trial at the last Assizes, all, against whom the verdict "guilty" was returned, were sentenced to imprisonment;
Some, who were sentenced to imprisonment, were also sentenced to hard labour.

Univ. "prisoners who were put on their trial at the last Assizes"; m = sentenced to imprisonment; x = against whom the verdict "guilty" was returned; y = sentenced to hard labour.

All x are m;
Some m are y.

There is no Conclusion.

[Review Tables VII, VIII (pp. 100, 101). Work Examples §1, 17–21 (p. 144); §4, 1–6 (p. 146); §5, 1–6 (p. 147).]

[§3] Given a Trio of Propositions of Relation, of which every two contain a Pair of codivisional Classes, and which are proposed as a Syllogism; to ascertain whether the proposed Conclusion is consequent from the proposed Premisses, and, if so, whether it is complete

The Rules, for doing this, are as follows:

(1) Take the proposed Premisses, and ascertain, by the process described at p. 110, what Conclusion, if any, is consequent from them.

(2) If there be *no* Conclusion, say so.

(3) If there *be* a Conclusion, compare it with the proposed Conclusion, and pronounce accordingly.

I will now work out, in their briefest form, as models for the Reader to imitate in working examples, six Problems.

(1)

All soldiers are strong;
All soldiers are brave.
   Some strong men are brave.

Univ. "men"; m = soldiers; x = strong; y = brave.

All m are x;
All m are y.
Some x are y.

∴ Some x are y.

Hence proposed Conclusion is right.

(2)

I admire these pictures;

When I admire anything I wish to examine it thoroughly.

I wish to examine some of these pictures thoroughly.

Univ. "things"; m = admired by me; x = these pictures; y = things which I wish to examine thoroughly.

All x are m;
All m are y.
Some x are y.

∴ All x are y.

Hence proposed Conclusion is *incomplete*, the *complete* one being "I wish to examine *all* these pictures thoroughly."

(3)

None but the brave deserve the fair;

Some braggarts are cowards.

Some braggarts do not deserve the fair.

Univ. "persons"; m = brave; x = deserving of the fair; y = braggarts.

No m' are x;
Some y are m'.
Some y are x'.

∴ Some y are x'.

Hence proposed Conclusion is right.

(4)

All soldiers can march;

Some babies are not soldiers.

Some babies cannot march.

Univ. "persons"; m = soldiers; x = able to march; y = babies.

All m are x;
Some y are m'.
Some y are x'.

There is no Conclusion.

(5)

All selfish men are unpopular;

All obliging men are popular.

All obliging men are unselfish.

Univ. "men"; m = popular; x = selfish; y = obliging.

All x are m';
All y are m.
All y are x'.

∴ All x are y';
All y are x'.

Hence proposed Conclusion is *incomplete*, the *complete* one containing, in addition, "All selfish men are disobliging."

(6)

No one, who means to go by the train and cannot get a conveyance, and has not enough time to walk to the station, can do
without running;

This party of tourists mean to go by the train and cannot get a
conveyance, but they have plenty of time to walk to the
station.

This party of tourists need not run.

Univ. "persons meaning to go by the train, and unable to get a conveyance"; m = having enough time to walk to the station; x = needing to
run; y = these tourists.

No m' are x';
All y are m.
All y are x'.

There is no
Conclusion.

[Here is *another* opportunity, gentle Reader, for playing a trick on your
innocent friend.   Put the proposed Syllogism before him, and ask him
what he thinks of the Conclusion.

He will reply "Why, it's perfectly correct, of course!   And if your
precious Logic-book tells you it *isn't*, don't believe it!   You don't mean to
tell me those tourists *need* to run?   If *I* were one of them, and knew the
Premisses to be true, I should be *quite* clear that *I* needn't run—and
I *should walk*!"

And *you* will reply "But suppose there was a mad bull behind you?"

And then your innocent friend will say "Hum! Ha! I must think that
over a bit!"

You may then explain to him, as a convenient *test* of the soundness of a
Syllogism, that, if circumstances can be invented which, without
interfering with the truth of the *Premisses*, would make the *Conclusion* false,
the Syllogism *must* be unsound.]

[Review Tables V–VIII (pp. 98–101).   Work Examples §4, 7–12 (p. 146);
§5, 7–12 (p. 147); §6, 1–10 (p. 153); §7, 1–6 (pp. 154, 155).]

BOOK VI
THE METHOD OF
SUBSCRIPTS

Chapter I ❧ Introductory

Let us agree that x_1 shall mean "Some existing Things have the Attribute x," i.e. (more briefly) "Some x exist"; also that xy_1 shall mean "Some xy exist," and so on.   Such a Proposition may be called an **Entity**.

[Note that, when there are *two* letters in the expression, it does not in the least matter which stands *first*: xy_1 and yx_1 mean exactly the same.]

Also that x_0 shall mean "No existing Things have the Attribute x," i.e. (more briefly) "No x exist"; also that xy_0 shall mean "No xy exist," and so on.   Such a Proposition may be called a **Nullity**.
Also that † shall mean "and."

[Thus ab_1 † cd_0 means "Some ab exist and no cd exist."]

Also that ¶ shall mean "would, if true, prove." [1]

[Thus, x_0 ¶ xy_0 means "The Proposition 'No x exist' would, if true, prove the Proposition 'No xy exist.'"]

---

[1] The symbol ¶ is first used by Carroll,   *Euclid and His Modern Rivals*. in approximately this sense, in his

When two Letters are both of them accented, or both *not* accented, they are said to have **Like Signs**, or to be **Like**: when one is accented, and the other not, they are said to have **Unlike Signs**, or to be **Unlike**.

Chapter II ※ Representation of Propositions of Relation

Let us take, first, the Proposition "Some x are y."

This, we know, is equivalent to the Proposition of Existence "Some xy exist." (See p. 86.) Hence it may be represented by the expression xy_1.

The Converse Proposition "Some y are x" may of course be represented by the *same* expression, viz. xy_1.

Similarly we may represent the three similar Pairs of Converse Propositions, viz.

$$\text{Some } x \text{ are } y' = \text{Some } y' \text{ are } x,$$
$$\text{Some } x' \text{ are } y = \text{Some } y \text{ are } x',$$
$$\text{Some } x' \text{ are } y' = \text{Some } y' \text{ are } x'.$$

Let us take, next, the Proposition "No x are y."

This, we know, is equivalent to the Proposition of Existence "No xy exist." (See p. 88.) Hence it may be represented by the expression xy_0.

The Converse Proposition "No y are x" may of course be represented by the *same* expression, viz. xy_0.

Similarly we may represent the three similar Pairs of Converse Propositions, viz.

$$\text{No } x \text{ are } y' = \text{No } y' \text{ are } x,$$
$$\text{No } x' \text{ are } y = \text{No } y \text{ are } x',$$
$$\text{No } x' \text{ are } y' = \text{No } y' \text{ are } x'.$$

Let us take, next, the Proposition "All x are y."

Now it is evident that the Double Proposition of Existence "Some x exist and no xy' exist" tells us that *some* x-Things exist, but that *none* of them have the Attribute y': that is, it tells us that *all* of them have the Attribute y: that is, it tells us that "All x are y."

Also it is evident that the expression $x_1 \dagger xy'_0$ represents this Double Proposition.

Hence it also represents the Proposition "All x are y."

[The Reader will perhaps be puzzled by the statement that the Proposition "All x are y" is equivalent to the Double Proposition "Some x exist and no xy' exist," remembering that it was stated, at p. 88, to be equivalent to the Double Proposition "Some x are y and no x are y' " (i.e. "Some xy exist and no xy' exist"). The explanation is that the Proposition "Some xy exist" contains *superfluous information*. "Some x exist" is enough for our purpose.]

This expression may be written in a shorter form, viz. $x_1y'_0$, since *each* Subscript takes effect back to the *beginning* of the expression.

Similarly we may represent the seven similar Propositions

All x are y',
All x' are y,
All x' are y',
All y are x,
All y are x',
All y' are x,
All y' are x'.

[The Reader should make out all these for himself.]

It will be convenient to remember that, in translating a Proposition, beginning with "All," from abstract form into subscript form, or *vice versa*, the Predicate *changes sign* (that is, changes from positive to negative, or else from negative to positive).

[Thus, the Proposition "All y are x' " becomes y_1x_0, where the Predicate changes from x' to x.

Again, the expression $x'_1y'_0$ becomes "All x' are y," where the Predicate changes from y' to y.]

Chapter III ⚶ Syllogisms

[§1] Representation of Syllogisms

We already know how to represent each of the three Propositions of a Syllogism in subscript form. When that is done, all we need, besides, is to write the three expressions in a row, with † between the Premisses, and ¶ before the Conclusion.

[Thus the Syllogism

$$\text{No } x \text{ are } m';$$
$$\text{All } m \text{ are } y.$$
$$\therefore \text{ No } x \text{ are } y'.$$

may be represented thus:

$$xm'_0 \dagger m_1 y'_0 \,\P\, xy'_0$$

When a Proposition has to be translated from concrete form into subscript form, the Reader will find it convenient, just at first, to translate it into *abstract* form, and *thence* into subscript form. But, after a little practice, he will find it quite easy to go straight from concrete form to subscript form.]

[§2] Formulæ for solving Problems in Syllogisms

When once we have found, by Diagrams, the Conclusion to a given Pair of Premisses, and have represented the Syllogism in subscript form, we have a *Formula*, by which we can at once find, without having to use Diagrams again, the Conclusion to any *other* Pair of Premisses having the *same* subscript forms.

[Thus, the expression

$$xm_0 \dagger ym'_0 \,\P\, xy_0$$

is a *Formula*, by which we can find the Conclusion to any Pair of Premisses whose subscript forms are

$$xm_0 \dagger ym'_0$$

For example, suppose we had the Pair of Propositions

$$\text{No gluttons are healthy;}$$
$$\text{No unhealthy men are strong.}$$

proposed as Premisses.   Taking "men" as our Universe, and making m = healthy; x = gluttons; y = strong; we might translate the Pair into abstract form, thus:

No x are m;
No m' are y.

These, in subscript form, would be

$xm_0 \dagger m'y_0$

which are identical with those in our *Formula*.   Hence we at once know the Conclusion to be

xy_0

that is, in abstract form,

No x are y;

that is, in concrete form,

No gluttons are strong.]

I shall now take three different forms of Pairs of Premisses, and work out their Conclusions, once for all, by Diagrams; and thus obtain some useful Formulæ.   I shall call them Fig. I, Fig. II, and Fig. III.

Fig. I

This includes any Pair of Premisses which are both of them Nullities, and which contain Unlike Eliminands.

The simplest case is

$xm_0 \dagger ym'_0$

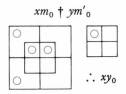

$\therefore xy_0$

In this case we see that the Conclusion is a Nullity, and that the Retinends have kept their Signs.

And we should find this Rule to hold good with *any* Pair of Premisses which fulfil the given conditions.

[The Reader had better satisfy himself of this, by working out, on Diagrams, several varieties, such as

$m_1x_0 \dagger ym'_0$ (which $\P\ xy_0$)
$xm'_0 \dagger m_1y_0$ (which $\P\ xy_0$)
$x'm_0 \dagger ym'_0$ (which $\P\ x'y_0$)
$m'_1x'_0 \dagger m_1y'_0$ (which $\P\ x'y'_0$).]

If either Retinend is asserted in the *Premisses* to exist, of course it may be so asserted in the *Conclusion*.

Hence we get two *Variants* of Fig. I, viz.

 (α) where *one* Retinend is so asserted;
 (β) where *both* are so asserted.

[The Reader had better work out, on Diagrams, examples of these two Variants, such as

$$m_1x_0 \dagger y_1m'_0 \text{ (which proves } y_1x_0\text{)}$$
$$x_1m'_0 \dagger m_1y_0 \text{ (which proves } x_1y_0\text{)}$$
$$x'_1m_0 \dagger y_1m'_0 \text{ (which proves } x'_1y_0 \dagger y_1x'_0\text{)}.]$$

The Formula, to be remembered, is

$$xm_0 \dagger ym'_0 \,\P\, xy_0$$

with the following two Rules:

 (1) *Two Nullities, with Unlike Eliminands, yield a Nullity, in which both Retinends keep their Signs.*
 (2) *A Retinend, asserted in the Premisses to exist, may be so asserted in the Conclusion.*

[Note that Rule (1) is merely the Formula expressed in words.]

Fig. II

This includes any Pair of Premisses, of which one is a Nullity and the other an Entity, and which contain Like Eliminands.

The simplest case is

$$xm_0 \dagger ym_1$$

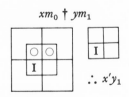

$$\therefore x'y_1$$

In this case we see that the Conclusion is an Entity, and that the Nullity-Retinend has changed its Sign.

And we should find this Rule to hold good with *any* Pair of Premisses which fulfil the given conditions.

[The Reader had better satisfy himself of this, by working out, on Diagrams, several varieties, such as

$$x'm_0 \dagger ym_1 \text{ (which } \mathbb{P} \, xy_1)$$
$$x_1m'_0 \dagger y'm'_1 \text{ (which } \mathbb{P} \, x'y'_1)$$
$$m_1x_0 \dagger y'm_1 \text{ (which } \mathbb{P} \, x'y'_1).]$$

The Formula, to be remembered, is,

$$xm_0 \dagger ym_1 \, \mathbb{P} \, x'y_1$$

with the following Rule:

A Nullity and an Entity, with Like Eliminands, yield an Entity, in which the Nullity-Retinend changes its Sign.

[Note that this Rule is merely the Formula expressed in words.]

Fig. III

This includes any Pair of Premisses which are both of them Nullities, and which contain Like Eliminands asserted to exist.

The simplest case is

$$xm_0 \dagger ym_0 \dagger m_1$$

[Note that m_1 is here stated *separately*, because it does not matter in *which* of the two Premisses it occurs: so that this includes the *three* forms $m_1x_0 \dagger ym_0$, $xm_0 \dagger m_1y_0$, and $m_1x_0 \dagger m_1y_0$.]

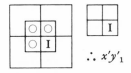

$$\therefore x'y'_1$$

In this case we see that the Conclusion is an Entity, and that *both* Retinends have changed their Signs.

And we should find this Rule to hold good with *any* Pair of Premisses which fulfil the given conditions.

[The Reader had better satisfy himself of this, by working out, on Diagrams, several varieties, such as

$$x'm_0 \dagger m_1y_0 \text{ (which } \mathbb{P} \, xy'_1)$$
$$m'_1x_0 \dagger m'y'_0 \text{ (which } \mathbb{P} \, x'y_1)$$
$$m_1x'_0 \dagger m_1y'_0 \text{ (which } \mathbb{P} \, xy_1).]$$

The Formula, to be remembered, is

$$xm_0 \dagger ym_0 \dagger m_1 \ \P \ x'y'_1$$

with the following Rule (which is merely the Formula expressed in words):

> *Two Nullities, with Like Eliminands asserted to exist, yield an Entity, in which both Retinends change their Signs.*

In order to help the Reader to remember the peculiarities and Formulæ of these three Figures, I will put them all together in one Table.

TABLE IX

Fig. I
$xm_0 \dagger ym'_0 \ \P \ xy_0$
Two Nullities, with Unlike Eliminands, yield a Nullity, in which both Retinends keep their Signs.   A Retinend, asserted in the Premisses to exist, may be so asserted in the Conclusion.
Fig. II
$xm_0 \dagger ym_1 \ \P \ x'y_1$
A Nullity and an Entity, with Like Eliminands, yield an Entity, in which the Nullity-Retinend changes its Sign.
Fig. III
$xm_0 \dagger ym_0 \dagger m_1 \ \P \ x'y'_1$
Two Nullities, with Like Eliminands asserted to exist, yield an Entity, in which both Retinends change their Signs.

I will now work out, by these Formulæ, as models for the Reader to imitate, some Problems in Syllogisms which have been already worked, by Diagrams, in Book V, Chap. II.

(1) [see p. 110]

No son of mine is dishonest;
People always treat an honest man with respect.

Univ. "men"; m = honest; x = my sons; y = treated with respect.

$$xm'_0 \dagger m_1 y'_0 \ \P \ xy'_0 \ \text{[Fig. I}$$

i.e. "No son of mine ever fails to be treated with respect."

(2) [see p. 111]

All cats understand French;
Some chickens are cats.

Univ. "creatures"; m = cats; x = understanding French; y = chickens.

$$m_1x'_0 \dagger ym_1 \, \P \, xy_1 \text{ [Fig. II}$$

i.e. "Some chickens understand French."

(3) [see p. 112]

All diligent students are successful;
All ignorant students are unsuccessful.

Univ. "students"; m = successful; x = diligent; y = ignorant.

$$x_1m'_0 \dagger y_1m_0 \, \P \, x_1y_0 \dagger y_1x_0 \text{ [Fig. I } (\beta)$$

i.e. "All diligent students are learned; and all ignorant students are idle."

(4) [see p. 115]

All soldiers are strong;
All soldiers are brave.
    Some strong men are brave.

Univ. "men"; m = soldiers; x = strong; y = brave.

$$m_1x'_0 \dagger m_1y'_0 \, \P \, xy_1 \text{ [Fig. III}$$

Hence proposed Conclusion is right.

(5) [see p. 116]

I admire these pictures;
When I admire anything, I wish to examine it thoroughly
    I wish to examine some of these pictures thoroughly.

Univ. "things"; m = admired by me; x = these; y = things which I wish to examine thoroughly.

$$x_1m'_0 \dagger m_1y'_0 \, \P \, x_1y'_0 \text{ [Fig. I } (\alpha)$$

Hence proposed Conclusion, xy_1, is *incomplete*, the *complete* one being "I wish to examine *all* these pictures thoroughly."

(6) [see p. 116]

None but the brave deserve the fair;
Some braggarts are cowards.
    Some braggarts do not deserve the fair.

Univ. "persons"; $m =$ brave; $x =$ deserving of the fair; $y =$ braggarts.

$$m'x_0 \dagger ym'_1 \mathbb{P} x'y_1 \text{ [Fig. II}$$

Hence proposed Conclusion is right.

(7) [see p. 117]

No one, who means to go by the train and cannot get a conveyance,
    and has not enough time to walk to the station, can do without
    running;
This party of tourists mean to go by the train and cannot get a
    conveyance, but they have plenty of time to walk to the station.
    This party of tourists need not run.

Univ. "persons meaning to go by the train, and unable to get a conveyance"; $m =$ having enough time to walk to the station; $x =$ needing to run; $y =$ these tourists.

$m'x'_0 \dagger y_1m'_0$ do not come under any of the three Figures. Hence it is necessary to return to the Method of Diagrams, as shown at p. 117. Hence there is no Conclusion.

[Work Examples §**4**, 12–20 (p. 146); §**5**, 13–24 (pp. 147, 148); §**6**, 1–6 (p. 153); §**7**, 1–3 (pp. 154, 155). Also read Note (A).]

Notes

(A)

One of the favourite objections, brought against the Science of Logic by its detractors, is that a Syllogism has no real validity as an argument, since it involves the Fallacy of *Petitio Principii* (i.e. "Begging the Question," the essence of which is that the whole Conclusion is involved in *one* of the Premisses).

This formidable objection is refuted, with beautiful clearness and simplicity, by these three Diagrams, which show us that, in each of the three Figures, the Conclusion is really involved in the *two* Premisses taken together, each contributing its share.

Thus, in Fig. I, the Premiss xm_0 empties the *Inner* Cell of the North-West Quarter, while the Premiss ym'_0 empties its *Outer* Cell. Hence it needs the two Premisses to empty the *whole* of the North-West Quarter, and thus to prove the Conclusion xy_0.

Again, in Fig. II, the Premiss xm_0 empties the Inner Cell of the North-West Quarter. The Premiss ym_1 merely tells us that the Inner Portion of the West Half is *occupied*, so that we may place a I in it, *somewhere*; but, if this were the *whole* of our information, we should not know in *which* Cell to place it, so that it would have to "sit on the fence": it is only when we learn, from the other Premiss, that the *upper* of these two Cells is *empty*, that we feel authorised to place the I in the *lower* Cell, and thus to prove the Conclusion $x'y_1$.

Lastly, in Fig. III, the information, that m exists, merely authorises us to place a I *somewhere* in the Inner Square—but it has a large choice of fences to sit upon! It needs the Premiss xm_0 to drive it out of the North Half of that Square; and it needs the Premiss ym_0 to drive it out of the West Half. Hence it needs the two Premisses to drive it into the Inner Portion of the South-East Quarter, and thus to prove the Conclusion $x'y'_1$.

[§3] Fallacies

Any argument which *deceives* us, by seeming to prove what it does not really prove, may be called a **Fallacy** (derived from the Latin verb *fallo* "I deceive"); but the particular kind, to be now discussed, consists of a Pair of Propositions, which are proposed as the Premisses of a Syllogism, but yield no Conclusion.

When each of the proposed Premisses is a Proposition in *I*, or *E*, or *A* (the only kinds with which we are now concerned) the Fallacy may be detected by the "Method of Diagrams," by simply setting them out on a Triliteral Diagram, and observing that they yield no information which can be transferred to the Biliteral Diagram.

But suppose we were working by the "Method of *Subscripts*," and had to deal with a Pair of proposed Premisses, which happened to be a "Fallacy," how could we be certain that they would not yield any Conclusion?

Our best plan is, I think, to deal with *Fallacies* in the same way as we have already dealt with *Syllogisms*: that is, to take certain forms of Pairs of Propositions, and to work them out, once for all, on the Triliteral Diagram, and ascertain that they yield *no* Conclusion; and then to record them, for future use, as *Formulæ for Fallacies*, just as we have already recorded our three *Formulæ for Syllogisms*.

Now, if we were to record the two Sets of Formulæ in the *same* shape, viz. by the Method of Subscripts, there would be considerable risk of confusing the two kinds. Hence, in order to keep them distinct, I propose to record the Formulæ for *Fallacies* in *words*, and to call them "Forms" instead of "Formulæ."

Let us now proceed to find, by the Method of Diagrams, three "Forms of Fallacies," which we will then put on record for future use. They are as follows:

(1) Fallacy of Like Eliminands not asserted to exist.
(2) Fallacy of Unlike Eliminands with an Entity-Premiss.
(3) Fallacy of two Entity-Premisses.

These shall be discussed separately, and it will be seen that each fails to yield a Conclusion.

(1) *Fallacy of Like Eliminands not asserted to exist*

It is evident that neither of the given Propositions can be an *Entity*, since that kind asserts the *existence* of both of its Terms (see p. 76). Hence they must both be *Nullities*.

Hence the given Pair may be represented by $(xm_0 \dagger ym_0)$, with or without x_1, y_1.

These, set out on Triliteral Diagrams, are

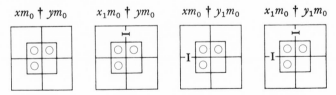

$$xm_0 \dagger ym_0 \qquad x_1m_0 \dagger ym_0 \qquad xm_0 \dagger y_1m_0 \qquad x_1m_0 \dagger y_1m_0$$

(2) *Fallacy of Unlike Eliminands with an Entity-Premiss*

Here the given Pair may be represented by $(xm_0 \dagger ym'_1)$ with or without x_1 or m_1.

These, set out on Triliteral Diagrams, are

$xm_0 \dagger ym'_1$ $x_1m_0 \dagger ym'_1$ $m_1x_0 \dagger ym'_1$

(3) *Fallacy of two Entity-Premisses*[1]

Here the given Pair may be represented by either $(xm_1 \dagger ym_1)$ or $(xm_1 \dagger ym'_1)$.

These, set out on Triliteral Diagrams, are

$xm_1 \dagger ym_1$ $xm_1 \dagger ym'_1$

[§4] Method of proceeding with a given Pair of Propositions

Let us suppose that we have before us a Pair of Propositions of Relation, which contain between them a Pair of codivisional Classes, and that we wish to ascertain what Conclusion, if any, is consequent from them. We translate them, if necessary, into subscript-form, and then proceed as follows:

(1) We examine their Subscripts, in order to see whether they are

(a) a Pair of Nullities; or

(b) a Nullity and an Entity; or

(c) a Pair of Entities.

---

[1] On a manuscript page preserved in the Library of Christ Church, Oxford, dated 1 February 1893, Carroll writes of fallacies:

"Every valid trinomial Syllogism must contain either

$\left.\begin{array}{c} xm_0 \\ ym'_0 \end{array}\right\}$

or

$\left.\begin{array}{c} xm_0 \\ ym_1 \end{array}\right\}$

"These should be reduced to Rules, so that fallacious Premisses might be convicted by some such phrases as 'undistributed middle,' 'four terms,' etc.

"The fallacy

$\left.\begin{array}{c} xm_1 \\ ym_1 \end{array}\right\}$

may be called 'the fallacy of two entities.'"

(2) If they are a Pair of Nullities, we examine their Eliminands, in order to see whether they are Unlike or Like.

If their Eliminands are *Unlike*, it is a case of Fig. I. We then examine their Retinends, to see whether one or both of them are asserted to *exist*. If *one* Retinend is so asserted, it is a case of Fig. I (α); if *both*, it is a case of Fig. I (β).

If their Eliminands are *Like*, we examine them, in order to see whether either of them is asserted to exist. If so, it is a case of Fig. III; if not, it is a case of "Fallacy of Like Eliminands not asserted to exist."

(3) If they are a Nullity and an Entity, we examine their Eliminands, in order to see whether they are Like or Unlike.

If their Eliminands are *Like*, it is a case of Fig. II; if *Unlike*, it is a case of "Fallacy of Unlike Eliminands with an Entity-Premiss."

(4) If they are a Pair of Entities, it is a case of "Fallacy of two Entity-Premisses."

[Work Examples §4, 1–11 (p. 146); §5, 1–12 (p. 147); §6, 7–12 (p. 153); §7, 7–12 (p. 155).]

BOOK VII
SORITESES

Chapter I ❧ Introductory

When a Set of three or more Biliteral Propositions are such that all their Terms are Species of the same Genus, and are also so related that two of them, taken together, yield a Conclusion, which, taken with another of them, yields another Conclusion, and so on, until all have been taken, it is evident that, if the original Set were true, the last Conclusion would *also* be true.

Such a Set, with the last Conclusion tacked on, is called a **Sorites**; the original Set of Propositions is called its **Premisses**; each of the intermediate Conclusions is called a **Partial Conclusion** of the Sorites; the last Conclusion is called its **Complete Conclusion**, or, more briefly, its **Conclusion**; the Genus, of which all the Terms are Species, is called its **Universe of Discourse**, or, more briefly, its **Univ.**; the Terms, used as Eliminands in the Syllogisms, are called its **Eliminands**; and the two Terms, which are *retained*, and therefore appear in the Conclusion, are called its **Retinends**.

[Note that each *Partial* Conclusion contains one or two *Eliminands*; but that the *Complete* Conclusion contains *Retinends* only.]

The Conclusion is said to be **consequent** from the Premisses; for which reason it is usual to prefix to it the word "Therefore" (or the symbol ∴).

[Note that the question, whether the Conclusion is or is not *consequent* from the Premisses, is not affected by the *actual* truth or falsity of any one of the

133

Propositions which make up the Sorites, but depends entirely on their *relationship to one another.*[1]

As a specimen-Sorites, let us take the following Set of five Propositions:

(1) No a are b';
(2) All b are c;
(3) All c are d;
(4) No e' are a';
(5) All h are e'

Here the first and second, taken together, yield "No a are c'."
This, taken along with the third, yields "No a are d'."
This, taken along with the fourth, yields "No d' are e'."
And this, taken along with the fifth, yields "All h are d."
Hence, if the original Set were true, this would *also* be true.
Hence the original Set, with this tacked on, is a *Sorites*; the original Set
    is its *Premisses*; the Proposition "All h are d" is its *Conclusion*; the Terms
    a, b, c, e are its *Eliminands*; and the Terms d and h are its *Retinends*.
Hence we may write the whole Sorites thus:

No a are b';
All b are c;
All c are d;
No e' are a';
All h are e'.
$\therefore$ All h are d

In the above Sorites, the three Partial Conclusions are the Propositions
"No a are c'," "No a are d'," "No d' are e'"; but, if the Premisses were
arranged in other ways, other Partial Conclusions might be obtained.
Thus, the order 41523 yields the Partial Conclusions "No e' are b',"
"All h are b," "All h are c." There are altogether *nine* Partial Conclusions
to this Sorites, which the Reader will find it an interesting task to make
out for himself.]

---

[1] Here Carroll refers to the important distinction between the *validity* of an argument (such as Syllogism or Sorites) and the *truth* of its component statements. In his Preface to the third edition of *Euclid and His Modern Rivals*, Carroll put the point somewhat more vividly: "The *validity* of a Syllogism is quite independent of the *truth* of its Premisses. 'I have sent for you, my dear Ducks,' said the worthy Mrs. Bond, 'to enquire with what sauce you would like to be eaten?' 'But we don't want to be *killed*!' cried the Ducks. '*You are wandering from the point*' was Mrs. Bond's perfectly logical reply."

Chapter II ❧ Problems in Soriteses

[§1] Introductory

The Problems we shall have to solve are of the following form:

> Given three or more Propositions of Relation, which are proposed as Premisses: to ascertain what Conclusion, if any, is consequent from them.

We will limit ourselves, at present, to Problems which can be worked by the Formulæ of Fig. I. (See p. 123.) Those that require *other* Formulæ are rather too hard for beginners.

Such Problems may be solved by either of two Methods, viz.

(1) The Method of Separate Syllogisms;
(2) The Method of Underscoring.

These shall be discussed separately.

[§2] Solution by Method of Separate Syllogisms

The Rules, for doing this, are as follows:

(1) Name the Universe of Discourse.
(2) Construct a Dictionary, making *a*, *b*, *c*, &c., represent the Terms.
(3) Put the Proposed Premisses into subscript form.
(4) Select two which, containing between them a pair of codivisional Classes, can be used as the Premisses of a Syllogism.
(5) Find their Conclusion by Formula.
(6) Find a third Premiss which, along with this Conclusion, can be used as the Premisses of a second Syllogism.
(7) Find a second Conclusion by Formula.
(8) Proceed thus, until all the proposed Premisses have been used.
(9) Put the last Conclusion, which is the Complete Conclusion of the Sorites, into concrete form.

[As an example of this process, let us take, as the proposed Set of Premisses,

(1) All the policemen on this beat sup with our cook;

135

(2) No man with long hair can fail to be a poet;
(3) Amos Judd has never been in prison;
(4) Our cook's "cousins" all love cold mutton;
(5) None but policemen on this beat are poets;
(6) None but her "cousins" ever sup with our cook;
(7) Men with short hair have all been in prison.

Univ. "men"; a = Amos Judd; b = cousins of our cook;
c = having been in prison; d = long-haired;
e = loving cold mutton; h = poets;
k = policemen on this beat; l = supping with our cook.

We now have to put the proposed Premisses into *subscript* form. Let us begin by putting them into *abstract* form. The result is

(1) All k are l;
(2) No d are h';
(3) All a are c';
(4) All b are e;
(5) No k' are h;
(6) No b' are l;
(7) All d' are c

And it is now easy to put them into *subscript* form, as follows:

(1) $k_1 l'_0$
(2) dh'_0
(3) $a_1 c_0$
(4) $b_1 e'_0$
(5) $k' h_0$
(6) $b' l_0$
(7) $d'_1 c'_0$

We now have to find a pair of Premisses which will yield a Conclusion. Let us begin with No. (1), and look down the list, till we come to one which we can take along with it, so as to form Premisses belonging to Fig. I. We find that No. (5) will do, since we can take k as our Eliminand. So our first syllogism is

(1) $k_1 l'_0$
(5) $k' h_0$
  $\therefore l' h_0 \ldots (8)$

We must now begin again with $l' h_0$, and find a Premiss to go along with it. We find that No. (2) will do, h being our Eliminand. So our next Syllogism is

(8) $l' h_0$
(2) dh'_0
  $\therefore l' d_0 \ldots (9)$

We have now used up Nos. (1), (5), and (2), and must search among the others for a partner for $l'd_0$. We find that No. (6) will do. So we write

(9) $l'd_0$
(6) $b'l_0$
$\therefore db'_0 \ldots (10)$

Now what can we take along with db'_0? No. (4) will do.

(10) db'_0
(4) $b_1 e'_0$
$\therefore de'_0 \ldots (11)$

Along with *this* we may take No. (7).

(11) de'_0
(7) $d'_1 c'_0$
$\therefore e'c'_0 \ldots (12)$

And along with *this* we may take No. (3).

(12) $e'c'_0$
(3) $a_1 c_0$
$\therefore a_1 e'_0$

This Complete Conclusion, translated into *abstract* form, is

All *a* are *e*;

and this, translated into *concrete* form, is

Amos Judd loves cold mutton.

In actually *working* this Problem, the above explanations would, of course, be omitted, and all, that would appear on paper, would be as follows:

(1) $k_1 l'_0$
(2) dh'_0
(3) $a_1 c_0$
(4) $b_1 e'_0$
(5) $k'h_0$
(6) $b'l_0$
(7) $d'_1 c'_0$

(1) $k_1 l'_0$
(5) $k'h_0$
$\therefore l'h_0 \ldots (8)$

(8) $l'h_0$
(2) dh'_0
$\therefore l'd_0 \ldots (9)$

(9) $l'd_0$
(6) $b'l_0$
$\therefore db'_0 \ldots (10)$

(10) db'_0
(4) $b_1 e'_0$
$\therefore de'_0 \ldots (11)$

(11) de'_0
(7) $d'_1 c'_0$
$\therefore e'c'_0 \ldots (12)$

(12) $e'c'_0$
(3) $a_1 c_0$
$\therefore a_1 e'_0$

Note that, in working a Sorites by this Process, we may begin with *any* Premiss we choose.]

[§3] Solution by Method of Underscoring

Consider the Pair of Premisses

$$xm_0 \dagger ym'_0$$

which yield the Conclusion xy_0.

We see that, in order to get this Conclusion, we must eliminate m and m', and write x and y together in one expression.

Now, if we agree to *mark* m and m' as eliminated, and to read the two expressions together, as if they were written in one, the two Premisses will then exactly represent the *Conclusion*, and we need not write it out separately.

Let us agree to mark the eliminated letters by *underscoring* them, putting a *single* score under the *first*, and a *double* one under the *second*.

The two Premisses now become

$$x\underline{m}_0 \dagger y\underline{\underline{m}}'_0$$

which we read as xy_0.

In copying out the Premisses for underscoring, it will be convenient to *omit all subscripts*. As to the O's we may always *suppose* them written, and, as to the I's, we are not concerned to know *which* Terms are asserted to *exist*, except those which appear in the *Complete* Conclusion; and for *them* it will be easy enough to refer to the original list.

[I will now go through the process of solving, by this method, the example worked in §2.

The Data are

$$\overset{1}{k_1}\overset{2}{l'_0} \dagger \overset{}{dh'_0} \dagger \overset{3}{a_1 c_0} \dagger \overset{4}{b_1 e'_0} \dagger \overset{5}{k'h_0} \dagger \overset{6}{b'l_0} \dagger \overset{7}{d'_1 c'_0}$$

The Reader should take a piece of paper, and write out this solution for himself. The first line will consist of the above Data; the second must be composed, bit by bit, according to the following directions.

We begin by writing down the first Premiss, with its numeral over it, but omitting the subscripts.

We have now to find a Premiss which can be combined with this, i.e., a Premiss containing either k' or l. The first we find is No. 5; and this we tack on, with a $\dagger$.

To get the *Conclusion* from these, k and k' must be eliminated, and what remains must be taken as one expression. So we *underscore* them, putting a *single* score under k, and a *double* one under k'. The result we read as $l'h$.

We must now find a Premiss containing either l or h'.   Looking along the row, we fix on No. 2, and tack it on.

Now these three Nullities are really equivalent to ($l'h \dagger dh'$), in which h and h' must be eliminated, and what remains taken as one expression. So we *underscore* them.   The result reads as $l'd$.

We now want a Premiss containing l or d'.   No. 6 will do.

These four Nullities are really equivalent to ($l'd \dagger b'l$).   So we underscore l' and l.   The result reads as db'.

We now want a Premiss containing d' or b.   No. 4 will do.

Here we underscore b' and b.   The result reads as de'.

We now want a Premiss containing d' or e.   No. 7 will do.

Here we underscore d and d'.   The result reads as $e'c'$.

We now want a Premiss containing e or c.   No. 3 will do—in fact *must* do, as it is the only one left.

Here we underscore c' and c; and, as the whole thing now reads as $e'a$, we may tack on $e'a_0$ as the *Conclusion*, with a ¶.

We now look along the row of Data, to see whether e' or a has been given as *existent*.   We find that a has been so given in No. 3.   So we add this fact to the Conclusion, which now stands as ¶ $e'a_0 \dagger a_1$, i.e. ¶ $a_1e'_0$; i.e. "All a are e."

If the Reader has faithfully obeyed the above directions, his written solution will now stand as follows:

$$\overset{1}{}\quad\overset{2}{}\quad\overset{3}{}\quad\overset{4}{}\quad\overset{5}{}\quad\overset{6}{}\quad\overset{7}{}$$
$$k_1l'_0 \dagger dh'_0 \dagger a_1c_0 \dagger b_1e'_0 \dagger k'h_0 \dagger b'l_0 \dagger d'_1c'_0$$

$$\overset{1}{}\quad\overset{5}{}\quad\overset{2}{}\quad\overset{6}{}\quad\overset{4}{}\quad\overset{7}{}\quad\overset{3}{}$$
$$\underline{kl'} \dagger \underline{k'h} \dagger \underline{dh'} \dagger \underline{b'l} \dagger \underline{be'} \dagger \underline{d'c'} \dagger \underline{ac} \ ¶ \ e'a_0 \dagger a_1 \text{ i.e. } ¶ \ a_1e'_0$$

i.e. "All a are e"

The Reader should now take a second piece of paper, and copy the Data only, and try to work out the solution for himself, beginning with some other Premiss.

If he fails to bring out the Conclusion $a_1e'_0$, I would advise him to take a third piece of paper, and *begin again!*]

I will now work out, in its briefest form, a Sorites of five Premisses, to serve as a model for the Reader to imitate in working examples.

(1) I greatly value everything that John gives me;
(2) Nothing but this bone will satisfy my dog;
(3) I take particular care of everything that I greatly value;
(4) This bone was a present from John;
(5) The things, of which I take particular care, are things I do *not* give to my dog.

Univ. "things"; a = given by John to me; b = given by me to my dog; c = greatly valued by me; d = satisfactory to my dog"; e = taken particular care of by me; h = this bone.

$$\begin{array}{ccccc} 1 & 2 & 3 & 4 & 5 \end{array}$$
$$a_1c'_0 \dagger h'd_0 \dagger c_1e'_0 \dagger h_1a'_0 \dagger e_1b_0$$

$$\begin{array}{ccccc} 1 & 3 & 4 & 2 & 5 \end{array}$$
$$\underline{ac'} \dagger \underline{ce'} \dagger \underline{ha'} \dagger \underline{h'd} \dagger \underline{eb} \; \P \; db_0$$

i.e. "Nothing, that I give my dog, satisfies him," or, "My dog is not satisfied with *anything* that I give him!"

[Note that, in working a Sorites by this process, we may begin with *any* Premiss we choose. For instance, we might begin with No. 5, and the result would then be

$$\begin{array}{ccccc} 5 & 3 & 1 & 4 & 2 \end{array}$$
$$\underline{eb} \dagger \underline{ce'} \dagger \underline{ac'} \dagger \underline{ha'} \dagger \underline{h'd} \; \P \; bd_0]$$

[Work Examples §**4**, 25–30 (p. 146); §**5**, 25–30 (p. 148); §**6**, 13–15 (p. 153); §**7**, 13–15 (p. 156); §**8**, 1–4, 13, 14, 19, 24 (pp. 158, 159); §**9**, 1–4, 26, 27, 40, 48 (pp. 160, 161, 165, 169).]

The Reader, who has successfully grappled with all the Examples hitherto set, and who thirsts, like Alexander the Great, for "more worlds to conquer," may employ his spare energies on the following seventeen Examination-Papers. He is recommended not to attempt more than *one* Paper on any one day. The answers to the questions about words and phrases may be found by referring to the Index at p. 491.

I. §**4**, 31 (p. 146); §**5**, 31–34 (p. 149); §**6**, 16, 17 (p. 154); §**7**, 16 (p. 156); §**8**, 5, 6 (p. 159); §**9**, 5, 22, 42 (pp. 161, 164, 169). What is "Classification"? And what is a "Class"?

II. §**4**, 32 (p. 146); §**5**, 35–38 (p. 149); §**6**, 18 (p. 154); §**7**, 17, 18 (p. 156); §**8**, 7, 8 (p. 159); §**9**, 6, 23, 43 (pp. 156, 161, 165). What are "Genus," "Species," and "Differentia"?

III. §**4**, 33 (p. 146); §**5**, 39–42 (p. 149); §**6**, 19, 20 (p. 154); §**7**, 19 (p. 156); §**8**, 9, 10 (p. 159); §**9**, 7, 24, 44 (pp. 160, 165, 170). What are "Real" and "Imaginary" Classes?

IV. §**4**, 34 (p. 146); §**5**, 43–46 (p. 149); §**6**, 21 (p. 154); §**7**, 20, 21 (p. 156); §**8**, 11, 12 (p. 159); §**9**, 8, 25, 45 (pp. 162, 165, 170).

What is "Division"?   When are Classes said to be "Co-divisional"?

V. §4, 35 (p. 146); §5, 47–50 (p. 150); §6, 22, 23 (p. 154); §7, 22 (p. 156); §8, 15, 16 (p. 159); §9, 9, 28, 46 (pp. 162, 166, 170). What is "Dichotomy"?   What arbitrary rule does one sometimes require?

VI. §4, 36 (p. 146); §5, 51–54 (p. 150); §6, 24 (p. 154); §7, 23, 24 (p. 156); §8, 17 (p. 159); §9, 10, 29, 47 (pp. 162, 166, 171). What is a "Definition"?

VII. §4, 37 (p. 146); §5, 55–58 (p. 150); §6, 25, 26 (p. 154); §7, 25 (p. 157); §8, 18 (p. 159); §9, 11, 30, 49 (pp. 162, 166, 171).   What are the "Subject" and the "Predicate" of a Proposition?   What is its "Normal" form?

VIII. §4, 38 (p. 146); §5, 59–62 (p. 150); §6, 27 (p. 154); §7, 26, 27 (p. 157); §8, 20 (p. 159); §9, 12, 31, 50 (pp. 163, 167, 172). What is a Proposition "in *I*"?   "In *E*"?   And "in *A*"?

IX. §4, 39 (p. 146); §5, 63–66 (p. 151); §6, 28, 29 (p. 154); §7, 28 (p. 157); §8, 21 (p. 159); §9, 13, 32, 51 (pp. 163, 167, 172). What is the "Normal" form of a Proposition of Existence?

X. §4, 40 (p. 146); §5, 67–70 (p. 151); §6, 30 (p. 154); §7, 29, 30 (p. 157); §8, 22 (p. 159); §9, 14, 33, 52 (pp. 163, 167, 173). What is the "Universe of Discourse"?

XI. §4, 41 (p. 146); §5, 71–74 (p. 151); §6, 31, 32 (p. 154); §7, 31 (p. 157); §8, 23 (p. 159); §9, 15, 34, 53 (pp. 163, 167, 173). What is implied, in a Proposition of Relation, as to the Reality of its Terms?

XII. §4, 42 (p. 146); §5, 75–78 (p. 151); §6, 33 (p. 154); §7, 32, 33 (p. 157); §8, 25 (p. 159); §9, 16, 35, 54 (pp. 163, 168, 173).   Explain the phrase "sitting on the fence."

XIII. §5, 79–83 (p. 152); §6, 34, 35 (p. 154); §7, 34 (p. 157); §8, 26 (p. 159); §9, 17, 36, 55 (pp. 163, 168, 173).   What are "Converse" Propositions?

XIV. §5, 84–88 (p. 152); §6, 36 (p. 154); §7, 35, 36 (p. 158); §8, 27 (p. 156); §9, 18, 37, 56 (pp. 164, 168, 174).   What are "Concrete" and "Abstract" Propositions?

XV. §**5**, 89–93 (p. 152); §**6**, 37, 38 (p. 154); §**7**, 37 (p. 158); §**8**, 28 (p. 159); §**9**, 19, 38, 57 (pp. 164, 168, 174). What is a "Syllogism"? And what are its "Premisses" and its "Conclusion"?

XVI. §**5**, 94–97 (p. 152); §**6**, 39 (p. 154); §**7**, 38, 39 (p. 158); §**8**, 29 (p. 160); §**9**, 20, 39, 58 (pp. 164, 169, 174). What is a "Sorites"? And what are its "Premisses," its "Partial Conclusions," and its "Complete Conclusion"?

XVII. §**5**, 98–101 (p. 153); §**6**, 40 (p. 154); §**7**, 40 (p. 158); §**8**, 30 (p. 160); §**9**, 21, 41, 59, 60 (pp. 164, 169, 175). What are the "Universe of Discourse," the "Eliminands," and the "Retinends," of a Syllogism? And of a Sorites?

BOOK VIII
EXAMPLES, ANSWERS, AND SOLUTIONS

[N.B. The numbers at the foot of each page indicate the pages where the corresponding answers or solutions may be found.]

Chapter I ❦ Examples

[§1] **Propositions of Relation, to be reduced to normal form**

1. I have been out for a walk.
2. I am feeling better.
3. No one has read the letter but John.
4. Neither you nor I are old.
5. No fat creatures run well.
6. None but the brave deserve the fair.
7. No one looks poetical unless he is pale.
8. Some judges lose their tempers.
9. I never neglect important business.
10. What is difficult needs attention.
11. What is unwholesome should be avoided.
12. All the laws passed last week relate to excise.

[Ans. 176; Sol. 187–189.]

13. Logic puzzles me.
14. There are no Jews in the house.
15. Some dishes are unwholesome if not well-cooked.
16. Unexciting books make one drowsy.
17. When a man knows what he's about, he can detect a sharper.
18. You and I know what we're about.
19. Some bald people wear wigs.
20. Those who are fully occupied never talk about their grievances.
21. No riddles interest me if they can be solved.

[§2] Pairs of Abstract Propositions, one in terms of x and m, and the other in terms of y and m, to be represented on the same Triliteral Diagram

1. No x are m;
   No m' are y.

2. No x' are m';
   All m' are y.

3. Some x' are m;
   No m are y.

4. All m are x;
   All m' are y'.

5. All m' are x;
   All m' are y'.

6. All x' are m';
   No y' are m.

7. All x are m;
   All y' are m'.

8. Some m' are x';
   No m are y.

9. All m are x';
   No m are y.

10. No m are x';
    No y are m'.

11. No x' are m';
    No m are y.

12. Some x are m;
    All y' are m.

13. All x' are m;
    All m are y.

14. Some x are m';
    All m are y.

15. No m' are x';
    All y are m.

16. All x are m';
    No y are m.

17. Some m' are x;
    No m' are y'.

18. All x are m';
    Some m' are y'.

19. All m are x;
    Some m are y'.

20. No x' are m;
    Some y are m.

21. Some x' are m';
    All y' are m.

22. No m are x;
    Some m are y.

23. No m' are x;
    All y are m'.

24. All m are x;
    No y' are m'.

25. Some m are x;
    No y' are m.

26. All m' are x';
    Some y are m'.

27. Some m are x';
    No y' are m'.

[Ans. 127, 178]

28. No *x* are *m'*;
    All *m* are *y'*.

29. No *x'* are *m*;
    No *m* are *y'*.

30. No *x* are *m*;
    Some *y'* are *m'*.

31. Some *m'* are *x*;
    All *y'* are *m*.

32. All *x* are *m'*;
    All *y* are *m*.

[§3] **Marked Triliteral Diagrams, to be interpreted in terms of *x* and *y***

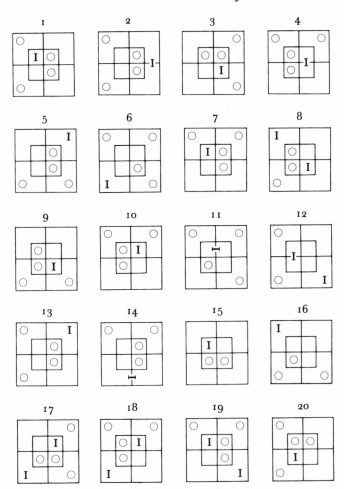

[Ans. 178.]

[§4] **Pairs of Abstract Propositions, proposed as Premisses**[1]:
Conclusions to be found

1. No *m* are *x'*;
   All *m'* are *y*.

2. No *m'* are *x'*;
   Some *m'* are *y'*.

3. All *m'* are *x*;
   All *m'* are *y'*.

4. No *x'* are *m'*;
   All *y'* are *m*.

5. Some *m* are *x'*;
   No *y* are *m*.

6. No *x'* are *m*;
   No *m* are *y*.

7. No *m* are *x'*;
   Some *y'* are *m*.

8. All *m'* are *x'*;
   No *m'* are *y*.

9. Some *x'* are *m'*;
   No *m* are *y'*.

10. All *x* are *m*;
    All *y'* are *m'*.

11. No *m* are *x*;
    All *y'* are *m'*.

12. No *x* are *m*;
    All *y* are *m*.

13. All *m'* are *x*;
    No *y* are *m*.

14. All *m* are *x*;
    All *m'* are *y*.

15. No *x* are *m*;
    No *m'* are *y*.

16. All *x* are *m'*;
    All *y* are *m*.

17. No *x* are *m*;
    All *m'* are *y*.

18. No *x* are *m'*;
    No *m* are *y*.

19. All *m* are *x*;
    All *m* are *y'*.

20. No *m* are *x*;
    All *m'* are *y*.

21. All *x* are *m*;
    Some *m'* are *y*.

22. Some *x* are *m*;
    All *y* are *m*.

23. All *m* are *x*;
    Some *y* are *m*.

24. No *x* are *m*;
    All *y* are *m*.

25. Some *m* are *x'*;
    No *m* are *y'*.

26. No *m* are *x'*;
    All *y* are *m*.

27. All *x* are *m'*;
    All *y'* are *m*.

28. All *m* are *x'*;
    Some *m* are *y*.

29. No *m* are *x*;
    All *y* are *m'*.

30. All *x* are *m*;
    Some *y* are *m*.

31. All *x* are *m*;
    All *y* are *m*.

32. No *x* are *m'*;
    All *m* are *y*.

33. No *m* are *x*;
    No *m* are *y*.

34. No *m* are *x'*;
    Some *y* are *m*.

35. No *m* are *x*;
    All *y* are *m*.

36. All *m* are *x'*;
    Some *y* are *m*.

37. All *m* are *x*;
    No *y* are *m*.

38. No *m* are *x*;
    No *m'* are *y*.

39. Some *m* are *x'*;
    No *m* are *y*.

40. No *x'* are *m*;
    All *y'* are *m*.

41. All *x* are *m'*;
    No *y* are *m'*.

42. No *m'* are *x*;
    No *y* are *m*.

[Ans. 179, 180; Sol. (1 to 12) 191-192; (1 to 42) 199-202.]

---

[1] In one of Carroll's own copies of *Symbolic Logic*, preserved in The Huntington Library, he sets each of these pairs of propositions into subscript form and works them out—in each case indicating the figure or fallacy involved. His manuscript answers are given below, p. 201.

[§5] **Pairs of Concrete Propositions, proposed as Premisses: Conclusions to be found**

1. I have been out for a walk;
   I am feeling better.

2. No one has read the letter but John;
   No one, who has *not* read it, knows what it is about.

3. Those who are not old like walking;
   You and I are young.

4. Your course is always honest;
   Your course is always the best policy.

5. No fat creatures run well;
   Some greyhounds run well.

6. Some, who deserve the fair, get their deserts;
   None but the brave deserve the fair.

7. Some Jews are rich;
   All Esquimaux are Gentiles.

8. Sugar-plums are sweet;
   Some sweet things are liked by children.

9. John is in the house;
   Everybody in the house is ill.

10. Umbrellas are useful on a journey;
    What is useless on a journey should be left behind.

11. Audible music causes vibration in the air;
    Inaudible music is not worth paying for.

12. Some holidays are rainy;
    Rainy days are tiresome.

13. No Frenchmen like plumpudding;
    All Englishmen like plumpudding.

14. No portrait of a lady, that makes her simper or scowl, is satisfactory;
    No photograph of a lady ever fails to make her simper or scowl.

[Ans. 180; Sol. (1–12) 192–195; 202–204.]

15. All pale people are phlegmatic;
    No one looks poetical unless he is pale.

16. No old misers are cheerful;
    Some old misers are thin.

17. No one, who exercises self-control, fails to keep his temper;
    Some judges lose their tempers.

18. All pigs are fat;
    Nothing that is fed on barley-water is fat.

19. All rabbits, that are not greedy, are black;
    No old rabbits are free from greediness.

20. Some pictures are not first attempts;
    No first attempts are really good.

21. I never neglect important business;
    Your business is unimportant.

22. Some lessons are difficult;
    What is difficult needs attention.

23. All clever people are popular;
    All obliging people are popular.

24. Thoughtless people do mischief;
    No thoughtful person forgets a promise.

25. Pigs cannot fly;
    Pigs are greedy.

26. All soldiers march well;
    Some babies are not soldiers.

27. No bride-cakes are wholesome;
    What is unwholesome should be avoided.

28. John is industrious;
    No industrious people are unhappy.

29. No philosophers are conceited;
    Some conceited persons are not gamblers.

30. Some excise laws are unjust;
    All the laws passed last week relate to excise.

[Ans. 180, 181; Sol. (18–24) 202–204.]

31. No military men write poetry;
    None of my lodgers are civilians.

32. No medicine is nice;
    Senna is a medicine.

33. Some circulars are not read with pleasure;
    No begging-letters are read with pleasure.

34. All Britons are brave;
    No sailors are cowards.

35. Nothing intelligible ever puzzles *me*;
    Logic puzzles me.

36. Some pigs are wild;
    All pigs are fat.

37. All wasps are unfriendly;
    All unfriendly creatures are unwelcome.

38. No old rabbits are greedy;
    All black rabbits are greedy.

39. Some eggs are hard-boiled;
    No eggs are uncrackable.

40. No antelope is ungraceful;
    Graceful creatures delight the eye.

41. All well-fed canaries sing loud;
    No canary is melancholy if it sings loud.

42. Some poetry is original;
    No original work is producible at will.

43. No country, that has been explored, is infested by dragons;
    Unexplored countries are fascinating.

44. No coals are white;
    No niggers are white.

45. No bridges are made of sugar;
    Some bridges are picturesque.

46. No children are patient;
    No impatient person can sit still.

[Ans. 181.]

47. No quadrupeds can whistle;
    Some cats are quadrupeds.

48. Bores are terrible;
    You are a bore.

49. Some oysters are silent;
    No silent creatures are amusing.

50. There are no Jews in the house;
    No Gentiles have beards a yard long.

51. Canaries, that do not sing loud, are unhappy;
    No well-fed canaries fail to sing loud.

52. All my sisters have colds;
    No one can sing who has a cold.

53. All that is made of gold is precious;
    Some caskets are precious.

54. Some buns are rich;
    All buns are nice.

55. All my cousins are unjust;
    All judges are just.

56. Pain is wearisome;
    No pain is eagerly wished for.

57. All medicine is nasty;
    Senna is a medicine.

58. Some unkind remarks are annoying;
    No critical remarks are kind.

59. No tall men have woolly hair;
    Niggers have woolly hair.

60. All philosophers are logical;
    An illogical man is always obstinate.

61. John is industrious;
    All industrious people are happy.

62. These dishes are all well-cooked;
    Some dishes are unwholesome if not well-cooked.

[Ans. 181–182.]

63. No exciting books suit feverish patients;
    Unexciting books make one drowsy.

64. No pigs can fly;
    All pigs are greedy.

65. When a man knows what he's about, he can detect a sharper;
    You and I know what we're about.

66. Some dreams are terrible;
    No lambs are terrible.

67. No bald creature needs a hairbrush;
    No lizards have hair.

68. All battles are noisy;
    What makes no noise may escape notice.

69. All my cousins are unjust;
    No judges are unjust.

70. All eggs can be cracked;
    Some eggs are hard-boiled.

71. Prejudiced persons are untrustworthy;
    Some unprejudiced persons are disliked.

72. No dictatorial person is popular;
    She is dictatorial.

73. Some bald people wear wigs;
    All your children have hair.

74. No lobsters are unreasonable;
    No reasonable creatures expect impossibilities.

75. No nightmare is pleasant;
    Unpleasant experiences are not eagerly desired.

76. No plumcakes are wholesome;
    Some wholesome things are nice.

77. Nothing that is nice need be shunned;
    Some kinds of jam are nice.

78. All ducks waddle;
    Nothing that waddles is graceful.

[Ans. 182.]

79. Sandwiches are satisfying;
Nothing in this dish is unsatisfying.

80. No rich man begs in the street;
Those who are not rich should keep accounts.

81. Spiders spin webs;
Some creatures, that do not spin webs, are savage.

82. Some of these shops are not crowded;
No crowded shops are comfortable.

83. Prudent travelers carry plenty of small change;
Imprudent travelers lose their luggage.

84. Some geraniums are red;
All these flowers are red.

85. None of my cousins are just;
All judges are just.

86. No Jews are mad;
All my lodgers are Jews.

87. Busy folk are not always talking about their grievances;
Discontented folk are always talking about their grievances.

88. None of my cousins are just;
No judges are unjust.

89. All teetotalers like sugar;
No nightingale drinks wine.

90. No riddles interest me if they can be solved;
All these riddles are insoluble.

91. All clear explanations are satisfactory;
Some excuses are unsatisfactory.

92. All elderly ladies are talkative;
All good-tempered ladies are talkative.

93. No kind deed is unlawful;
What is lawful may be done without scruple.

94. No babies are studious;
No babies are good violinists.

[Ans. 182, 183.]

95. All shillings are round;
All these coins are round.

96. No honest men cheat;
No dishonest men are trustworthy.

97. None of my boys are clever;
None of my girls are greedy.

98. All jokes are meant to amuse;
No Act of Parliament is a joke.

99. No eventful tour is ever forgotten;
Uneventful tours are not worth writing a book about.

100. All my boys are disobedient;
All my girls are discontented.

101. No unexpected pleasure annoys me;
Your visit is an unexpected pleasure.

[§6] Trios of Abstract Propositions, proposed as Syllogisms[2]: to be examined

1. Some x are m; No m are y'. Some x are y.
2. All x are m; No y are m'. No y are x'.
3. Some x are m'; All y' are m. Some x are y.
4. All x are m; No y are m. All x are y'.
5. Some m' are x'; No m' are y. Some x' are y'.
6. No x' are m; All y are m'. All y are x'.
7. Some m' are x'; All y' are m'. Some x' are y'.
8. No m' are x'; All y' are m'. All y' are x.
9. Some m are x'; No m are y. Some x' are y'.
10. All m' are x'; All m' are y. Some y are x'.
11. All x are m'; Some y are m. Some y are x'.
12. No x are m; No m' are y'. No x are y'.
13. No x are m; All y' are m. All y' are x'.

[Ans. 182, 183; Sol. (1–10) 195–197; 207–208.]

---

[2] In Carroll's copy of *Symbolic Logic* in The Huntington Library he marks each of these correct or fallacious, in the latter case specifying which fallacy is involved.

14. All *m′* are *x′*;	All *m′* are *y*.	Some *y* are *x′*.
15. Some *m* are *x′*;	All *y* are *m′*.	Some *x′* are *y′*.
16. No *x′* are *m*;	All *y′* are *m′*.	Some *y′* are *x*.
17. No *m′* are *x*;	All *m′* are *y′*.	Some *x′* are *y′*.
18. No *x′* are *m*;	Some *m* are *y*.	Some *x* are *y*.
19. Some *m* are *x*;	All *m* are *y*.	Some *y* are *x′*.
20. No *x′* are *m′*;	Some *m′* are *y′*.	Some *x* are *y′*.
21. No *m* are *x*;	All *m* are *y′*.	Some *x′* are *y′*.
22. All *x′* are *m*;	Some *y* are *m′*.	All *x′* are *y′*.
23. All *m* are *x*;	No *m′* are *y′*.	No *x′* are *y′*.
24. All *x* are *m′*;	All *m′* are *y*.	All *x* are *y*.
25. No *x* are *m′*;	All *m* are *y*.	No *x* are *y′*.
26. All *m* are *x′*;	All *y* are *m*.	All *y* are *x′*.
27. All *x* are *m*;	No *m* are *y′*.	All *x* are *y*.
28. All *x* are *m*;	No *y′* are *m′*.	All *x* are *y*.
29. No *x′* are *m*;	No *m′* are *y′*.	No *x′* are *y′*.
30. All *x* are *m*;	All *m* are *y′*.	All *x* are *y′*.
31. All *x′* are *m′*;	No *y′* are *m′*.	All *x′* are *y*.
32. No *x* are *m*;	No *y′* are *m′*.	No *x* are *y′*.
33. All *m* are *x′*;	All *y′* are *m*.	All *y′* are *x′*.
34. All *x* are *m′*;	Some *y* are *m′*.	Some *y* are *x*.
35. Some *x* are *m*;	All *m* are *y*.	Some *x* are *y*.
36. All *m* are *x′*;	All *y* are *m*.	All *y* are *x′*.
37. No *m* are *x′*;	All *m* are *y′*.	Some *x* are *y′*.
38. No *x* are *m*;	No *m* are *y′*.	No *x* are *y′*.
39. No *m* are *x*;	Some *m* are *y′*.	Some *x′* are *y′*.
40. No *m* are *x′*;	Some *y* are *m*.	Some *x* are *y*.

[§7] Trios of Concrete Propositions, proposed as Syllogisms[3]: to be examined

1. No doctors are enthusiastic;
 You are enthusiastic.

 You are not a doctor.

[Ans. 183; Sol. (§7) 197, 208.]

---

[3] As in previous note.

2. Dictionaries are useful;
   Useful books are valuable.
   　　Dictionaries are valuable.

3. No misers are unselfish.
   None but misers save egg-shells.
   　　No unselfish people save egg-shells.

4. Some epicures are ungenerous;
   All my uncles are generous.
   　　My uncles are not epicures.

5. Gold is heavy;
   Nothing but gold will silence him.
   　　Nothing light will silence him.

6. Some healthy people are fat;
   No unhealthy people are strong.
   　　Some fat people are not strong.

7. "I saw it in a newspaper."
   "All newspapers tell lies."
   　　It was a lie.

8. Some cravats are not artistic;
   I admire anything artistic.
   　　There are some cravats that I do not admire.

9. His songs never last an hour;
   A song, that lasts an hour, is tedious.
   　　His songs are never tedious.

10. Some candles give very little light;
    Candles are *meant* to give light.
    　　Some things, that are meant to give light, give very little.

11. All, who are anxious to learn, work hard;
    Some of these boys work hard.
    　　Some of these boys are anxious to learn.

12. All lions are fierce;
    Some lions do not drink coffee.
    　　Some creatures that drink coffee are not fierce.

[Ans. 183–184; Sol. 198–199; 208–210.]

13. No misers are generous;
    Some old men are ungenerous.
        Some old men are misers.

14. No fossil can be crossed in love;
    An oyster may be crossed in love.
        Oysters are not fossils.

15. All uneducated people are shallow;
    Students are all educated.
        No students are shallow.

16. All young lambs jump;
    No young animals are healthy, unless they jump.
        All young lambs are healthy.

17. Ill-managed business is unprofitable;
    Railways are never ill-managed.
        All railways are profitable.

18. No Professors are ignorant;
    All ignorant people are vain.
        No professors are vain.

19. A prudent man shuns hyænas;
    No banker is imprudent.
        No banker fails to shun hyænas.

20. All wasps are unfriendly;
    No puppies are unfriendly.
        Puppies are not wasps.

21. No Jews are honest;
    Some Gentiles are rich.
        Some rich people are dishonest.

22. No idlers win fame;
    Some painters are not idle.
        Some painters win fame.

23. No monkeys are soldiers;
    All monkeys are mischievous.
        Some mischievous creatures are not soldiers.

[Ans. 184; Sol. 211–213.]

24. All these bonbons are chocolate-creams;
All these bonbons are delicious.
  Chocolate-creams are delicious.

25. No muffins are wholesome;
All buns are unwholesome.
  Buns are not muffins.

26. Some unauthorised reports are false;
All authorised reports are trustworthy.
  Some false reports are not trustworthy.

27. Some pillows are soft;
No pokers are soft.
  Some pokers are not pillows.

28. Improbable stories are not easily believed;
None of his stories are probable.
  None of his stories are easily believed.

29. No thieves are honest;
Some dishonest people are found out.
  Some thieves are found out.

30. No muffins are wholesome;
All puffy food is unwholesome.
  All muffins are puffy.

31. No birds, except peacocks, are proud of their tails;
Some birds, that are proud of their tails, cannot sing.
  Some peacocks cannot sing.

32. Warmth relieves pain;
Nothing, that does not relieve pain, is useful in toothache.
  Warmth is useful in toothache.

33. No bankrupts are rich;
Some merchants are not bankrupts.
  Some merchants are rich.

34. Bores are dreaded;
No bore is ever begged to prolong his visit.
  No one, who is dreaded, is ever begged to prolong his visit.

[Ans. 184; Sol. 213–215.]

35. All wise men walk on their feet;
All unwise men walk on their hands.
　　No man walks on both.

36. No wheelbarrows are comfortable;
No uncomfortable vehicles are popular.
　　No wheelbarrows are popular.

37. No frogs are poetical;
Some ducks are unpoetical.
　　Some ducks are not frogs.

37A[4]. John never orders anything I ought to do;
Peter never orders anything I ought not to do.
　　John and Peter never give the same order.

38. No emperors are dentists;
All dentists are dreaded by children.
　　No emperors are dreaded by children.

39. Sugar is sweet;
Salt is not sweet.
　　Salt is not sugar.

40. Every eagle can fly;
Some pigs cannot fly.
　　Some pigs are not eagles.

[§8] Sets of Abstract Propositions, proposed as Premisses for Soriteses: Conclusions to be found

[N.B. At the end of this Section instructions are given for varying these Examples.]

1	2	3	4
1. No *c* are *d*;	1. All *d* are *b*;	1. No *b* are *a*;	1. No *b* are *c*;
2. All *a* are *d*;	2. No *a* are *c'*;	2. No *c* are *d'*;	2. All *a* are *b*;
3. All *b* are *c*.	3. No *b* are *c*.	3. All *d* are *b*.	3. No *c'* are *d*.

[Ans. 184–185; Sol. 215–216.]

---

[4] This example appears as a manuscript substitution for Example 37 in Carroll's own copy of *Symbolic Logic* preserved in the Huntington Library.

5

1. All b' are a';
2. No b are c;
3. No a' are d.

6

1. All a are b';
2. No b' are c;
3. All d are a.

7

1. No d are b';
2. All b are a;
3. No c are d'.

8

1. No b' are d;
2. No a' are b;
3. All c are d.

9

1. All b' are a;
2. No a are d;
3. All b are c.

10

1. No c are d;
2. All b are c;
3. No a are d'.

11

1. No b are c;
2. All d are a;
3. All c' are a'.

12

1. No c are b';
2. All c' are d';
3. All b are a.

13

1. All d are e;
2. All c are a;
3. No b are d';
4. All e are a'.

14

1. All c are b;
2. All a are e;
3. All d are b';
4. All a' are c.

15

1. No b' are d;
2. All e are c;
3. All b are a;
4. All d' are c'.

16

1. No a' are e;
2. All d are c';
3. All a are b;
4. All e' are d.

17

1. All d are c;
2. All a are e;
3. No b are d';
4. All c are e'.

18

1. All a are b;
2. All d are e;
3. All a' are c';
4. No b are e.

19

1. No b are c;
2. All e are h;
3. All a are b;
4. No d are h;
5. All e' are c.

20

1. No d are h';
2. No c are e;
3. All h are b;
4. No a are d';
5. No b are e'.

21

1. All b are a;
2. No d are h;
3. No c are e;
4. No a are h';
5. All c' are b.

22

1. All e are d';
2. No b' are h';
3. All c' are d;
4. All a are e;
5. No c are h.

23

1. All b' are a';
2. No d are e';
3. All h are b';
4. No c are e;
5. All d' are a.

24

1. All h' are k';
2. No b' are a;
3. All c are d;
4. All e are h';
5. No d are k';
6. No b are c'.

25

1. All a are d;
2. All k are b;
3. All e are h;
4. No a' are b;
5. All d are c;
6. All h are k.

26

1. All a' are h;
2. No d' are k';
3. All e are b';
4. No h are k;
5. All a are c';
6. No b' are d.

27

1. All e are d';
2. No h are b;
3. All a' are k;
4. No c are e';
5. All b' are d;
6. No a are c'.

28

1. No a' are k;
2. All e are b;
3. No h are k';
4. No d' are c;
5. No a are b;
6. All c' are h.

[Ans. 185; Sol. 216–218.]

29	30
1. No *e* are *k*;	1. All *n* are *m*;
2. No *b'* are *m*;	2. All *a'* are *e*;
3. No *a* are *c'*;	3. No *c'* are *l*;
4. All *h'* are *e*;	4. All *k* are *r'*;
5. All *d* are *k*;	5. No *a* are *h'*;
6. No *c* are *b*;	6. No *d* are *l'*;
7. All *d'* are *l*;	7. No *c* are *n'*;
8. No *h* are *m'*.	8. All *e* are *b*;
	9. All *m* are *r*;
	10. All *h* are *d*.

[N.B. In each Example, in Sections 8 and 9, it is possible to begin with *any* Premiss, at pleasure, and thus to get as many different Solutions (all of course yielding the *same* Complete Conclusion) as there are Premisses in the Example.   Hence §8 really contains 129 different Examples, and §9 contains 273.]

[§9] Sets of Concrete Propositions, proposed as Premisses for Soriteses: Conclusions to be found

1

(1) Babies are illogical;

(2) Nobody is despised who can manage a crocodile;

(3) Illogical persons are despised.

Univ. "persons"; *a* = able to manage a crocodile; *b* = babies; *c* = despised; *d* = logical.

2

(1) My saucepans are the only thing I have that are made of tin;

(2) I find all *your* presents very useful;

(3) None of my saucepans are of the slightest use.

Univ. "things of mine"; *a* = made of tin; *b* = my saucepans; *c* = useful; *d* = your presents.

[Ans. 185; Sol. 218–219.]

3

(1) No potatoes of mine, that are new, have been boiled;
(2) All my potatoes in this dish are fit to eat;
(3) No unboiled potatoes of mine are fit to eat.

Univ. "my potatoes"; a = boiled; b = eatable; c = in this dish; d = new.

4

(1) There are no Jews in the kitchen;
(2) No Gentiles say "shpoonj";
(3) My servants are all in the kitchen.

Univ. "persons"; a = in the kitchen; b = Jews; c = my servants; d = saying "shpoonj."

5

(1) No ducks waltz;
(2) No officers ever decline to waltz;
(3) All my poultry are ducks.

Univ. "creatures"; a = ducks; b = my poultry; c = officers; d = willing to waltz.

6

(1) Every one who is sane can do Logic;
(2) No lunatics are fit to serve on a jury;
(3) None of *your* sons can do Logic.

Univ. "persons"; a = able to do Logic; b = fit to serve on a jury; c = sane; d = your sons.

7

(1) There are no pencils of mine in this box;
(2) No sugar-plums of mine are cigars;
(3) The whole of my property, that is not in this box, consists of cigars.

Univ. "things of mine"; a = cigars; b = in this box; c = pencils; d = sugar-plums.

[Ans. 185; Sol. 219.]

8

(1) No experienced person is incompetent;
(2) Jenkins is always blundering;
(3) No competent person is always blundering.

Univ. "persons"; a = always blundering; b = competent; c = experienced; d = Jenkins.

9

(1) No terriers wander among the signs of the zodiac;
(2) Nothing, that does not wander among the signs of the zodiac, is a comet;
(3) Nothing but a terrier has a curly tail.

Univ. "things"; a = comets; b = curly-tailed; c = terriers; d = wandering among the signs of the zodiac.

10

(1) No one takes in the *Times*, unless he is well-educated;
(2) No hedge-hogs can read;
(3) Those who cannot read are not well-educated.

Univ. "creatures"; a = able to read; b = hedge-hogs; c = taking in the *Times*; d = well-educated.

11

(1) All puddings are nice;
(2) This dish is a pudding;
(3) No nice things are wholesome.

Univ. "things"; a = nice; b = puddings; c = this dish; d = wholesome.

12

(1) My gardener is well worth listening to on military subjects;
(2) No one can remember the battle of Waterloo, unless he is very old;
(3) Nobody is really worth listening to on military subjects, unless he can remember the battle of Waterloo.

Univ. "persons"; a = able to remember the battle of Waterloo; b = my gardener; c = well worth listening to on military subjects; d = very old.

[Ans. 185; Sol. 219–220.]

13

(1) All humming-birds are richly coloured;
(2) No large birds live on honey;
(3) Birds that do not live on honey are dull in colour.

Univ. "birds"; a = humming-birds; b = large; c = living on honey; d = richly coloured.

14

(1) No Gentiles have hooked noses;
(2) A man who is a good hand at a bargain always makes money;
(3) No Jew is ever a bad hand at a bargain.

Univ. "persons"; a = good hands at a bargain; b = hook-nosed; c = Jews; d = making money.

15

(1) All ducks in this village, that are branded B, belong to Mrs. Bond;
(2) Ducks in this village never wear lace collars, unless they are branded B;
(3) Mrs. Bond has no gray ducks in this village.

Univ. "ducks in this village"; a = belonging to Mrs. Bond; b = branded B; c = gray; d = wearing lace collars.

16

(1) All the old articles in this cupboard are cracked;
(2) No jug in this cupboard is new;
(3) Nothing in this cupboard, that is cracked, will hold water.

Univ. "things in this cupboard"; a = able to hold water; b = cracked; c = jugs; d = old.

17

(1) All unripe fruit is unwholesome;
(2) All these apples are wholesome;
(3) No fruit, grown in the shade, is ripe.

Univ. "fruit"; a = grown in the shade; b = ripe; c = these apples; d = wholesome.

[Ans. 185; Sol. 220.]

18

(1) Puppies, that will not lie still, are always grateful for the loan of a skipping-rope;

(2) A lame puppy would not say "thank you" if you offered to lend it a skipping-rope;

(3) None but lame puppies ever care to do worsted-work.

Univ. "puppies"; a = caring to do worsted-work; b = grateful for the loan of a skipping-rope; c = lame; d = willing to lie still.

19

(1) No name in this list is unsuitable for the hero of a romance;

(2) Names beginning with a vowel are always melodious;

(3) No name is suitable for the hero of a romance, if it begins with a consonant.

Univ. "names"; a = beginning with a vowel; b = in this list; c = melodious; d = suitable for the hero of a romance.

20

(1) All members of the House of Commons have perfect self-command;

(2) No M.P., who wears a coronet, should ride in a donkey-race;

(3) All members of the House of Lords wear coronets.

Univ. "M.P.'s"; a = belonging to the House of Commons; b = having perfect self-command; c = one who may ride in a donkey-race; d = wearing a coronet.

21

(1) No goods in this shop, that have been bought and paid for, are still on sale;

(2) None of the goods may be carried away, unless labeled "sold";

(3) None of the goods are labeled "sold," unless they have been bought and paid for.

Univ. "goods in this shop"; a = allowed to be carried away; b = bought and paid for; c = labeled "sold"; d = on sale.

22

(1) No acrobatic feats, that are not announced in the bills of a circus, are ever attempted there;

[Ans. 185; Sol. 220–221.]

(2) No acrobatic feat is possible, if it involves turning a quadruple somersault;

(3) No impossible acrobatic feat is ever announced in a circus bill.

Univ. "acrobatic feats"; a = announced in the bills of a circus; b = attempted in a circus; c = involving the turning of a quadruple somersault; d = possible.

23

(1) Nobody, who really appreciates Beethoven, fails to keep silence while the Moonlight-Sonata is being played;

(2) Guinea-pigs are hopelessly ignorant of music;

(3) No one, who is hopelessly ignorant of music, ever keeps silence while the Moonlight-Sonata is being played.

Univ. "creatures"; a = guinea-pigs; b = hopelessly ignorant of music; c = keeping silence while the Moonlight-Sonata is being played; d = really appreciating Beethoven.

24

(1) Coloured flowers are always scented;

(2) I dislike flowers that are not grown in the open air;

(3) No flowers grown in the open air are colourless.

Univ. "flowers"; a = coloured; b = grown in the open air; c = liked by me; d = scented.

25

(1) Showy talkers think too much of themselves;

(2) No really well-informed people are bad company;

(3) People who think too much of themselves are not good company.

Univ. "persons"; a = good company; b = really well-informed; c = showy talkers; d = thinking too much of one's self.

26

(1) No boys under 12 are admitted to this school as boarders;

(2) All the industrious boys have red hair;

(3) None of the day-boys learn Greek;

(4) None but those under 12 are idle.

Univ. "boys in this school"; a = boarders; b = industrious; c = learning Greek; d = red-haired; e = under 12.

[Ans. 185, 186; Sol. 221.]

27

(1) The only articles of food, that my doctor allows me, are such as are not very rich;
(2) Nothing that agrees with me is unsuitable for supper;
(3) Wedding-cake is always very rich;
(4) My doctor allows me all articles of food that are suitable for supper.

Univ. "articles of food"; a = agreeing with me; b = allowed by my doctor; c = suitable for supper; d = very rich; e = wedding-cake.

28

(1) No discussions in our Debating-Club are likely to rouse the British Lion, so long as they are checked when they become too noisy;
(2) Discussions, unwisely conducted, endanger the peacefulness of our Debating-Club;
(3) Discussions, that go on while Tomkins is in the Chair, are likely to rouse the British Lion;
(4) Discussions in our Debating-Club, when wisely conducted, are always checked when they become too noisy.

Univ. "discussions in our Debating-Club"; a = checked when too noisy; b = dangerous to the peacefulness of our Debating-Club; c = going on while Tomkins is in the chair; d = likely to rouse the British Lion; e = wisely conducted.

29

(1) All my sons are slim;
(2) No child of mine is healthy who takes no exercise;
(3) All gluttons, who are children of mine, are fat;
(4) No daughter of mine takes any exercise.

Univ. "my children"; a = fat; b = gluttons; c = healthy; d = sons; e = taking exercise.

30

(1) Things sold in the street are of no great value;
(2) Nothing but rubbish can be had for a song;
(3) Eggs of the Great Auk are very valuable;
(4) It is only what is sold in the street that is really *rubbish*.

Univ. "things"; a = able to be had for a song; b = eggs of the Great Auk; c = rubbish; d = sold in the street; e = very valuable.

[Ans. 186; Sol. 221–222.]

31

(1) No books sold here have gilt edges, except what are in the front shop;
(2) All the *authorised* editions have red labels;
(3) All the books with red labels are priced at 5s. and upwards;
(4) None but *authorised* editions are ever placed in the front shop.

Univ. "books sold here"; a = authorised editions; b = gilt-edged; c = having red labels; d = in the front shop; e = priced at 5s. and upwards.

32

(1) Remedies for bleeding, which fail to check it, are a mockery;
(2) Tincture of Calendula is not to be despised;
(3) Remedies, which will check the bleeding when you cut your finger, are useful;
(4) All mock remedies for bleeding are despicable.

Univ. "remedies for bleeding"; a = able to check bleeding; b = despicable; c = mockeries; d = Tincture of Calendula; e = useful when you cut your finger.

33

(1) None of the unnoticed things, met with at sea, are mermaids;
(2) Things entered in the log, as met with at sea, are sure to be worth remembering;
(3) *I* have never met with anything worth remembering, when on a voyage;
(4) Things met with at sea, that are noticed, are sure to be recorded in the log.

Univ. "things met with at sea"; a = entered in log; b = mermaids; c = met with by me; d = noticed; e = worth remembering.

34

(1) The only books in this library, that I do *not* recommend for reading, are unhealthy in tone;
(2) The bound books are all well-written;
(3) All the romances are healthy in tone;
(4) I do not recommend you to read any of the unbound books.

Univ. "books in this library"; a = bound; b = healthy in tone; c = recommended by me; d = romances; e = well-written.

[Ans. 186; Sol. 222.]

35

(1) No birds, except ostriches, are 9 feet high;
(2) There are no birds in this aviary that belong to any one but *me*;
(3) No ostrich lives on mince-pies;
(4) I have no birds less than 9 feet high.

Univ. "birds"; a = in this aviary; b = living on mince-pies; c = my; d = 9 feet high; e = ostriches.

36

(1) A plum-pudding, that is not really solid, is mere porridge;
(2) Every plum-pudding, served at my table, has been boiled in a cloth;
(3) A plum-pudding that is mere porridge is indistinguishable from soup;
(4) No plum-puddings are really solid, except what are served at *my* table.

Univ. "plum-puddings"; a = boiled in a cloth; b = distinguishable from soup; c = mere porridge; d = really solid; e = served at my table.

37

(1) No interesting poems are unpopular among people of real taste;
(2) No modern poetry is free from affectation;
(3) All *your* poems are on the subject of soap-bubbles;
(4) No affected poetry is popular among people of real taste;
(5) No ancient poem is on the subject of soap-bubbles.

Univ. "poems"; a = affected; b = ancient; c = interesting; d = on the subject of soap-bubbles; e = popular among people of real taste; h = written by you.

38

(1) All the fruit at this Show, that fails to get a prize, is the property of the Committee;
(2) None of my peaches have got prizes;
(3) None of the fruit, sold off in the evening, is unripe;
(4) None of the ripe fruit has been grown in a hot-house;
(5) All fruit, that belongs to the Committee, is sold off in the evening.

Univ. "fruit at this Show"; a = belonging to the Committee; b = getting prizes; c = grown in a hot-house; d = my peaches; e = ripe; h = sold off in the evening.

[Ans. 186; Sol. 222.]

39

(1) Promise-breakers are untrustworthy;
(2) Wine-drinkers are very communicative;
(3) A man who keeps his promises is honest;
(4) No teetotalers are pawnbrokers;
(5) One can always trust a very communicative person.

Univ. "persons"; a = honest; b = pawnbrokers; c = promise-breakers; d = trustworthy; e = very communicative; h = wine-drinkers.

40

(1) No kitten, that loves fish, is unteachable;
(2) No kitten without a tail will play with a gorilla;
(3) Kittens with whiskers always love fish;
(4) No teachable kitten has green eyes;
(5) No kittens have tails unless they have whiskers.

Univ. "kittens"; a = green-eyed; b = loving fish; c = tailed; d = teachable; e = whiskered; h = willing to play with a gorilla.

41

(1) All the Eton men in this College play cricket;
(2) None but the Scholars dine at the higher table;
(3) None of the cricketers row;
(4) *My* friends in this College all come from Eton;
(5) All the Scholars are rowing-men.

Univ. "men in this College"; a = cricketers; b = dining at the higher table; c = Etonians; d = my friends; e = rowing-men; h = Scholars.

42

(1) There is no box of mine here that I dare open;
(2) My writing-desk is made of rose-wood;
(3) All my boxes are painted, except what are here;
(4) There is no box of mine that I dare not open, unless it is full of live scorpions;
(5) All my rose-wood boxes are unpainted.

Univ. "my boxes"; a = boxes that I dare open; b = full of live scorpions; c = here; d = made of rose-wood; e = painted; h = writing-desks.

[Ans. 186; Sol. 222–223.]

43

(1) Gentiles have no objection to pork;
(2) Nobody who admires pigsties ever reads Hogg's poems;
(3) No Mandarin knows Hebrew;
(4) Every one, who does not object to pork, admires pigsties;
(5) No Jew is ignorant of Hebrew.

Univ. "persons"; a = admiring pigsties; b = Jews; c = knowing Hebrew; d = Mandarins; e = objecting to pork; h = reading Hogg's poems.

44

(1) All writers, who understand human nature, are clever;
(2) No one is a true poet unless he can stir the hearts of men;
(3) Shakespeare wrote "Hamlet";
(4) No writer, who does not understand human nature, can stir the hearts of men;
(5) None but a true poet could have written "Hamlet."

Univ. "writers"; a = able to stir the hearts of men; b = clever; c = Shakespeare; d = true poets; e = understanding human nature; h = writer of "Hamlet."

45

(1) I despise anything that cannot be used as a bridge;
(2) Everything, that is worth writing an ode to, would be a welcome gift to me;
(3) A rainbow will not bear the weight of a wheel-barrow;
(4) Whatever can be used as a bridge will bear the weight of a wheel-barrow;
(5) I would not take, as a gift, a thing that I despise.

Univ. "things"; a = able to bear the weight of a wheel-barrow; b = acceptable to me; c = despised by me; d = rainbows; e = useful as a bridge; h = worth writing an ode to.

46

(1) When I work a Logic-example without grumbling, you may be sure it is one that I can understand;
(2) These Soriteses are not arranged in regular order, like the examples I am used to;

[Ans. 186; Sol. 223.]

(3) No easy example ever makes my head ache;

(4) I ca'n't understand examples that are not arranged in regular order, like those I am used to;

(5) I never grumble at an example, unless it gives me a headache.

Univ. "Logic-examples worked by me"; a = arranged in regular order, like the examples I am used to; b = easy; c = grumbled at by me; d = making my head ache; e = these Soriteses; h = understood by me.

47

(1) Every idea of mine, that cannot be expressed as a Syllogism, is really ridiculous;

(2) None of my ideas about Bath-buns are worth writing down;

(3) No idea of mine, that fails to come true, can be expressed as a Syllogism;

(4) I never have any really ridiculous idea, that I do not at once refer to my solicitor;

(5) My dreams are all about Bath-buns;

(6) I never refer any idea of mine to my solicitor, unless it is worth writing down.

Univ. "my ideas"; a = able to be expressed as a Syllogism; b = about Bath-buns; c = coming true; d = dreams; e = really ridiculous; h = referred to my solicitor; k = worth writing down.

48

(1) None of the pictures here, except the battle-pieces, are valuable;

(2) None of the unframed ones are varnished;

(3) All the battle-pieces are painted in oils;

(4) All those that have been sold are valuable;

(5) All the English ones are varnished;

(6) All those in frames have been sold.

Univ. "the pictures here"; a = battle-pieces; b = English; c = framed; d = oil-paintings; e = sold; h = valuable; k = varnished.

49

(1) Animals, that do not kick, are always unexcitable;

(2) Donkeys have no horns;

(3) A buffalo can always toss one over a gate;

[Ans. 186; Sol. 223–224.]

(4) No animals that kick are easy to swallow;
(5) No hornless animal can toss one over a gate;
(6) All animals are excitable, except buffaloes.

Univ. "animals"; a = able to toss one over a gate; b = buffaloes; c = donkeys; d = easy to swallow; e = excitable; h = horned; k = kicking.

50

(1) No one, who is going to a party, ever fails to brush his hair;
(2) No one looks fascinating, if he is untidy;
(3) Opium-eaters have no self-command;
(4) Every one, who has brushed his hair, looks fascinating;
(5) No one wears white kid gloves, unless he is going to a party;
(6) A man is always untidy, if he has no self-command.

Univ. "persons"; a = going to a party; b = having brushed one's hair; c = having self-command; d = looking fascinating; e = opium-eaters; h = tidy; k = wearing white kid gloves.

51

(1) No husband, who is always giving his wife new dresses, can be a cross-grained man;
(2) A methodical husband always comes home for his tea;
(3) No one, who hangs up his hat on the gas-jet, can be a man that is kept in proper order by his wife;
(4) A good husband is always giving his wife new dresses;
(5) No husband can fail to be cross-grained, if his wife does not keep him in proper order;
(6) An unmethodical husband always hangs up his hat on the gas-jet.

Univ. "husbands"; a = always coming home for his tea; b = always giving his wife new dresses; c = cross-grained; d = good; e = hanging up his hat on the gas-jet; h = kept in proper order; k = methodical.

52

(1) Everything, not absolutely ugly, may be kept in a drawing-room;
(2) Nothing, that is encrusted with salt, is ever quite dry;
(3) Nothing should be kept in a drawing-room, unless it is free from damp;

[Ans. 186; Sol. 224.]

(4) Bathing-machines are always kept near the sea;

(5) Nothing, that is made of mother-of-pearl, can be absolutely ugly;

(6) Whatever is kept near the sea gets encrusted with salt.

Univ. "things"; a = absolutely ugly; b = bathing-machines; c = encrusted with salt; d = kept near the sea; e = made of mother-of-pearl; h = quite dry; k = things that may be kept in a drawing-room.

53

(1) I call no day "unlucky," when Robinson is civil to me;

(2) Wednesdays are always cloudy;

(3) When people take umbrellas, the day never turns out fine;

(4) The only days when Robinson is uncivil to me are Wednesdays;

(5) Everybody takes his umbrella with him when it is raining;

(6) My "lucky" days always turn out fine.

Univ. "days"; a = called by me "lucky"; b = cloudy; c = days when people take umbrellas; d = days when Robinson is civil to me; e = rainy; h = turning out fine; k = Wednesdays.

54

(1) No shark ever doubts that it is well fitted out;

(2) A fish, that cannot dance a minuet, is contemptible;

(3) No fish is quite certain that it is well fitted out, unless it has three rows of teeth;

(4) All fishes, except sharks, are kind to children.

(5) No heavy fish can dance a minuet;

(6) A fish with three rows of teeth is not to be despised.

Univ. "fishes"; a = able to dance a minuet; b = certain that he is well fitted out; c = contemptible; d = having three rows of teeth; e = heavy; h = kind to children; k = sharks.

55

(1) All the human race, except my footmen, have a certain amount of common-sense;

(2) No one, who lives on barley-sugar, can be anything but a mere baby;

(3) None but a hop-scotch player knows what real happiness is;

(4) No mere baby has a grain of common sense;

[Ans. 186; Sol. 224.]

(5) No engine-driver ever plays hop-scotch;

(6) No footman of mine is ignorant of what true happiness is.

Univ. "human beings"; a = engine-drivers; b = having common sense; c = hop-scotch players; d = knowing what real happiness is; e = living on barley-sugar; h = mere babies; k = my footmen.

56

(1) I trust every animal that belongs to me;

(2) Dogs gnaw bones;

(3) I admit no animals into my study, unless they will beg when told to do so;

(4) All the animals in the yard are mine;

(5) I admit every animal, that I trust, into my study;

(6) The only animals, that are really willing to beg when told to do so, are dogs.

Univ. "animals"; a = admitted to my study; b = animals that I trust; c = dogs; d = gnawing bones; e = in the yard; h = my; k = willing to beg when told.

57

(1) Animals are always mortally offended if I fail to notice them;

(2) The only animals that belong to *me* are in that field;

(3) No animal can guess a conundrum, unless it has been properly trained in a Board-School;

(4) None of the animals in that field are badgers;

(5) When an animal is mortally offended, it always rushes about wildly and howls;

(6) I never notice any animal, unless it belongs to me;

(7) No animal, that has been properly trained in a Board-School, ever rushes about wildly and howls.

Univ. "animals"; a = able to guess a conundrum; b = badgers; c = in that field; d = mortally offended; e = my; h = noticed by me; k = properly trained in a Board-School; l = rushing about wildly and howling.

58

(1) I never put a cheque, received by me, on that file, unless I am anxious about it;

[Ans. 186–187; Sol. 224–225.]

(2) All the cheques received by me, that are not marked with a cross, are payable to bearer;

(3) None of them are ever brought back to me, unless they have been dishonoured at the Bank;

(4) All of them, that are marked with a cross, are for amounts of over £100;

(5) All of them, that are not on that file, are marked "not negotiable";

(6) No cheque of yours, received by me, has ever been dishonoured;

(7) I am never anxious about a cheque, received by me, unless it should happen to be brought back to me;

(8) None of the cheques received by me, that are marked "not negotiable," are for amounts of over £100.

Univ. "cheques received by me"; a = brought back to me; b = cheques that I am anxious about; c = honoured; d = marked with a cross; e = marked "not negotiable"; h = on that file; k = over £100; l = payable to bearer; m = your.

59

(1) All the dated letters in this room are written on blue paper;

(2) None of them are in black ink, except those that are written in the third person;

(3) I have not filed any of them that I can read;

(4) None of them, that are written on one sheet, are undated;

(5) All of them, that are not crossed, are in black ink;

(6) All of them, written by Brown, begin with "Dear Sir";

(7) All of them, written on blue paper, are filed;

(8) None of them, written on more than one sheet, are crossed;

(9) None of them, that begin with "Dear Sir," are written in the third person.

Univ. "letters in this room"; a = beginning with "Dear Sir"; b = crossed; c = dated; d = filed; e = in black ink; h = in third person; k = letters that I can read; l = on blue paper; m = on one sheet; n = written by Brown.

60

(1) The only animals in this house are cats;

(2) Every animal is suitable for a pet, that loves to gaze at the moon;

[Ans. 187; Sol. 225.]

(3) When I detest an animal, I avoid it;

(4) No animals are carnivorous, unless they prowl at night;

(5) No cat fails to kill mice;

(6) No animals ever take to me, except what are in this house;

(7) Kangaroos are not suitable for pets;

(8) None but carnivora kill mice;

(9) I detest animals that do not take to me;

(10) Animals, that prowl at night, always love to gaze at the moon.

Univ. "animals"; a = avoided by me; b = carnivora; c = cats; d = detested by me; e = in this house; h = kangaroos; k = killing mice; l = loving to gaze at the moon; m = prowling at night; n = suitable for pets; r = taking to me.

Chapter II ❧ Answers

Answers to §1

1. All . . . . *Sign of Quantity*

   persons represented by the Name "I" (or I's)   *Subject*

   are . . . . *Copula*

   persons who have been out for a walk . . . *Predicate*

   or more briefly,

   All | I's | are | persons who have been out for a walk.

2. All | I's | are | persons who feel better.

3. No | persons who are not John | are | persons who have read the letter.

4. No | Members of the Class "you and I" | are | old persons.

5. No | fat creatures | are | creatures that run well.

6. No | not-brave persons | are | persons deserving of the fair.

7. No | not-pale persons | are | persons who look poetical.

[Ex. 143; Sol. 187–188.]

8. Some | judges | are | persons who lose their tempers.

9. All | I's | are | persons who do not neglect important business.

10. All | difficult things | are | things that need attention.

11. All | unwholesome things | are | things that should be avoided.

12. All | laws passed last week | are | laws relating to excise.

13. All | logical studies | are | things that puzzle me.

14. No | persons in the house | are | Jews.

15. Some | not well-cooked dishes | are | unwholesome dishes.

16. All | unexciting books | are | books that make one drowsy.

17. All | men who know what they're about | are | men who can detect a sharper.

18. All | Members of the Class "you and I" | are | persons who know what they're about.

19. Some | bald persons | are | persons accustomed to wear wigs.

20. All | fully occupied persons | are | persons who do not talk about their grievances.

21. No | riddles that can be solved | are | riddles that interest me.

Answers to §2

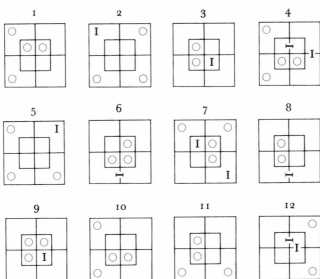

[Ex. 143–144; Sol. 188–192.]

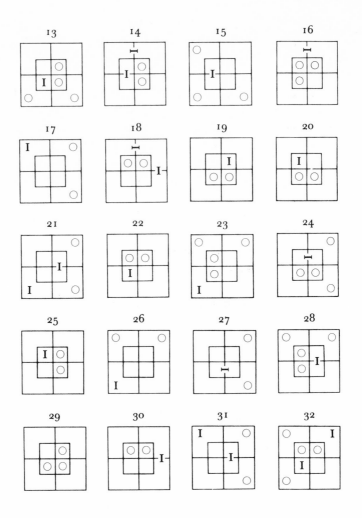

Answers to §3

1. Some xy exist, or some x are y, or some y are x.
2. No information.
3. All y' are x'.
4. No xy exist, &c.
5. All y' are x.
6. All x' are y.
7. All x are y.
8. All x' are y', and all y are x.
9. All x' are y'.
10. All x are y'.
11. No information.
12. Some $x'y'$ exist, &c.
13. Some xy' exist, &c.

[Ex. 144–145.]

14. No xy' exist, &c.
15. Some xy exist, &c.
16. All y are x.
17. All x' are y, and all y' are x.

18. All x are y' and all y are x'.
19. All x are y, and all y' are x'.
20. All y are x'.

Answers to §4

1. No x' are y'.
2. Some x' are y'.
3. Some x are y'.
4. [No Concl.   Fallacy of Like Eliminands not asserted to exist.]
5. Some x' are y'.
6. [No Concl.   Fallacy of Like Eliminands not asserted to exist.]
7. Some x are y'.
8. Some x' are y'.
9. [No Concl.   Fallacy of Unlike Eliminands with an Entity-Premiss.]
10. All x are y, and all y' are x'.
11. [No Concl.   Fallacy of Like Eliminands not asserted to exist.]
12. All y are x'.
13. No x' are y.
14. No x' are y'.
15. No x are y.
16. All x are y', and all y are x'.
17. No x are y'.
18. No x are y.
19. Some x are y'.
20. No x are y'
21. Some y are x'.
22. [No Concl.   Fallacy of Unlike Eliminands with an Entity-Premiss.]
23. Some x are y.
24. All y are x'.
25. Some y are x'.
26. All y are x.
27. All x are y, and all y' are x'.
28. Some y are x'.
29. [No Concl.   Fallacy of Like Eliminands not asserted to exist.]
30. [No Concl.   Fallacy of Unlike Eliminands with an Entity-Premiss.]

[Ex. 145–146; Sol. 191–192; 199–200.]

31. [No Concl. Fallacy of Like Eliminands not asserted to exist.]
32. No x are y'.
33. [No Concl. Fallacy of Like Eliminands not asserted to exist.]
34. Some x are y.
35. All y are x'.
36. Some y are x'.
37. Some x are y'
38. No x are y.
39. Some x' are y'.
40. All y' are x.
41. All x are y'.
42. No x are y.

Answers to §5

1. Somebody who has been out for a walk is feeling better.
2. No one but John knows what the letter is about.
3. You and I like walking.
4. Honesty is sometimes the best policy.
5. Some greyhounds are not fat.
6. Some brave persons get their deserts.
7. Some rich persons are not Esquimaux.
8. [No Concl. Fallacy of Unlike Eliminands with an Entity-Premiss.]
9. John is ill.
10. Some things, that are not umbrellas, should be left behind on a journey.
11. No music is worth paying for, unless it causes vibration in the air.
12. Some holidays are tiresome.
13. Englishmen are not Frenchmen.
14. No photograph of a lady is satisfactory.
15. No one looks poetical unless he is phlegmatic.
16. Some thin persons are not cheerful.
17. Some judges do not exercise self-control.
18. Pigs are not fed on barley-water.
19. Some black rabbits are not old.
20. [No Concl. Fallacy of Unlike Eliminands with an Entity-Premiss.]
21. [No Concl. Fallacy of Like Eliminands not asserted to exist.]

[Ex. 146–148; Sol. 192–195; 202–203.]

22. Some lessons need attention.
23. [No Concl.   Fallacy of Like Eliminands not asserted to exist.]
24. No one, who forgets a promise, fails to do mischief.
25. Some greedy creatures cannot fly.
26. [No Concl.   Fallacy of Unlike Eliminands with an Entity-Premiss.]
27. No bride-cakes are things that need not be avoided.
28. John is happy.
29. Some people, who are not gamblers, are not philosophers.
30. [No Concl.   Fallacy of Unlike Eliminands with an Entity-Premiss.]
31. None of my lodgers write poetry.
32. Senna is not nice.
33. [No Concl.   Fallacy of Unlike Eliminands with an Entity-Premiss.]
34. [No Concl.   Fallacy of Like Eliminands not asserted to exist.]
35. Logic is unintelligible.
36. Some wild creatures are fat.
37. All wasps are unwelcome.
38. All black rabbits are young.
39. Some hard-boiled things can be cracked.
40. No antelopes fail to delight the eye.
41. All well-fed canaries are cheerful.
42. Some poetry is not producible at will.
43. No country infested by dragons fails to be fascinating.
44. [No Concl.   Fallacy of Like Eliminands not asserted to exist.]
45. Some picturesque things are not made of sugar.
46. No children can sit still.
47. Some cats cannot whistle.
48. You are terrible.
49. Some oysters are not amusing.
50. Nobody in the house has a beard a yard long.
51. Some ill-fed canaries are unhappy.
52. My sisters cannot sing.
53. [No Concl.   Fallacy of Unlike Eliminands with an Entity-Premiss.]
54. Some rich things are nice.
55. My cousins are none of them judges, and judges are none of them cousins of mine.
56. Something wearisome is not eagerly wished for.
57. Senna is nasty.
58. [No Concl.   Fallacy of Unlike Eliminands with an Entity-Premiss.]

[Ex. 148–150; Sol. 204–205.]

59. Niggers are not any of them tall.
60. Some obstinate persons are not philosophers.
61. John is happy.
62. Some unwholesome dishes are not present here (i.e. cannot be spoken of as "these").
63. No books suit feverish patients unless they make one drowsy.
64. Some greedy creatures cannot fly.
65. You and I can detect a sharper.
66. Some dreams are not lambs.
67. No lizard needs a hairbrush.
68. Some things, that may escape notice, are not battles.
69. My cousins are not any of them judges.
70. Some hard-boiled things can be cracked.
71. [No Concl. Fallacy of Unlike Eliminands with an Entity-Premiss.]
72. She is unpopular.
73. Some people, who wear wigs, are not children of yours.
74. No lobsters expect impossibilities.
75. No nightmare is eagerly desired.
76. Some nice things are not plumcakes.
77. Some kinds of jam need not be shunned.
78. All ducks are ungraceful.
79. [No Concl. Fallacy of Like Eliminands not asserted to exist.]
80. No man, who begs in the street, should fail to keep accounts.
81. Some savage creatures are not spiders.
82. [No Concl. Fallacy of Unlike Eliminands with an Entity-Premiss.]
83. No travelers, who do not carry plenty of small change, fail to lose their luggage.
84. [No Concl. Fallacy of Unlike Eliminands with an Entity-Premiss.]
85. Judges are none of them cousins of mine.
86. All my lodgers are sane.
87. Those who are busy are contented, and discontented people are not busy.
88. None of my cousins are judges.
89. No nightingale dislikes sugar.
90. [No Concl. Fallacy of Like Eliminands not asserted to exist.]
91. Some excuses are not clear explanations.
92. [No Concl. Fallacy of Like Eliminands not asserted to exist.]
93. No kind deed need cause scruple.

[Ex. 150–152; Sol. 205–206.]

94. [No Concl.   Fallacy of Like Eliminands not asserted to exist.]
95. [No Concl.   Fallacy of Like Eliminands not asserted to exist.]
96. No cheats are trustworthy.
97. No clever child of mine is greedy.
98. Some things, that are meant to amuse, are not Acts of Parliament.
99. No tour, that is ever forgotten, is worth writing a book about.
100. No obedient child of mine is contented.
101. Your visit does not annoy me.

Answers to §6

   1. Conclusion right.
   2. No Concl.   Fallacy of Like Eliminands not asserted to exist.
3, 4, 5. Concl. right.
   6. No Concl.   Fallacy of Like Eliminands not asserted to exist.
   7. No Concl.   Fallacy of Unlike Eliminands with an Entity-Premiss.
8–15. Concl. right.
   16. No Concl.   Fallacy of Like Eliminands not asserted to exist.
17–21. Concl. right.
   22. Concl. wrong: the right one is "Some x are y."
23–27. Concl. right.
   28. No Concl.   Fallacy of Like Eliminands not asserted to exist.
29–33. Concl. right.
   34. No Concl.   Fallacy of Unlike Eliminands with an Entity-Premiss.
35, 36, 37. Concl. right.
   38. No Concl.   Fallacy of Like Eliminands not asserted to exist.
39, 40. Concl. right.

Answers to §7

1, 2, 3. Concl. right.
4. Concl. wrong: right one is "Some epicures are not uncles of mine."
5. Concl. right.
6. No Concl.   Fallacy of Unlike Eliminands with an Entity-Premiss.

[Ex. 152–155; Sol. 206–209.]

7. Concl. wrong: right one is "The publication, in which I saw it, tells lies."

8. No Concl. Fallacy of Unlike Eliminands with an Entity-Premiss.

9. Concl. wrong: right one is "Some tedious songs are not his."

10. Concl. right.

11. No Concl. Fallacy of Unlike Eliminands with an Entity-Premiss.

12. Concl. wrong: right one is "Some fierce creatures do not drink coffee."

13. No Concl. Fallacy of Unlike Eliminands with an Entity-Premiss.

14. Concl. right.

15. Concl. wrong: right one is "Some shallow persons are not students."

16. No Concl. Fallacy of Like Eliminands not asserted to exist.

17. Concl. wrong: right one is "Some business, other than railways, is unprofitable."

18. Concl. wrong: right one is "Some vain persons are not Professors."

19. Concl. right.

20. Concl. wrong: right one is "Wasps are not puppies."

21. No Concl. Fallacy of Unlike Eliminands with an Entity-Premiss.

22. No Concl. Same Fallacy.

23. Concl. right.

24. Concl. wrong: right one is "Some chocolate-creams are delicious."

25. No Concl. Fallacy of Like Eliminands not asserted to exist.

26. No Concl. Fallacy of Unlike Eliminands with an Entity-Premiss.

27. Concl. wrong: right one is "Some pillows are not pokers."

28. Concl. right.

29. No Concl. Fallacy of Unlike Eliminands with an Entity-Premiss.

30. No Concl. Fallacy of Like Eliminands not asserted to exist.

31. Concl. right.

32. No Concl. Fallacy of Like Eliminands not asserted to exist.

33. No Concl. Fallacy of Unlike Eliminands with an Entity-Premiss.

34. Concl. wrong: right one is "Some dreaded persons are not begged to prolong their visits."

35. Concl. wrong: right one is "No man walks on neither."

36. Concl. right.

37. No Concl. Fallacy of Unlike Eliminands with an Entity-Premiss.

38. Concl. wrong: right one is "Some persons, dreaded by children, are not emperors."

39. Concl. incomplete: the omitted portion is "Sugar is not salt."

40. Concl. right.

[Ex. 155–158; Sol. 209–216.]

Answers to §8

1. $a_1b_0 \dagger b_1a_0$	2. d_1a_0	3. ac_0	4. a_1d_0
5. cd_0	6. d_1c_0	7. $a'c_0$	8. $c_1a'_0$
9. $c'd_0$	10. b_1a_0	11. d_1b_0	12. $a'd_0$
13. c_1b_0	14. $d_1e'_0$	15. $e_1a'_0$	16. $b'c_0$
17. a_1b_0	18. d_1c_0	19. a_1d_0	20. ac_0
21. de_0	22. $a_1b'_0$	23. h_1c_0	24. e_1a_0
25. $e_1c'_0$	26. $e_1c'_0$	27. hk'_0	28. $e_1d'_0$
29. $l'a_0$	30. $k_1b'_0$		

Answers to §9

1. Babies cannot manage crocodiles.
2. *Your* presents to me are not made of tin.
3. All my potatoes in this dish are old ones.
4. My servants never say "shpoonj."
5. My poultry are not officers.
6. None of *your* sons are fit to serve on a jury.
7. No pencils of mine are sugar-plums.
8. Jenkins is inexperienced.
9. No comet has a curly tail.
10. No hedge-hog takes in the *Times*.
11. This dish is unwholesome.
12. My gardener is very old.
13. All humming-birds are small.
14. No one with a hooked nose ever fails to make money.
15. No gray ducks in this village wear lace collars.
16. No jug in this cupboard will hold water.
17. These apples were grown in the sun.
18. Puppies, that will not lie still, never care to do worsted work.
19. No name in this list is unmelodious.
20. No M.P. should ride in a donkey-race, unless he has perfect self-command.
21. No goods in this shop, that are still on sale, may be carried away.
22. No acrobatic feat, which involves turning a quadruple somersault, is ever attempted in a circus.

[Ex. 158–164; Sol. 216–221.]

23. Guinea-pigs never really appreciate Beethoven.
24. No scentless flowers please me.
25. Showy talkers are not really well-informed.
26. None but red-haired boys learn Greek in this school.
27. Wedding-cake always disagrees with me.
28. Discussions, that go on while Tomkins is in the chair, endanger the peacefulness of our Debating-Club.
29. All gluttons, who are children of mine, are unhealthy.
30. An egg of the Greak Auk is not to be had for a song.
31. No books sold here have gilt edges, unless they are priced at 5s. and upwards.
32. When you cut your finger, you will find Tincture of Calendula useful.
33. *I* have never come across a mermaid at sea.
34. All the romances in this library are well-written.
35. No bird in this aviary lives on mince-pies.
36. No plum-pudding, that has not been boiled in a cloth, can be distinguished from soup.
37. All *your* poems are uninteresting.
38. None of my peaches have been grown in a hot-house.
39. No pawnbroker is dishonest.
40. No kitten with green eyes will play with a gorilla.
41. All *my* friends dine at the lower table.
42. My writing-desk is full of live scorpions.
43. No Mandarin ever reads Hogg's poems.
44. Shakespeare was clever.
45. Rainbows are not worth writing odes to.
46. These Sorites-examples are difficult.
47. All my dreams come true.
48. All the English pictures here are painted in oils.
49. Donkeys are not easy to swallow.
50. Opium-eaters never wear white kid gloves.
51. A good husband always comes home for his tea.
52. Bathing-machines are never made of mother-of-pearl.
53. Rainy days are always cloudy.
54. No heavy fish is unkind to children.
55. No engine-driver lives on barley-sugar.
56. All the animals in the yard gnaw bones.
57. No badger can guess a conundrum.

[Ex. 165–174; Sol. 221–225.]

58. No cheque of yours, received by me, is payable to order.

59. I cannot read any of Brown's letters.

60. I always avoid a kangaroo.

Chapter III ⚡ Solutions

[§1] **Propositions of Relation reduced to normal form**

Solutions for §1

1. The Univ. is "persons." The Individual I may be regarded as a Class, of persons, whose peculiar Attribute is "represented by the Name 'I'," and may be called the Class of I's. It is evident that this Class cannot possibly contain more than one Member: hence the Sign of Quantity is "all." The verb "have been" may be replaced by the phrase "are persons who have been." The Proposition may be written thus:

All . . . . *Sign of Quantity*
I's . . . . *Subject*
are . . . . *Copula*
persons who have been out for a walk   *Predicate*

or, more briefly,

All | I's | are | persons who have been out for a walk.

2. The Univ. and the Subject are the same as in Ex. 1. The Proposition may be written

All | I's | are | persons who feel better.

3. Univ. is "persons." The Subject is evidently the Class of persons from which John is *excluded*: i.e. it is the Class containing all persons who are *not* John. The Sign of Quantity is "no." The verb

[Ex. 143; Ans. 176.]

"has read" may be replaced by the phrase "are persons who have read."

The Proposition may be written

> No | persons who are not John | are | persons
> who have read the letter.

4. Univ. is "persons." The Subject is evidently the Class of persons whose only two Members are "you and I." Hence the Sign of Quantity is "no."

The Proposition may be written

> No | Members of the Class "you and I" | are |
> old persons.

5. Univ. is "creatures." The verb "run well" may be replaced by the phrase "are creatures that run well."

The Proposition may be written

> No | fat creatures | are | creatures that run
> well.

6. Univ. is "persons." The Subject is evidently the Class of persons who are *not* brave. The verb "deserve" may be replaced by the phrase "are deserving of."

The Proposition may be written

> No | not-brave persons | are | persons deserv-
> ing of the fair.

7. Univ. is "persons." The phrase "looks poetical" evidently belongs to the *Predicate*: and the *Subject* is the Class, of persons, whose peculiar Attribute is "*not*-pale."

The Proposition may be written

> No | not-pale persons | are | persons who look
> poetical.

8. Univ. is "persons."

The Proposition may be written

> Some | judges | are | persons who lose their
> tempers.

[Ex. 143; Ans. 176–177.]

9. Univ. is "persons." The phrase "never neglect" is merely a stronger form of the phrase "am a person who does not neglect."
The Proposition may be written

> All | I's | are | persons who do not neglect important business.

10. Univ. is "things." The phrase "what is difficult" (i.e. "that which is difficult") is equivalent to the phrase "all difficult things."
The Proposition may be written

> All | difficult things | are | things that need attention.

11. Univ. is "things." The phrase "what is unwholesome" may be interpreted as in Ex. 10.
The Proposition may be written

> All | unwholesome things | are | things that should be avoided.

12. Univ. is "laws." The Predicate is evidently a Class whose peculiar Attribute is "relating to excise."
The Proposition may be written

> All | laws passed last week | are | laws relating to excise.

13. Univ. is "things." The Subject is evidently the Class, of studies, whose peculiar Attribute is "logical": hence the Sign of Quantity is "all."
The Proposition may be written

> All | logical studies | are | things that puzzle me.

14. Univ. is "persons." The Subject is evidently "persons in the house."
The Proposition may be written

> No | persons in the house | are | Jews.

[Ex. 143–144; Ans. 177.]

15. Univ. is "dishes." The phrase "if not well-cooked" is equivalent to the Attribute "not well-cooked."
The Proposition may be written

> Some | not well-cooked dishes | are | unwhole-
> some dishes.

16. Univ. is "books." The phrase "make one drowsy" may be replaced by the phrase "are books that make one drowsy." The Sign of Quantity is evidently "all."
The Proposition may be written

> All | unexciting books | are | books that make
> one drowsy.

17. Univ. is "men." The Subject is evidently "a man who knows what he's about"; and the word "when" shows that the Proposition is asserted of *every* such man, i.e. of *all* such men. The verb "can" may be replaced by "are men who can."
The Proposition may be written

> All | men who know what they're about | are |
> men who can detect a sharper.

18. The Univ. and the Subject are the same as in Ex. 4.
The Proposition may be written

> All | Members of the Class "*you* and I" | are |
> persons who know what they're about.

19. Univ. is "persons." The verb "wear" may be replaced by the phrase "are accustomed to wear."
The Proposition may be written

> Some | bald persons | are | persons accus-
> tomed to wear wigs.

20. Univ. is "persons." The phrase "never talk" is merely a stronger form of "are persons who do not talk."
The Proposition may be written

> All | fully occupied persons | are | persons who
> do not talk about their grievances.

[Ex. 144; Ans. 177.]

21. Univ. is "riddles."   The phrase "if they can be solved" is equivalent to the Attribute "that can be solved."

   The Proposition may be written

> No | riddles that can be solved | are | riddles that interest me.

[§2] **Method of Diagrams**

Solutions for §4, *Nos.* 1–12

1. No *m* are *x*';
   All *m*' are *y*.

∴ No *x*' are *y*'.

2. No *m*' are *x*;
   Some *m*' are *y*'.

∴ Some *x* are *y*'.

3. All *m*' are *x*;
   All *m*' are *y*'.

∴ Some *x* are *y*'.

4. No *x*' are *m*';
   All *y*' are *m*.

There is no Conclusion.

5. Some *m* are *x*';
   No *y* are *m*.

∴ Some *x*' are *y*'.

6. No *x*' are *m*;
   No *m* are *y*.

There is no Conclusion.

[Ex. 144, 146; Ans. 177, 179.]

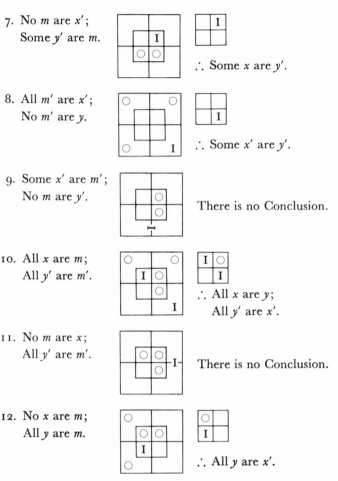

7. No *m* are *x'*;
   Some *y'* are *m*.

   ∴ Some *x* are *y'*.

8. All *m'* are *x'*;
   No *m'* are *y*.

   ∴ Some *x'* are *y'*.

9. Some *x'* are *m'*;
   No *m* are *y'*.

   There is no Conclusion.

10. All *x* are *m*;
    All *y'* are *m'*.

    ∴ All *x* are *y*;
       All *y'* are *x'*.

11. No *m* are *x*;
    All *y'* are *m'*.

    There is no Conclusion.

12. No *x* are *m*;
    All *y* are *m*.

    ∴ All *y* are *x'*.

Solutions for §5, *Nos.* 1–12

1. I have been out for a walk;
   I am feeling better.

Univ. is "persons"; *m* = the Class of I's; *x* = persons who have been out for a walk; *y* = persons who are feeling better.

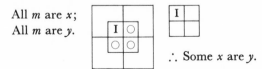

All *m* are *x*;
All *m* are *y*.

∴ Some *x* are *y*.

i.e. Somebody, who has been out for a walk, is feeling better.

[Ex. 146, 147; Ans. 179, 180.]

2. No one has read the letter but John;

No one, who has *not* read it, knows what it is about.

Univ. is "persons"; m = persons who have read the letter; x = the Class of Johns; y = persons who know what the letter is about.

No x' are m;
No m' are y.

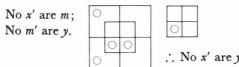

∴ No x' are y.

i.e. No one, but John, knows what the letter is about.

3. Those who are not old like walking;

You and I are young.

Univ. is "persons"; m = old; x = persons who like walking; y = you and I.

All m' are x;
All y are m'.

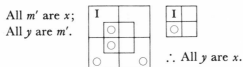

∴ All y are x.

i.e. You and I like walking.

4. Your course is always honest;

Your course is always the best policy.

Univ. is "courses"; m = your; x = honest; y = courses which are the best policy.

All m are x;
All m are y.

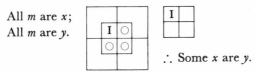

∴ Some x are y.

i.e. Honesty is sometimes the best policy.

5. No fat creatures run well;

Some greyhounds run well.

Univ. is "creatures"; m = creatures that run well; x = fat; y = grey-hounds.

No x are m;
Some y are m.

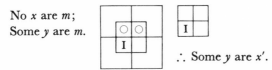

∴ Some y are x'.

i.e. Some greyhounds are not fat.

[Ex. 147; Ans. 180.]

6. Some, who deserve the fair, get their deserts;
   None but the brave deserve the fair.

Univ. is "persons"; m = persons who deserve the fair; x = persons who get their deserts; y = brave.

Some m are x;
No y' are m.

∴ Some y are x.

i.e. Some brave persons get their deserts.

7. Some Jews are rich;
   All Esquimaux are Gentiles.

Univ. is "persons"; m = Jews; x = rich; y = Esquimaux.

Some m are x;
All y are m'.

∴ Some x are y'.

i.e. Some rich persons are not Esquimaux.

8. Sugar-plums are sweet;
   Some sweet things are liked by children.

Univ. is "things"; m = sweet; x = sugar-plums; y = things that are liked by children.

All x are m;
Some m are y.

There is no Conclusion.

9. John is in the house;
   Everybody in the house is ill.

Univ. is "persons"; m = persons in the house; x = the Class of Johns; y = ill.

All x are m;
All m are y.

∴ All x are y.

i.e. John is ill.

[Ex. 147; Ans. 180.]

10. Umbrellas are useful on a journey;
    What is useless on a journey should be left behind.

Univ. is "things"; m = useful on a journey; x = umbrellas; y = things that should be left behind.

All x are m;
All m' are y.

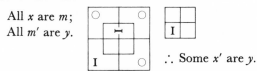

∴ Some x' are y.

i.e. Some things, that are not umbrellas, should be left behind on a journey.

11. Audible music causes vibration in the air;
    Inaudible music is not worth paying for.

Univ. is "music"; m = audible; x = music that causes vibration in the air; y = worth paying for.

All m are x;
All m' are y'.

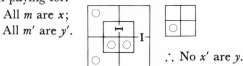

∴ No x' are y.

i.e. No music is worth paying for, unless it causes vibration in the air.

12. Some holidays are rainy;
    Rainy days are tiresome.

Univ. is "days"; m = rainy; x = holidays; y = tiresome.

Some x are m;
All m are y.

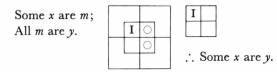

∴ Some x are y.

i.e. Some holidays are tiresome.

Solutions for §6, Nos. 1–10

1

Some x are m; No m are y'.   Some x are y.

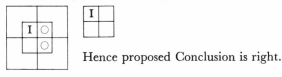

Hence proposed Conclusion is right.

[Ex. 147, 153; Ans. 180, 183.]

2

All *x* are *m*; No *y* are *m'*.   No *y* are *x'*.

There is no Conclusion.

3

Some *x* are *m'*; All *y'* are *m*.   Some *x* are *y*.

Hence proposed Conclusion is right.

4

All *x* are *m*; No *y* are *m*.   All *x* are *y'*.

Hence proposed Conclusion is right.

5

Some *m'* are *x'*; No *m'* are *y*.   Some *x'* are *y'*.

Hence proposed Conclusion is right.

6

No *x'* are *m*; All *y* are *m'*.   All *y* are *x*.

There is no Conclusion.

[Ex. 153; Ans. 183.]

7

Some *m'* are *x'*; All *y'* are *m'*.   Some *x'* are *y'*.

 I   There is no Conclusion.

8

No *m'* are *x'*; All *y'* are *m'*.   All *y'* are *x*.

Hence proposed Conclusion is right.

9

Some *m* are *x'*; No *m* are *y*.   Some *x'* are *y'*.

Hence proposed Conclusion is right.

10

All *m'* are *x'*; All *m'* are *y*.   Some *y* are *x'*.

Hence proposed Conclusion is right.

Solutions for §7, Nos. 1–6

1

No doctors are enthusiastic;
You are enthusiastic.

You are not a doctor.

Univ. "persons"; *m* = enthusiastic; *x* = doctors; *y* = you.

[Ex. 153–154; Ans. 183.]

No x are m;
All y are m.
All y are x'.

∴ All y are x'.

Hence proposed Conclusion is right.

2

All dictionaries are useful;
Useful books are valuable.
 Dictionaries are valuable.

Univ. "books"; m = useful; x = dictionaries; y = valuable.

All x are m;
All m are y.
All x are y.

∴ All x are y.

Hence proposed Conclusion is right.

3

No misers are unselfish;
None but misers save egg-shells.
 No unselfish people save egg-shells.

Univ. "people"; m = misers; x = selfish; y = people who save egg-shells.

No m are x';
No m' are y.
No x' are y.

∴ No x' are y.

Hence proposed Conclusion is right.

4

Some epicures are ungenerous;
All my uncles are generous.
 My uncles are not epicures.

Univ. "persons"; m = generous; x = epicures; y = my uncles.

Some x are m';
All y are m.
All y are x'.

∴ Some x are y'.

[Ex. 155; Ans. 183.]

Hence proposed Conclusion is wrong, the right one being "Some epicures are not uncles of mine."

5

Gold is heavy;
Nothing but gold will silence him.
    Nothing light will silence him.

Univ. "things"; m = gold; x = heavy; y = able to silence him.

      All m are x;
      No m' are y.
      No x' are y.

∴ No x' are y.

Hence proposed Conclusion is right.

6

Some healthy people are fat;
No unhealthy people are strong.
    Some fat people are not strong.

Univ. "persons"; m = healthy; x = fat; y = strong.

      Some m are x;
      No m' are y.
      Some x are y'.

There is no Conclusion.

[§3] Method of Subscripts

Solutions for §4

1. $mx'_0 \dagger m'_1 y'_0 \P x'y'_0$ [Fig. I
   i.e. No x' are y'.

2. $m'x_0 \dagger m'y'_1 \P x'y'_1$ [Fig. II
   i.e. Some x' are y'.

3. $m'_1 x'_0 \dagger m'_1 y_0 \P xy'_1$ [Fig. III
   i.e. Some x are y'.

4. $x'm'_0 \dagger y'_1 m'_0 \P$ nothing.
   [Fallacy of Like Eliminands not asserted to exist.]

5. $mx'_1 \dagger ym_0 \P x'y'_1$ [Fig. II
   i.e. Some x' are y'.

6. $x'm_0 \dagger my_0 \P$ nothing.
   [Fallacy of Like Eliminands not asserted to exist.]

[Ex. 155, 146; Ans. 199, 179.]

7. $mx'_0 \dagger y'm_1 \P xy'_1$ [Fig. II
i.e. Some x are y'.

9. $x'm'_1 \dagger my_0 \P$ nothing.
[Fallacy of Unlike Eliminands
with an Entity-Premiss.]

11. $mx_0 \dagger y'_1m_0 \P$ nothing.
[Fallacy of Like Eliminands
not asserted to exist.]

13. $m'_1x'_0 \dagger ym_0 \P x'y_0$ [Fig. I
i.e. No x' are y.

15. $xm_0 \dagger m'y_0 \P xy_0$ [Fig. I
i.e. No x are y.

17. $xm_0 \dagger m'_1y'_0 \P xy'_0$ [Fig. I
i.e. No x are y'.

19. $m_1x'_0 \dagger m_1y_0 \P xy'_1$ [Fig. III
i.e. Some x are y'.

21. $x_1m'_0 \dagger m'y_1 \P x'y_1$ [Fig. II
i.e. Some x' are y.

23. $m_1x'_0 \dagger ym_1 \P xy_1$ [Fig. II
i.e. Some x are y.

25. $mx'_1 \dagger my'_0 \P x'y_1$ [Fig. II
i.e. Some x' are y.

27. $x_1m_0 \dagger y'_1m'_0 \P (x_1y'_0 \dagger y'_1x_0)$
[Fig. I (β)
i.e. All x are y, and all y' are x'.

29. $mx_0 \dagger y_1m_0 \P$ nothing.
[Fallacy of Like Eliminands
not asserted to exist.]

31. $x_1m'_0 \dagger y_1m'_0 \P$ nothing.
[Fallacy of Like Eliminands
not asserted to exist.]

8. $m'_1x_0 \dagger m'y_0 \P x'y'_1$ [Fig. III
i.e. Some x' are y'.

10. $x_1m'_0 \dagger y'_1m_0 \P x_1y'_0 \dagger y'_1x_0$
[Fig. I (β)
i.e. All x are y, and all y' are x'

12. $xm_0 \dagger y_1m'_0 \P y_1x_0$ [Fig. I (α)
i.e. All y are x'.

14. $m_1x'_0 \dagger m'_1y'_0 \P x'y'_0$ [Fig. I
i.e. No x' are y'.

16. $x_1m_0 \dagger y_1m'_0 \P (x_1y_0 \dagger y_1x_0)$
[Fig. I (β)
i.e. All x are y' and all y are x'.

18. $xm'_0 \dagger my_0 \P xy_0$ [Fig. I
i.e. No x are y.

20. $mx_0 \dagger m'_1y'_0 \P xy'_0$ [Fig. I
i.e. No x are y'.

22. $xm_1 \dagger y_1m'_0 \P$ nothing.
[Fallacy of Unlike Eliminands
with an Entity-Premiss.]

24. $xm_0 \dagger y_1m'_0 \P y_1x_0$ [Fig. I (α)
i.e. All y are x'.

26. $mx'_0 \dagger y_1m'_0 \P y_1x'_0$ [Fig. I (α)
i.e. All y are x.

28. $m_1x_0 \dagger my_1 \P x'y_1$ [Fig. II
i.e. Some x' are y.

30. $x_1m'_0 \dagger ym_1 \P x'y_1$ [Fig. II
i.e. Some y are x'.

32. $xm_0 \dagger m_1y'_0 \P xy'_0$ [Fig. I
i.e. No x are y'.

[Ex. 146; Ans. 179–180.]

§4.

1. $mx_0' \dagger m_1' y_0' \, \mathbb{P} \, xy_0' \, [\text{I}$

2. $m'x_0 \dagger m_1' y_1' \, \mathbb{P} \, x'y_1' \, [\text{II}$

3. $m_1' x_0' \dagger m_1' y_0 \, \mathbb{P} \, xy_1' \, [\text{III}$

4. $x'm_0' \dagger y_1' m_0' \quad \delta\lambda$

5. $mx_1' \dagger ym_0 \, \mathbb{P} \, x'y_1' [\text{II}$

6. $x'm_0 \dagger my_0 \quad \delta\lambda$

7. $mx_0' \dagger y'm_1 \, \mathbb{P} \, xy_1' [\text{II}$

8. $m_1' x_0 \dagger m'y_0 \, \mathbb{P} \, x'y_1' [\text{III}$

9. $x'm_1' \dagger my_0' \quad \delta\varepsilon$

10. $x_1' m_0' \dagger y_1' m_0 \, \mathbb{P} \, x y_0'$
$\dagger y_1' x_0 [\text{I}\beta$

11. $mx_0 \dagger y_1' m_0 \quad \delta\lambda$

12. $xm_0 \dagger y_1 m_0' \, \mathbb{P} \, y_1 \, x_0 [\text{I}.\alpha$

13. $m_1' x_0' \dagger ym_0 \, \mathbb{P} \, x'y_0 [\text{I}$

14. $m_1 x_0' \dagger m_1' y_0' \, \mathbb{P} \, xy_0' [\text{I}$

15. $xm_0 \dagger m'y_0 \, \mathbb{P} \, xy_0 [\text{I}$

16. $x_1 m_0 \dagger y_1 m_0' \, \mathbb{P} \, x_1 y_0$
$\dagger y_1 x_0 [\text{I}\beta$

17. $xm_0 \dagger m_1' y_0' \, \mathbb{P} \, xy_0' [\text{I}$

18. $xm_0' \dagger my_0 \, \mathbb{P} \, xy_0 [\text{I}$

19. $m_1 x_0' \dagger m_1 y_0 \, \mathbb{P} \, xy_1' [\text{III}$

20. $mx_0 \dagger m_1' y_0' \, \mathbb{P} \, xy_0' [\text{I}$

21. $x_1 m_0' \dagger m' y_1 \, \mathbb{P} \, x'y_1 [\text{II}$

22. $x m_1 \dagger y_1 m_0 \quad \delta\varepsilon$

23. $m_1 x_0' \dagger ym_1 \, \mathbb{P} \, xy_1 [\text{II}$

24. $xm_0 \dagger y_1 m_0' \, \mathbb{P} \, y_1 x_0 [\text{I}\alpha$

25. $mx_1' \dagger my_0' \, \mathbb{P} \, x'y_1 [\text{II}$

26. $mx_0' \dagger y_1 m_0' \, \mathbb{P} \, y_1 x_0' [\text{I}$

27. $x_1 m_0 \dagger y_1' m_0' \, \mathbb{P} \, x_1 y_0'$
$\dagger y_1' x_0 \, [\text{I}\beta$

28. $m_1 x_0 \dagger my_1 \, \mathbb{P} \, x'y_1 [\text{II}$

29. $mx_0 \dagger y_1 m_0 \quad \delta\lambda$

30. $x_1 m_0' \dagger y_1 m' \, \mathbb{P} \, xy_1 [\text{II}$

31. $x_1 m_0' \dagger y_1 m_0' \quad \delta\lambda$

32. $xm_0' \dagger m_1 y_0' \, \mathbb{P} \, xy_0' [\text{I}$

33. $mx_0 \dagger my_0 \quad \delta\lambda$

34. $mx_0' \dagger ym_1 \, \mathbb{P} \, xy_1 [\text{II}$

35. $mx_0 \dagger y_1 m_0' \, \mathbb{P} \, y_1 x_0 [\text{I}\alpha$

36. $m_1 x_0 \dagger ym_1 \, \mathbb{P} \, x'y_1 [\text{II}$

37. $m_1 x_0' \dagger ym_0 \, \mathbb{P} \, xy_1' [\text{III}$

38. $mx_0' \dagger m'y_0 \, \mathbb{P} \, xy_0 [\text{I}$

39. $mx_1 \dagger my_0 \, \mathbb{P} \, xy_1' [\text{II}$

40. $x'm_0 \dagger y_1 m_0' \, \mathbb{P} \, y_1' x_0' [\text{I}\alpha$

41. $x_1 m_0 \dagger ym_0' \, \mathbb{P} \, x_1 y_0 [\text{I}\alpha$

42. $m'x_0 \dagger ym_0 \, \mathbb{P} \, xy_0 [\text{I}$

In early editions of *Symbolic Logic*, Part I, §4 was not rendered into subscript form. Here is a specimen of Carroll's own working out into subscript form of the examples in this section.   See Book VIII, Chapter III §3 for the version that appeared in the Fourth Edition. (Henry E. Huntington Library)

33. mx_0 † my_0 ⫟ nothing.
[Fallacy of Like Eliminands
not asserted to exist.]

34. mx'_0 † ym_1 ⫟ xy_1 [Fig. II
i.e. Some x are y.

35. mx_0 † $y_1m'_0$ ⫟ y_1x_0 [Fig. I (α)
i.e. All y are x'.

36. m_1x_0 † ym_1 ⫟ $x'y_1$ [Fig. II
i.e. Some x' are y.

37. $m_1x'_0$ † ym_0 ⫟ xy'_1 [Fig. III
i.e. Some x are y'.

38. mx_0 † $m'y_0$ ⫟ xy_0 [Fig. I
i.e. No x are y.

39. mx'_1 † my_0 ⫟ $x'y'_1$ [Fig. II
i.e. Some x' are y'.

40. $x'm_0$ † $y'_1m'_0$ ⫟ $y'_1x'_0$ [Fig. I (α)
i.e. All y' are x.

41. x_1m_0 † ym'_0 ⫟ x_1y_0 [Fig. I (α)
i.e. All x are y'.

42. $m'x_0$ † ym_0 ⫟ xy_0 [Fig. I
i.e. No x are y.

Solutions for §5, *Nos.* 13–24

13. No Frenchmen like plumpudding;
All Englishmen like plumpudding.

Univ. "men"; m = liking plumpudding; x = French; y = English.

$$xm_0 \text{ † } y_1m'_0 \text{ ⫟ } y_1x_0 \text{ [Fig. I (α)}$$

i.e. Englishmen are not Frenchmen.

14. No portrait of a lady, that makes her simper or scowl, is
satisfactory;
No photograph of a lady ever fails to make her simper or scowl.

Univ. "portraits of ladies"; m = making the subject simper or scowl;
x = satisfactory; y = photographic.

$$mx_0 \text{ † } ym'_0 \text{ ⫟ } xy_0 \text{ [Fig. I}$$

i.e. No photograph of a lady is satisfactory.

15. All pale people are phlegmatic;
No one looks poetical unless he is pale.

Univ. "people"; m = pale; x = phlegmatic; y = looking poetical.

$$m_1x'_0 \text{ † } m'y_0 \text{ ⫟ } x'y_0 \text{ [Fig. I}$$

i.e. No one looks poetical unless he is phlegmatic.

[Ex. 146–148; Ans. 180–181.]

16. No old misers are cheerful;
   Some old misers are thin.

Univ. "persons"; m = old misers; x = cheerful; y = thin.

$$mx_0 \dagger my_1 \,\P\, x'y_1 \text{ [Fig. II}$$

i.e. Some thin persons are not cheerful.

17. No one, who exercises self-control, fails to keep his temper;
   Some judges lose their tempers.

Univ. "persons"; m = keeping their tempers; x = exercising self-control; y = judges.

$$xm'_0 \dagger ym'_1 \,\P\, x'y_1 \text{ [Fig. II}$$

i.e. Some judges do not exercise self-control.

18. All pigs are fat;
   Nothing that is fed on barley-water is fat.

Univ. is "things"; m = fat; x = pigs; y = fed on barley-water.

$$x_1m'_0 \dagger ym_0 \,\P\, x_1y_0 \text{ [Fig. I } (\alpha)$$

i.e. Pigs are not fed on barley-water.

19. All rabbits, that are not greedy, are black;
   No old rabbits are free from greediness.

Univ. is "rabbits"; m = greedy; x = black; y = old.

$$m'_1x'_0 \dagger ym'_0 \,\P\, xy'_1 \text{ [Fig. III}$$

i.e. Some black rabbits are not old.

20. Some pictures are not first attempts;
   No first attempts are really good.

Univ. is "things"; m = first attempts; x = pictures; y = really good.

$$xm'_1 \dagger my_0 \,\P\, \text{nothing.}$$

[Fallacy of Unlike Eliminands with an Entity-Premiss.]

21. I never neglect important business;
   Your business is unimportant.

Univ. is "business"; m = important; x = neglected by me; y = your.

$$mx_0 \dagger y_1m_0 \,\P\, \text{nothing.}$$

[Fallacy of Like Eliminands not asserted to exist.]

[Ex. 148; Ans. 180.]

22. Some lessons are difficult;
   What is difficult needs attention.

Univ. is "things"; m = difficult; x = lessons; y = needing attention.

$$xm_1 \dagger m_1y'_0 \text{ ⫤ } xy_1 \text{ [Fig. II]}$$

i.e. Some lessons need attention.

23. All clever people are popular;
   All obliging people are popular.

Univ. is "people"; m = popular; x = clever; y = obliging.

$$x_1m'_0 \dagger y_1m'_0 \text{ ⫤ nothing.}$$

[Fallacy of Like Eliminands not asserted to exist.]

24. Thoughtless people do mischief;
   No thoughtful person forgets a promise.

Univ. is "persons"; m = thoughtful; x = mischievous; y = forgetful of promises.

$$m'_1x'_0 \dagger my_0 \text{ ⫤ } x'y_0$$

i.e. No one, who forgets a promise, fails to do mischief.

Solutions[1] for §5, Nos. 1–12 and 25–101

1.	III	$m_1x'_0 \dagger m_1y'_0 \text{ ⫤ } xy_1$
2.	I	$x'm_0 \dagger m'y_0 \text{ ⫤ } x'y_0$
3.	I(α)	$m'_1x'_0 \dagger y_1m_0 \text{ ⫤ } y_1x'_0$
4.	III	$m_1x'_0 \dagger m_1y'_0 \text{ ⫤ } xy_1$
5.	II	$xm_0 \dagger ym_1 \text{ ⫤ } yx'_1$
6.	II	$mx_1 \dagger y'm_0 \text{ ⫤ } yx_1$
7.	II	$mx_1 \dagger y_1m_0 \text{ ⫤ } xy'_1$
8.	$\delta\varepsilon$	$x_1m'_0 \dagger my_1$
9.	I(α)	$x_1m'_0 \dagger m_1y'_0 \text{ ⫤ } x_1y'_0$
10.	III	$x_1m'_0 \dagger m'_1y'_0 \text{ ⫤ } x'y_1$

[Ex. 147–148; Ans. 180–181.]

---

[1] Previously published editions do not give solutions to these problems. The solutions given here are taken from Carroll's own manuscript annotations on a copy of *Symbolic Logic*, Part I, preserved in the Henry E. Huntington Library, Pasadena, and from a galley sheet preserved in the Library of Christ Church, Oxford.

11. I $m_1x'_0$ † m'_1y_0 ℙ $x'y_0$
12. II xm_1 † $m_1y'_0$ ℙ xy_1

25. III m_1x_0 † $m_1y'_0$ ℙ yx'_1
26. $\delta\varepsilon$ $m_1x'_0$ † ym'_1
27. I xm_0 † $m'_1y'_0$ ℙ xy'_0
28. I(α) $x_1m'_0$ † my'_0 ℙ $x_1y'_0$
29. II xm_0 † my'_1 ℙ $x'y'_1$
30. $\delta\varepsilon$ mx'_1 † $y_1m'_0$
31. I mx_0 † ym'_0 ℙ yx_0
32. I(α) mx_0 † $y_1m'_0$ ℙ y_1x_0
33. $\delta\varepsilon$ xm'_1 † ym_0
34. $\delta\lambda$ $x_1m'_0$ † ym'_0
35. I(α) xm_0 † $y_1m'_0$ ℙ y_1x_0
36. II mx_1 † $m_1y'_0$ ℙ xy_1
37. I(α) x_1m_0 † m'_1y_0 ℙ x_1y_0
38. I(α) xm_0 † $y_1m'_0$ ℙ y_1x_0
39. II mx_1 † my'_0 ℙ xy_1
40. I xm'_0 † $m_1y'_0$ ℙ xy'_0
41. I(α) $x_1m'_0$ † my_0 ℙ x_1y_0
42. II xm_1 † my_0 ℙ xy'_1
43. I mx_0 † $m'_1y'_0$ ℙ xy'_0
44. $\delta\lambda$ xm_0 † ym_0
45. II mx_0 † my_1 ℙ yx'_1
46. I xm_0 † $m'y_0$ ℙ xy_0
47. II mx_0 † ym_1 ℙ yx'_1
48. I(α) $m_1x'_0$ † $y_1m'_0$ ℙ $y_1x'_0$
49. II xm_1 † my_0 ℙ xy'_1
50. I mx_0 † $m'y_0$ ℙ xy_0
51. III m'_1x_0 † ym'_0 ℙ $y'x'_1$
52. I(α) $x_1m'_0$ † my_0 ℙ x_1y_0
53. $\delta\varepsilon$ $x_1m'_0$ † ym_1
54. II mx_1 † $m_1y'_0$ ℙ xy_1
55. I(β) x_1m_0 † $y_1m'_0$ ℙ x_1y_0 † y_1x_0
56. III $m_1x'_0$ † my_0 ℙ xy'_1
57. I(α) $m_1x'_0$ † $y_1m'_0$ ℙ $y_1x'_0$
58. $\delta\varepsilon$ mx'_1 † ym_0
59. I(α) xm_0 † $y_1m'_0$ ℙ y_1x_0

[Ex. 147–150; Ans. 180–182.]

60.	III	$x_1m'_0 \dagger m'_1y'_0 \;\mathbb{P}\; yx'_1$
61.	I(α)	$x_1m'_0 \dagger m_1y'_0 \;\mathbb{P}\; x_1y'_0$
62.	II	$x_1m'_0 \dagger m'y'_1 \;\mathbb{P}\; x'y'_1$
63.	I	$mx_0 \dagger m'_1y'_0 \;\mathbb{P}\; xy'_0$
64.	III	$mx_0 \dagger m_1y'_0 \;\mathbb{P}\; yx'_1$
65.	I(α)	$m_1x'_0 \dagger y_1m'_0 \;\mathbb{P}\; y_1x'_0$
66.	II	$xm_1 \dagger ym_0 \;\mathbb{P}\; xy'_1$
67.	I	$m'x_0 \dagger ym_0 \;\mathbb{P}\; yx_0$
68.	III	$x_1m'_0 \dagger m'_1y'_0 \;\mathbb{P}\; x'y_1$
69.	I(α)	$x_1m_0 \dagger ym'_0 \;\mathbb{P}\; x_1y_0$
70.	II	$m_1x'_0 \dagger my_1 \;\mathbb{P}\; yx_1$
71.	$\delta\varepsilon$	$m_1x_0 \dagger m'y_1$
72.	I(α)	$mx_0 \dagger y_1m'_0 \;\mathbb{P}\; y_1x_0$
73.	II	$m'x_1 \dagger y_1m'_0 \;\mathbb{P}\; y'x_1$
74.	I	$xm'_0 \dagger my_0 \;\mathbb{P}\; xy_0$
75.	I	$xm_0 \dagger m'_1y_0 \;\mathbb{P}\; xy_0$
76.	II	$xm_0 \dagger my_1 \;\mathbb{P}\; x'y_1$
77.	II	$mx_0 \dagger ym_1 \;\mathbb{P}\; yx'_1$
78.	I(α)	$x_1m'_0 \dagger my_0 \;\mathbb{P}\; x_1y_0$
79.	$\delta\lambda$	$x_1m'_0 \dagger ym'_0$
80.	I	$mx_0 \dagger m'_1y'_0 \;\mathbb{P}\; xy'_0$
81.	II	$x_1m'_0 \dagger m'y_1 \;\mathbb{P}\; x'y_1$
82.	$\delta\varepsilon$	$xm'_1 \dagger my_0$
83.	I	$m_1x'_0 \dagger m'_1y'_0 \;\mathbb{P}\; x'y'_0$
84.	$\delta\varepsilon$	$xm_1 \dagger y_1m'_0$
85.	I(α)	$xm_0 \dagger y_1m'_0 \;\mathbb{P}\; y_1x_0$
86.	I(α)	$mx_0 \dagger y_1m'_0 \;\mathbb{P}\; y_1x_0$
87.	I(β)	$x_1m_0 \dagger y'_1m'_0 \;\mathbb{P}\; x_1y'_0 \dagger y'_1x_0$
88.	I	$xm_0 \dagger ym'_0 \;\mathbb{P}\; xy_0$
89.	I	$m'_1x'_0 \dagger ym_0 \;\mathbb{P}\; yx'_0$
90.	$\delta\lambda$	$mx_0 \dagger y_1m_0$
91.	II	$x_1m'_0 \dagger ym'_1 \;\mathbb{P}\; yx'_1$
92.	$\delta\lambda$	$x_1m'_0 \dagger y_1m'_0$
93.	I	$xm'_0 \dagger m_1y'_0 \;\mathbb{P}\; xy'_0$
94.	$\delta\lambda$	$mx_0 \dagger my_0$
95.	$\delta\lambda$	$x_1m'_0 \dagger y_1m'_0$
96.	I	$mx_0 \dagger m'y_0 \;\mathbb{P}\; xy_0$
97.	I	$mx_0 \dagger m'y_0 \;\mathbb{P}\; xy_0$

[Ex. 150–153; Ans. 182–183.]

98. III $m_1x'_0 \dagger ym_0 \, \mathbb{P} \, xy'_1$

99. I $mx_0 \dagger m'_1y_0 \, \mathbb{P} \, xy_0$

100. I $m_1x_0 \dagger m'_1y_0 \, \mathbb{P} \, xy_0$

101. I$(\alpha)^2$ $m'x_0 \dagger y_1m_0 \, \mathbb{P} \, y_1x_0$

Solutions for §6

1. $xm_1 \dagger my'_0 \, \mathbb{P} \, xy_1$ [Fig. II] Concl. right.

2. $x_1m'_0 \dagger ym'_0$ Fallacy of Like Eliminands not asserted to exist.

3. $xm'_1 \dagger y'_1m'_0 \, \mathbb{P} \, xy_1$ [Fig. II] Concl. right.

4. $x_1m'_0 \dagger ym_0 \, \mathbb{P} \, x_1y_0$ [Fig. I (α)] Concl. right.

5. $m'x'_1 \dagger m'y_0 \, \mathbb{P} \, x'y'_1$ [Fig. II] Concl. right.

6. $x'm_0 \dagger y_1m_0$ Fallacy of Like Eliminands not asserted to exist.

7. $m'x'_1 \dagger y'_1m_0$ Fallacy of Unlike Eliminands with an Entity-Premiss.

8. $m'x'_0 \dagger y'_1m_0 \, \mathbb{P} \, y'_1x'_0$ [Fig. I (α)] Concl. right.

9. $mx'_1 \dagger my_0 \, \mathbb{P} \, x'y'_1$ [Fig. II] Concl. right.

10. $m'_1x_0 \dagger m'_1y'_0 \, \mathbb{P} \, x'y_1$ [Fig. III] Concl. right.

11. $x_1m_0 \dagger ym_1 \, \mathbb{P} \, x'y_1$ [Fig. II] Concl. right.

12. $xm_0 \dagger m'y'_0 \, \mathbb{P} \, xy'_0$ [Fig. I] Concl. right.

13. $xm_0 \dagger y'_1m'_0 \, \mathbb{P} \, y'_1x_0$ [Fig. I (α)] Concl. right.

14. $m'_1x_0 \dagger m'_1y'_0 \, \mathbb{P} \, x'y_1$ [Fig. III] Concl. right.

15. $mx'_1 \dagger y_1m_0 \, \mathbb{P} \, x'y'_1$ [Fig. II] Concl. right.

16. $x'm_0 \dagger y'_1m_0$ Fallacy of Like Eliminands not asserted to exist.

17. $m'x_0 \dagger m'_1y_0 \, \mathbb{P} \, x'y'_1$ [Fig. III] Concl. right.

18. $x'm_0 \dagger my_1 \, \mathbb{P} \, xy_1$ [Fig. II] Concl. right.

19. $mx'_1 \dagger m_1y'_0 \, \mathbb{P} \, x'y_1$ [Fig. II] Concl. right.

20. $x'm'_0 \dagger m'y'_1 \, \mathbb{P} \, xy'_1$ [Fig. II] Concl. right.

21. $mx_0 \dagger m_1y_0 \, \mathbb{P} \, x'y'_1$ [Fig. III] Concl. right.

22. $x'_1m'_0 \dagger ym'_1 \, \mathbb{P} \, xy_1$ [Fig. II] Concl. wrong: the right one is "Some x are y."

[Ex. 153, 154; Ans. 183.]

---

[2] KEY. Carroll employs the following key, written out in his hand in the Huntington Library copy of *Symbolic Logic*:

α = Concl. right
β = incomplete

γ = Concl. wrong
δ = No Concl.
λ = Fallacy of Like ...
ε = Fallacy of Unlike & with Entity-Prem.

23. $m_1 x'_0 \dagger m'y'_0 \; \P \; x'y'_0$ [Fig. I]   Concl. right.

24. $x_1 m_0 \dagger m'_1 y'_0 \; \P \; x_1 y'_0$ [Fig. I (α)]   Concl. right.

25. $xm'_0 \dagger m_1 y'_0 \; \P \; xy'_0$ [Fig. I]   Concl. right.

26. $m_1 x_0 \dagger y_1 m'_0 \; \P \; y_1 x_0$ [Fig. I (α)]   Concl. right.

27. $x_1 m'_0 \dagger my'_0 \; \P \; x_1 y'_0$ [Fig. I (α)]   Concl. right.

28. $x_1 m'_0 \dagger y'm'_0$ Fallacy of Like Eliminands not asserted to exist.

29. $x'm_0 \dagger m'y'_0 \; \P \; x'y'_0$ [Fig. I]   Concl. right.

30. $x_1 m'_0 \dagger m_1 y_0 \; \P \; x_1 y_0$ [Fig. I (α)]   Concl. right.

31. $x'_1 m_0 \dagger y'm'_0 \; \P \; x'_1 y'_0$ [Fig. I (α)]   Concl. right.

32. $xm_0 \dagger y'm'_0 \; \P \; xy'_0$ [Fig. I]   Concl. right.

33. $m_1 x_0 \dagger y'_1 m'_0 \; \P \; y'_1 x_0$ [Fig. I (α)]   Concl. right.

34. $x_1 m_0 \dagger ym'_1$ Fallacy of Unlike Eliminands with an Entity-Premiss.

35. $xm_1 \dagger m_1 y'_0 \; \P \; xy_1$ [Fig. II]   Concl. right.

36. $m_1 x_0 \dagger y_1 m'_0 \; \P \; y_1 x_0$ [Fig. I (α)]   Concl. right.

37. $mx'_0 \dagger m_1 y_0 \; \P \; xy'_1$ [Fig. III]   Concl. right.

38. $xm_0 \dagger my'_0$ Fallacy of Like Eliminands not asserted to exist.

39. $mx_0 \dagger my'_1 \; \P \; x'y'_1$ [Fig. II]   Concl. right.

40. $mx'_0 \dagger ym_1 \; \P \; xy_1$ [Fig. II]   Concl. right.

Solutions for §7

1. No doctors are enthusiastic;
   You are enthusiastic.

   You are not a doctor.

Univ. "persons"; m = enthusiastic; x = doctors; y = you.

$$xm_0 \dagger y_1 m'_0 \; \P \; y_1 x_0 \quad \text{[Fig. I (α)}$$

Conclusion right.

2. Dictionaries are useful;
   Useful books are valuable.

   Dictionaries are valuable.

Univ. "books"; m = useful; x = dictionaries; y = valuable.

$$x_1 m'_0 \dagger m_1 y'_0 \; \P \; x_1 y'_0 \quad \text{[Fig. I (α)}$$

Conclusion right.

[Ex. 154, 155; Ans. 183.]

3. No misers are unselfish;
   None but misers save egg-shells.
   No unselfish people save egg-shells.

Univ. "people"; m = misers; x = selfish; y = people who save egg-shells.

$$mx'_0 \dagger m'y_0 \,\P\, x'y_0 \text{ [Fig. I}$$

Conclusion right.

4. Some epicures are ungenerous;
   All my uncles are generous.
   My uncles are not epicures.

Univ. "persons"; m = generous; x = epicures; y = my uncles.

$$xm'_1 \dagger y_1m'_0 \,\P\, xy'_1 \text{ [Fig. II}$$

Conclusion wrong: right one is "Some epicures are not uncles of mine."

5. Gold is heavy;
   Nothing but gold will silence him.
   Nothing light will silence him.

Univ. "things"; m = gold; x = heavy; y = able to silence him.

$$m_1x'_0 \dagger m'y_0 \,\P\, x'y_0 \text{ [Fig. I}$$

Conclusion right.

6. Some healthy people are fat;
   No unhealthy people are strong.
   Some fat people are not strong.

Univ. "people"; m = healthy; x = fat; y = strong.

$$mx_1 \dagger m'y_0$$

No Conclusion.   [Fallacy of Unlike Eliminands with an Entity-Premiss.]

7. I saw it in a newspaper;
   All newspapers tell lies.
   It was a lie.

Univ. "publications"; m = newspapers; x = publications in which I saw it; y = telling lies.

$$x_1m'_0 \dagger m_1y'_0 \,\P\, x_1y'_0 \text{ [Fig. I } (\alpha)$$

Conclusion wrong: right one is "The publication, in which I saw it, tells lies."

[Ex. 155; Ans. 183–184.]

8. Some cravats are not artistic;
   I admire anything artistic.
   There are some cravats that I do not admire.

Univ. "things"; m = artistic; x = cravats; y = things that I admire.

$$xm'_1 \dagger m_1y'_0$$

No Conclusion.   [Fallacy of Unlike Eliminands with an Entity-Premiss.]

9. His songs never last an hour;
   A song, that lasts an hour, is tedious.
   His songs are never tedious.

Univ. "songs"; m = lasting an hour; x = his; y = tedious.

$$x_1m_0 \dagger m_1y'_0 \mathbb{P} x'y_1 \text{ [Fig. III}$$

Conclusion wrong: right one is "Some tedious songs are not his."

10. Some candles give very little light;
    Candles are *meant* to give light.
    Some things, that are meant to give light, give very little.

Univ. "things"; m = candles; x = giving &c.; y = meant &c.

$$mx_1 \dagger m_1y'_0 \mathbb{P} xy_1 \text{ [Fig. II}$$

Conclusion right.

11. All, who are anxious to learn, work hard;
    Some of these boys work hard.
    Some of these boys are anxious to learn.

Univ. "persons"; m = hard-working; x = anxious to learn; y = these boys.

$$x_1m'_0 \dagger ym_1$$

No Conclusion.   [Fallacy of Unlike Eliminands with an Entity-Premiss.]

12. All lions are fierce;
    Some lions do not drink coffee.
    Some creatures that drink coffee are not fierce.

Univ. "creatures"; m = lions; x = fierce; y = creatures that drink coffee.

$$m_1x'_0 \dagger my'_1 \mathbb{P} xy'_1 \text{ [Fig. II}$$

Conclusion wrong: right one is "Some fierce creatures do not drink coffee."

[Ex. 155; Ans. 184.]

13. No misers are generous;
   Some old men are ungenerous.
   Some old men are misers.

Univ. "persons"; m = generous; x = misers; y = old men.

$$xm_0 \dagger ym'_1$$

No Conclusion.   [Fallacy of Unlike Eliminands with an Entity-Premiss.]

14. No fossil can be crossed in love;
   An oyster may be crossed in love.
   Oysters are not fossils.

Univ. "things"; m = things that can be crossed in love; x = fossils; y = oysters.

$$xm_0 \dagger y_1m'_0 \; \P \; y_1x_0 \; [\text{Fig. I } (\alpha)$$

Conclusion right.

15. All uneducated people are shallow;
   Students are all educated.
   No students are shallow.

Univ. "people"; m = educated; x = shallow; y = students.

$$m'_1x'_0 \dagger y_1m'_0 \; \P \; xy'_1 \; [\text{Fig. III}$$

Conclusion wrong: right one is "Some shallow people are not students."

16. All young lambs jump;
   No young animals are healthy, unless they jump.
   All young lambs are healthy.

Univ. "young animals"; m = young animals that jump; x = lambs; y = healthy.

$$x_1m'_0 \dagger m'y_0$$

No Conclusion.   [Fallacy of Like Eliminands not asserted to exist.]

17. Ill-managed business is unprofitable;
   Railways are never ill-managed.
   All railways are profitable.

Univ. "business"; m = ill-managed; x = profitable; y = railways.

$$m_1x_0 \dagger y_1m_0 \; \P \; x'y'_0 \; [\text{Fig. III}$$

Conclusion wrong: right one is "Some business, other than railways, is unprofitable."

[Ex. 156; Ans. 184.]

18. No Professors are ignorant;
    All ignorant people are vain.
    No Professors are vain.

Univ. "people"; m = ignorant; x = Professors; y = vain.

$$xm_0 \dagger m_1 y'_0 \; ⫣ \; x'y_1 \; [\text{Fig. III}$$

Conclusion wrong: right one is "Some vain persons are not Professors."

19. A prudent man shuns hyænas;
    No banker is imprudent.
    No banker fails to shun hyænas.

Univ. "men"; m = prudent; x = shunning hyænas; y = bankers.

$$m_1 x'_0 \dagger ym'_0 \; ⫣ \; x'y_0 \; [\text{Fig. I}$$

Conclusion right.

20. All wasps are unfriendly;
    No puppies are unfriendly.
    No puppies are wasps.

Univ. "creatures"; m = friendly; x = wasps; y = puppies.

$$x_1 m_0 \dagger ym'_0 \; ⫣ \; x_1 y_0 \; [\text{Fig. I } (\alpha)$$

Conclusion incomplete: complete one is "Wasps are not puppies."

21. No Jews are honest;
    Some Gentiles are rich.
    Some rich people are dishonest.

Univ. "persons"; m = Jews; x = honest; y = rich.

$$mx_0 \dagger m'y_1$$

No Conclusion.   [Fallacy of Unlike Eliminands with an Entity-Premiss.]

22. No idlers win fame;
    Some painters are not idle.
    Some painters win fame.

Univ. "persons"; m = idlers; x = persons who win fame; y = painters.

$$mx_0 \dagger ym'_1$$

No Conclusion.   [Fallacy of Unlike Eliminands with an Entity-Premiss.]

[Ex. 156; Ans. 184.]

23. No monkeys are soldiers;
   All monkeys are mischievous.
   Some mischievous creatures are not soldiers.

Univ. "creatures"; m = monkeys; x = soldiers; y = mischievous.

$$mx_0 \dagger m_1 y'_0 \parallel x'y_1 \text{ [Fig. III}$$

Conclusion right.

24. All these bonbons are chocolate-creams;
   All these bonbons are delicious.
   Chocolate-creams are delicious.

Univ. "food"; m = these bonbons; x = chocolate-creams; y = delicious.

$$m_1 x'_0 \dagger m_1 y'_0 \parallel xy_1 \text{ [Fig. III}$$

Conclusion wrong, being in excess of the right one, which is "*Some* chocolate-creams are delicious."

25. No muffins are wholesome;
   All buns are unwholesome.
   Buns are not muffins.

Univ. "food"; m = wholesome; x = muffins; y = buns.

$$xm_0 \dagger y_1 m_0$$

No Conclusion.   [Fallacy of Like Eliminands not asserted to exist.]

26. Some unauthorised reports are false;
   All authorised reports are trustworthy.
   Some false reports are not trustworthy.

Univ. "reports"; m = authorised; x = true; y = trustworthy.

$$m'x'_1 \dagger m_1 y'_0$$

No Conclusion.   [Fallacy of Unlike Eliminands with an Entity-Premiss.]

27. Some pillows are soft;
   No pokers are soft.
   Some pokers are not pillows.

Univ. "things"; m = soft; x = pillows; y = pokers.

$$xm_1 \dagger ym_0 \parallel xy'_1 \text{ [Fig. II}$$

Conclusion wrong: right one is "Some pillows are not pokers."

[Ex. 156–157; Ans. 184.]

28. Improbable stories are not easily believed;
     None of his stories are probable.
     None of his stories are easily believed.

Univ. "stories"; m = probable; x = easily believed; y = his.

$$m'_1 x_0 \dagger y m_0 \ \mathbb{P} \ xy_0 \ \text{[Fig. I}$$

Conclusion right.

29. No thieves are honest;
     Some dishonest people are found out.
     Some thieves are found out.

Univ. "people"; m = honest; x = thieves; y = found out.

$$x m_0 \dagger m' y_1$$

No Conclusion.   [Fallacy of Unlike Eliminands with an Entity-Premiss.]

30. No muffins are wholesome;
     All puffy food is unwholesome.
     All muffins are puffy.

Univ. is "food"; m = wholesome; x = muffins; y = puffy.

$$x m_0 \dagger y_1 m_0$$

No Conclusion.   [Fallacy of Like Eliminands not asserted to exist.]

31. No birds, except peacocks, are proud of their tails;
     Some birds, that are proud of their tails, cannot sing.
     Some peacocks cannot sing.

Univ. "birds"; m = proud of their tails; x = peacocks; y = birds that can sing.

$$x' m_0 \dagger m y'_1 \ \mathbb{P} \ xy'_1 \ \text{[Fig. II}$$

Conclusion right.

32. Warmth relieves pain;
     Nothing, that does not relieve pain, is useful in toothache.
     Warmth is useful in toothache.

Univ. "applications"; m = relieving pain; x = warmth; y = useful in toothache.

$$x_1 m'_0 \dagger m' y_0$$

No Conclusion.   [Fallacy of Like Eliminands not asserted to exist.]

[Ex. 157; Ans. 184.]

33. No bankrupts are rich;
     Some merchants are not bankrupts.
     Some merchants are rich.

Univ. "persons"; m = bankrupts; x = rich; y = merchants.

$$mx_0 \dagger ym'_1$$

No Conclusion.   [Fallacy of Unlike Eliminands with an Entity-Premiss.]

34. Bores are dreaded;
     No bore is ever begged to prolong his visit.
     No one, who is dreaded, is ever begged to prolong his visit.

Univ. "persons"; m = bores; x = dreaded; y = begged to prolong their visits.

$$m_1x'_0 \dagger my_0 \parallel xy'_1 \text{ [Fig. III}$$

Conclusion wrong: the right one is "Some dreaded persons are not begged to prolong their visits."

35. All wise men walk on their feet;
     All unwise men walk on their hands.
     No man walks on both.

Univ. "men"; m = wise; x = walking on their feet; y = walking on their hands.

$$m_1x'_0 \dagger m'_1y'_0 \parallel x'y'_0 \text{ [Fig. I}$$

Conclusion wrong: right one is "No man walks on neither."

36. No wheelbarrows are comfortable;
     No uncomfortable vehicles are popular.
     No wheelbarrows are popular.

Univ. "vehicles"; m = comfortable; x = wheelbarrows; y = popular.

$$xm_0 \dagger m'x_0 \parallel xy_0 \text{ [Fig. I}$$

Conclusion right.

37. No frogs are poetical;
     Some ducks are unpoetical.
     Some ducks are not frogs.

Univ. "creatures"; m = poetical; x = frogs; y = ducks.

$$xm_0 \dagger ym'_1$$

No Conclusion.   [Fallacy of Unlike Eliminands with an Entity-Premiss.]

[Ex. 157–158; Ans. 184.]

38. No emperors are dentists;
   All dentists are dreaded by children.

   No emperors are dreaded by children.

Univ. "persons"; m = dentists; x = emperors; y = dreaded by children.

$$xm_0 \dagger m_1 y'_0 \, ⫴ \, x'y_1 \text{ [Fig. III}$$

Conclusion wrong: right one is "Some persons, dreaded by children, are not emperors."

39. Sugar is sweet;
   Salt is not sweet.

   Salt is not sugar.

Univ. "things"; m = sweet; x = sugar; y = salt.

$$x_1 m'_0 \dagger y_1 m_0 \, ⫴ \, (x_1 y_0 \dagger y_1 x_0) \text{ [Fig. I } (\beta)$$

Conclusion incomplete: omitted portion is "Sugar is not salt."

40. Every eagle can fly;
   Some pigs cannot fly.

   Some pigs are not eagles.

Univ. "creatures"; m = creatures that can fly; x = eagles; y = pigs.

$$x_1 m'_0 \dagger ym'_1 \, ⫴ \, x'y_1 \text{ [Fig. II}$$

Conclusion right.

Solutions for §8

	1	2	3		1	2	3	

1. $cd_0 \dagger a_1 d'_0 \dagger b_1 c'_0$; $\underline{cd} \dagger a\underline{d}' \dagger b\underline{c}' \, ⫴ \, ab_0 \dagger a_1 \dagger b_1$ i.e. $⫴ \, a_1 b_0 \dagger b_1 a_0$

2. $d_1 b'_0 \dagger ac'_0 \dagger bc_0$; $d\underline{b}' \dagger \underline{bc} \dagger a\underline{c}' \, ⫴ \, da_0 \dagger d_1$ i.e. $⫴ \, d_1 a_0$

3. $ba_0 \dagger cd'_0 \dagger d_1 b'_0$; $\underline{ba} \dagger d\underline{b}' \dagger c\underline{d}' \, ⫴ \, ac_0$

4. $bc_0 \dagger a_1 b'_0 \dagger c'd_0$; $\underline{bc} \dagger a\underline{b}' \dagger \underline{c}'d \, ⫴ \, ad_0 \dagger a_1$ i.e. $⫴ \, a_1 d_0$

5. $b'_1 a_0 \dagger bc_0 \dagger a'd_0$; $\underline{b'a} \dagger \underline{bc} \dagger \underline{a}'d \, ⫴ \, cd_0$

[Ex. 158–159; Ans. 184, 185.]

$$\begin{array}{ccc} 1 & 2 & 3 \end{array} \qquad \begin{array}{ccc} 1 & 2 & 3 \end{array}$$
6. $a_1b_0 † b'c_0 † d_1a'_0$; $\underline{ab} † \underline{b}'c † d\underline{a}'$ ℙ $cd_0 † d_1$ i.e. ℙ d_1c_0

$$\begin{array}{ccc} 1 & 2 & 3 \end{array} \qquad \begin{array}{ccc} 1 & 2 & 3 \end{array}$$
7. $db'_0 † b_1a'_0 † cd'_0$; $\underline{db}' † \underline{b}a' † c\underline{d}'$ ℙ $a'c_0$

$$\begin{array}{ccc} 1 & 2 & 3 \end{array} \qquad \begin{array}{ccc} 1 & 2 & 3 \end{array}$$
8. $b'd_0 † a'b_0 † c_1d'_0$ $\underline{b}'\underline{d} † a'\underline{b} † c\underline{d}'$ ℙ $a'c_0 † c_1$ i.e. ℙ $c_1a'_0$

$$\begin{array}{ccc} 1 & 2 & 3 \end{array} \qquad \begin{array}{ccc} 1 & 2 & 3 \end{array}$$
9. $b'_1a'_0 † ad_0 † b_1c'_0$; $\underline{b}'\underline{a}' † \underline{a}d † \underline{b}c'$ ℙ dc'_0

$$\begin{array}{ccc} 1 & 2 & 3 \end{array} \qquad \begin{array}{ccc} 1 & 2 & 3 \end{array}$$
10. $cd_0 \quad b_1c'_0 † ad'_0$; $\underline{cd} † \underline{bc}' † \underline{a}\underline{d}'$ ℙ $ba_0 † b_1$ i.e. ℙ b_1a_0

$$\begin{array}{ccc} 1 & 2 & 3 \end{array} \qquad \begin{array}{ccc} 1 & 3 & 2 \end{array}$$
11. $bc_0 † d_1a'_0 † c'_1a_0$; $\underline{bc} † \underline{c}'\underline{a} † d\underline{a}'$ ℙ $bd_0 † d_1$ i.e. ℙ d_1b_0

$$\begin{array}{ccc} 1 & 2 & 3 \end{array} \qquad \begin{array}{ccc} 1 & 2 & 3 \end{array}$$
12. $cb'_0 † c'_1d_0 † b_1a'_0$; $\underline{cb}' † \underline{c}'d † \underline{b}a'$ ℙ da'_0

$$\begin{array}{cccc} 1 & 2 & 3 & 4 \end{array} \qquad \begin{array}{cccc} 1 & 3 & 4 & 2 \end{array}$$
13. $d_1e'_0 † c_1a'_0 † bd'_0 † e_1a_0$; $\underline{de}' † \underline{bd}' † \underline{ea} † \underline{ca}'$ ℙ $bc_0 † c_1$ i.e. ℙ c_1b_0

$$\begin{array}{cccc} 1 & 2 & 3 & 4 \end{array} \qquad \begin{array}{cccc} 1 & 3 & 4 & 2 \end{array}$$
14. $c_1b'_0 † a_1c'_0 † d_1b_0 † a'_1c'_0$; $\underline{cb}' † \underline{db} † \underline{a}'\underline{c}' † \underline{ae}'$ ℙ $de'_0 † d_1$ i.e. ℙ $d_1e'_0$

$$\begin{array}{cccc} 1 & 2 & 3 & 4 \end{array} \qquad \begin{array}{cccc} 1 & 3 & 4 & 2 \end{array}$$
15. $b'd_0 † e_1c'_0 † b_1a'_0 † d'_1c_0$; $\underline{b}'\underline{d} † \underline{b}a' † \underline{d}'\underline{c} † e\underline{c}'$ ℙ $a'e_0 † e_1$ i.e. ℙ $e_1a'_0$

$$\begin{array}{cccc} 1 & 2 & 3 & 4 \end{array} \qquad \begin{array}{cccc} 1 & 3 & 4 & 2 \end{array}$$
16. $a'c_0 † d_1c_0 † a_1b'_0 † e'_1d'_0$; $\underline{a}'\underline{e} † \underline{a}b' † \underline{e}'\underline{d}' † \underline{dc}$ ℙ $b'c_0$

$$\begin{array}{cccc} 1 & 2 & 3 & 4 \end{array} \qquad \begin{array}{cccc} 1 & 3 & 4 & 2 \end{array}$$
17. $d_1c'_0 † a_1e'_0 † bd'_0 † c_1e_0$; $\underline{dc}' † \underline{bd}' † \underline{ce} † \underline{ae}'$ ℙ $ba_0 † a_1$ i.e. ℙ a_1b_0

$$\begin{array}{cccc} 1 & 2 & 3 & 4 \end{array} \qquad \begin{array}{cccc} 1 & 3 & 4 & 2 \end{array}$$
18. $a_1b'_0 † d_1e'_0 † a'_1c_0 † bc$; $\underline{ab}' † \underline{a}'c † \underline{be} † d\underline{e}'$ ℙ $cd_0 † d_1$ i.e. ℙ d_1c_0

$$\begin{array}{ccccc} 1 & 2 & 3 & 4 & 5 \end{array} \qquad \begin{array}{ccccc} 1 & 3 & 5 & 2 & 4 \end{array}$$
19. $bc_0 † c_1h'_0 † a_1b'_0 † dh_0 † e'_1c'_0$ $\underline{bc} † a\underline{b}' † \underline{e}'\underline{c}' † \underline{eh}' † d\underline{h}$ ℙ $ad_0 † a_1$
  i.e. ℙ a_1d_0

$$\begin{array}{ccccc} 1 & 2 & 3 & 4 & 5 \end{array} \qquad \begin{array}{ccccc} 1 & 3 & 4 & 5 & 2 \end{array}$$
20. $dh'_0 † ce_0 † h_1b'_0 † ad'_0 † be'_0$; $\underline{dh}' † \underline{hb}' † \underline{ad}' † \underline{be}' † c\underline{e}$ ℙ ac_0

[Ex. 159; Ans. 185.]

$$\begin{array}{ccccc} 1 & 2 & 3 & 4 & 5 \end{array}$$
21. $b_1a'_0$ † dh_0 † ce_0 † ah'_0 † $c'_1b'_0$;

$$\begin{array}{ccccc} 1 & 4 & 2 & 5 & 3 \end{array}$$
$\underline{ba}'$ † $\underline{ah}'$ † $\underline{dh}$ † $\underline{c'b}'$ † $\underline{ce}$ ⫟ de_0

$$\begin{array}{ccccc} 1 & 2 & 3 & 4 & 5 \end{array}$$
22. e_1d_0 † $b'h'_0$ † $c'_1d'_0$ † $a_1e'_0$ † ch;

$$\begin{array}{ccccc} 1 & 3 & 4 & 5 & 2 \end{array}$$
$\underline{ed}$ † $\underline{cd}'$ † $\underline{ae}'$ † $\underline{ch}$ † $b'\underline{h}'$ ⫟ ab'_0 † a_1

i.e. ⫟ $a_1b'_0$

$$\begin{array}{ccccc} 1 & 2 & 3 & 4 & 5 \end{array}$$
23. b'_1a_0 † de'_0 † h_1b_0 † ce_0 † $d'_1a'_0$;

$$\begin{array}{ccccc} 1 & 3 & 5 & 2 & 4 \end{array}$$
$\underline{b'a}$ † $h\underline{b}$ † $\underline{d'a}'$ † $\underline{de}'$ † $\underline{ce}$ ⫟ hc_0 † h_1

i.e. ⫟ h_1c

$$\begin{array}{cccccc} 1 & 2 & 3 & 4 & 5 & 6 \end{array}$$
24. h'_1k_0 † $b'a_0$ † $c_1d'_0$ † e_1h_0 † dk'_0 † bc'_0;

$$\begin{array}{cccccc} 1 & 4 & 5 & 3 & 6 & 2 \end{array}$$
$\underline{h'k}$ † $e\underline{h}$ † $\underline{dk}'$ † $\underline{cd}'$ † $\underline{bc}'$ † $\underline{b}'a$ ⫟ ea_0 † e_1 i.e. ⫟ e_1a_0

$$\begin{array}{cccccc} 1 & 2 & 3 & 4 & 5 & 6 \end{array}$$
25. $a_1d'_0$ † $k_1b'_0$ † $e_1h'_0$ † $a'b_0$ † $d_1c'_0$ † $h_1k'_0$;

$$\begin{array}{cccccc} 1 & 4 & 2 & 5 & 6 & 3 \end{array}$$
$\underline{ad}'$ † $\underline{a'b}$ † $\underline{kb}'$ † $\underline{dc}'$ † $\underline{hk}'$ † $e\underline{h}'$ ⫟ $c'e_0$ † e_1 i.e. ⫟ $e_1c'_0$

$$\begin{array}{cccccc} 1 & 2 & 3 & 4 & 5 & 6 \end{array}$$
26. $a'_1h'_0$ † $d'k'_0$ † e_1b_0 † hk_0 † a_1c_0 † $b'd_0$;

$$\begin{array}{cccccc} 1 & 4 & 2 & 5 & 6 & 3 \end{array}$$
$\underline{a'h}'$ † $\underline{hk}$ † $\underline{d'k}'$ † $\underline{ac}'$ † $\underline{b'd}$ † $e\underline{b}$ ⫟ $c'e_0$ † e_1 i.e. ⫟ e_1c_0

$$\begin{array}{cccccc} 1 & 2 & 3 & 4 & 5 & 6 \end{array}$$
27. e_1d_0 † hb_0 † $a'_1k'_0$ † ce'_0 † $b'_1d'_0$ † ac'_0;

$$\begin{array}{cccccc} 1 & 4 & 5 & 2 & 6 & 3 \end{array}$$
$\underline{ed}$ † $\underline{ce}'$ † $\underline{b'd}'$ † $h\underline{b}$ † $\underline{ac}'$ † $\underline{a'k}'$ ⫟ hk'_0

$$\begin{array}{cccccc} 1 & 2 & 3 & 4 & 5 & 6 \end{array}$$
28. $a'k_0$ † $e_1b'_0$ † hk'_0 † $d'c_0$ † ab_0 † $c'_1h'_0$;

$$\begin{array}{cccccc} 1 & 3 & 5 & 2 & 6 & 4 \end{array}$$
$\underline{a'k}$ † $\underline{hk}'$ † $\underline{ab}$ † $e\underline{b}'$ † $\underline{c'h}'$ † $d'\underline{c}$ ⫟ ed'_0 † e_1 i.e. ⫟ $e_1d'_0$

$$\begin{array}{cccccccc} 1 & 2 & 3 & 4 & 5 & 6 & 7 & 8 \end{array}$$
29. ek_0 † $b'm_0$ † ac'_0 † $h'_1e'_0$ † $d_1k'_0$ † cb_0 † $d'_1l'_0$ † hm'_0;

$$\begin{array}{cccccccc} 1 & 4 & 5 & 7 & 8 & 2 & 6 & 3 \end{array}$$
$\underline{ek}$ † $h'\underline{e}'$ † $\underline{dk}'$ † $\underline{d'l}'$ † $\underline{hm}'$ † $b'\underline{m}$ † $c\underline{b}$ † $a\underline{c}'$ ⫟ $l'a_0$

[Ex. 159–160; Ans. 185.]

$$\begin{array}{cccccccccc} 1 & 2 & 3 & 4 & 5 & 6 & 7 & 8 & 9 & 10 \end{array}$$

30. $n_1m'_0 \dagger a'_1e'_0 \dagger c'l_0 \dagger k_1r_0 \dagger ah'_0 \dagger dl'_0 \dagger cn'_0 \dagger e_1b'_0 \dagger m_1r'_0 \dagger h_1d'_0;$

$$\begin{array}{cccccccccc} 1 & 7 & 3 & 6 & 9 & 4 & 10 & 5 & 2 & 8 \end{array}$$

$\underline{nm}' \dagger \underline{cn}' \dagger \underline{c'l} \dagger \underline{dl}' \dagger \underline{mr}' \dagger \underline{kr} \dagger \underline{hd}' \dagger \underline{ah}' \dagger \underline{a'e}' \dagger \underline{eb}' \ \mathbb{P} \ kb'_0 \dagger k_1$ i.e. $\mathbb{P}k_1b'_0$

Solutions for §9

$$\begin{array}{ccccccc} 1 & 2 & 3 & & 1 & 3 & 2 \end{array}$$

1. $b_1d_0 \dagger ac_0 \dagger d'_1c'_0; \qquad \underline{bd} \dagger \underline{d'c}' \dagger \underline{ac} \ \mathbb{P} \ ba_0 \dagger b_1,$ i.e. $\mathbb{P} \ b_1a_0$

i.e. Babies cannot manage crocodiles.

$$\begin{array}{ccccccc} 1 & 2 & 3 & & 1 & 3 & 2 \end{array}$$

2. $a_1b'_0 \dagger d_1c'_0 \dagger bc_0; \qquad \underline{ab}' \dagger \underline{bc} \dagger \underline{dc}' \ \mathbb{P} \ ad_0 \dagger d_1,$ i.e. $\mathbb{P} \ d_1a_0$ & $ad_0 \dagger a_1,$

i.e. $\mathbb{P} \ a_1d_0$

i.e. *Your* presents to me are not made of tin.

$$\begin{array}{ccccccc} 1 & 2 & 3 & & 1 & 3 & 2 \end{array}$$

3. $da_0 \dagger c_1b'_0 \dagger a'b_0; \qquad \underline{da} \dagger \underline{a'b} \dagger \underline{cb}' \ \mathbb{P} \ dc_0 \dagger c_1,$ i.e. $\mathbb{P} \ c_1d_0$

i.e. All my potatoes in this dish are old ones.

$$\begin{array}{ccccccc} 1 & 2 & 3 & & 1 & 2 & 3 \end{array}$$

4. $ba_0 \dagger b'd_0 \dagger c_1a'_0; \qquad \underline{ba} \dagger \underline{b'd} \dagger \underline{ca}' \ \mathbb{P} \ dc_0 \dagger c_1,$ i.e. $\mathbb{P} \ c_1d_0$

i.e. My servants never say "shpoonj."

$$\begin{array}{ccccccc} 1 & 2 & 3 & & 1 & 2 & 3 \end{array}$$

5. $ad_0 \dagger cd'_0 \dagger b_1a'_0; \qquad \underline{ad} \dagger \underline{cd}' \dagger \underline{ba}' \ \mathbb{P} \ cb_0 \dagger b_1,$ i.e. $\mathbb{P} \ b_1c_0$

i.e. My poultry are not officers.

$$\begin{array}{ccccccc} 1 & 2 & 3 & & 1 & 2 & 3 \end{array}$$

6. $c_1a'_0 \dagger c'b_0 \dagger da_0; \qquad \underline{ca}' \dagger \underline{c'b} \dagger \underline{da} \ \mathbb{P} \ bd_0$

i.e. None of *your* sons are fit to serve on a jury.

$$\begin{array}{ccccccc} 1 & 2 & 3 & & 1 & 3 & 2 \end{array}$$

7. $cb_0 \dagger da_0 \dagger b'_1a'_0; \qquad \underline{cb} \dagger \underline{b'a}' \dagger \underline{da} \ \mathbb{P} \ cd_0$

i.e. No pencils of mine are sugarplums.

$$\begin{array}{ccccccc} 1 & 2 & 3 & & 1 & 3 & 2 \end{array}$$

8. $cb'_0 \dagger d_1a'_0 \dagger ba_0; \qquad \underline{cb}' \dagger \underline{ba} \dagger \underline{da}' \ \mathbb{P} \ cd_0 \dagger d_1,$ i.e. $\mathbb{P} \ d_1c_0$

i.e. Jenkins is inexperienced.

[Ex. 160–162; Ans. 185.]

     1   2   3   1   2   3

9. cd_0 † $d'a_0$ † $c'b_0$; $\underline{cd}$ † $\underline{d}'a$ † $\underline{c}'b$ ⊩ ab_0

i.e. No comet has a curly tail.

     1   2   3   1   3   2

10. $d'c_0$ † ba_0 † a'_1d_0; $\underline{d}'c$ † $\underline{a}'\underline{d}$ † $\underline{ba}$ ⊩ cb_0

i.e. No hedgehog takes in the *Times*.

     1   2   3   1   2   3

11. $b_1a'_0$ † $c_1b'_0$ † ad_0; $\underline{ba}'$ † $c\underline{b}'$ † $\underline{ad}$ ⊩ cd_0 † c_1, i.e. ⊩ c_1d_0

i.e. This dish is unwholesome.

     1   2   3   1   3   2

12. $b_1c'_0$ † $d'a_0$ † $a'c_0$; $b\underline{c}'$ † $\underline{a}'\underline{c}$ † $d'\underline{a}$ ⊩ bd'_0 † b_1, i.e. ⊩ $b_1d'_0$

i.e. My gardener is very old.

     1   2   3   1   3   2

13. $a_1d'_0$ † bc_0 † c'_1d_0; $a\underline{d}'$ † $\underline{c}'\underline{d}$ † $b\underline{c}$ ⊩ ab_0 † a_1, i.e. ⊩ a_1b_0

i.e. All humming-birds are small.

     1   2   3   1   3   2

14. $c'b_0$ † $a_1d'_0$ † ca'_0; $\underline{c}'b$ † $\underline{ca}'$ † $\underline{a}d'$ ⊩ bd'_0

i.e. No one with a hooked nose ever fails to make money.

     1   2   3   1   2   3

15. $b_1a'_0$ † b'_1d_0 † ca_0; $\underline{ba}'$ † $\underline{b}'d$ † $c\underline{a}$ ⊩ dc_0

i.e. No gray ducks in this village wear lace collars.

     1   2   3   1   2   3

16. $d_1b'_0$ † cd'_0 † ba_0; $\underline{db}'$ † $c\underline{d}'$ † $\underline{b}a$ ⊩ ca_0

i.e. No jug in this cupboard will hold water.

     1   2   3   1   2   3

17. b'_1d_0 † $c_1d'_0$ † ab_0; $\underline{b}'\underline{d}$ † $c\underline{d}'$ † $a\underline{b}$ ⊩ ca_0 † c_1, i.e. ⊩ c_1a_0

i.e. These apples were grown in the sun.

     1   2   3   1   2   3

18. $d'_1b'_0$ † c_1b_0 † $c'a_0$; $d'\underline{b}'$ † $c\underline{b}$ † $\underline{c}'a$ ⊩ $d'a_0$ † d'_1, i.e. ⊩ d'_1a_0

i.e. Puppies, that will not lie still, never care to do worsted-work.

     1   2   3   1   3   2

19. bd'_0 † $a_1c'_0$ † $a'd_0$; $b\underline{d}'$ † $\underline{a}'\underline{d}$ † $\underline{a}c'$ ⊩ bc'_0

i.e. No name in this list is unmelodious.

[Ex. 162–164; Ans. 185.]

    1   2   3   1   3   2

20. $a_1b'_0 \dagger dc_0 \dagger a'_1d'_0;$ $\underline{ab}' \dagger \underline{a}'\underline{d}' \dagger \underline{dc}\ \P\ b'c_0$

    i.e. No M.P. should ride in a donkey-race, unless he has perfect self-command.

    1   2   3   1   3   2

21. $bd_0 \dagger c'a_0 \dagger b'c_0;$ $\underline{bd} \dagger \underline{b}'\underline{c} \dagger \underline{c}'a\ \P\ da_0$

    i.e. No goods in this shop, that are still on sale, may be carried away.

    1   2   3   1   3   2

22. $a'b_0 \dagger cd_0 \dagger d'a_0;$ $\underline{a}'b \dagger \underline{d}'\underline{a} \dagger \underline{cd}\ \P\ bc_0$

    i.e. No acrobatic feat, which involves turning a quadruple somersault, is ever attempted in a circus.

    1   2   3   1   3   2

23. $dc'_0 \dagger a_1b'_0 \dagger bc_0;$ $\underline{dc}' \dagger \underline{bc} \dagger \underline{ab}'\ \P\ da_0 \dagger a_1,$ i.e. $\P\ a_1d_0$

    i.e. Guinea-pigs never really appreciate Beethoven.

    1   2   3   1   3   2

24. $a_1d'_0 \dagger b'_1c_0 \dagger ba'_0;$ $\underline{ad}' \dagger \underline{ba}' \dagger \underline{b}'c\ \P\ d'c_0$

    i.e. No scentless flowers please me.

    1   2   3   1   3   2

25. $c_1d'_0 \dagger ba'_0 \dagger d_1a_0;$ $\underline{cd}' \dagger \underline{da} \dagger \underline{ba}'\ \P\ cb_0 \dagger c_1,$ i.e. $\P\ c_1b_0$

    i.e. Showy talkers are not really well-informed.

    1   2   3   4   1   3   4   2

26. $ea_0 \dagger b_1d'_0 \dagger a'_1c_0 \dagger e'b'_0;$ $\underline{ea} \dagger \underline{a}'\underline{c} \dagger \underline{e}'\underline{b}' \dagger \underline{bd}'\ \P\ cd'_0$

    i.e. None but red-haired boys learn Greek in this school.

    1   2   3   4   1   3   4   2

27. $b_1d_0 \dagger ac'_0 \dagger e_1d'_0 \dagger c_1b'_0;$ $\underline{bd} \dagger \underline{ed}' \dagger \underline{cb}' \dagger \underline{ac}'\ \P\ ea_0 \dagger e_1,$ i.e. $\P\ e_1a_0$

    i.e. Wedding-cake always disagrees with me.

    1   2   3   4   1   3   4   2

28. $ad_0 \dagger e'_1b'_0 \dagger c_1d'_0 \dagger e_1a'_0;$ $\underline{ad} \dagger \underline{cd}' \dagger \underline{ea}' \dagger \underline{e}'b\ \P\ cb'_0 \dagger c_1,$ i.e. $\P\ c_1b'_0$

    i.e. Discussions, that go on while Tomkins is in the chair, endanger the peacefulness of our Debating-Club.

    1   2   3   4   1   3   4   2

29. $d_1a_0 \dagger e'c_0 \dagger b_1a'_0 \dagger d'e_0;$ $\underline{da} \dagger \underline{ba}' \dagger \underline{d}'\underline{e} \dagger \underline{e}'c\ \P\ bc_0 \dagger b_1,$ i.e. $\P\ b_1c_0$

    i.e. All the gluttons in my family are unhealthy.

[Ex. 164–166; Ans. 185–186.]

30. $\overset{1}{}\quad\overset{2}{}\quad\overset{3}{}\quad\overset{4}{}\qquad\overset{1}{}\quad\overset{3}{}\quad\overset{4}{}\quad\overset{2}{}$

    $d_1e_0 \dagger c'a_0 \dagger b_1e'_0 \dagger c_1d'_0 \qquad \underline{de} \dagger \underline{be}' \dagger \underline{cd}' \dagger \underline{c}'a \ \P\ ba_0 \dagger b_1$, i.e. $\P\ b_1a_0$

    i.e. An egg of the Great Auk is not to be had for a song.

31. $\overset{1}{}\quad\overset{2}{}\quad\overset{3}{}\quad\overset{4}{}\qquad\overset{1}{}\quad\overset{4}{}\quad\overset{2}{}\quad\overset{3}{}$

    $d'b_0 \dagger a_1c'_0 \dagger c_1e'_0 \dagger a'd_0;\qquad \underline{d}'b \dagger \underline{a}'\underline{d} \dagger \underline{ac}' \dagger \underline{c}e' \ \P\ be'_0$

    i.e. No books sold here have gilt edges unless they are priced at 5s. and upwards.

32. $\overset{1}{}\quad\overset{2}{}\quad\overset{3}{}\quad\overset{4}{}\qquad\overset{1}{}\quad\overset{3}{}\quad\overset{4}{}\quad\overset{2}{}$

    $a'_1c'_0 \dagger d_1b_0 \dagger a_1e'_0 \dagger c_1b'_0;\qquad \underline{a}'\underline{c}' \dagger \underline{a}e' \dagger \underline{c}b' \dagger \underline{db} \ \P\ e'd_0 \dagger d_1$, i.e. $\P\ d_1e'_0$

    i.e. When you cut your finger, you will find Tincture of Calendula useful.

33. $\overset{1}{}\quad\overset{2}{}\quad\overset{3}{}\quad\overset{4}{}\qquad\overset{1}{}\quad\overset{4}{}\quad\overset{2}{}\quad\overset{3}{}$

    $d'b_0 \dagger a_1e'_0 \dagger ec_0 \dagger d_1a'_0;\qquad \underline{d}'b \dagger \underline{da}' \dagger \underline{ae}' \dagger \underline{e}c \ \P\ bc_0$

    i.e. *I* have never come across a mermaid at sea.

34. $\overset{1}{}\quad\overset{2}{}\quad\overset{3}{}\quad\overset{4}{}\qquad\overset{1}{}\quad\overset{3}{}\quad\overset{4}{}\quad\overset{2}{}$

    $c'_1b_0 \dagger a_1c'_0 \dagger d_1b'_0 \dagger a'_1c_0;\qquad \underline{c}'\underline{b} \dagger \underline{db}' \dagger \underline{a}'\underline{c} \dagger \underline{a}e' \ \P\ de'_0 \dagger d_1$, i.e. $\P\ d_1e'_0$

    i.e. All the romances in this library are well-written.

35. $\overset{1}{}\quad\overset{2}{}\quad\overset{3}{}\quad\overset{4}{}\qquad\overset{1}{}\quad\overset{3}{}\quad\overset{4}{}\quad\overset{2}{}$

    $e'd_0 \dagger c'a_0 \dagger eb_0 \dagger d'c_0;\qquad \underline{e}'\underline{d} \dagger \underline{e}b \dagger \underline{d}'\underline{c} \dagger \underline{c}'a \ \P\ ba_0$

    i.e. No bird in this aviary lives on mince-pies.

36. $\overset{1}{}\quad\overset{2}{}\quad\overset{3}{}\quad\overset{4}{}\qquad\overset{1}{}\quad\overset{3}{}\quad\overset{4}{}\quad\overset{2}{}$

    $d'_1c'_0 \dagger e_1a'_0 \dagger c_1b_0 \dagger e'd_0;\qquad \underline{d}'\underline{c}' \dagger \underline{c}b \dagger \underline{e}'\underline{d}' \dagger \underline{e}a' \ \P\ ba'_0$

    i.e. No plum-pudding, that has not been boiled in a cloth, can be distinguished from soup.

37. $\overset{1}{}\quad\overset{2}{}\quad\overset{3}{}\quad\overset{4}{}\quad\overset{5}{}\qquad\overset{1}{}\quad\overset{4}{}\quad\overset{2}{}\quad\overset{5}{}\quad\overset{3}{}$

    $ce'_0 \dagger b'a'_0 \dagger h_1d'_0 \dagger ac_0 \dagger bd_0;\qquad \underline{c}e' \dagger \underline{ac} \dagger \underline{b}'\underline{a}' \dagger \underline{bd} \dagger \underline{hd}' \ \P\ ch_0 \dagger h_1$,

                                         i.e. $\P\ h_1c_0$

    i.e. All *your* poems are uninteresting.

38. $\overset{1}{}\quad\overset{2}{}\quad\overset{3}{}\quad\overset{4}{}\quad\overset{5}{}\qquad\overset{1}{}\quad\overset{2}{}\quad\overset{5}{}\quad\overset{3}{}\quad\overset{4}{}$

    $b'_1a'_0 \dagger db_0 \dagger he'_0 \dagger ec_0 \dagger a_1h'_0;\qquad \underline{b}'\underline{a}' \dagger \underline{db} \dagger \underline{ah}' \dagger \underline{he}' \dagger \underline{e}c \ \P\ dc_0$

    i.e. None of my peaches have been grown in a hothouse.

39. $\overset{1}{}\quad\overset{2}{}\quad\overset{3}{}\quad\overset{4}{}\quad\overset{5}{}\qquad\overset{1}{}\quad\overset{3}{}\quad\overset{5}{}\quad\overset{2}{}\quad\overset{4}{}$

    $c_1d_0 \dagger h_1e'_0 \dagger c'_1a'_0 \dagger h'b_0 \dagger e_1d'_0;\qquad \underline{c}'\underline{d} \dagger \underline{c}'a' \dagger \underline{ed}' \dagger \underline{he}' \dagger \underline{h}'b \ \P\ a'b_0$

    i.e. No pawnbroker is dishonest.

[Ex. 166–169; Ans. 186.]

$\quad$ 1 $\quad$ 2 $\quad$ 3 $\quad$ 4 $\quad$ 5 $\qquad$ 1 $\quad$ 3 $\quad$ 4 $\quad$ 5 $\quad$ 2

.40. ad'_0 † $c'h_0$ † $c_1a'_0$ † db_0 † $e'c_0$; $\quad$ $\underline{ad}'$ † $\underline{ea}'$ † $\underline{db}$ † $\underline{e'c}$ † $\underline{c'h}$ ¶ bh_0

i.e. No kitten with green eyes will play with a gorilla.

$\quad$ 1 $\quad$ 2 $\quad$ 3 $\quad$ 4 $\quad$ 5 $\qquad$ 1 $\quad$ 3 $\quad$ 4 $\quad$ 5 $\quad$ 2

41. $c_1a'_0$ † $h'b_0$ † ae_0 † $d_1c'_0$ † $h_1e'_0$; $\quad$ $\underline{ca}'$ † $\underline{ae}$ † $\underline{dc}'$ † $\underline{he}'$ † $\underline{h}'b$ ¶ db_0 † d_1,

$\hfill$ i.e. ¶ d_1b_0

i.e. All *my* friends in this College dine at the lower table.

$\quad$ 1 $\quad$ 2 $\quad$ 3 $\quad$ 4 $\quad$ 5 $\qquad$ 1 $\quad$ 3 $\quad$ 4 $\quad$ 5 $\quad$ 2

42. ca_0 † $h_1d'_0$ † $c'_1e'_0$ † $b'a'_0$ † d_1e_0; $\quad$ $\underline{ca}$ † $\underline{c'e}'$ † $b'\underline{a}'$ † $\underline{dc}$ † hd' ¶ $b'h_0$ † h_1,

$\hfill$ i.e. ¶ $h_1b'_0$

i.e. My writing-desk is full of live scorpions.

$\quad$ 1 $\quad$ 2 $\quad$ 3 $\quad$ 4 $\quad$ 5 $\qquad$ 1 $\quad$ 4 $\quad$ 2 $\quad$ 5 $\quad$ 3

43. b_1e_0 † ah_0 † dc_0 † $e'_1a'_0$ † bc'_0; $\quad$ $\underline{b'e}$ † $\underline{e'a}'$ † $\underline{ah}$ † $\underline{bc}'$ † $\underline{dc}$ ¶ hd_0

i.e. No Mandarin ever reads Hogg's poems.

$\quad$ 1 $\quad$ 2 $\quad$ 3 $\quad$ 4 $\quad$ 5 $\qquad$ 1 $\quad$ 4 $\quad$ 2 $\quad$ 5 $\quad$ 3

44. $e_1b'_0$ † $a'd_0$ † $c_1h'_0$ † $e'a_0$ † $d'h_0$; $\quad$ $\underline{eb}'$ † $\underline{e'a}$ † $\underline{a'd}$ † $\underline{d'h}$ † $\underline{ch}'$ ¶ $b'c_0$ † c_1,

$\hfill$ i.e. ¶ $c_1b'_0$

i.e. Shakespeare was clever.

$\quad$ 1 $\quad$ 2 $\quad$ 3 $\quad$ 4 $\quad$ 5 $\qquad$ 1 $\quad$ 4 $\quad$ 3 $\quad$ 5 $\quad$ 2

45. $e'_1c'_0$ † hb'_0 † d_1a_0 † $c_1a'_0$ † c_1b_0; $\quad$ $\underline{e'c}'$ † $\underline{ea}'$ † $\underline{da}$ † $\underline{cb}$ † hb' ¶ dh_0 † d_1,

$\hfill$ i.e. ¶ d_1h_0

i.e. Rainbows are not worth writing odes to.

$\quad$ 1 $\quad$ 2 $\quad$ 3 $\quad$ 4 $\quad$ 5 $\qquad$ 1 $\quad$ 4 $\quad$ 2 $\quad$ 5 $\quad$ 3

46. $c'_1h'_0$ † e_1a_0 † bd_0 † a'_1h_0 † $d'c_0$; $\quad$ $\underline{e'h}'$ † $\underline{a'h}$ † ea † $\underline{d'c}$ † bd ¶ eb_0 † e_1,

$\hfill$ i.e. ¶ e_1b_0

i.e. These Sorites-examples are difficult.

$\quad$ 1 $\quad$ 2 $\quad$ 3 $\quad$ 4 $\quad$ 5 $\quad$ 6 $\qquad$ 1 $\quad$ 3 $\quad$ 4 $\quad$ 6 $\quad$ 2 $\quad$ 5

47. $a'_1e'_0$ † bk_0 † $c'a_0$ † eh'_0 † $d_1b'_0$ † $k'h_0$; $\quad$ $\underline{a'e}'$ † $c'\underline{a}$ † $\underline{eh}'$ † $\underline{k'h}$ † $\underline{bk}$ † db'

$\hfill$ ¶ $c'd_0$ † d_1, i.e. ¶ $d_1c'_0$

i.e. All my dreams come true.

$\quad$ 1 $\quad$ 2 $\quad$ 3 $\quad$ 4 $\quad$ 5 $\quad$ 6 $\qquad$ 1 $\quad$ 3 $\quad$ 4 $\quad$ 6 $\quad$ 2

48. $a'h_0$ † $c'k_0$ † $a_1d'_0$ † $e_1h'_0$ † $b_1k'_0$ † $c_1e'_0$; $\quad$ $\underline{a'h}$ † $\underline{ad}'$ † $\underline{eh}'$ † $\underline{ce}'$ † $\underline{c'k}$ †

$\hfill$ 5

$\hfill$ $b\underline{k}'$ ¶ $d'b_0$ † b_1, i.e. ¶ $b_1d'_0$

i.e. All the English pictures here are painted in oils.

[Ex. 169–171; Ans. 186.]

      1   2   3   4   5   6   1   4   6   3   5

49. $k'_1e_0 \dagger c_1h_0 \dagger b_1a'_0 \dagger kd_0 \dagger h'a_0 \dagger b'_1e'_0$; $\underline{k'e} \dagger \underline{kd} \dagger \underline{b'e'} \dagger \underline{ba'} \dagger \underline{h'a}$

                                                  2

                                      $\dagger \underline{ch} \,\P\, dc_0 \dagger c_1$, i.e. $\P\, c_1d_0$

i.e. Donkeys are not easy to swallow.

      1   2   3   4   5   6   1   4   2   5   6   3

50. $ab'_0 \dagger h'd_0 \dagger e_1c_0 \dagger b_1d'_0 \dagger a'k_0 \dagger c_1h_0$; $\underline{ab'} \dagger \underline{bd} \dagger \underline{h'd} \dagger \underline{a'k} \dagger \underline{c'h} \dagger \underline{ec}$

                                            $\P\, ke_0 \dagger e_1$, i.e. $\P\, e_1k_0$

i.e. Opium-eaters never wear white kid gloves.

      1   2   3   4   5   6   1   4   5   3   6   2

51. $bc_0 \dagger k_1a'_0 \dagger ch_0 \dagger d_1b'_0 \dagger h'c'_0 \dagger k'_1e'_0$; $\underline{bc} \dagger \underline{db'} \dagger \underline{h'c'} \dagger \underline{eh} \dagger \underline{k'e'} \dagger \underline{ka'}$

                                            $\P\, da'_0 \dagger d_1$, i.e. $\P\, d_1a'_0$

i.e. A good husband always comes home for his tea.

      1   2   3   4   5   6   1   3   2   6   4

52. $a'_1k'_0 \dagger ch_0 \dagger h'k'_0 \dagger b_1d'_0 \dagger ea_0 \dagger d_1c'_0$; $\underline{a'k'} \dagger \underline{h'k} \dagger \underline{ch} \dagger \underline{dc'} \dagger \underline{bd'}$

                                                5

                                      $\dagger ea \,\P\, be_0 \dagger b_1$, i.e. $\P\, b_1e_0$

i.e. Bathing-machines are never made of mother-of-pearl.

      1   2   3   4   5   6   1   4   2   6   3

53. $da'_0 \dagger k_1b'_0 \dagger c_1h_0 \dagger d'_1k'_0 \dagger e_1c'_0 \dagger a_1h'_0$; $\underline{da'} \dagger \underline{d'k'} \dagger \underline{kb'} \dagger \underline{ah'} \dagger \underline{ch}$

                                                5

                                      $\dagger \underline{ec'} \,\P\, b'e_0 \dagger e_1$, i.e. $\P\, e_1b'_0$

i.e. Rainy days are always cloudy.

      1   2   3   4   5   6   1   3   4   6   2

54. $kb'_0 \dagger a'_1c'_0 \dagger d'b_0 \dagger k'_1h'_0 \dagger ea_0 \dagger d_1c_0$; $\underline{kb'} \dagger \underline{d'b} \dagger \underline{k'h'} \dagger \underline{dc} \dagger \underline{a'c'}$

                                                5

                                      $\dagger \underline{ea} \,\P\, h'e_0$

i.e. No heavy fish is unkind to children.

      1   2   3   4   5   6   1   4   2   6   3   5

55. $k'_1b'_0 \dagger eh'_0 \dagger c'd_0 \dagger hb_0 \dagger ac_0 \dagger kd'_0$; $\underline{k'b'} \dagger \underline{hb} \dagger \underline{eh'} \dagger \underline{kd'} \dagger \underline{c'd'} \dagger \underline{ac}$

                                            $\P\, ea_0$

i.e. No engine-driver lives on barley-sugar.

      1   2   3   4   5   6   1   4   5   3   6

56. $h_1b'_0 \dagger c_1d'_0 \dagger k'a_0 \dagger e_1h'_0 \dagger b_1a'_0 \dagger k_1c'_0$; $\underline{hb'} \dagger \underline{eh'} \dagger \underline{ba'} \dagger \underline{k'a} \dagger \underline{kc'}$

                                                2

                                      $\dagger \underline{cd'} \,\P\, ed'_0 \dagger e_1$, i.e. $\P\, e_1d'_0$

i.e. All the animals in the yard gnaw bones.

[Ex. 171–174; Ans. 186.]

57. $h'_1d'_0 \dagger e_1c'_0 \dagger k'a_0 \dagger cb_0 \dagger d_1l'_0 \dagger e'h_0 \dagger kl_0$; $\underline{hd}' \dagger \underline{dl}' \dagger \underline{kl} \dagger \underline{k}'a$

$$\dagger \underline{e'h} \dagger \underline{ec}' \dagger \underline{cb} \ \P \ ab_0$$

(positions above the first group: 1 2 3 4 5 6 7; above the second: 1 5 7 3 · 6 2 4)

i.e. No badger can guess a conundrum.

58. $b'h_0 \dagger d'_1l'_0 \dagger ca_0 \dagger d_1k'_0 \dagger h'_1e'_0 \dagger mc'_0 \dagger a'b_0 \dagger ek_0$;

$\underline{b'h} \dagger \underline{h'e}' \dagger \underline{a'b} \dagger \underline{ca} \dagger \underline{mc}' \dagger \underline{ek} \dagger \underline{dk}' \dagger \underline{d}'l' \ \P \ ml'_0$

(positions: 1 2 3 4 5 6 7 8; second group: 1 5 7 3 6 8 4 2)

i.e. No cheque of yours, received by me, is payable to order.

59. $c_1l'_0 \dagger h'e_0 \dagger kd_0 \dagger mc'_0 \dagger b'_1e'_0 \dagger n_1a'_0 \dagger l_1d'_0 \dagger m'b_0 \dagger ah_0$;

$\underline{cl}' \dagger \underline{mc}' \dagger \underline{ld}' \dagger \underline{kd} \dagger \underline{m'b} \dagger \underline{b'e}' \dagger \underline{h'e} \dagger \underline{ah} \dagger \underline{na}' \ \P \ kn_0$

(positions: 1 2 3 4 5 6 7 8 9; second group: 1 4 7 3 8 5 2 9 6)

i.e. I cannot read any of Brown's letters.

60. $e_1c'_0 \dagger l_1n'_0 \dagger d_1a'_0 \dagger m'b_0 \dagger ck'_0 \dagger c'r_0 \dagger h_1n_0 \dagger b'k_0 \dagger r'_1d'_0 \dagger m_1l'_0$;

$\underline{ec}' \dagger \underline{ck}' \dagger \underline{e'r} \dagger \underline{b'k} \dagger \underline{m'b} \dagger \underline{r'd}' \dagger \underline{da}' \dagger \underline{ml}' \dagger \underline{ln}' \dagger \underline{hn} \ \P \ a'h_0 \dagger h_1,$

(positions: 1 2 3 4 5 6 7 8 9 10; second group: 1 5 6 8 4 9 3 10 2 7)

i.e. $\P \ h_1a'_0$

i.e. I always avoid a kangaroo.

"*He thought he saw a Kangaroo*
   That worked a coffee-mill:
He looked again, and found it was
   A Vegetable-Pill.
'*Were I to swallow this,*' *he said,*
   '*I should be very ill!*'"

(From *Sylvie and Bruno*)

[Ex. 174–176; Ans. 186–187.]

SYMBOLIC LOGIC

Part Two
Advanced

BY LEWIS CARROLL

Arrangement and Annotations
by the Editor

Louisa, Margaret, and Henrietta Dodgson, sisters of Lewis Carroll. The sister on the left, Louisa, is one with whom he corresponded about many of his logical puzzles. (Gernsheim Collection, Humanities Research Center, University of Texas, Austin)

BOOK IX
SOME ACCOUNT OF
PARTS II AND III[1]

In Part II, in addition to treating of such matters as the "Existential Import" of Propositions, the use of a *negative* Copula, and the theory that two negative Premisses prove nothing, I shall also extend the range of Syllogisms and of Sorites, by introducing Propositions containing *alternatives* (such as "Not-all x are y"), Propositions containing three or more Terms (such as "All ab are c," which, taken along with "Some bc' are d" would prove "Some d are a'"), &c. I shall also discuss Sorites containing Entities, and the *very* puzzling subjects of Hypotheticals, Dilemmas, and Paradoxes. I hope, in the course of Part II, to go over all the ground usually traversed in the text-books used in our Schools and Universities, and to enable my Readers to solve Problems of the same kind as, and far harder than, those that are at present set in their Examinations.

In Part III[2] I hope to deal with many curious and out-of-the-way subjects, some of which are not even alluded to in any of the treatises I have met with. In this Part will be found such matters as the Analysis of Propositions into their Elements (let the Reader, who has never gone into this branch of the subject, try to make out for himself what additional

---

[1] The contents of Books IX and X have been published previously as an "Appendix to Teachers" for Part I, fourth edition. Please consult editor's Introduction for details of arrangement.

[2] There is no evidence that Part III ever reached manuscript stage. Possibly some of the materials arranged here as parts of Part II were, however, intended by Carroll for Part III.

Proposition would be needed to convert "Some *a* are *b*" into "Some *a* are *bc*"), the treatment of Numerical and Geometrical Problems, the construction of Problems, and the solution of Syllogisms and Sorites containing Propositions more complex than any that I have used in Part II.

BOOK X
INTRODUCTORY

Chapter I ❧ Introductory

There are several matters which need to be explained to Readers, into whose hands this book may fall, in order that they may thoroughly understand what my Symbolic Method *is*, and in what respects it differs from the many other Methods already published.

These matters are as follows:

The "Existential Import" of Propositions.
The use of "is-not" (or "are-not") as a Copula.
The theory "two Negative Premisses prove nothing."
Euler's Method of Diagrams.
Venn's Method of Diagrams.
My Method of Diagrams.
The solution of a Syllogism by various Methods.
My Method of treating Syllogisms and Sorites.

Chapter II ※ The Existential Import of Propositions

The writers, and editors, of the Logical text-books which run in the ordinary grooves—to whom I shall hereafter refer by the (I hope inoffensive) title "The Logicians"—take, on this subject, what seems to me to be a more humble position than is at all necessary. They speak of the Copula of a Proposition "with bated breath," almost as if it were a living, conscious Entity, capable of declaring for itself what it chose to mean, and that we, poor human creatures, had nothing to do but to ascertain *what* was its sovereign will and pleasure, and submit to it.

In opposition to this view, I maintain that any writer of a book is fully authorised in attaching any meaning he likes to any word or phrase he intends to use.[1] If I find an author saying, at the beginning of his book, "Let it be understood that by the word *black* I shall always mean *white*, and that by the word *white* I shall always mean *black*," I meekly accept his ruling, however injudicious I may think it.

And so, with regard to the question whether a Proposition is or is not to be understood as asserting the existence of its Subject, I maintain that every writer may adopt his own rule, provided of course that it is consistent with itself and with the accepted facts of Logic.

Let us consider certain views that may *logically* be held, and thus settle which of them may *conveniently* be held; after which I shall hold myself free to declare which of them *I* intend to hold.

The *kinds* of Proposition, to be considered, are those that begin with "some," with "no," and with "all." These are usually called Propositions "in *I*," "in *E*," and "in *A*."

First, then, a Proposition in *I* may be understood as asserting, or else as *not* asserting, the existence of its Subject. (By "existence" I mean of course whatever kind of existence suits its nature. The two Propositions, "*dreams* exist" and "*drums* exist," denote two totally different kinds of

---

[1] Here in *Symbolic Logic* there reappears the nominalism of Humpty Dumpty in *Through the Looking-Glass*, in which Humpty Dumpty declares to Alice, "When *I* use a word it means just what I choose it to mean—neither more nor less." When Alice objects—"The question is whether you *can* make words mean so many different things"— Humpty Dumpty replies, "The question is which is to be master—that's all." See Martin Gardner's discussion in *The Annotated Alice* (New York: Clarkson Potter, 1960), pp. 268ff.

"existence." A *dream* is an aggregate of ideas, and exists only in the *mind of a dreamer*; whereas a *drum* is an aggregate of wood and parchment, and exists in the *hands of a drummer*.)

First, let us suppose that I "asserts" (i.e. "asserts the existence of its Subject").

Here, of course, we must regard a Proposition in A as making the *same* assertion, since it necessarily *contains* a Proposition in I.[2]

We now have I and A "asserting." Does this leave us free to make what supposition we choose as to E? My answer is "No. We are tied down to the supposition that E does *not* assert." This can be proved as follows:

If possible, let E "assert." Then (taking x, y, and z to represent Attributes) we see that, if the Proposition "No xy are z" be true, some things exist with the Attributes x and y: i.e. "Some x are y."

Also, we know that, if the Proposition "Some xy are z" be true, the same result follows.

But these two Propositions are Contradictories, so that one or other of them *must* be true. Hence this result is *always* true: i.e. the Proposition "Some x are y" is *always* true!

Quod est absurdum. (See Note A to this Book.)

We see, then, that the supposition "I asserts" necessarily leads to "A asserts, but E does not." And this is the *first* of the various views that may conceivably be held.

Next, let us suppose that I does *not* "assert." And, along with this, let us take the supposition that E *does* "assert."

Hence the Proposition "No x are y" means "Some x exist, and none of them are y"; i.e. "*all* of them are *not-y*," which is a Proposition in A. We also know, of course, that the Proposition "All x are not-y" proves "No x are y." Now two Propositions, each of which proves the other, are *equivalent*. Hence every Proposition in A is equivalent to one in E, and therefore "*asserts*."[3]

---

[2] Carroll begs the main question of this section, which is precisely whether it is indeed convenient to regard propositions in A as "necessarily containing" propositions in I. His discussion depends on the assumption of the two main issues: (1) whether every proposition in A contains a proposition in I; and (2) whether every proposition in A is equivalent to a proposition in I and E. These assumptions prevent him from even considering the convention adopted by contemporary logicians that I asserts, and A and E do not.

[3] The convention adopted by contemporary logicians is that every proposition in A is indeed equivalent to one in E, but that *neither* asserts.

Hence our *second* conceivable view is "*E* and *A* assert, but *I* does not."

This view does not seem to involve any necessary contradiction with itself or with the accepted facts of Logic. But, when we come to *test* it, as applied to the actual *facts* of life, we shall find, I think, that it fits in with them so badly that its adoption would be, to say the least of it, singularly inconvenient for ordinary folk.

Let me record a little dialogue I have just held with my friend Jones, who is trying to form a new Club, to be regulated on strictly *Logical* principles.

Author: "Well, Jones! Have you got your new Club started yet?"

Jones (*rubbing his hands*): "You'll be glad to hear that some of the Members (mind, I only say *some*) are millionaires! Rolling in gold, my boy!"

Author: "That sounds well. And how many Members have entered?"

Jones (*staring*): "None at all. We haven't got it started yet. What makes you think we have?"

Author: "Why, I thought you said that some of the Members ——"

Jones (*contemptuously*): "You don't seem to be aware that we're working on strictly *Logical* principles. A *Particular* Proposition does *not* assert the existence of its Subject. I merely meant to say that we've made a Rule not to admit *any* Members till we have at least *three* Candidates whose incomes are over ten thousand a year!"

Author: "Oh, *that's* what you meant, is it? Let's hear some more of your Rules."

Jones: "Another is, that no one, who has been convicted seven times of forgery, is admissible."

Author: "And here, again, I suppose you don't mean to assert there *are* any such convicts in existence?"

Jones: "Why that's exactly what I *do* mean to assert! Don't you know that a Universal Negative *asserts* the existence of its Subject? *Of course* we didn't make that Rule till we had satisfied ourselves that there are several such convicts now living."

The Reader can now decide for himself how far this *second* conceivable view would fit in with the facts of life. He will, I think, agree with me that Jones' view, of the "Existential Import" of Propositions, would lead to some inconvenience.

Thirdly, let us suppose that neither *I* nor *E* "asserts."

Now the supposition that the two Propositions, "Some *x* are *y*" and "No *x* are not-*y*," do not "assert," necessarily involves the supposition that "All *x* are *y*" does *not* "assert," since it would be absurd to suppose that they assert, when combined, more than they do when taken separately.

Hence the *third* (and last) of the conceivable views is that neither *I*, nor *E*, nor *A*, "asserts."

The advocates of this third view would interpret the Proposition "Some *x* are *y*" to mean "If there were any *x* in existence, some of them *would* be *y*"; and so with *E* and *A*.

It admits of proof that this view, as regards *A*, conflicts with the accepted facts of Logic.

Let us take the Syllogism *Darapti*, which is universally accepted as valid. Its form is

All *m* are *x*;

All *m* are *y*

∴ Some *y* are *x*.

This they would interpret as follows:

If there were any *m* in existence, all of them would be *x*;

If there were any *m* in existence, all of them would be *y*.

∴ If there were any *y* in existence, some of them would be *x*.

That this Conclusion does *not* follow has been so briefly and clearly explained by Mr. Keynes (in his *Formal Logic*, dated 1894, pp. 356, 357), that I prefer to quote his words:

"*Let no proposition imply the existence either of its subject or of its predicate.*
"Take, as an example, a syllogism in *Darapti*:

All *M* is *P*,

All *M* is *S*,

∴ Some *S* is *P*.

"Taking *S, M, P*, as the minor, middle, and major terms respectively, the conclusion will imply that, if there is any *S*, there is some *P*. Will the premisses also imply this? If so, then the syllogism is valid; but not otherwise.

"The Conclusion implies that if *S* exists *P* exists, but, consistently with the premisses, *S* may be existent while *M* and *P* are both non-existent. An implication is, therefore, contained in the conclusion, which is not justified by the premisses."

This seems to *me* entirely clear and convincing. Still, "to make sicker," I may as well throw the above (*soi-disant*) Syllogism into a concrete form, which will be within the grasp of even a *non*-logical Reader.

Let us suppose that a Boys' School has been set up, with the following system of Rules:

All boys in the First (the highest) Class are to do French, Greek, and Latin. All in the Second Class are to do Greek only. All in the Third Class are to do Latin only.

Suppose also that there *are* boys in the Third Class, and in the Second; but that no boy has yet risen into the First.

It is evident that there are no boys in the School doing French: still we know, by the Rules, what would happen if there *were* any.

We are authorised, then, by the *Data*, to assert the following two Propositions:

If there were any boys doing French, all of them would be doing Greek;

If there were any boys doing French, all of them would be doing Latin.

And the Conclusion, according to "The Logicians," would be

If there were any boys doing Latin, some of them would be doing Greek.

Here, then, we have two *true* Premisses and a *false* Conclusion (since we know that there *are* boys doing Latin, and that *none* of them are doing Greek.)   Hence the argument is *invalid*.[4]

Similarly it may be shown that this "non-existential" interpretation destroys the validity of *Disamis, Datisi, Felapton,* and *Fresison.*

Some of "The Logicians" will, no doubt, be ready to reply "But we are not *Aldrichians*!   Why should *we* be responsible for the validity of the Syllogisms of so antiquated an author as Aldrich?"[5]

Very good.   Then, for the *special* benefit of these "friends" of mine (with what ominous emphasis that name is sometimes used!   "I must have a private interview with *you*, my young *friend*," says the bland Dr.

---

[4] Carroll uses a similar argument against Fowler in the letter appended to this section.
[5] The reference is to Henry Aldrich's *Artis Logicae Compendium,* published in 1691, but still in widespread use in Oxford in the second half of the nineteenth century, having been reprinted with notes by Henry Mansel (1820–1871) in 1862.

Birch, "in my library at 9 A.M. tomorrow.   And you will please to be *punctual!*"), for their *special* benefit, I say, I will produce *another* charge against this "non-existential" interpretation.

It actually invalidates the ordinary Process of "Conversion," as applied to Propositions in *I*.

Every logician, Aldrichian or otherwise, accepts it as an established fact that "Some *x* are *y*" may be legitimately converted into "Some *y* are *x*."

But is it equally clear that the Proposition "If there *were* any *x*, some of them *would* be *y*" may be legitimately converted into "If there *were* any *y*, some of them would be *x*"?   I trow not.

The example I have already used—of a Boy's School with a non-existent First Class—will serve admirably to illustrate this new flaw in the theory of "The Logicians."

Let us suppose that there is yet *another* Rule in this School, viz. "In each Class, at the end of the Term, the head boy and the second boy shall receive prizes."

This Rule entirely authorises us to assert (in the sense in which "The Logicians" would use the words) "Some boys in the First Class will receive prizes," for this simply means (according to them) "If there *were* any boys in the First Class, some of them *would* receive prizes."

Now the Converse of this Proposition is, of course, "Some boys, who will receive prizes, are in the First Class," which means (according to "The Logicians") "If there *were* any boys about to receive prizes, some of them *would* be in the First Class" (which Class we know to be *empty*).

Of this Pair of Converse Propositions, the first is undoubtedly *true*: the second, *as* undoubtedly, *false*.

It is always sad to see a batsman knock down his own wicket: one pities him, as a man and a brother, but, as a *cricketer*, one can but pronounce him "Out!"

We see, then, that, among all the conceivable views we have here considered, there are only *two* which can *logically* be held, viz.

> *I* and *A* "assert," but *E* does not.
> *E* and *A* "assert," but *I* does not.

The *second* of these I have shown to involve great practical inconvenience.

The *first* is the one adopted in this book.

Some further remarks on this subject will be found in Note B to this Book.

Letter from Lewis Carroll to T. Fowler[6]

Ch. Ch.
Nov. 13/85

DEAR FOWLER,

I find a statement in your Logic that puzzles me much: & I shall be grateful for your view thereon.

You assert that the copula "are" does *not* connote the actual *existence* of the subject. According to this view the Propositions "all *x* are *y*," "some *x* are *y*," mean, in Aldrich's forms, "*if any x exist*, all of them are *y*," "*if any x exist*, some of them are *y*."

Now suppose my (empty) purse to be lying on the table, and that I say

"All the sovereigns in that purse are made of gold;
All the sovereigns in that purse are my property;
∴ Some of my property is made of gold."

That is (according to your interpretation of the copula),

"*If there are sovereigns in that purse*, they are all made of gold;
If there are sovereigns in that purse, they are all my property;
∴ *If I have any property*, some of it is made of gold."

It seems to me that, though these two premisses are *true*, the conclusion may very easily be *false*: it might easily happen that I *had* much "property," but that *none* of it was "made of gold."

Sincerely yours,
C. L. DODGSON

Chapter III ☙ The Use of "Is-not" (or "Are-not") as a Copula

Is it better to say "John *is-not* in-the-house" or "John *is* not-in-the-house"? "Some of my acquaintances *are-not* men-I-should-like-to-be-seen-with"

---

[6] The original of this letter to Fowler, the author of *The Elements of Inductive Logic*, and well-known critic of Jevons, is in the Morris L. Parrish Collection, Princeton University Library.

or "Some of my acquaintances *are* men-I-should-*not*-like-to-be-seen-with"? That is the sort of question we have now to discuss.

This is no question of Logical Right and Wrong: it is merely a matter of *taste*, since the two forms mean exactly the same thing.   And here, again, "The Logicians" seem to me to take a much too humble position.   When they are putting the final touches to the grouping of their Proposition, just before the curtain goes up, and when the Copula—always a rather fussy "heavy father," asks them "Am *I* to have the 'not,' or will you tack it on to the Predicate?" they are much too ready to answer, like the subtle cab-driver, "Leave it to *you*, Sir!"   The result seems to be, that the grasping Copula constantly gets a "not" that had better have been merged in the Predicate, and that Propositions are differentiated which had better have been recognised as precisely similar.   Surely it is simpler to treat "Some men are Jews" and "Some men are Gentiles" as being, both of them, *affirmative* Propositions, instead of translating the latter into "Some men are-not Jews," and regarding it as a *negative* Proposition?

The fact is, "The Logicians" have somehow acquired a perfectly *morbid* dread of negative Attributes, which makes them shut their eyes, like frightened children, when they come across such terrible Propositions as "All not-*x* are *y*"; and thus they exclude from their system many very useful forms of Syllogisms.

Under the influence of this unreasoning terror, they plead that, in Dichotomy by Contradiction, the *negative* part is too large to deal with, so that it is better to regard each Thing as either included in, or excluded from, the *positive* part.   I see no force in this plea: and the facts often go the other way.   As a personal question, dear Reader, if *you* were to group your acquaintances into the two Classes, men that you *would* like to be seen with, and men that you would *not* like to be seen with, do you think the latter group would be so *very* much the larger of the two?

For the purposes of Symbolic Logic, it is so *much* the most convenient plan to regard the two sub-divisions, produced by Dichotomy, on the *same* footing, and to say, of any Thing, either that it "is" in the one, or that it "is" in the other, that I do not think any Reader of this book is likely to demur to my adopting that course.

Chapter IV ❧ The Theory that Two Negative Premisses Prove Nothing

This I consider to be *another* craze of "The Logicians," fully as morbid as their dread of a negative Attribute.

It is, perhaps, best refuted by the method of *Instantia Contraria*. Take the following Pairs of Premisses:

None of my boys are conceited;
None of my girls are greedy.

None of my boys are clever;
None but a clever boy could solve this problem.

None of my boys are learned;
Some of my boys are not choristers.

[This last Proposition is, in *my* system, an *affirmative* one, since *I* should read it "are not-choristers"; but, in dealing with "The Logicians," I may fairly treat it as a *negative* one, since *they* would read it "are-not choristers."]

If you, dear Reader, declare, after full consideration of these Pairs of Premisses, that you cannot deduce a Conclusion from *any* of them—why, all I can say is that, like the Duke in *Patience*, you "will have to be contented with our heart-felt sympathy"! (See p. 253.)

Chapter V ❧ Euler's Method of Diagrams

Diagrams seem to have been used, at first, to represent *Propositions* only. In Euler's well-known Circles, each was supposed to contain a Class, and the Diagram consisted of two Circles, which exhibited the relations, as to inclusion and exclusion, existing between the two Classes.

Thus, the Diagram, here given, exhibits the two Classes, whose respective Attributes are *x* and *y*, as so related to each other that the following Propositions are all simultaneously true:

> All *x* are *y*,
> No *x* are not-*y*,
> Some *x* are *y*,
> Some *y* are not-*x*,
> Some not-*y* are not-*x*,

and, of course, the Converses of the last four.

Similarly, with this Diagram, the following Propositions are true:

> All *y* are *x*,
> No *y* are not-*x*,
> Some *y* are *x*,
> Some *x* are not-*y*,
> Some not-*x* are not *y*

and, of course, the Converses of the last four.

Similarly, with this Diagram, the following are true:

> All *x* are not-*y*,
> All *y* are not-*x*,
> No *x* are *y*,
> Some *x* are not-*y*,
> Some *y* are not-*x*,
> Some not-*x* are not-*y*,

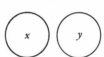

and the Converses of the last four.

Similarly, with this Diagram, the following are true:

> Some *x* are *y*,
> Some *x* are not-*y*,
> Some not-*x* are *y*,
> Some not-*x* are not-*y*,

and, of course, their four Converses.

Note that *all* Euler's Diagrams assert "Some not-*x* are not-*y*." Apparently it never occurred to him that it might *sometimes* fail to be true!

Now, to represent "All *x* are *y*," the first of these Diagrams would suffice.   But to represent any *Particular* Proposition, at least *three* Diagrams would be needed (in order to include all the possible cases), and, for "Some not-*x* are not-*y*," all the *four*.

Chapter VI ⚡ Venn's Method of Diagrams

Let us represent not-*x* by *x'*.

Mr. Venn's Method of Diagrams is a great advance on the above Method.

He uses the last of the above Diagrams to represent *any* desired relation between *x* and *y*, by simply shading a Compartment known to be *empty*, and placing a + in one known to be *occupied*.

Thus, he would represent the three Propositions "Some *x* are *y*," "No *x* are *y*," and "All *x* are *y*," as follows:[1]

It will be seen that, of the *four* Classes, whose peculiar Sets of Attributes are *xy*, *xy'*, *x'y*, and *x'y'*, only *three* are here provided with closed Compartments, while the *fourth* is allowed the rest of the Infinite Plane to range about in!

This arrangement would involve us in very serious trouble, if we ever attempted to represent "No *x'* are *y'*." Mr. Venn *once* (at p. 281) encounters this awful task; but evades it, in a quite masterly fashion, by the simple foot-note, "We have not troubled to shade the outside of this diagram"!

---

[1] Carroll seriously misdescribes Venn's position here.   In *Symbolic Logic* (London: Macmillan, 1894), Chapter VI, pp. 157ff., Venn quite explicitly denies that Propositions in *A*, in the symbolic logic which he is developing, have existential import.   Thus his diagram for "All *x* are *y*" is thus:

See also Venn's *Symbolic Logic*, p. 122.

To represent *two* Propositions (containing a common Term) *together*, a *three*-letter Diagram is needed. This is the one used by Mr. Venn.

Here, again, we have only *seven* closed Compartments, to accommodate the *eight* Classes whose peculiar Sets of Attributes are *xym*, *xym'*, &c.

"With four terms in request," Mr. Venn says, "the most simple and symmetrical diagram seems to me that produced by making four ellipses intersect one another in the desired manner." This, however, provides only *fifteen* closed compartments.

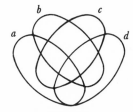

For *five* letters, "The simplest diagram I can suggest," Mr. Venn says, "is one like this (the small ellipse in the centre is to be regarded as a portion of the *outside* of *c*; i.e. its four component portions are inside *b* and *d*, but are no part of *c*). It must be admitted that such a diagram is not quite so simple to draw as one might wish it to be; but then consider what the alternative is if one undertakes to deal with five terms and all their combinations—nothing short of the disagreeable task of writing out, or in some way putting before us, all the 32 combinations involved."

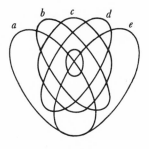

This Diagram gives us 31 closed compartments.

For *six* letters, Mr. Venn suggests that we might use *two* Diagrams, like the above, one for the *f* part, and the other for the not-*f* part, of all the other combinations. "This," he says, "would give the desired 64 subdivisions." This, however, would only give 62 closed Compartments, and *one* infinite area, which the two Classes, *a'b'c'd'e'f* and *a'b'c'd'e'f'*, would have to share between them.

Beyond *six* letters Mr. Venn does not go.[2]

---

[2] Carroll is hardly fair to Venn here. For cases involving more than six letters, Venn suggests the use of rectangular figures. See his *Symbolic Logic*, 1894, page 140.

Chapter VII ⚡ My Method of Diagrams

My Method of Diagrams *resembles* Mr. Venn's, in having separate Compartments assigned to the various Classes, and in marking these Compartments as *occupied* or as *empty*; but it *differs* from his Method, in assigning a *closed* area to the *Universe of Discourse*, so that the Class which, under Mr. Venn's liberal sway, has been ranging at will through Infinite Space, is suddenly dismayed to find itself "cabin'd, cribb'd, confined," in a limited Cell like any other Class! Also, I use *rectilinear*, instead of *curvilinear*, Figures; and I mark an *occupied* Cell with I (meaning that there is at least *one* Thing in it), and an *empty* Cell with a O (meaning that there is *no* Thing in it).

For *two* letters, I use this Diagram, in which the North Half is assigned to x, the South to not-x (or x'), the West to y, and the East to y'. Thus the North-West Cell contains the xy-Class, the North-East Cell the xy' Class, and so on.

For *three* letters, I subdivide these four Cells, by drawing an *Inner* Square, which I assign to m, the *Outer* Border being assigned to m'. I thus get the *eight* Cells that are needed to to accommodate the eight Classes, whose peculiar Sets of Attributes are xym, xym', &c.

This last Diagram is the most complex that I used in the *Elementary* Part of my *Symbolic Logic*.

For *four* letters (which I call a, b, c, d) I use this Diagram; assigning the North Half to a (and of course the rest of the Diagram to a'), the West Half to b, the Horizontal Oblong to c, and the Upright Oblong to d. We have now got 16 Cells.

For *five* letters (adding e) I subdivide the 16 Cells of the previous Diagram by *oblique* partitions, assigning all the *upper* portions to e, and all the *lower* portions to e'. Here, I admit, we lose the advantage of having the e-Class all *together*, "in a ring-fence," like the other four Classes. Still, it is very easy to find; and the operation of erasing it is nearly as easy as that of erasing any other Class. We have now got 32 Cells.

For *six* letters (adding *h*, as I avoid *tailed* letters) I substitute upright crosses for the oblique partitions, assigning the four portions, into which each of the 16 Cells is thus divided, to the four Classes *eh*, *eh′*, *e′h*, *e′h′*. We have now got 64 Cells.

For *seven* letters (adding *k*) I add, to each upright cross, a little inner square. All these 16 little squares are assigned to the *k*-Class, and all

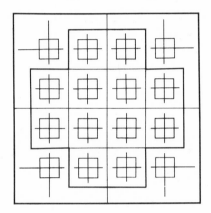

outside them to the *k′*-Class; so that the 8 little Cells (into which each of the 16 Cells is divided) are respectively assigned to the eight Classes *ehk*, *ehk′*, &c. We have now got 128 Cells.

For *eight* letters (adding *l*) I place, in each of the 16 Cells, a *lattice*, which is reduced copy of the whole Diagram; and just as the 16 large Cells of the whole Diagram are assigned to the 16 Classes, *abcd*, *abcd′*, so

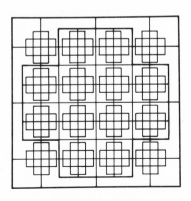

the 16 little Cells of each lattice are assigned to the 16 Classes *ehkl, ehkl'*, &c. Thus, the lattice in the North-West corner serves to accommodate the 16 Classes *abc'd'ehkl, abc'd'eh'kl'*, &c. The Octoliteral Diagram contains 256 Cells.

For *nine* letters, I place two Octoliteral Diagrams side by side, assigning one of them to *m*, and the other to *m'*. We have now got 512 Cells.

Finally, for *ten* letters, I arrange four Octoliteral Diagrams, like the above, in a square, assigning them to the four Classes *mn, mn', m'n, m'n'*. We have now got 1024 Cells.

Chapter VIII ❧ Solution of a Syllogism by Various Methods

The best way, I think, to exhibit the differences between these various Methods of solving Syllogisms will be to take a concrete example, and solve it by each Method in turn. Let us take, as our example, No. 29 (see Book VIII, Chapter I, §5).

No philosophers are conceited;
Some conceited persons are not gamblers.
∴ Some persons, who are not gamblers, are not philosophers.

(1) Solution by ordinary Method

These Premisses, as they stand, will give no Conclusion, as they are both negative.

If by Permutation or Obversion, we write the Minor Premiss thus,

Some conceited persons are not-gamblers,

we can get a Conclusion in Fresison, viz.

No philosophers are conceited;
Some conceited persons are not-gamblers.
∴ Some not-gamblers are not philosophers.

This can be proved by reduction to *Ferio*, thus:

No conceited persons are philosophers;
Some not-gamblers are conceited.
∴ Some not-gamblers are not philosophers.

The validity of *Ferio* follows directly from the Axiom "*De Omni et Nullo.*"

(2) Symbolic Representation

Before proceeding to discuss other Methods of Solution, it is *necessary* to translate our Syllogism into an *abstract* form.

Let us take "persons" as our "Universe of Discourse"; and let x = philosophers, m = conceited, and y = gamblers.

Then the Syllogism may be written thus:

No x are m;
Some m are y'.
∴ Some y' are x'.

(3) Solution by Euler's Method of Diagrams

The Major Premiss requires only *one* Diagram, viz.

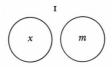

The Minor requires *three*, viz.

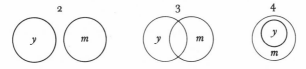

The combination of Major and Minor, in every possible way, requires *nine*, viz.

Figs. 1 and 2 give

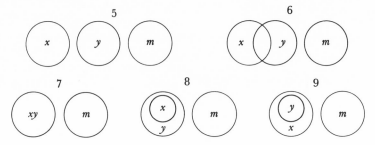

Figs. 1 and 3 give

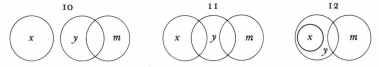

Figs. 1 and 4 give

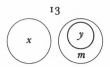

From this group (Figs. 5 to 13) we have, by disregarding *m*, to find the relation of *x* and *y*. On examination we find that Figs. 5, 10, and 13 express the relation of entire mutual exclusion; that Figs. 6 and 11 express partial inclusion and partial exclusion; that Fig. 7 expresses coincidence; that Figs. 8 and 12 express entire inclusion of *x* in *y*; and that Fig. 9 expresses entire inclusion of *y* in *x*.

We thus get five Biliteral Diagrams for *x* and *y*, viz.

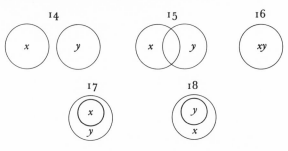

where the only Proposition, represented by them all, is "Some not-*y* are not-*x*," i.e. "Some persons, who are not gamblers, are not philosophers"— a result which Euler would hardly have regarded as a valuable one, since he seems to have assumed that a Proposition of this form is *always* true!

(4) Solution by Venn's Method of Diagrams

The following Solution has been kindly supplied to me by Mr. Venn himself.

"The Minor Premiss declares that some of the constituents in *my'* must be saved: mark these constituents with a cross.

"The Major declares that all *xm* must be destroyed; erase it.
"Then, as some *my'* is to be saved, it must clearly be *my'x'*.   That is, there must exist *my'x'*; or, eliminating *m, y'x'*.   In common phraseology,

"Some *y'* are *x'*, or 'Some not-gamblers are not-philosophers.'"

---

(5) Solution by my Method of Diagrams

The first Premiss asserts that no *xm* exist: so we mark the *xm*-Compartment as empty, by placing a O in each of its Cells.

The second asserts that some *my'* exist: so we mark the *my'*-Compartment as occupied, by placing a I in its only available Cell.

The only information, that this gives us as to *x* and *y*, is that the *x'y'*-Compartment is occupied, i.e. that some *x'y'* exist.

Hence "Some *x'* are *y'*": i.e. "Some persons, who are not philosophers, are not gamblers."

(6) Solution by my Method of Subscripts

$$xm_0 \dagger my'_1 \P x'y'_1,$$

i.e. "Some persons, who are not philosophers, are not gamblers."

Chapter IX ❧ My Method of Treating Syllogisms and Sorites

Of all the strange things, that are to be met with in the ordinary text-books of Formal Logic, perhaps the strangest is the violent contrast one finds to exist between their ways of dealing with these two subjects. While they have elaborately discussed no less than *nineteen* different forms of *Syllogisms* —each with its own special and exasperating Rules, while the whole constitutes an almost useless machine, for practical purposes, many of the Conclusions being incomplete, and many quite legitimate forms being ignored—they have limited *Sorites* to *two* forms only, of childish simplicity; and these they have dignified with special *names*, apparently under the impression that no other possible forms existed!

As to Syllogisms, I find that their nineteen forms, with about a score of others which they have ignored, can all be arranged under *three* forms, each with a very simple Rule of its own; and the only question the Reader has to settle in working any one of the 101 Examples given at Book VIII, Chapter 1, §5 is "Does it belong to Fig. I, II, or III?"

As to *Sorites*, the only two forms recognised by the textbooks are the *Aristotelian*, whose Premisses are a series of Propositions in *A*, so arranged that the Predicate of each is the Subject of the next, and the *Goclenian*, whose Premisses are the very same series, written backwards. Goclenius, it seems, was the first who noticed the startling fact that it does not affect the force of a Syllogism to invert the order of its Premisses, and who applied this discovery to a Sorites. If we assume (as surely we may?) that he is the *same* man as that transcendent genius who first noticed that 4 times 5 is the same thing as 5 times 4, we may apply to him what somebody (Edmund Yates, I think it was) has said of Tupper, viz. "Here is a man who, beyond all others of his generation, has been favored with Glimpses of the Obvious!"

These puerile—not to say infantine—forms of a Sorites I have, in this book, ignored from the very first, and have not only admitted freely Propositions in *E*, but have purposely stated the Premisses in random order, leaving to the Reader the useful task of arranging them, for himself, in an order which can be worked as a series of regular Syllogisms. In doing this, he can begin with *any one* of them he likes.

I have tabulated, for curiosity, the various orders in which the Premisses of the Aristotelian Sorites

(1) All *a* are *b*;
(2) All *b* are *c*;
(3) All *c* are *d*;
(4) All *d* are *e*;
(5) All *e* are *h*.
∴ All *a* are *h*.

may be syllogistically arranged, and I find there are no less than sixteen such orders, viz., 12345, 21345, 23145, 23415, 23451, 32145, 32415, 32451, 34215, 34251, 34521, 43215, 43251, 43521, 45321, 54321. Of these the *first* and the *last* have been dignified with names; but the other *fourteen*—first enumerated by an obscure Writer on Logic, towards the end of the Nineteenth Century—remain without a name!

Notes to Book X

(A) [See p. 233]

It may, perhaps, occur to the Reader, who has studied Formal Logic, that the argument, here applied to the Propositions *I* and *E*, will apply equally well to the Propositions *I* and *A* (since, in the ordinary text-books, the Propositions "All *xy* are *z*" and "Some *xy* are not *z*" are regarded as Contradictories). Hence it may appear to him that the argument might have been put as follows:

We now have *I* and *A* "asserting." Hence, if the Proposition "All *xy* are *z*" be true, some things exist with the Attributes *x* and *y*: i.e. "Some *x* are *y*."

Also we know that, if the Proposition "Some *xy* are not-*z*" be true, the same result follows.

But these two Propositions are Contradictories, so that one or other of them *must* be true. Hence this result is *always* true: i.e. the Proposition "Some *x* are *y*" is *always* true!

Quod est absurdum. Hence *I* cannot assert.

I may as well give here what seems to me to be an irresistible proof that this view (that *A* and *I* are Contradictories), though adopted in the ordinary text-books, is untenable. The proof is as follows:

With regard to the relationship existing between the Class *xy* and the two Classes *z* and not-*z*, there are *four* conceivable states of things, viz.

(1) Some *xy* are *z*, and some are not-*z*;
(2) Some *xy* are *z*, and none are not-*z*;
(3) No *xy* are *z*, and some are not-*z*;
(4) No *xy* are *z*, and none are not-*z*.

Of these four, No. (2) is equivalent to "All *xy* are *z*," No. 3 is equivalent to "All *xy* are not-*z*," and No. 4 is equivalent to "No *xy* exist."

Now it is quite undeniable that, of these *four* states of things, each is, *a priori*, *possible*, some *one must* be true, and the other three *must* be false.

Hence the Contradictory to (2) is "Either (1) or (3) or (4) is true." Now the assertion "Either (1) or (3) is true" is equivalent to "Some *xy* are not-*z*"; and the assertion "(4) is true" is equivalent to "No *xy* exist." Hence the Contradictory to "All *xy* are *z*" may be expressed as the Alternative Proposition "Either some *xy* are not-*z*, or no *xy* exist," but *not* as the Categorical Proposition "Some *y* are not-*z*."

(B) [See p. 237 at end of Chapter 2]

There are yet *other* views current among "The Logicians," as to the "Existential Import" of Propositions, which have not been mentioned in this Section.

One is, that the Proposition "Some *x* are *y*" is to be interpreted, neither as "Some *x* exist and are *y*," nor yet as "If there *were* any *x* in existence, some of them would be *y*," but merely as "Some *x* can be *y*; i.e. the Attributes *x* and *y* are compatible." On *this* theory, there would be nothing offensive in my telling my friend Jones "Some of your brothers are swindlers"; since, if he indignantly retorted "What do you *mean* by such insulting language, you scoundrel?," I should calmly reply, "I merely mean that the thing is *conceivable*—that some of your brothers *might possibly* be swindlers." But it may well be doubted whether such an explanation would *entirely* appease the wrath of Jones!

Another view is, that the Proposition "All *x* are *y*" *sometimes* implies the actual *existence* of *x*, and *sometimes* does *not* imply it and that we cannot tell, without having it in *concrete* form, *which* interpretation we are to give it. This view is, I think, strongly supported by common usage.

(C) [See p. 240, Chapter 4.]

The three Conclusions are

No conceited child of mine is greedy;
None of my boys could solve this problem;
Some unlearned boys are not choristers.

BOOK XI
SYMBOLS,
LOGICAL CHARTS[1]

Chapter I 🙣 Logical Symbols

[1] The purpose of this "Book" is to present and review certain of Carroll's basic logical notions, and to introduce some logical charts and other information from Carroll's papers for Part II that never reached finished form but are nonetheless useful in dealing with the material in the books that follow.

Although Carroll developed neither a propositional calculus nor a calculus of classes in the modern sense, his logic contains near-equivalents of the basic logical symbols used in contemporary propositional and class calculi. Professional logicians will notice that Carroll *tends* to use his symbols as "metalinguistic" abbreviations—just as most of Aristotelian logic is metalinguistic. Thus these symbols cannot be identified with the object-linguistic symbols used in contemporary calculi of propositions and classes. Nonetheless, straightforward interpretations can

be given to most of these symbols so as to permit them to function in propositional and functional calculi.

Some of this basic symbolic notation has been introduced in Part I. Other notation is introduced in this chapter. The notation not previously introduced is taken from two sources: printed charts, reproduced below, intended to be included in Part II, and Carroll's logical notebook. (The originals of both are preserved at Princeton University, in the Morris L. Parrish Collection.)

We have already encountered *negation, conjunction,* and a form of *implication.*

For *negation,* Carroll appends the prime sign (′) to whatever is denied or negated.

For *conjunction,* he uses the dagger (†), to symbolise "and."

For what I have called a "form of" *implication,* Carroll uses the "reversed

255

paragraph sign" (⫣), which he describes as meaning "would, if true, prove." Professional logicians will notice that Carroll's use of this symbol is not entirely consistent. And it is clear from his notebooks that his understanding of the issues involved here was rather murkier than that of the typical contemporary logician: he uses object-linguistic notation for implication interchangeably with metalinguistic notation for derivability. And he has not satisfactorily solved the problem of incorporating hypothetical and categorical propositions and inferences in a single deductive system. One finds, for instance, in the notebooks the following:

$$\alpha \equiv xyz$$

i.e.,

$$\alpha \;⫣\; xyz \quad \text{and} \quad xyz \;⫣\; \alpha$$
$$\alpha_1(xyz)'_0 \quad \text{and} \quad xyz_1\alpha'_0$$

It would, however, be anachronistic to take Carroll to task for this. Certainly the tendency in his writing is to interpret any inference $a \;⫣\; b$ *materially*: as being false if and only if a is true and b false. Therefore the contemporary student will not go far wrong if he simply reads ⫣ in the contemporary sense of "if ..., then ...," in object-linguistic contexts.

To symbolise Propositions in I, E, A, Carroll has introduced subscript numbers: Thus

a_1 means "There exists some a";
a_0 means "No a exist";
$a_1b'_0$ means "All a are b."

Three additional symbolic notations are now introduced.

For *alternation*, Carroll uses the section sign (§) to symbolise "or" in the nonexclusive sense. Thus "$a \;\S\; b$" is read

either a or b (or both).

For *equivalence*, Carroll introduces the triple-bar ($\equiv$). Thus one may interpret $a \equiv b$ as

$$a \;⫣\; b \;\dagger\; b \;⫣\; a$$

Finally, to introduce "Not all a are b," Carroll needs $a_0b'_1$. This last needs some explanation. The denial of a statement in A, "All a are b," must within Carroll's approach, wherein statements in A have existential import, be a denial of the two combined statements of the A proposition. A proposition in A, e.g.,

All a are b or $a_1b'_0$

is equivalent for Carroll to the two statements:

Some a is b and No a is not-b

or

$$ab_1 \;\dagger\; ab'_0$$

The denial of this, using DeMorgan's Law, is

$$ab_0 \;\S\; ab'_1$$

That is, either there are no ab, or some a is not b. And this idea Carroll symbolises by $a_0b'_1$.

Throughout Part II, the letters that may be combined using the symbols just given can, when it suits Carroll's convenience, represent statements as well as terms. In Part I, letters were used only to name terms.

[On one manuscript page, a fragment from some longer treatise, preserved in the Dodgson Family Collection at Guildford, Carroll gives an alternate rendering of "all" propositions as follows:

"... I shall be able to exhibit the facts more clearly by using the following abbreviations:
"Denoting a term which asserts the possession of some property

(such as 'straightness') by a single letter (such as a), I shall denote the term which denies it by not-a, or, yet more briefly by a'. And I shall denote the logical copula 'is,' which asserts that the possession, or non-possession, of some one prop-

erty, is necessarily followed by the possession, or non-possession, of some other, by the symbol ⫛. Thus, if a stand for 'human' and b for 'mortal,' the time-honoured proposition "all men are mortal' may be abbreviated into a ⫛ b. . . ."]

Chapter II ⚹ Figures or Forms[1]

There are six separate Figures or Forms in which Conclusions are validly derived from Pairs of Premisses.

[1] Material supplementary to Part I, Book VI, providing formulae for solving syllogistic problems and also formulae for fallacies, survives in manuscript in two places: the Library of Christ Church, Oxford, and the Warren Weaver Collection at the Humanities Research Center of the University of Texas.

In Oxford only a sheaf of manuscript pages remains; the item in Texas is rather more complete, being a copy-book of some 209 pages in which Carroll entered in manuscript, between June 10, 1886 and February 17, 1894, a kind of catalogue of forms and fallacies together with examples. (The copy-book in which Carroll entered this material was a publisher's dummy copy of *Euclid and His Modern Rivals*, and is catalogued as such. The manuscript material, however, deals exclusively with logic and has nothing to do with geometry.) In both cases, however, the manuscript is very rough draft and there would be no point to reproducing

it here. What is presented here is a composite of the material contained in these sources. The chief advance over Part I is Carroll's treatment of "not-all" statements, both in valid and in fallacious inference. The "not-all" Figures—which are, to the best of my knowledge, unique to Carroll—are forced on him by his doctrine of existential import. A "not-all" statement, that is, the denial of an "all" statement—e.g., "All x is y"—is on Carroll's account, as explained in the preceding chapter, the denial of *two* statements: "Some x is y" *and* "No x is not-y." And this is, using De Morgan's law, "Either no x is y or some x is not-y." In Carroll's symbolism, $xy_0 \S xy'_1$— which is in turn equivalent to $x_0 y'_1$— may be read "Not-all x ⟍ is y." In contemporary logical usage, wherein the doctrine of existential import is abandoned, matters are less complicated. "All x is y" is simply xy'_0; and the denial of this, i.e., "Not-all x is y," is simply xy'_1—that is, "Some x is not-y."

Fig. I

$xm_0 \dagger ym'_0 \,\P\, xy_0$

Two Nullities, with Unlike Eliminands, yield a Nullity, in which both Retinends keep their signs.

A Retinend, asserted in the Premisses to exist, may be so asserted in the conclusion.

Hence we get two *Variants* of Fig. I, viz.

> (α)   where *one* Retinend is so asserted;
> (β)   where *both* are so asserted.

Fig. I (α)

$x_1 m_0 \dagger ym'_0 \,\P\, x_1 y_0$

Fig. I (β)

$x_1 m_0 \dagger y_1 m'_0 \,\P\, x_1 y_0 \dagger y_1 x_0$

Fig. II

$xm_0 \dagger ym_1 \,\P\, yx'_1$

A Nullity and an Entity, with Like Eliminands, yield an Entity, in which the Nullity-Retinend changes its sign.

Fig. III

$xm_0 \dagger m_1 y'_0 \,\P\, yx'_1$

or to say the same thing,

$xm_0 \dagger my'_0 \dagger m_1 \,\P\, yx'_1$

Two Nullities, with Like Eliminands asserted to exist, yield an Entity, in which both Retinends change their signs.

Fig. IV

$xm_0 \dagger (ym'_0 \,\S\, ym_1) \,\P\, yx_0 \,\S\, yx'_1$

which is to say,

$xm_0 \dagger y_0 m_1 \,\P\, y_0 x'_1$

Thus "No x are m" and "No y are not-m or some y are m" prove that either "No y are x" or "Some y are not-x." And this is the same as saying, "No x are m" and "Not-all y are not-m" prove that "Not-all y are x."

Fig. V

$$m_1x_0 \dagger (my'_0 \S my_1) \, \mathbb{P} \, yx'_1$$

which is to say,

$$m_1x_0 \dagger m_0y_1 \, \mathbb{P} \, yx'_1$$

Thus "All m are not-x" and "No m are not-y" or "Some m are y" prove "Some y are not-x." And this is the same as saying, "All m are not-x" and "Not-all m are not-y" prove "Some y are not-x."

Figs. IV and V may be treated according to the same Rule: Treating a Not-all as an Entity, we may write:

> A Nullity and an Entity with Like Eliminands yield an Entity in which the Nullity-Retinend changes its sign.

> If the possibility of the non-existence of a Retinend is asserted in the Premisses, the same possibility may be asserted in the Conclusion.

An alternative Rule, with the same result, is this:

> Given a Pair of Premisses which are a Nullity and a Not-all, state the two separate possibilities of the Not-all, and find a Conclusion from the Nullity and each possibility or alternative of the Not-all separately. Combine these two alternative Conclusions either as an Entity or as a Not-all, as the case may be.

Thus, in Fig. IV,

$$xm_0 \dagger ym'_0 \, \mathbb{P} \, yx_0$$

whereas

$$xm_0 \dagger ym_1 \, \mathbb{P} \, yx'_1$$

Combining the two alternative Conclusions we reach $yx_0 \S yx'_1$, which is equivalent to $y_0x'_1$.

And in Fig. V,

$$m_1x_0 \dagger my'_0 \, \mathbb{P} \, yx'_1$$

whereas

$$m_1x_0 \dagger my_1 \, \mathbb{P} \, yx'_1$$

Combining these two alternative Conclusions we reach $yx'_1 \S yx'_1$, which is equivalent simply to yx'_1.

In Fig. V, m_1 and m_0 cancel each other.

Fig. VI

Two Premisses with no middle term.[2]

Chapter III ✗ Fallacies[1]

Fallacies [1]

Limiting the meaning of "Fallacy" to "a Pair of Premisses, one containing m, x (with or without accents), and the other m, y, and leading to no conclusion," I think we have only five kinds to deal with.

(1) In the Syllogism

$$\left. \begin{array}{c} xm_0 \\ ym'_0 \end{array} \right\} \quad \therefore xy_0$$

---

[2] Although Carroll lists this among his six figures he provides no examples. My own guess is that he intended this figure to cover those inferences which are detailed in Chapter IV below, in the logical charts. To take two examples:

$$x_0 y_1 \dagger (xy_0 \S xy'_0) \, \| \, xy'_0$$

That is, from "Not all x are y'" and "Either no x are y or no x are y'" one may infer "No x are y'."

Another example would be

$$x_0 y_1 \dagger x_1 \, \| \, xy_1$$

That is, from "Not all x are y'" and "Some x exist," one may infer "Some x are y."

For further examples the reader is referred to Charts I through V in Chapter IV.

[1] The material on fallacies presented here is drawn from manuscript remains in Christ Church, Oxford. The three sections consist in fairly connected narrative, adding to the material already presented in Book VI a treatment of fallacies involving "Not-all." The manuscript is dated November 11, 1888.

the only essential feature is that the middles shall have unlike signs. This yields the Fallacy

$$\left.\begin{array}{l} xm_0 \\ ym_0 \end{array}\right\}$$

where no existence is assigned to m.   (This condition is needed, since

$$\left.\begin{array}{l} xm_0 \\ m_1 y_0 \end{array}\right\}$$

is a logical Pair of Premisses.)

(2) In the Syllogism

$$\left.\begin{array}{l} xm_0 \\ ym_0 \end{array}\right\} \quad (m \text{ being assumed to exist}) \quad \therefore x'y'_1$$

the only other essential feature is that the middles have like signs.   This yields the Fallacy

$$\left.\begin{array}{l} xm_0 \\ ym_0 \end{array}\right\}$$

where no existence is assigned to m.   (The omission of the *other* essential feature would not yield a Fallacy, since

$$\left.\begin{array}{l} xm_0 \\ ym'_0 \end{array}\right\}$$

is a logical Pair of Premisses, whatever be assumed as to *m*'s existence or nonexistence.)

(3) In the Syllogism

$$\left.\begin{array}{l} xm_0 \\ ym_1 \end{array}\right\} \quad \therefore x'y_1$$

the only essential feature is that the middles have like signs.   This yields the Fallacy

$$\left.\begin{array}{l} xm_0 \\ ym'_1 \end{array}\right\}$$

(4) A Pair of Premisses, both ending in $_1$, gives no conclusion, and so is a Fallacy, whether the middles have like signs or not.

(5) In the Syllogism

$$\left.\begin{array}{l} xm_0 \\ y_0 m_1 \end{array}\right\} \quad \therefore y_0 x'_1$$

the only essential feature is that the middles have like signs.   This yields
the Fallacy

$$\left.\begin{array}{l} xm_0 \\ y_0m'_1 \end{array}\right\}$$

(6) In the Syllogism

$$\left.\begin{array}{l} xm_0 \\ m_1y_0 \end{array}\right\} \quad \therefore x'y'_1$$

the only essential feature is that the middles have like signs.   This yields
the Fallacy

$$\left.\begin{array}{l} xm_0 \\ m'_0y_1 \end{array}\right\}$$

Fallacies [2]

Hence the five Fallacies, needing names, are as follows:

$$\text{I.} \quad \left.\begin{array}{l} xm_0 \\ ym_0 \end{array}\right\}$$

where no existence is assigned to m.

$$\text{II.} \quad \left.\begin{array}{l} xm_0 \\ ym'_1 \end{array}\right\}$$

III.   Two "particular" Premisses

$$\text{IV.} \quad \left.\begin{array}{l} xm_0 \\ y_0m'_1 \end{array}\right\}$$

$$\text{V.} \quad \left.\begin{array}{l} xm_0 \\ m'_0y_1 \end{array}\right\}$$

Instances of these Fallacies are here given:

I.   No square-shillings are bright;
   No square-shillings are heavy.

II.   No Jews are honest;
    Some Gentiles are poor.

III.   Some Jews are honest;
    Some Gentiles are poor.

IV. No Jews are honest; }
     Not all merchants are Jews. }

V. No Jews are honest; }
    Not all dishonest men are poor. }

Fallacies [3]

These five Fallacies may really be classed as *four*, since the last two come under the same description.

I propose to call these four Fallacies

- (α) Premisses universal, middles alike.
- (β) Premisses universal and particular, middles unlike.
- (γ) Premisses particular.
- (δ) Premisses universal and not-all, middles unlike.

A more plausible set of instances would be

I. All lions are wild; }
    All tigers are wild. }

II. No Jews are honest; }
     Some poor men are not Jews. }

III. Some Jews are honest; }
      Some Jews are poor. }

IV. No Jews are honest; }
     Not all merchants are Jews. }

V. All Jews are dishonest; }
    Not all dishonest men are poor. }

Chapter IV ❦ Logical Charts[1]

[1] The existence of the seven Logical Charts reproduced below is noted   briefly in the *Lewis Carroll Handbook*. Previously it has not been possible to

interpret them. Interpretation becomes fairly routine in the light of the
newly discovered remains of Part II, and
it seems obvious that these charts were
intended for use in Part II. There
may have been more charts printed
which have not been preserved. Fur-

ther charts on these lines in Carroll's
hand are preserved in his notebook.

Charts I to V deal with the logical
combinations of *bi*literal statements.
Charts VI and VII deal with the logical
combinations of *tri*literal statements.

LOGICAL CHART I

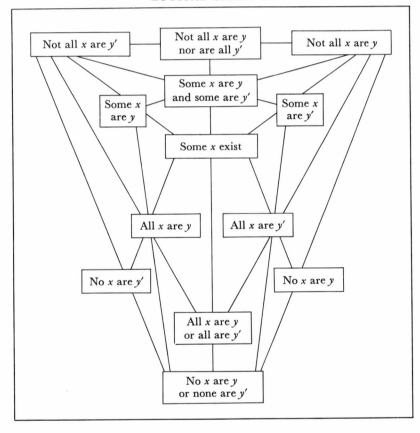

LOGICAL CHART II

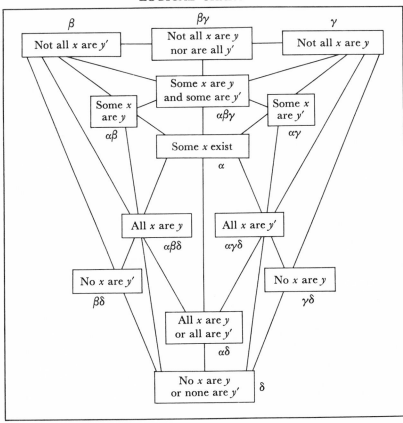

LOGICAL CHART III

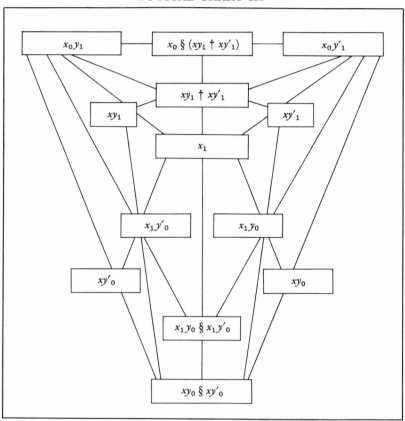

LOGICAL CHART IV

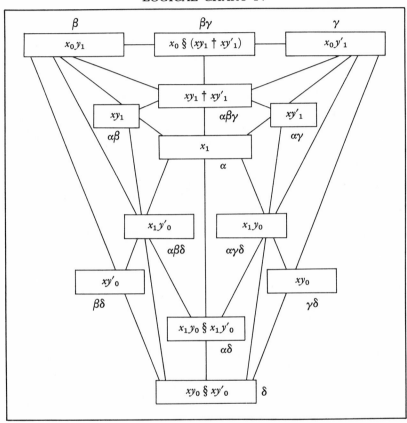

LOGICAL CHART V

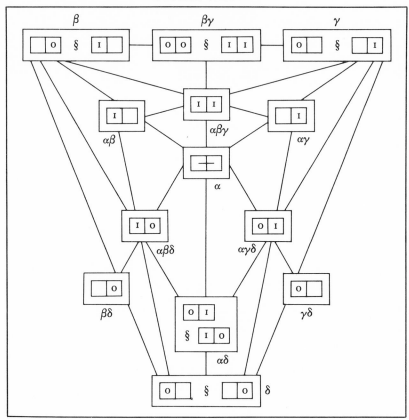

Interpretation of Charts I–V

These five diagrams or "Logical Charts" may be superimposed. All indicate various interrelationships among biliteral statements.

The first chart sets out relationships among biliteral statements. The second chart attaches Greek letters to each component statement of the first diagram, showing how from four statements taken as basic, α, β, γ, and δ, the remaining statements are compounded. Chart III represents the first chart in subscript form; and Chart IV represents the second chart in subscript form.

Of special interest in reading these charts are Carroll's use of the sign, introduced here, for alternation ("or"): §, and his treatment of statements of the form "Not all *a* are *b*." Both features are combined in the three top compartments: β, on the left, $\beta\gamma$, in the middle, and γ, on the right; β and γ represent, respectively, "Not all x are y'" and "Not all x are y." The conjunction of these two, $\beta\gamma$, "Not all x are y nor are all y'," has to be thrown into subscript form as follows, using alternation: $x_0 \,§\, (xy_1 \,\dagger\, xy'_1)$; that is, when β and γ both obtain, then either there are no x or some x are y and some x are not.

The double boxes in Chart V may puzzle the reader for a moment. They turn out to be the *top halves* of a Carroll Biliteral Diagram. Take $\beta\delta$ as an example. No x are y' would be represented diagrammatically, as explained in Part I, as illustrated above.

The two top compartments are shown in $\beta\delta$. All other points in Chart V are to be similarly interpreted.

The reader will want to notice the geometry of the charts. Take α as the apex of a regular tetrahedron, with β, γ, and δ as the base corners. Each of the three triangular faces $\alpha\beta\gamma$, $\alpha\gamma\delta$, $\alpha\delta\beta$ is its own miniature world of logical implication. The tetrahedron as a whole gives fifteen cases of Fig. VI, since for every straight line in the tetrahedron, the formula in its middle is the conclusion derivable from the formulae at the two ends. Thus these charts provide a handy ready reckoner for a figure for which there is no easy rule.

The tetrahedron looks like the following diagram.

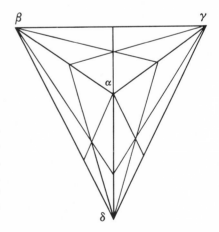

Interpretation of Chart VI

The sixth chart represents combinations of triliteral statements, single lines indicating biliteral connections and double lines indicating triliteral connections. Thus "All x are m'" may be derived from the two statements

"No x are m" and "Some x exist," and as indicated by the single lines, only two terms are involved here.

On the other hand, "Not all x are y" is derived from the two statements "No y are m'" and "Not all x are m," the inference here, as indicated by the double lines, involving three terms. These connections can of course be represented in subscript form. For example,

$$ym'_0 \dagger x_0m'_1 \,\P\, x_0y'_1$$

that is, "No y are m'" and "Not all x are m" would, if true, prove "Not all x are y," by the formula of Fig. V.

I have added Charts VI* and VI** to show how these charts may be used to illustrate Figs. I through VI. Chart VI*, besides putting Chart VI into subscript form, also shows Figs. I, Iα, II, and IV. Examples of what I interpret as the sixth figure also occur.

Chart VI** shows Figs. II, III, and V and, once again, illustrates what we interpret to be the sixth figure.

LOGICAL CHART VI

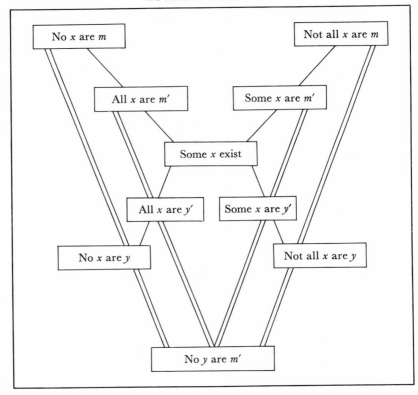

LOGICAL CHART VI*

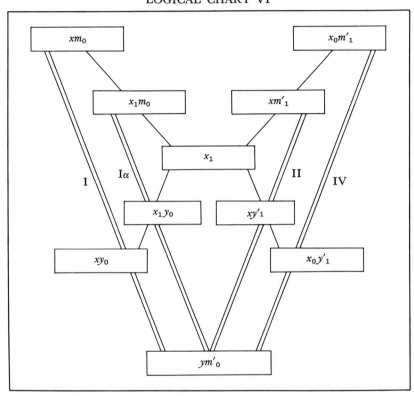

LOGICAL CHART VI**

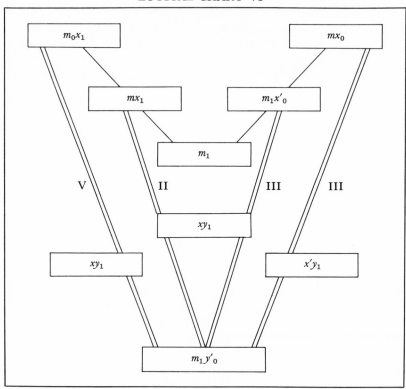

Interpretation of Chart VII

LOGICAL CHART VII

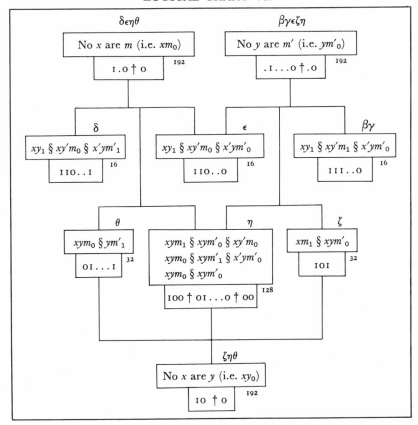

The interpretation of Chart VII is less clear, and although I suspect that there is a relatively simple interpretation of it, I have not been able to figure it out. Perhaps one of the readers of this book will be able to decipher it. To start him on his way, here are a few things about the chart that I have noticed. First of all, the bottom compartment, "No x are y," is derivable from the top two compartments ("No x are m" and "No y are m'"). That is,

$$xm_0 \dagger ym'_0 \ \mathbb{P} \ xy_0$$

Second, the three end compartments just mentioned, $(\delta\varepsilon\eta\theta)$, $(\beta\gamma\varepsilon\zeta\eta)$, and $(\zeta\eta\theta)$, are the logical products, by crossmultiplication, of the contents designated by the Greek letters heading them. For example, the contents of box $\delta\varepsilon\eta\theta$ is the logical product of the contents of boxes δ, ε, η, and θ.

Third, the small numbers attached to the individual compartments add up in the same way that the Greek letters conjoin. Thus,

$$\delta + \varepsilon + \eta + \theta = \delta\varepsilon\eta\theta$$

and

$$16 + 16 + 128 + 32 = 192$$

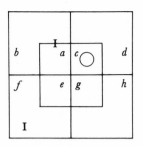

Finally, one can—provided one is prepared to deviate from Carroll's *original* rules—plot the larger numbers underneath each compartment onto Lewis Carroll triliteral diagrams. The reason I mention deviation from Carroll's original rules is that the rules given in Part I concern the plotting of *conjunctions* on diagrams, whereas here we are plotting *disjunctions* (statements connected by "or"). Presumably it was Carroll's aim, either in a chapter that is now missing or in a part of the book that was never written, to teach his readers how to put disjunctions onto his diagrams, and how to calculate with them. We may get some sketchy idea of how this worked as follows, using δ.

The task is to plot $xy_1 \S xy'm_0 \S x'ym'_1$ on a triliteral diagram. Plotting in the information given, we obtain the following diagram.

Reading the numbers entered in the box in alphabetical order, as indicated on the diagram, and entering dots where no numbers are entered, we reach 110..1—which is the number assigned to the δ compartment.

In this Lewis Carroll diagram, the only compartments used are a, b, c, and f. It turns out that these are the only compartments used throughout Chart VII, and they are the ones emptied by the three end compartments $(xm_0, ym'_0,$ and $xy_0)$. None of the disjuncts in any of the boxes or compartments on the chart, in short, gives us information about any compartment of the diagram not declared empty in one or other of the three end compartments.

In the pages from his notebooks illustrated opposite, and on pages 276 and 277, Carroll constructs further logical charts of the same type illustrated above. These charts, perhaps preliminary or supplementary to those set in type, may be interpreted as explained above. (**Morris L. Parrish Collection, Princeton University Library**)

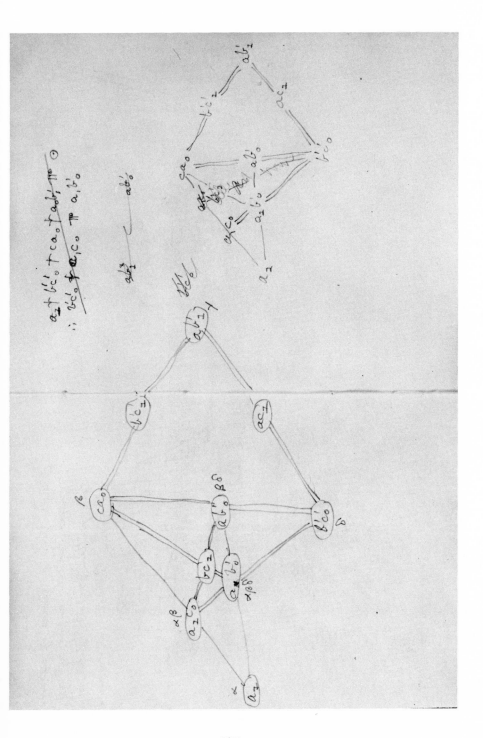

275

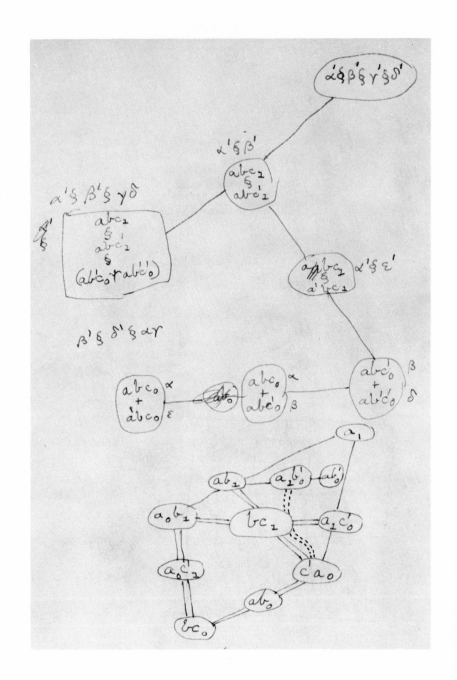

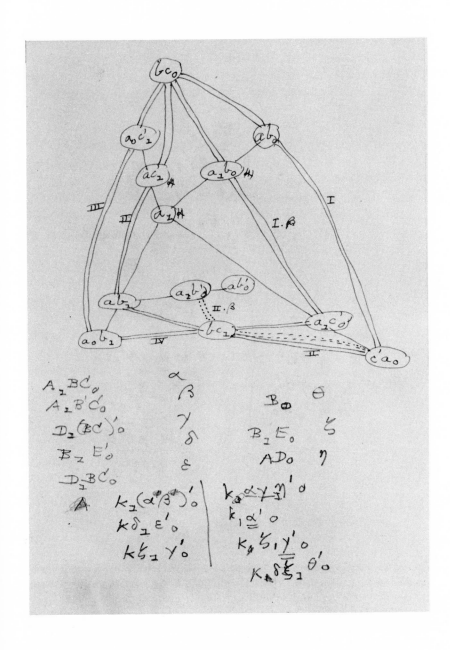

$$\dfrac{m\ a}{2}$$

$$\left.\begin{array}{l}a_1\\ ab_0\\ ac_0\end{array}\right\}\ \P\ b'c'_1$$

$$\therefore\ a_1\dagger ab_0\dagger ac_0\dagger b'c'_1\ \P\ \odot$$

$(1)\quad \left.\begin{array}{l}a_1 b_0\\ a c_0\end{array}\right\}\ \P\ b'c'_1$

$(2)\quad \left.\begin{array}{l}a_1 b_0\\ b'c'_0\end{array}\right\}\ \P\ ac_1$

$\left[\ \text{it really proves}\ a_1 c'_0\right.$
$\qquad\qquad i.e.\ ac'_0\dagger ac_1$
So the condensed form only
gives part of conclusion.

$(3)\quad \left.\begin{array}{l}ab_0\\ ac_0\\ b'c'_0\end{array}\right\}\ \P\ a_0 \equiv \left.\begin{array}{l}a\left(b'c'\right)'_0\\ b'c'_0\end{array}\right\}\ \P\ a_0$

$(4)\quad \left.\begin{array}{l}ab_0\\ b'c'_0\end{array}\right\}\ \P\ a_0 c_1$
$\qquad\qquad\left[\ \text{it really proves}\ ac'_0\right.$

$\big/$ the above condensed form is
of no practical use — a_0 (1) is
the only result worth notice.
(3) is a ~~similar~~ trio of premisses

Crucial to the argument of the next book, in which Carroll tackles more complicated multiliteral statements, is the assumption that a series of premisses when conjoined to the denial of the validly derived conclusion of those premisses yields absurdity. On the page from his notebook reproduced here we find him using this assumption, which is valid generally, in a triliteral argument. Thus when

$$a_1 \dagger ab_0 \dagger ac_0 \P b'c'_1$$

then $\quad a_1 \dagger ab_0 \dagger ac_0 \dagger b'c'_0 \P\odot$

BOOK XII
THE METHOD
OF TREES[1]

Chapter I ⚡ Introductory

The essential character of an ordinary Sorites-Problem may be described as follows. Our *Data* are certain Nullities, involving Attributes, some of which occur both in the *positive* and in the *negative* form, and are the *Eliminands*; while others occur in *one* form only, and are the *Retinends*. And our *Quaesitum* is to *annul* the aggregate of the Retinends (i.e. to prove it to be a *Nullity*).[2]

---

[1] Carroll sent the galley proofs of this book to John Cook Wilson on November 6, 1896, with the request that he return them. Fortunately he did not, and they are now in the possession of Mr. John Sparrow, All Souls College, Oxford.

The method presented in this book dates from July 16, 1894, when Carroll wrote in his *Diary*, "Today has proved to be an epoch in my Logical work. It occurred to me to try a complex Sorites by the method I have been using for ascertaining what cells, if any, survive for possible occupation when certain nullities are given. I took one of 40 premisses, with 'pairs within pairs,' & many bars, & worked it like a genealogy, each term proving all its descendents. It came out beautifully, & much shorter than the method I have used hitherto—I think of calling it the 'Genealogical Method.'"

[2] The definition given here of an "ordinary Sorites Problem" applies only to such problems in Fig. I. Thus a third method, the Method of Trees, is added to the Method of Separate Syllogisms and the Method of Underscoring described in Book VII, Chapter 2. But in this book we are still limited to the first figure.

Hitherto we have done this by a *direct* Process: that is, we have begun with two of the given Nullities, containing a pair of Eliminands differing only in *sign* (e.g. *a* and *a'*), and we have treated them as the Premisses of a Syllogism in Fig. I, and have combined them so as to form a new Nullity, not containing the Eliminands: This *Partial Conclusion* we have then combined, in the same way, with some other given Nullity: and in this way we have proceeded, gradually turning out the Eliminands, till finally we have proved, as our *Complete Conclusion*, a Nullity consisting of the aggregate of the *Retinends*.

In the *Method of Trees* this process is *reversed*. Its essential feature is that it involves a *Reductio ad Absurdum*. That is, we begin by assuming, *argumenti gratia*, that the aggregate of the Retinends (which we wish to prove to be a *Nullity*) is an *Entity*: from this assumption we deduce a certain result: this result we show to be *absurd*: and hence we infer that our original assumption was *false*, i.e. that the aggregate of the Retinends is a *Nullity*.

Chapter II ❧ Sorites-Problems with Biliteral Premisses

As the simplest possible example of this Method, let us take the original typical Syllogism in Fig. I, viz.

$$xm_0 \dagger ym'_0 \mathbb{P} xy_0$$

Here our *Data* are the two Nullities, xm_0 and ym'_0 involving the Attribute *m* both in the *positive* and in the *negative* form: and our *Quaesitum* is the Nullity xy_0.

We begin by assuming that the aggregate xy is an *Entity*: i.e. we assume that some existing Thing has *both* the Attributes *x* and *y*.

Now the *first* Premiss tells us that *x* is incompatible with *m*. Hence the "Thing" under consideration, which is assumed to have the Attribute *x*, *cannot* have the Attribute *m*. But it is bound to have one of the two *m* or *m'*, since these constitute an *Exhaustive Division* of the whole Universe. Hence it *must* have the Attribute *m'*.

Similarly, from the *second* Premiss, we can prove, as our *second* result, that the "Thing" under consideration has the Attribute *m*.

These two results, taken together, give us the startling assertion that this "Thing" has *both* the Attributes, *m* and *m'*, *at once*; i.e. we get

$$xy_1 \ ⫤ \ xym'm_1$$

Now we know that *m* and *m'* are *Contradictories*: hence this result is evidently *absurd*: so we go back to our original assumption (that the aggregate *xy* was an Entity), and we say "hence *xy* cannot be an *Entity*: that is, it is a *Nullity*."

Now let us arrange this argument in the form of a *Tree*.

I must explain, to begin with, that all the Trees, in this system, grow *head-downwards*: the Root is at the *top*, and the Branches are *below*. If it be objected that the name "Tree" is a misnomer, my answer is that I am only following the example of all writers on *Genealogy*. A *Genealogical* "Tree" *always* grows *downwards*: then why may not a *Logical* "Tree" do likewise?

Well, then, I put the *Root* of my Tree at the top. It consists of the aggregate *xy*: and the mere writing down of these two Letters is to be understood to mean (using the regular form of a *Reductio ad Absurdum*) "The aggregate *xy* shall be a *Nullity*: for, if not, let it be an *Entity*; that is, let a certain existing Thing have the two Attributes, *x* and *y*."

Underneath this *xy* I then place the Letter *m'* (this is part of the *Stem* of our Tree): and on its left-hand side I place the Number 1, followed by a full-stop, so that our Tree is now

$$\boxed{\begin{array}{c} xy \\ 1.m' \end{array}}$$

The meaning of this is, that the "Thing," which is assumed to have the two Attributes *x* and *y*, *must also* have the Attribute *m'*: and the Number 1 refers you to the *first* Premiss as my authority for this assertion.

Next, I place the Letter *m* on the right-hand side of *m'*, and the Number 2, followed by a comma, on the *left*-hand side of the 1, so that our Tree now is

$$\boxed{\begin{array}{c} xy \\ 2,1.m'm \end{array}}$$

This means that the Thing *must also* have the Attribute *m* (i.e. that *xym'm* is an *Entity*), and that my authority, for asserting this, is the *second* Premiss. (Observe that the two *Letters*, in the lower line, are to be read *from left to right*, but the two *Reference-Numbers from right to left*.)

Now we know that *m'* and *m* are *Contradictories*: hence it is impossible for an Aggregate, which contains them *both*, to be an *Entity*: hence it is a *Nullity*. And *this* fact I indicate by drawing a little *circle* (representing a *nought*) underneath, so that our Tree now is

$$xy$$
$$2,1.m'm$$
$$\bigcirc$$

The meaning of the circle is "The aggregate of Attributes, beginning at the Root, down to this point, is a *Nullity*."

Next, I place, underneath the little circle, the Conclusion $\therefore xy_0$, so that the Tree now is

$$xy$$
$$2,1.m'm$$
$$\bigcirc$$
$$\therefore xy_0$$

The meaning of the last line is "We have now proved, from the assumption that *xy* was an *Entity*, that this aggregate, *xym'm*, must be an *Entity*. But it is evidently a *Nullity*. Which is *absurd*. Hence our assumption was *false*. Hence we have a right to say "Therefore *xy* is a *Nullity*."

I will now exhibit, in one view, the whole Tree, bit by bit, with the meaning of each bit set against it.

xy	If possible, let *xy* be an *Entity*: i.e., let some existing Thing have the two Attributes *x* and *y*.
$2,1.m'm$	Then, by Premisses 1, 2, this Thing must *also* have the Attributes *m'* and *m*; i.e., *xym'm* must be an *Entity*.
$\bigcirc$	Now this aggregate (*xym'm*) is a *Nullity* (since it contains *m'* and *m*, which we know to be *Contradictories*).
$\therefore xy_0$	This result, that *xym'm* is both an *Entity* and a *Nullity*, is absurd. Hence our original assumption was *false*. Therefore *xy* is a *Nullity*.

All this magnificent machinery, used to prove one single Syllogism, may perhaps remind the Reader of the proverbial absurdity of using a Nasmyth-hammer to crack a nut: but we shall find, when we get a little further in the subject, and begin to deal with more complex Problems, that our machinery is none too costly for the purpose.

My next example shall be a Sorites-Problem, with *five* Premisses, but still keeping to that childishly simple kind of Premiss (the *only* kind, as I pointed out in Part I, pp. 250–251, with which the ordinary Logical text-books venture to deal), the *Biliteral* Nullity. I will take, from Book VIII, Chapter III, §3, 8 of Part I, the twenty-third Example, viz.

$$\overset{1}{b'_1 a_0} \dagger \overset{2}{de'_0} \dagger \overset{3}{h_1 b_0} \dagger \overset{4}{ce_0} \dagger \overset{5}{d'_1 a'_0}$$

Here we can easily see, by inspection, that a, b, d, e, are the four *Eliminands*, and that c and h are *Retinends*. (As the Reader already knows, we cannot have more than *four* Eliminands, with *five* Premisses, though of course the number of *Retinends* is unlimited.)

I begin by placing ch at the top of the paper, as the *Root*. And I then look through the Premisses for the Letter c. I find it in No. 4, which tells me that c and e are *incompatible*. Hence the Thing which I have assumed to have the Attributes c and h, *cannot* have the Attribute e. Hence it *must* have the Attribute e'. And this I express by placing e' underneath with the Reference-Number 4 on the left.

The Tree is now

$$\boxed{\begin{array}{c} ch \\ 4.e' \end{array}}$$

Next, I look for h among the Premisses. I find it in No. 3, which author-ises me to say that b' is *another* Attribute that the Thing *must* have (since it cannot have b). So I place b' in the same line with e', and its Reference-Number 3, followed by a comma, away to the left.

The Tree is now

$$\boxed{\begin{array}{c} ch \\ 3,4.e'b' \end{array}}$$

Next, I look for e' and b' among the Premisses. I find them in Nos. 2 and 1, which authorise me to assert that d' and a' are *also* necessary Attributes of the Thing; that is, to assert that the whole aggregate $che'b'd'a'$ is an *Entity*.

The Tree is now

$$
\boxed{
\begin{array}{c}
ch \\
3,4.e'b' \\
1,2.d'a'
\end{array}
}
$$

Next, I look for d' and a' among the Premisses. I find them *together*, in No. 5, which asserts that the pair $d'a'$ is a *Nullity*, and therefore authorises me to assert that the whole aggregate $che'b'd'a'$ is a *Nullity*.

The tree is now

$$
\boxed{
\begin{array}{c}
ch \\
3,4.e'b' \\
1,2.d'a' \\
5.\bigcirc
\end{array}
}
$$

Hence I may write underneath this, $\therefore ch_0$, and the Tree is complete.

I now examine the Premisses, to see whether either c or h is given as *existing*. I find that, in No. 3, h is so given. So I write the full Conclusion thus:

$$
\therefore ch_0 \dagger h_1; \quad \text{i.e. } h_1 c_0
$$

I will now exhibit, in one view, the whole Tree, in the same form as in the previous example.

ch	If possible let ch be an *Entity*: i.e. let some existing Thing have the two Attributes c and h.
$3,4.e'b'$	Then, by Premisses 4, 3, this Thing must *also* have the Attributes e' and b'.
$1,2.d'a'$	Hence, by Premisses 2, 1, it must *also* have the Attributes d' and a': the aggregate $che'b'd'a'$ must be an *Entity*.
5. $\bigcirc$	Now, by Premiss 5, this aggregate ($che'b'd'a'$) is a *Nullity* (since it contains the aggregate $d'a'$, which we know, by Premiss 5, to be a *Nullity*).
$\therefore ch_0 \dagger h_1$; i.e. $h_1 c_0$	(This result, that $che'b'd'a'$ is both an *Entity* and a *Nullity*, is *absurd*. Hence our original assumption was *false*.) Therefore ch is a *Nullity*. And we also know that h exists. Hence "All h are c'."

Here it will be well to pause for a moment in order to point out the beautiful fact that this "Tree" argument may be *verified*, by converting the *Tree* into a *Sorites*. And this may be done by the extremely simple rule of beginning at the *lower* end, and taking the rows of Reference-numbers *upwards* instead of *downwards*, viz. in the order 5, 2, 1, 4, 3.[1] The result will be

$$5 \quad 2 \quad 1 \quad 4 \quad 3$$
$$d'a' \dagger de' \dagger b'a \dagger ce \dagger hb$$

which proves ch_0, as the Reader will see for himself, if he will take the trouble to copy it out, and to underscore the Eliminands.

Chapter III ☜ Sorites-Problems with Triliteral and Multiliteral Premisses

The Sorites-Problems, hitherto discussed, have involved *Biliteral* Premisses only: the admission of *Triliteral*, and *Multiliteral*, Premisses introduces a new feature in the construction of Trees, which needs some preliminary explanation.

Suppose we are in the course of constructing a Tree, and have just proved that the existing "Thing," which we have assumed to possess the Retinends, must also possess the Attribute *a*. If, on looking up *a* in the Register, we find a Premiss containing it along with only *one* other Eliminand, *b*, of course we conclude, as in the previous Chapter, that, since the "Thing" *cannot* have the Attribute *b*, it *must* have the Contradictory of *b*, i.e. *b'*. But suppose there is no such Premiss: suppose the only one we can find, containing *a*, contains *two* other Eliminands, *b* and *c*, what conclusion can we draw from *this* Nullity? We may say, of course, "Since the Thing *cannot* have the Pair of Attributes *bc*, it *must* have the

---

[1] This sentence has been corrected following the rendering of a memorandum dated November 13, 1896, preserved in the Dodgson Family Collection in the Guildford Museum and Muniment Room.

Contradictory to it." But what *is* the Contradictory to a *Pair* of Attributes? The simplest way, I think, of answering this question, is to imagine our Univ. divided, by two successive Dichotomies, for these two Attributes. We know that this will give us the *four* Classes, *bc*, *bc'*, *b'c*, *b'c'*; and that in *one* of these four the Thing is bound to be; and that it is barred, by the Nullity we have just found, from being in the *first* of these four Classes. Hence it *must* be in some one of the other *three*, which together constitute the *Contradictory* to the Class *bc*: i.e. it *must* have some one of the *three* Pairs of Attributes, *bc'*, *b'c*, *b'c'*.

Now we might, if we liked, state the result in this way, and proceed to consider what would happen in each of these *three* events. But it would be a cumbrous process. If we were to treat a *Quadriliteral* Nullity on the same principle, we should have to allow the Thing the choice of *seven* different events, each of which we should have to investigate separately; and, with a *Quintiliteral* Nullity there would be *fifteen*!

But we may easily *group* these *three* Classes under *two* headings: and the simplest way of doing so is to remember that *bc* is the *only* one, of these four Pairs of Attributes, which contains neither *b'* nor *c'*: i.e., every *other* Pair contains either *b'* or *c'*. Hence we are authorised to say the Thing *must* have either *b'* or *c'*. In other words we may say the Thing must have either the Contradictory of *b* or the Contradictory of *c*.[1]

[Similarly, if the Nullity contained *ab'c*, we should say the Thing must have either *b* or *c'*. If the Nullity contained *ab'c'*, we should say the Thing *must* have either *b* or *c*.]

The Reader will easily see that the *three* possible Pairs, *bc'*, *b'c*, *b'c'*, can be grouped under these *two* headings. Under *b'* we can place *b'c* and *b'c'*; and under *c'* we can place *bc'* and *b'c'*.

This is, of course, a case of *overlapping*, or what is called "Cross Division," since *b'c'* appears under *both* headings. Now there is no reason to be so lavish of accommodation for this pampered Class *b'c'*: it ought to be quite content with *one* appearance. So we may fairly say it shall *not* appear under the heading *b'*: *that* heading shall contain the Class *b'c* only. This result we can secure by tacking on to *b'* the Letter *c*; so that the two

---

[1] When defining the "Contradictory of a Pair of Attributes," e.g., *(a'b')'*, Carroll observes what contemporary logicians call "DeMorgan's Laws." He makes this clear in a letter to John Cook Wilson of November 11, 1896, where he explains, " *(BC')'* is equivalent to *(B'* or *C)*; and *(B'C)'* is equivalent to *(B* or *C')*."

headings will be $b'c$ and c'.   Or we may, if we prefer it, say it shall *not* appear under the heading c': *that* heading shall contain the Class bc' only. And *this* result we can secure by tacking on c' the Letter b; so that the two headings will be b' and $c'b$.   It is worthwhile to note that, in *each* case, we tack on, to *one* of the single Letters, the *Contradictory* of the *other*: this fact should be remembered as a *rule*.

[Thus, if we found a Premiss proving that the Thing *could not* have the Pair of Attributes $b'c$, we might say it *must* have b or c'.   And we might afterwards tack on, at pleasure, either c to b, making the two headings bc and c', or b' to c', making them b and $c'b'$.]

We have now got a Rule of Procedure, to be observed whenever we are obliged to *divide* our Tree into *two* Branches, and, instead of saying the Thing *must* have this *one* Attribute, we say it *must* have one or other of these *two* Attributes.

I will now take some Sorites-Problems containing "Barred" Premisses. We shall find that the Method of Trees saves us a great deal of the trouble entailed by the earlier process.[2]   In that earlier process we were obliged to keep a careful watch on all the Barred Premisses, so as to be sure not to use any such Premiss until all its "Bars" had appeared in that Sorites. In this new Method, the Barred Premisses all take care of themselves: and we shall see, when we come to "verify" our Tree, by translating it into Sorites-form that no Barred Premiss will venture to make its appearance until all its Bars have been duly accounted for.

My first example shall be

$$\overset{1}{d'n'_1m'_0} \dagger \overset{2}{ka'_1c'_0} \dagger \overset{3}{le_1m_0} \dagger \overset{4}{dh_1k'_0} \dagger \overset{5}{h'la'_0} \dagger \overset{6}{hm'_1b'_0} \dagger \overset{7}{a'bn_0} \dagger \overset{8}{am'_1e_0}$$

Here we see that some of the Letters occur more than once: for instance, h occurs in Nos. 4 and 6, in the *positive* form, and in No. 5 in the *negative* form.   Hence, when we ask the question, as to any particular Letter, "In *which* of the Premisses does it occur?", we should have to interrupt the construction of our Tree, in order to hunt through the whole Set of Premisses.   To avoid this necessity, it will be convenient to draw up, once for all, a "Register of Attributes," from which we get, at a glance,

---

[2] The method of "Barred Premisses" is not discussed again in the surviving manuscript, but was apparently a method for treating multiliteral sori- teses in the first figure which is related to the underscoring method presented in Part I.   For an example see Book XIII, Chapter XII.

the required information. The rule, for making such a Register, is as follows:

> At the left margin of the paper draw a short vertical line, and above it, a little to the right, place the letter *a*: and under it place *two* rows of numbers, the *upper* row referring to the Premises where *a* occurs in the *positive* form, and the *lower* to those where it occurs in the *negative* form: then draw another short vertical, to divide the *a*'s from the *b*'s, write *b* over the next space, and proceed as before.

Thus, in the present example, after drawing the first vertical and writing *a* above, we look through the Premises, to see which of them contain *a* or *a'*. In No. 2, we find *a'*: so we write 2 in the *lower* line: in Nos. 5 and 7, we find two more: so we write 5, 7, still in the *lower* line: lastly, in No. 8, we find *a*: so we write 8 in the *upper* line: then we draw another vertical, and write *b* over the next space. The beginning of the Register will now be

$$\begin{array}{c|c}
a & b \\
8 & \\
2, 5, 7 &
\end{array}$$

I recommend my Reader to copy out these seven Premises at the top of a large sheet of paper, and underneath them to construct a Register of Attributes for himself, which he can then compare with the one here given, to satisfy himself that he has made no mistake. The Register is as follows:

$$\begin{array}{c|cc|cc|cc|c|cc|c}
a & b & c & d & e & h & k & l & m & & n \\
8 & 7 & & 4 & 3, 8 & 4, 6 & 2 & 3, 5 & 3 & & 7 \\
2, 5, 7 & 6 & 2 & 1 & & 5 & 4 & & 1, 6, 8 & & 1
\end{array}$$

This result we had better *verify*, before going further, by the following rule:

> Name the Letters in No. 1, in alphabetical order: then look them up in the Register, and see that 1 occurs in its proper place under each. Then name the Letters in No. 2: and so on.

Thus, in this example, we look at No. 1, and say (naming the letters in alphabetical order) "*d*-dash, *n*-dash, *m*-dash." Then we look up *d*, *n*, and *m* in the Register, and satisfy ourselves that *each* of them has a 1 under it in the *lower* line. Then we look at No. 2, and say "*a*-dash, *c*-dash, *k*," and proceed as before.

This Register not only enables us to see, at a glance, in *which* Premisses any particular Letter occurs; but it also tells us that this Sorites-Problem contains *seven* Eliminands (every Letter, that has numbers under it in *both* rows, is an Eliminand), and *three* Retinends.   It also tells us that there are *three* Barred Premisses; since, under *a*, we see that No. 8 is barred by Nos. 2, 5, and 7; under *h*, that No. 5 is barred by Nos. 4 and 6; and, under *m*, that No. 3 is barred by Nos. 1, 6, and 8.   But these are *now* trifles, about which we need not trouble ourselves!

In working this Tree, I shall adopt a new plan, which I think the Reader will find beautifully clear and intelligible.   Instead of exhibiting the Tree, piecemeal, as I proceed, I shall simply give my *soliloquy* as I work it out, with the "stage-directions" (given in italics, between square brackets) showing what I *do*: and, if the Reader will simply take a piece of paper, and pen and ink, and will copy, at the top of his paper, the eight Premisses and the Register, and will then, while reading my soliloquy, follow the stage-directions, and thus *do all the things himself*, he will find that he has constructed the Tree for himself: and he can *then*, for his own satisfaction, compare his finished result with mine.   (Note that the letters [R.R.] will be used to represent the stage-direction *I refer to Register.*)

My soliloquy is as follows:

"So!   *Eight* Premisses, and every one of them *triliteral*!   However, there are *seven* Eliminands: so there ca'n't be any superfluous Premisses.   Well, the Conclusion *ought* to be $c'el_0$, of course."

[*I write, under the Register,* "There are 8 Premisses, 7 Eliminands, and 3 Retinends.   *Then, under that in the middle,* I write $c'el$.]

"Now, what can we do with c'?"

[R.R.]

"It occurs in 2 only: and *that* tells me that it ca'n't[3] be ka': so of course it *must* be (taking them in alphabetical order) a or k'.   That would force me to divide the Tree at the very Root!   Let's try e."

[R.R.]

---

[3] In a memorandum on these galley proofs dated November 13, 1896, Carroll explains his spelling of "can't" as follows: "Abbreviate 'do not,' 'can not,' 'shall not,' drawing a ver-tical line through, to indicate where the first word *ends*.   Also, remembering that 'Is't so' is *accepted* as an abbreviation for 'Is it so?,' interpret 'Can't be so.' "

TREE 1

$$
\begin{array}{c}
c'el \\
3.m' \\
8.a' \\
5,2.k'h \\
6,4.d'b \\
7,1.nn' \\
\bigcirc
\end{array}
$$

"It occurs in 3 and 8: and in 3 it is kind enough to have *another* Retinend with it, and only *one* Eliminand! Well, *this* Premiss tells us that *el ca'n't* be *m*: so of course it *must* be *m'*. Well, there's *one* Letter for the Stem, at any rate!"

[*I place m' underneath c, and the Reference-Number 3, followed by a full-stop, on its left.*]

"Let's see if *l* gives us any other *certainty* for the second row."

[R.R.]

"No! No. 5 is the only other Premiss: and *that* would 'divide' between *a* and *h*. We must go on to the third row. What will *m'* do for us?"

[R.R.]

"*Hm*! There's good choice here! Nos. 1, 6, and 8. No. 1 divides between *d* and *n*. No. 6 divides between *b* and *h'*. No. 8 is more gracious: we've got both *m'* and *e* already: so this gives us *a'*."

[*I place a' under m' with 8 on the left.*]

"Well, now, what will *a'* do for us?"

[R.R.]

"*Again* we have ample choice! No. 2 does beautifully, as we've got *c* upstairs: so *that* gives *k'* for the fourth row."

[*I place k' under a' with 2 on the left.*]

"Any more results from *a'*?"

"Yes. No. 5, *h'la'*$_0$, and we've got *l* upstairs: so *that* gives us *h*."

[*I place h on the right of k', and 5, followed by a comma, away to the left.*]

"Any more?   No. 7 is the other one: and *that* would have to divide, as we haven't got either b or n upstairs: so we'll let it alone.   Now for the *fifth* row.   What will k' do for us?"

[R.R.]

"No. 4 is the only one: and that will do grandly, as we've got both h and k': so it gives us d' as a *certainty*."

[*I place d' under k', and 4 on the left.*]

"And what will h do for us?"

[R.R.]

"It occurs in Nos. 4 and 6.   But we've just *used* No. 4.   Let's try No. 6. Yes, that gives us b, as we have m' upstairs."

[*I place b to the right of d', and 6 away on the left.*]

"Now for the *sixth* row.   What will d' do?"

[R.R.]

"No. 1's the only one: *that* gives us n to follow, as we've got m' upstairs."

[*I place n under d', with l on the left.*]

"And will b do us any good?"

[R.R.]

"Yes, b gives us n', as we've got a' upstairs."

[*I place n' on the right of n, with 7 away to the left.*]

"Come! that finishes the thing: nn' is an absurdity!"

[*I draw a little circle under nn'.*]

"So now we've proved $c'el_0$.   The next thing is to examine the Premisses, and see if any of these three are given as *existing*."

[*I inspect the Premisses, by the help of the Register.*]

"c' occurs in No. 2 only—*non*-existent: e occurs in Nos. 3 and 8—and *exists* in No. 3, along with l.   So we get $c'el_0 \dagger le_1$; that is, $le_1c'_0$; that is, All le are c; and my task is done!"

[*I write, underneath the little circle, $\therefore c'el_0 \dagger le_1$; i.e. $le_1c'_0$; i.e. All le are c.*]

Here ends my soliloquy. If the Reader will now turn to p. 290, he will see what the Tree *ought* to look like: and, between *that* and the Tree he has constructed for himself, I *hope* he will find a considerable family-likeness! He should then *verify* his Tree, by writing out the eight Premisses in the *reverse* order (i.e. in the order 1, 7, 4, 6, 2, 5, 8, 3), omitting all subscripts, and underscoring whatever letters he can eliminate: and the final result *ought* to be $c'el_0$.

My second example shall be

$$\begin{matrix} 1 & 2 & 3 & 4 & 5 & 6 & 7 \\ hm_1k_0 & \dagger\ d'e'c'_0 & \dagger\ hk'a'_0 & \dagger\ bl_1h'_0 & \dagger\ ck_1m'_0 & \dagger\ hc'e_0 & \dagger\ ba_1k'_0 \end{matrix}$$

a	b	c	d	e	h	k	l	m
7	4, 7	5			6	1, 3, 6	1, 5	4	1
3		2, 6	2	2	4		3, 7		5

I will now construct the Tree, soliloquising as I do so.

"*Six* Eliminands, are there? And *seven* Premisses—none too many. And *three* Retinends, *b*, *d'*, and *l*. Well, those will make the *Root*."

[*I take a piece of paper, and write bd'l in the middle at the top.*]

"Now, then, what will *b* do for us?"

[R.R.]

"No. 4—why, that gives us a certainty at once! *b* and *l* are *both* of them *Retinends*."

[*I place h under b, with 4 on the left.*]

"No. 7?"

[R.R.]

"Divides. Now for *d'*. No. 2?"

[R.R.]

"Divides. And now for *l*. No. 4? We've got it already. So that ends our *second* row. Now for the *third*. What will *h* do? No. 1?"

[R.R.]

"Divides. No. 3?"

[R.R.]

"Ditto.   No. 6?"

[R.R.]

"Ditto.   We *must* divide, this time: let's go back to No. 1: 'first come, first served,' you know."

[*I draw a short line (say $\frac{1}{8}$ inch long) downwards from h; and, across the lower end of it, I draw a horizontal line (say 3 inches long); under it I write 1, and, from its ends, I draw two more short downward lines; and under them I write k' and m'.*]

"Now, shall we tack an *m* on to the *k'*?   Or shall we tack a *k* on to the *m'*? Let's see if either of them would be of any future use."

[R.R.]

"Well, *m* only occurs in No. 1, and *that* we've just used: so *m'* can be of no further use: but *k* occurs in No. 5 *also*: so perhaps it *may* be of use, further down."

[*I tack on k to m'.*]

Here I cease to soliloquise, for a moment, in order to inform my Reader that the *meaning* of this division of the Tree into two Branches is to assert that the (supposed) existing "Thing," which has the Attributes *bd'lh*, *must also* have *either* the single Attribute *k'* (which it may follow up with *m* or with *m'*, whichever it likes), *or else* the Pair of Attributes *m'k*.   I resume my soliloquy.

"Now, in the left-hand branch, what will *k'* do for us?"

[R.R.]

"It occurs in No. 3.   That'll do very nicely: we've got *h* and *k'* already, down this Branch: so that gives us *a*."

[*I place a under k', with 3 on the left.*]

"It also occurs in No. 7: and this gives us *another* certainty, as we've got *b* upstairs: so this gives us *a'*."

[*I tack on a' to a, and place a 7, followed by a comma, to the left of the 3.*]

"Well, *that* Branch is annulled, anyhow!"

[*I draw a circle under the aa'.*]

"Now for the right-hand Branch. What will m' do for us?"

[R.R.]

"It occurs in No. 5 only. However, that gives us a *certainty*, as we've got both k and m': so we *must* have c' to follow."

[*I place c' under the m', with 5 on its left.*]

"Now, what will c' lead to?"

[R.R.]

"It occurs in No. 2, and in No. 6. In No. 2, it gives us e to follow, as we've got d' upstairs; and, in No. 6, it gives us e' to follow, as we've got h upstairs."

[*I write ee' under c', with 6, 2 on the left.*]

"Well, that annuls the *right*-hand Branch: so the Tree is finished!"

[*I draw a circle under the ee'.*]

"So now we've got $bd'l_0$: let's see which of them *exist* in the Premisses."

[*I refer to the Premisses, the Register telling me where the Retinends occur.*]

"No. 4 gives us bl as *existing*: that'll do very well."

[*I write, underneath the Tree, $\therefore$ $bd'l_0$ † bl_1; i.e. $bl_1 d'_0$; i.e. All bl are d.*]

My reader may now refer to the Tree, given at p. 295, and see if he has drawn his correctly.

Observe that this Tree, though not containing a single word of English, expresses *symbolically* the whole of the following argument.

If possible, let $bd'l$ be an *Entity*; i.e. let there be a certain existing Thing, which has all three Attributes. Then, by No. 4, this same Thing *must also* have the Attribute h. Hence, by No. 1, it must *also* have *either k' or $m'k$*. If it chooses k', then, by Nos. 3 and 7, it must *also* have aa', which is absurd: if it chooses $m'k$, then, by Nos. 5, 2, and 6, it must *also* have $c'ee'$, which is absurd.

More briefly, if an existing Thing has the Attributes $bd'l$, it *must* also have *either $hk'aa'$ or $hm'kc'ee'$*. But each of these aggregates is impossible.

Hence *bd'l cannot* be an *Entity*.

Therefore it is a *Nullity*.

Tree 2[4]

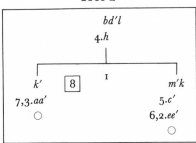

Here ends my soliloquy; and there is no logical *necessity* to do anything more: still it is very *satisfactory* to "verify" the Tree, by translating it into Sorites-form. There will be *two* Partial Conclusions, which I shall number as 9 and 10. But I must pause here, to instruct my Reader how to deal with *Branches*, in verifying a Tree. The simple Rule is, when there are two Branches, of which *one* is headed by a *single* Letter, and the *other* by a *Pair*, to take the *single* Letter first, turn it into a Sorites, and record its Partial Conclusion: then take the *double*-Letter Branch: turn it also into a Sorites—but there's no need to *record* its result, as we may go on at once with the Premiss used in the Branching: then take the recorded result of the *single*-Letter Branch: then we can go "upstairs," if there is any *Stem* leading down to the Branching. Thus, in the present instance, of the two main Branches, we take *k'* first. So our *first* Sorites consists of 3 and 7. So we draw a small square against *k'*, on the right side of it; and in that square we write 8. Our final Sorites will begin, in the *m'k*-Branch, with Nos. 2, 6, and 5. This takes us up to *m'k*. Then we cross

---

[4] *Illustration* to exhibit One of Carroll's Trees. The question: Do

$$\begin{array}{cccc} \text{I} & 2 & 3 & 4 \\ hm_1k_0 \dagger & d'e'c'_0 \dagger & hk'a'_0 \dagger & bl_1h'_0 \\ & 5 & 6 & 7 \\ & \dagger ck_1m'_0 \dagger & hc'e_0 \dagger & ba_1k'_0 \end{array}$$

prove $bl_1d'_0$?

The method: Assume that the Premisses are true and the Conclusion false; i.e., assume that *bld'* is an Entity: bld'_1, and reduce to absurdity.

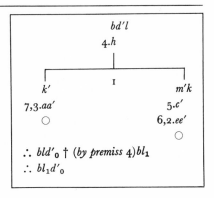

the bridge, by means of No. 1: then take in No. 8: then we can go upstairs, and take No. 4: and that *ought* to give us the desired Conclusion.

The following summary exhibits these two Soriteses in a handy form:

$$3,7 \; \P \; hk'b_0 \ldots (8); \qquad 2,6,5,1,8,4 \; \P \; d'bl_0$$

The Reader should satisfy himself that this is correct, by copying the above, substituting, for the reference-numbers, the actual Premisses, and underscoring all the Eliminands. The result ought to be as follows:

$$\begin{array}{cc} 3 & 7 \\ hk'\underline{a}' \; \dagger \; b\underline{ak}' & \P \; hk'b_0 \ldots (8); \end{array}$$

$$\begin{array}{cccccc} 2 & 6 & 5 & 1 & 8 & 4 \\ d'\underline{e}'\underline{c}' \; \dagger \; \underline{hc}'\underline{e} \; \dagger \; \underline{ckm}' \; \dagger \; \underline{hmk} \; \dagger \; \underline{hk}'b \; \dagger \; bl\underline{h}' & \P \; d'bl_0 \end{array}$$

I will now work out a rather harder Problem.

Let us take the Sorites,

$$\begin{array}{cccccccc} 1 & 2 & 3 & 4 & 5 & 6 & 7 & 8 \\ knl'_0 \; \dagger \; ch_1e'_0 \; \dagger \; bl'a'_0 \; \dagger \; d_1e'n'_0 \; \dagger \; ahc'_0 \; \dagger \; nb_1k'_0 \; \dagger \; le'_1m_0 \; \dagger \; d'h'n'_0 \end{array}$$

a	b	c	d	e	h	k	l	m	n
5	3, 6	2	4		2, 5	1	7	7	1, 6
3		5	8	2, 4, 7	8	6	1, 3		4, 8

There are eight Premisses, seven Eliminands, and three Retinends.

My soliloquy is as follows:

"No superfluous Premisses, *this* time. *Two* Barred Premisses, and a Barred Group! But no matter: the *Tree* will take care of all *that*!"

[*I write be'm as the Root.*]

"Now, what will *b* do for us?"

[R.R.]

"In 3 it divides: and in 7 it divides. Let's try *e'*."

[R.R.]

"In 2 it divides; but 7 suits us better: both *e'* and *m* are Retinends: so the Thing, that's got *all* the Retinends, *ca'n't* be *l*, and therefore *must* be *l'*."

[*I write l' under b, with a 7 on the left.*]

"Will *m* give us any more certainties?"

[R.R.]

"No: it only occurs in 7, which we've just used.   Now, what will *l'* do for us?"

[R.R.]

"It occurs in 1 and 3.   In 1, it divides: but we've better luck in 3, as *b*'s a Retinend.   So that gives us *a* to go on with."

[*I write a under l', with a 3 on the left.*]

"Now for *a*."

[R.R.]

"It occurs in 5 only: and that divides.   Well, there's no help for it, *this* time!   We must divide between *c* and *h'*."

[*I draw a short line downwards from a: across the lower end of it I draw a horizontal line: under the middle of this line I write a 5: from its ends I draw two short downward lines: and under them I write c and h'.*]

"Now, we've got the right to tack on *c'* to the *h'*, or *h* to the *c*, whichever we like.   Shall we do either?   Let's see if either of them would be of any use, further down."

[R.R.]

"*c'* is no use: it only occurs in 5, the one we're using.   But *h* occurs also in 2: so we'd better tack it on."

[*I tack on h to the c.*]

"Now what will *c*, or *h*, do for us?"

[R.R.]

"*c* occurs in 2—and *h* along with it: and *e'* is a Retinend: so that gives us a Nullity at once."

[*I draw a small circle under ch, with 2 on the left.*]

"Now, what can we do with *h'*?"

[R.R.]

"Well it divides in 8; and I'm afraid there's no help for it, as that's the *only* one it occurs in."

[*I make a Branching under h', with 8 under the middle of it, and d and n under the ends.*]

"Now shall we tack on d' to n? Or n' to d? Let's see if d' could be of any use further down."

[R.R.]

"No, it couldn't. Could n'?"

[R.R.]

"Yes, it *might*. Very well, then we'll tack it on, on the chance."

[*I tack on n' to d.*]

"Well, there's no use going back to the left-hand Branch: it's extinct. So we must go on with *this* one. Will d help us at all?"

[R.R.]

"Yes! It occurs in 4, along with n' and a Retinend. So here we get *another Nullity*!"

[*I draw a small circle under dn', with 4 on the left.*]

"Now there's only *one* Branch left to attend to. What can we do with n?"

[R.R.]

"n occurs in 1 and 6. In 1 it gives us k', and we've got l' upstairs: and in 6 it gives us k, as we've got b upstairs. And $k'k$ is an obvious *absurdity*. So this brings the whole thing to an end."

[*I write $k'k$ under n, with 6, 1 on the left.*]

"Well, that proves $be'm$ to be a *Nullity*. But do any of them exist *separately*?"

[R.R.]

"Yes, each *one* exists, by itself: but we're not told that any *two* exist together. Well, let's make b exist, then."

[*I write, underneath the Tree, $\therefore$ $be'm_0 \dagger b_1$; i.e. $b_1e'm_0$; i.e. All b are e or m'.*]

"So now the Tree is in full leaf!"

TREE 3

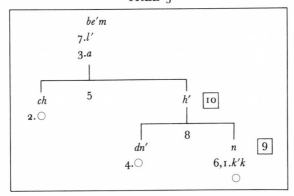

The Reader can now look above, and compare his Tree with the one there depicted.

The Verification of this tree shall now be given in a second soliloquy:

"Well, now to *verify* our result.   Where are the Partial Conclusions to come?   At the first Branching, of course we must take h' first: and, at the second Branching, we must take n first.   So the first Partial Conclusion must be at n: and it must be No. 9, as we've got eight Premisses."

[*I draw a small square on the right side of n, and in it I write* 9.]

"That first Sorites consists of Nos. 1 and 6.   Then, for the second Sorites, we must take the *two*-Letter Branch—the dn'-Branch.   So we take No. 4: then cross the bridge with 8: then take in 9: then we go upstairs, and record the result as No. 10."

[*I draw a small square against h', and in it I write* 10.]

"Then, for the final Sorites, we must begin with 2: then cross the bridge with 5: then take in 10; then we go upstairs, and take 3 and 7: and that *ought* to prove $be'm_0$."

The Reader should now write out these three Soriteses, in full according to the following summary, and do all the necessary underscoring, and thus satisfy himself that they really *do* prove the Conclusion.

$$1, 6 \ {\P} \ nl'b_0 \ldots (9); \qquad 4, 8, 9 \ {\P} \ e'h'l'b_0 \ldots (10);$$
$$2, 5, 10, 3, 7 \ {\P} \ e'bm_0$$

I will now take a still harder Problem, and solve it in the same way.

$$\begin{array}{ccccccc}
1 & 2 & 3 & 4 & 5 & 6 & 7
\end{array}$$
$$an_1b'_0 \dagger wm_1l'_0 \dagger csn_0 \dagger ar_1v'_0 \dagger e_1c'l'_0 \dagger mh_1t'_0 \dagger k_1n'_0$$

$$\begin{array}{ccccccc}
8 & 9 & 10 & 11 & 12 & 13 & 14
\end{array}$$
$$\dagger\, dr_1a'e'_0 \dagger rt_1w'_0 \dagger el'_1n'_0 \dagger a's'_0 \dagger db_1m'_0 \dagger v_1e'k'_0 \dagger bw'_1h'_0$$

a	b	c	d	e	h	k	l
1, 4	12, 14	3	8, 12	5, 10	6	7	
8, 11	1	5		8, 13	14	13	2, 5, 10

m	n	r	s	t	v	w
2, 6	1, 3	4, 8, 9	3	9	13	2
12	7, 10		11	6	4	9, 14

There are fourteen Premisses, twelve Eliminands, and three Retinends.

The Reader should now take a large sheet of paper, and copy the above fourteen Premisses at the top: then put the book aside, and make and verify his own Register: then compare it with mine: then copy the words, "There are fourteen &c.": and *then* he will be able to understand the following soliloquy:

"Fourteen Premisses, and only *twelve* Eliminands? There *may* be a superfluous Premiss. And *three* Retinends."

[*I write dl′r underneath the words* "There are &c.," *in the middle.*]

"Now for *d*. No. 8? It occurs there, along with *another* Retinend, *l*; but, even with that help, it has to divide. Let's try the other Premisses containing Retinends. They are Nos. 12, 2, 5, 10, 4, 8, and 9. No, it's no use! They all divide! So let's gq back to No. 8."

[*I make a Branching under d, with 8 under the middle of the horizontal, and a and e under the ends.*]

"Now, we may tack on *a′* to *e*, or *e′* to *a*, whichever we like. Will either of them do any good? Well, *a′* might be used further down—and so might *e′*. Then it doesn't matter *which* we take. Let's move *from left to right*— moving the other way would seem like writing *backwards*!"

[*I tack on a′ to e.*]

"Now, what does *a* give us? It occurs in 1 and 4. In 1, it divides. But, in 4, it gives us *v*, as we've got *r* upstairs."

[*I write v under a, with 4 on the left.*]

"Now for the right-hand Branch. Is *e* of any use? It's in 5, and 10. In 5, it gives us *c*, in 10, it gives us *n*."

[*I write cn under ea', with* 10, 5, *on the left.*]

"And will its partner, *a'*, help us? It occurs in 8 and 11; but of course 8 is no good, as we've used it in the Branching. However, 11 gives us another Letter *s*: so we've actually landed *three* fish in one haul *this* time!"

[*I place s on the right of cn, with* 11 *away on the left.*]

"Now we go back to *v*. Well, *that* only occurs in 13: so it's got to divide, I'm afraid!"

[*I make a Branching under v with* 13 *under the middle of it, and e and k under the ends.*]

"Now, is it worthwhile tacking on an *e'* or a *k'*? I see *e'* occurs in 8; but we couldn't use 8, down *this* Branch, as it would want *a'*, and we've got an *a* upstairs: so *that's* no good. Where does *k'* occur? Nowhere else, besides 13, I see. Then there's no use tacking on *either*. So we'll let them alone. Now we go back to our grand haul, *cns*. Where does *c* occur? No. 3? Why, that actually slays all three at once!"

[*I draw a circle under cns, with* 3, *as its authority, on the left.*]

"Now we return to *e*. Let's see: we've had *e* somewhere before. Oh, there it is, in the right-hand Branch! So this *e* can *perhaps* make use of the annulment of the earlier one, *provided that* the other *e* didn't need its partner, *a'*, to help to annul it, since *this e* has got *a* as a partner. *Did* it need it? What Premisses does *a'* occur in? Nos. 8 and 11. And was either of them used in the annulment? Yes, we used 11. Then I'm afraid this new *e* ca'n't get any help from the old one. It must manage its own annulment. What can we do with it? It occurs in 5 and 10. In 5, it gives us *c*: in 10, it gives us *n*."

[*I write cn under e with* 10, 5, *on the left.*]

"But we ca'n't tack on an *s*, *this* time, as we haven't got an *a'* to help us! Let's go to the *k*-Branch. What will *k* do? It occurs in 7 only: and *that* gives us *n*."

[*I write n under k, with* 7 *on the left.*]

"Now back to the left-hand again. What will *c* do? It occurs in 3—along with *n* luckily: so that gives us *s'*."

[*I write s' under c, with 3 on the left.*]

"And will *c*'s partner, *n*, do anything for us? Yes in 1, it gives us *b*, as we've got an *a* upstairs."

[*I write b after s', with 1, away to the left of the 3.*]

"Now back to the *k*-Branch. What can we do with *n*? Why, we've got another *n*, on the same level, in the *e*-Branch! So this one had better *wait* on the chance of being able to avail itself of the annulment of the other."

[*I place a dot under n, to indicate that it is "waiting."*]

"Now to the left again. What can we do with *s'b*? Well, *s'* only occurs in 11, and *that* needs an *a'*: so *s'* gives us no assistance. Will *b* do any good? It occurs in 12 and 14. In 12, it gives us *m*: in 14, it divides."

[*I write m under s'b, with 12, on the left.*]

"Any other Branch to go to? No, the other one is waiting: we must stick to this one till it's finished. What can we do with *m*? Well, it occurs in 2 and 6. In 2, it gives us *w'*: in 6, it divides."

[*I write w' under m, with 2 on the left.*]

"Now for *w'*. It occurs in 9 and 14. In 9, it gives us *t'*: in 14, it gives us *h*."

[*I write t'h under w', with 14, 9, on the left.*]

"Now, what will *t'* do? It occurs in 6 only: but *there* it comes along with *h*, and we've got *m* upstairs: so *that* annuls this Branch."

[*I draw a circle under t'h, with 6, on the left.*]

"Now, we've got an *n* in the other Branch, patiently waiting to learn the fate of its namesake on *this* Branch. So, now that *this n* has got itself annulled, the question is whether the waiting *n* can use the *same* annulment, in which case we need only *refer* to it, without taking the trouble to write it out again. Now this new *n* has the same ancestors as the old *n*, with the exception of its brother *c*, and its father *e*. So, if the left-hand *n* managed to get annulled *without* using either of these two kinsmen, then its annulment will serve for the right-hand one: if not I'm afraid the new n must devise an annulment of its own.   Now, *was c or e* used in that annulment?"

[R.R.]

"Yes! c was used in the very next row! it gave us $s'n$.   So *this n* will have to devise an annulment for itself—no, stay!   That s' was of no further use!   So, after all, c was *not* used in the annulment.   Well, then, was e used?"

[R.R.]

"No, e only occurs in 5 and 10; and neither of those was used in the annulment.   So, after all this new n *can* use the old annulment."

[*I draw a little square against the cn in the e-Branch, and another little square under the n in the k-Branch, just where I placed the dot.*]

"So now the Tree is complete, and we've proved the Nullity $dl'r_0$.   Now, are any of these Letters given as *existent*?   Let's see."

[*I examine the Premisses containing them.*]

"Yes, dr exist, *together*, in No. 8."

[*I write, under the Tree, $\therefore$ $dl'r_0$ † dr_1; i.e. $dr_1l'_0$; i.e. All dr are l.*]

TREE 4

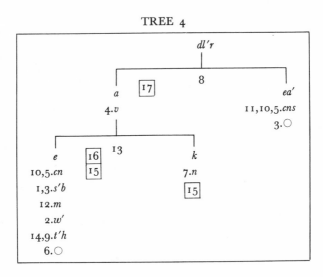

Here ends my soliloquy. But we had better *verify* our result, by translating our Tree into Sorites-form. This shall be done in a supplementary soliloquy.

"Well, now to *verify* this Tree. And first, what *reference-number* must be put under the *n* that we kept waiting so long? To answer this question, we must first settle in what *order* we're going to take the Soriteses that are to prove our Partial Conclusions. Let's see. At the first Branching, of course it's the *a*-Branch that must be proved first, as it's a *single*-Letter one, and the other is a *double*-Letter one. At the second branching, *both* are single-Letters: but of course we must take the *e*-Branch first, as it's the only one we can *prove*, to begin with, since it ends in a *circle*. So the first Sorites must run up as far as *cn*, and then record its result, for the benefit of the waiting *n*: that Sorites will consist of Nos. 6, 9, 14, 2, 12, 3, and 1. But wait a moment! *Will* it contain No. 3? No, of course it won't! No. 3 only served to give us *s'*, and *s'* turned out to be useless! Then the first Sorites will simply be 6, 9, 14, 2, 12, and 1. And we must call its result No. 15, as there are fourteen Premisses."

[*I write* 15 *in the little square against cn, in the e-Branch, and another* 15 *in the little square under n, in the k-Branch.*]

"Then the *second* Sorites had better take in the whole of the *e*-Branch, and record its result at the top. So *it* will be a *very* short one—merely containing 15 and 10: of course missing 5, as *that* was only wanted for the useless *c*."

[*I draw a little square against e, and in it I write* 16.]

"Then the third Sorites will have to work its way up the *k*-Branch. That is, it must begin with 15: then take 7: then cross the bridge, by means of 13: then take in 16: then go upstairs and take 4: and then we shall have to record its result."

[*I draw a little square against the a, at the top of the great left-hand Branch, and in it I write* 17.]

"And the *final* Sorites must of course run up the *ea'*-Branch. So it will begin with 3, 5, 10, 11: then cross the 8 bridge: then take in 17: and *that* ought to finish the thing, as there's no stem above that first Branching. So the four Soriteses will run as follows:

6, 9, 14, 2, 12, 1 ¶ 15;   15, 10 ¶ 16;   15, 7, 13, 16, 4 ¶ 17;
3, 5, 10, 11, 8, 17 ¶ $dl'r_0$."

The Reader should now write out these Soriteses, *in full,* and do all the necessary underscoring, and satisfy himself that they do really prove the desired Conclusion.

I will now go through a really long and hard Problem[5] of this kind, soliloquy fashion, and I think that the Reader, if he has the patience to work it through, taking my soliloquy as his guide, will then find himself fully competent to solve any *ordinary* Sorites-Problem: those, that have *special* features, will be considered in subsequent chapters.

The twenty-four Premisses of this Problem are as follows:

$$\overset{\text{I}}{Cl_1E'_0} \dagger \overset{2}{Av'_1D_0} \dagger \overset{3}{k_1m'_0} \dagger \overset{4}{lC'_1(b'n')'_0} \dagger \overset{5}{dsb_1t'_0} \dagger$$

$$\overset{6}{tD_1w'_0} \dagger \overset{7}{dr'a'_1A'_0} \dagger \overset{8}{vw_1B_0} \dagger \overset{9}{em'_1(r'b')'_0} \dagger \overset{10}{Ha_1c'_0} \dagger$$

$$\overset{11}{dtmav'_0} \dagger \overset{12}{dst_1A'_0} \dagger \overset{13}{Dn'r'b'_1z_0} \dagger \overset{14}{cE'z_0} \dagger \overset{15}{bs'_1l'e'_0} \dagger$$

$$\overset{16}{atE_1v'_0} \dagger \overset{17}{rDh'_1e'_0} \dagger \overset{18}{mt'_1D_0} \dagger \overset{19}{Anl'_1c'_0} \dagger \overset{20}{rdk'_1h_0} \dagger$$

$$\overset{21}{ztB'_1d_0} \dagger \overset{22}{nl'_1H'_0} \dagger \overset{23}{Et'_1z_0} \dagger \overset{24}{dzrA'_1a'_0}$$

Before making the Register, it may be well to point out that No. 4 means "All lC' are $b'n'$"; i.e. "All lC' are b', *and* all lC' are n'." Hence this

---

[5] A letter from Carroll to John Cook Wilson of November 6, 1896, as well as other correspondence and an undated "P.S." that must have been written in 1896, indicates that this problem is a variant of one due to Wilson. The letter of November 6 follows:

Ch. Ch. Nov. 6/96

MY DEAR WILSON,

I think I forgot to mention, in sending you that batch of Problems, that the "Active Jew" is No. 29.

I now enclose a proof of my "Method of Trees." Kindly return it when done with. You will find *your* Problem "treed" as the climax. The "peculiarities" therein, for which I value it (as I don't know how to *construct* a Problem containing such phenomena), and which you vainly besought me to describe (regarding my silence as a proof that I had been reading Mrs. Radcliffe's "Mysteries of Adolpho"), are those three places where I have inserted a double-line. I think you will see, if you have the patience to read so far, that it was *impossible*, without first explaining the "Method," to give an intelligible account of the "peculiarities."

Truly yours,
C. L. DODGSON

Premiss really contains *two* distinct Propositions, which we might, if we chose, symbolise as $lC'_1 b_0 \dagger lC'_1 n_0$ (so that b and n must be reckoned as appearing in the *positive* form in this Premiss). If I have to use the *whole* Premiss at once, I shall refer to it as 4, simply; but, if I have to use either part *by itself*, I shall refer to it as 4*, or as 4**. Similar remarks will apply to No. 9. Hence the *actual* number of Premisses is twenty-six.

I recommend the Reader to copy these Premisses at the top of a large sheet of paper, and then to make the Register for himself, without looking at mine; then to verify it, by the method he has already learned (see p. 285); and lastly to compare it with the Register here given.

a	b	c	d	e
10, 11, 16	4, 5, 9, 15	14	5, 7, 11, 12, 20, 21, 24	9
7, 24	13	10, 19		15, 17

h	k	l	m	n	r	s
20	3	1, 4	11, 18	4, 19, 22	9, 17, 20, 24	5, 12
17	20	15, 19, 22	3, 9	13	7, 13	15

t	v	w	z	
6, 11, 12, 16, 21	8	8	13, 14, 21, 23, 24	
5, 18, 23	2, 11, 16	6		

A	B	C	D	E	H
2, 19	8	1	2, 6, 13, 17, 18	16, 23	10
7, 12, 24	21	4		1, 14	22

My soliloquy is as follows:

"Twenty-six Premisses, nineteen Eliminands, and three Retinends, d, z, and D. So there are *six* extra Premisses. Looks as if there *might* be some superfluous ones: and perhaps a *Retinend* might be spared: let's try."

[*I ascertain, taking each Retinend in turn, what Premisses would be lost by its omission: but I find they go faster than the Eliminands, and so give up the quest.*]

"No: there seems no chance of getting rid of a Retinend. So now for our Tree."

[*I write dzD at top of available space in middle.*]

"Now what can we do with d? It occurs in 5, 7, 11, 12, 20, 21, 24. Alas, they *all* divide! And so do the z's: and so do the great D's. Well, there's no help for it: we must divide at the very first start! Let's get a

biliteral division, if we *can*.   No. 21 is the first I can find, as it contains *two*
Retinends: so it merely divides for *t* and *B'*."

[*I make a wide Branching under d: under the middle of the horizontal line I write
21, and under the two ends I write t' and B.*]

"Now, is there any use tacking on *t* or *B'*?   Let's see.   Yes, *t can* be of
further use, but *B'* of none."

[*I tack on t to B.*]

"Now, for the *t'*-Branch.   5 divides, but 18 doesn't: it gives us *m'*.   And
23 gives us *E'*.   That's a good beginning."

[*I write m'E' under t', with 23, 18 on the left.*]

"Now for the *Bt*-Branch.   *B* only occurs in 8; and *that* divides.   However, *t* helps us in 6, and gives us *w*: in all the other Premisses it divides."

[*I write w under Bt, with 6 on the left.*]

"Now we go back to the *t'*-Branch.   What will *m'* and *E'* do for us?
m' occurs in 3, and that gives us *k'*.   In 9 it divides, even if we take 9
piecemeal.   *E'* divides in 1, but in 14 it gives us *c'*.   That'll do capitally."

[*I write k'c' under m'E', with 14, 3 on the left.*]

"Now for the *Bt*-Branch again.   What will *w* do?   It occurs in 8, and
gives us *v'*."

[*I write v' under w, with 8 on the left.*]

"Now we go back to the *t'*-Branch again.   What can we do with *k'* and
c'?   *k'* only occurs in 20, and *that* divides.   *c'* occurs in 10 and 19, but
they both divide.   Then we will take *k'*: *that* will give us *h'* and *r'* for our
Branches."

[*I make a Branching under k'c': under the middle of it I write 20, and under the
ends I write h' and r'.*]

"Now would either *h* or *r* be of any further use?   *h* won't, but *r* occurs in
three other Premisses."

[*I tack on r to h'.*]

"Now back to the *Bt*-Branch.   What will v' do?   It occurs in 2, 11, and 16.   In 2 it gives us A'.   In 11 and 16 it divides."

[*I write A' under v', with 2 on the left.*]

"Now back to that last Branching.   What will $h'r$ do? h' occurs in 17; and that gives us e at once, as we've got *three* of the four letters already. And r occurs in 9 (which we must break up, and take $em'r_0$ by itself), and that gives us e'.   No use troubling about 24: we've got our Nullity already."

[*I write ee' under h'r, with 9*, 17' on the left.   And under ee' I draw a little circle.*]

"Come, there's *one* Branch annulled already!   The r'-Branch is the only one we have to go on with, at present.   Let's see what r' does for us. It occurs in 7 and 13, and *both* divide.   Let's take 7."

[*I make a Branching under r': under the middle I write 7, and under the ends I write a and A.*]

"Now, would a' or A' be of further use?   Well, a' occurs in 24; but *there* it wants A' as a partner, which of course it can't have: so *it's* no use. Great A' occurs in 12 and 24; but in 12 it wants t, which it can't have; and 24 we *know* to be useless.   So there's no tacking on to be done, *this* time!   Now we go back to A'.   In 7 it divides: in 12 it gives us s': in 24 it divides."

[*I write s' under A', with 12 on the left.*]

"Now back to the left again.   What will a do for us?   In 10 it gives us H', as we've got c' upstairs.   We can't use 11, as it wants t, and we've got t' upstairs: and 16 wants E, and we've got E' upstairs: so 10's the only one."

[*I write H' under a, with 10 on the left.*]

"Now for the A-Branch. A gives us v in 2: in 19 it divides: a' occurs only in 24 (besides 7, which made the Branching) and there it wants A': so we can't use it."

[*I write v under A, with 2 on the left.*]

"Now away to the right again.   What will s' do?""

[R.R.]

"It occurs *only* in 15, and there, alas, it divides into *three* Branches! That's a very cumbrous process, and a thing to be avoided as long as possible. So let's draw a double-line under *s'*, to show that we've rejected its guidance for the present, and 'hark back' for something that will divide into *two* Branches."

[*I draw a double-line under s'.*]

"Now, will *A'* serve our purpose? Yes, that'll do very well: in 7 it divides into *a* and *r*. And we must remember, in case we succeed in annulling this Branch, to examine whether we've used this *s'* anywhere below; for, if not, No. 12 will be a superfluous Premiss—unless it happens to be used in the left-hand Branch."

[*I write A' under the double-line: and under A' I make a Branching, with 7 under the middle of it, and a and r under the ends.*]

"Now, would *a'*, or *r'*, be of any further use? Yes, *a'* could be used in 24: that will do."

[*I tack on a' to r.*]

"And *r'* could be used in 13. Which will be best? I see that *a* has appeared before. Now we go back to the left. What will *H'* do? It occurs *only* in 22; and *there* it divides. This is a *very* branchy Tree!"

[*I make a Branching under H', with 22 under the middle of it, and l and n' under the ends.*]

"Now, will *l'* or *n* be of further use? Yes, *each* of them might. *l'* occurs in 15 and 19; and neither of those demand impossible partners. And *n* occurs in 4 and 19. In 4 we could use it, as it wants *l* for a partner; but not in 19, as *there* it demands *l'*. Well, it's arbitrary *which* we tack on: let's keep *l* as the *single* Letter."

[*I tack on l' to n'.*]

"Now for the other Branch. What can we do with *v*? Well, it occurs *only* in 8. So we've no choice."

[*I make a Branching under v, with 8 under the middle of it, and w' and B' under the ends.*]

"Would *w* or *B* be of further use? No, *neither* of them. So we go away to the right again, and try our luck with the *Bt*-Branch. What can we do with *a*? It occurs in 10, 11, and 16. In 10, it divides: but in 11 it gives us *m'*: and in 16 it gives us *E'*."

[*I write m'E' under a, with* 16, 11 *on the left.*]

"Now for *ra'*. What will *r* do? In 9 it divides: in 17, ditto: in 20, ditto: but in 24 it gives us a Nullity!"

[*I draw a small circle under ra', with* 24 *on the left.*]

"Now we go back to the extreme left-hand again, and take the first Branch we find, that's still growing. What will *l* do for us? In 1, it gives us *C'*. No. 4 we ca'n't use, *yet*; though we shall be able to, *next* time we come this way."

[*I write C' under l, with* 1 *on the left.*]

"Now for *n'l'*. *n'* occurs in 13, which *looks* alarming, it's so full of Letters: however, we've got all but *one*, upstairs! So that gives us *b*: *l'* occurs in 15; but *that* would divide. It also occurs in 19; but *there* it wants *n* for a partner.[6] Well, we've got *one* Letter, anyhow!"

[*I write b under n'l', with* 13 *on the left.*]

"Now for *w'*. Well, *w'* occurs *only* in 6: and *there* it wants *t* for a partner, and ca'n't have it! So *this* Branch won't grow any further. Will the *B'*-Branch be more vigorous? No, not a bit of it! It only occurs in 21, and there it demands *t* for a partner! So *both* these Branches come to a deadlock. Well, there's nothing for it but to draw a double-line under each, and 'hark back' for some ancestor that will give us a Branching (for of course it ca'n't give us any *single* Letter) that we've not yet used."

[*I draw a double-line under w', and another under B'.*]

"Now, to hark back. Will *v* do? No. Will *A*? Yes, it will: we've not used 19 yet. So of course No. 2 would be a superfluous Premiss, were it not that it happens to be used in the *other* Branch."

---

[6] In a memorandum of November 13, 1896, addressed to Louisa Dodgson, Carroll replies as follows to a query whether this sentence ought not to have been written: "occurs in both 19 and 22, but in each wants *n* for a partner." Carroll replies "No. It's no use considering 22, as it was used for the *Branch*. I've made a mem. to explain that rule somewhere. I wish I could find a better word than "Branching"; yet a *Branch* doesn't grow so!"

[*In the open space under the two double lines I repeat A, and under it I make a fresh Branching, with* 19 *under the middle of it, and l and n' under the two ends.*]

"But stay! We've had *both* these Letters before! There they are, away on the left, supplied by No. 22, and calling H' their father! Well, these are *very* affectionate children: they don't seem to mind *who* is to be called their father, so long as *somebody* will own them! Well, *one* of the two sets must wait, anyhow, and see what happens to the other set. Which shall it be? This new set? Well, it could only utilise the experiences of the *other l* and *n'*, *provided* that they don't use, in their annulment, either *a* or H', for those do *not* occur in the ancestral line of this new set. This we must look into. I see that *a* occurs in 10, 11, and 16. It ca'n't use 10 again, as it used *that* before we got down to *l* and *n'*. No. 11 it ca'n't use, because that wants *t*: and No. 16 it ca'n't use, because it wants *E*. Well, *a* is safe, then. And H' occurs *only* in 22, which it uses in branching. So this new set of *l* and *n' may* wait."

[*I place dots under them.*]

"Now we go back to the *Bt*-Branch. What will *m'* do for us? It occurs in 3 and 9. In 3 it gives us k': in 9 it divides. And what will E' do? In 1 it divides: but in 14 it gives us c'."

[*I write k'c' under m'E', with* 14, 3 *on the left.*]

"Now we return to the extreme left. What will C' do? C' occurs only in 4; but that's very helpful, as it gives us *two* fresh Letters at once, b' and n'."

[*I write b'n' under C', with* 4 *on the left.*]

"Now for *b*. Well, *b* occurs in no less than *four* Premisses. It ca'n't use 4, as *that* would want *l* as a partner: but it *can* use 5; and that gives us s'. Also it *can* use 9 (or rather the second *bit* of 9); and *that* gives us e'. No. 15 it ca'n't use *yet*."

[*I write s'e' under b, with* 9**, 5 *on the left.*]

"Now we return to the *Bt*-Branch. What can we do with k'? It only occurs in 20, and *that* divides. Is *c'* of any use? Yes, in 10 it gives us H': 19 it ca'n't use."

[*I write H' under k'c', with* 10 *on the left.*]

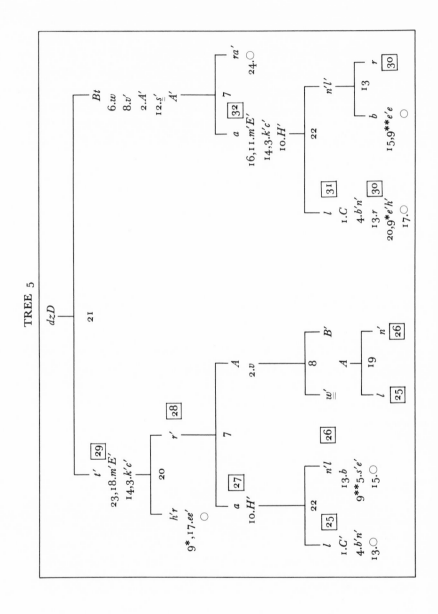

TREE 5

"Now we return to the extreme left.   What can we do with $b'n'$?   Well, b' occurs in 13, along with n', and also with D, r', and z, *all* of which we've got upstairs!   So here's *another* Nullity!"

[*I draw a small circle under $b'n'$, with 13 on the left.*]

"Now for $s'e'$.   Well, s' occurs in 15, which gives us *another* Nullity!"

[*I draw a small circle under $s'e'$, with 15 on the left.*]

"Come!   That finishes up *all* the branches on this side, except the two that are waiting, l and n'; and those we *know* are all right: we've discussed *that* matter already."

[*I draw two little squares, to hold reference-numbers, on the right-hand sides of the l and $n'l'$ which stand at the tops of the two branches just annulled: and under the new l and n' I draw two similar little squares, which will contain the same two reference-numbers.*]

"Now there's nothing left but the Bt-Branch.   What can we do with H'?   Can we utilise, for its benefit, the H' that has already appeared, higher up, in the left-hand Branch?   I must examine the Branches dependent from the earlier H', and refer to the List of Premisses, to see whether all these, used in its annulment, can lawfully be used *here*."

[*I do so.*]

"No, I find that the earlier uses 13 in *both* the Branches dependent from it: and that requires r': and *that* we haven't got *here*.   So *this* H' must get annulled in some other way.   What can we do with it?   Well, we must divide *here*."

[*I make a Branching under H', with 22 under the middle of it, and l and n' under the ends.*]

"Now, would l' or n be of any further use?   Yes, l' would."

[*I tack on l' to n'.*]

"Now what will l do?   In 1 it gives us C': 4 it ca'n't use *yet*."

[*I write C' under l, with 1 on the left.*]

"Now for $n'l'$.   What will n' do?   It only occurs in 13, and there it divides.   Let's try l'.   In 15 it divides: 19 it can't use—nor 22.   Well, then, we *must* divide.   Let's do it with 13."

[*I make a Branching under $n'l'$, with 13 under the middle of it, and b and r under the ends.*]

"Now, would b' or r' be of any further use? No, neither of them: so there's no tacking on to be done. Now for C'. In 4 it gives us two Letters at once, b' and n'."

[I write $b'n'$ under C', with 4 on the left.]

"Now for that Branching. What will b do? It ca'n't use 4—nor 5, since we've got s' upstairs: in 9 it gives us e': and in 15 it gives us e. So we've finished *that* Branch."

[I write $e'e$ under b, with 15, 9 on the left, and a small circle underneath.]

"Now for r. In 9 it gives us e': 17 it ca'n't use yet: in 20 it gives us h': 24 it ca'n't use."

[I write $e'h'$ under r, with 20, 9 on the left.]

"Now back to the l-Branch. Our last entry was $b'n'$. What will b' do? In 13 it gives us r: that's all it will do."

[I write r under $b'n'$, with 13 on the left.]

"Now back to the extreme right. What will e' do? In 15 it gives b'; but in 17 it gives us a *Nullity*! So we needn't trouble about 15."

[I draw a small circle under $e'h'$, with 17 on the left.]

"Now there's nothing left but the l-Branch. Our last entry was r: and, as we've just annulled an r on the extreme right, we may as well utilise it, if possible. Let's see if this new r can lawfully use 9, 20, and 17."

[I examine them.]

"Yes, it *can*."

[I draw a small square against the r at the top of the right-hand Branch, and another one, to hold the same reference-number, under the new r.][7]

"So now the Tree is finished! And we've proved dzD to be a *Nullity*. Let's see if any of them exist *separately*."

[I examine the List of Premisses.]

"Yes, dz exists in 24. So now for our Conclusion."

---

[7] Several steps are omitted by Carroll here.

[*I write, in the space below the Tree,* $\therefore dzD_0 \dagger dz_1$; i.e. dz_1D_0; i.e. All dz are D'.]

"Now, *was* No. 12 superfluous, after all?"

[*I examine the Tree.*]

"No, it wasn't: we had to use that s' in order to bring in No. 15. So, 'now my task is fairly done, I can fly or I can run'—only, I *ca'n't* fly, and, on the whole, I prefer *not* to run!"

Here ends my long (and, I fear, tedious) soliloquy. But does not my exhausted Reader, who has patiently obeyed all its instructions, feel a certain glow of pride at having constructed so splendid a Tree—such a veritable Monarch of the Forest?

We have now completed the *Solution* of this Problem. But it is always desirable to *verify* every such Tree, by translating it into Sorites-form: this will require a supplementary soliloquy, with stage-directions as before.

"Now let's *verify* this Tree. At Branching 21 I take the t'-Branch first: and in it, at Branching 20, I take r' first. Under r', at Branching 7, a and A are *both* single Letters. Well, let's take a first. Under a, of course I take l first: and, as that ends with a circle, we can begin with that Branch, which must be numbered 25, as there are 24 Premisses."

[*I write* 25 *in the little square placed against* l, *in the South-West corner, and another* 25 *in the little square placed under the* l *which belongs to Branching* 19.]

"Now, which Partial Conclusion shall we take for 26? Best take the other part of Branching 22."

[*I write* 26 *in the little square placed against* $n'l'$, *under Branching* 22, *in the South-West corner, and another* 26 *in the little square placed under the* n' *belonging to Branching* 19.]

"Then of course we go up this Branch for 27. The Sorites will begin with 26: then cross by bridge 22: then take in 25: then upstairs, and take in 10 —and there you are!"

[*I draw a little square against the* a *under Branching* 7, *which depends from* r': *and in it I write* 27.]

"Then, for 28, of course we must work up to r', just above. The Sorites will be—we must take the A-Branch first, as it isn't yet worked up to the top—the Sorites will be 26 (we *must* take the n'-Branch *first*, as it refers to the *biliteral* Branch $n'l'$): then cross by 19: then take in 25: then, upstairs and take in 2. Now we've got to A. Then cross by the 7-bridge: then take in 27: that finishes it."

[*I draw a little square against the r', that stands over Branching* 7, *and in it I write* 28.]

"Then, 29 must come at the top of the t'-Branch. The sorites must begin with the circle at the foot of the $h'r$-Branch. So it will be 17, 9*: then the 20-bridge: then take in 28: then upstairs, and take 3, 14, 18, and 23. That gives us 29."

[*I draw a little square against the t', at the top of the left-hand Branch, and in it I write* 29.]

"Now for the great Bt-Branch. At Branching 7 of course we take a: and, under it, at Branching 22, we take l: and that ends in a circle: so let's begin there. But we mustn't do it all at once: a Partial Conclusion must be recorded at r, for the benefit of the r-Branch just to the right, so the Sorites will be 17, 9*, and 20."

[*I write* 30 *in the little square placed against r, and another* 30 *in the little square placed below the r-Branch on the right.*]

"Then we had better have 31 at the top of this same Branch: and the Sorites will be 30, 13, 4, and 1."

[*I draw a little square against the l at the top of this Branch, and in it I write* 31.]

"Well, now for the $n'l'$-Branch. It doesn't matter *which* we take first, b or r: both are *single* Letters: but b wants working up: so of course we begin *there*. Our Sorites will be 9**, 15: then bridge 13: then take in 30: that brings us up to $n'l'$: then bridge 22: then take in 31: then upstairs, taking 10, 3, 14, 11, 16: then we must record, as a is the *single*-Letter Branch."

[*I draw a little square against the a, and in it I write* 32.]

"Now, there's only *one* more Sorites wanted: so there'll be no more recording to do. Our final Sorites must begin with 24, to take in the ra'-Branch: then cross by the bridge 7: then take in 32: then—do we go up to A' at once? Or do we take in s'? Oh, I remember! We are *not* to miss s': it's used down below.   Well, then, the Sorites goes on with 12, 2, 8, 6: then bridge 21: then take in 29: and that *ought* to give us our final Nullity dzD_0!' "

[*I write out these nine Soriteses, and do all the underscoring, and at last reach the desired Conclusion, when I smile a satisfied smile, and lay down my pen with a sigh of relief.*]

The Method of Trees
APPENDIX

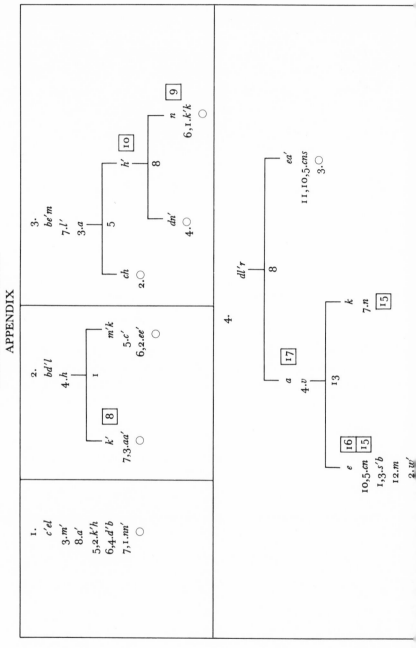

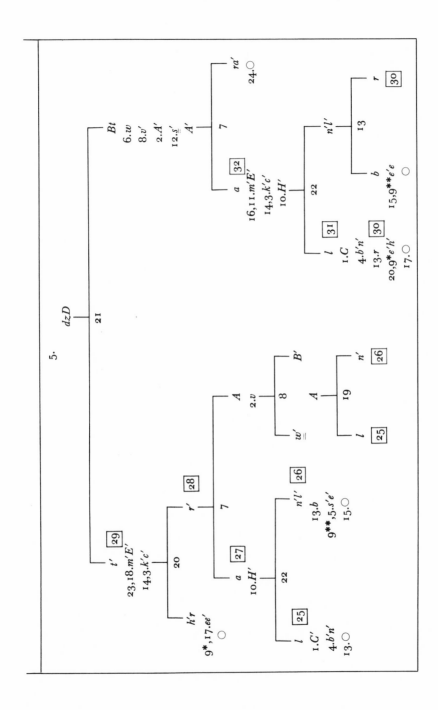

BOOK XIII
SOME PROBLEMS TO BE SOLVED BY THE METHODS OF PART II[1]

Chapter I ⚶ Introductory

[1] Eight problems in this book (Chapters III–X) present versions of problems that Carroll introduced in the "Appendix Addressed to Teachers" in successive editions of Part I of *Symbolic Logic* to provide his readers with a "taste of what is coming" in Part II. In addition to the versions given in the fourth edition, I have appended, where interesting, earlier versions of some of the problems.

Several of these problems were attempted by John Cook Wilson; and from Carroll's letters to Wilson we can get some idea, indicated below where appropriate, of his own answers to these problems, and of the way in which he deploys the "Method of Trees," as explained in the preceding book, to solve certain problems. In the present book the Method of Trees is applied not only to problems in the first figure, but also to rather more complicated problems that contain entity premisses.

I have also incorporated some problems from Carroll's papers on logic, printed privately by him for circulation among his friends, where I could clarify the existing text by introducing them or where there was some indication that Carroll had intended to incorporate them into the final version of *Symbolic Logic*.

Although a few of the problems in this book are quite easy, most of them are moderately difficult and some of them are extremely hard. I have provided solutions to some of the problems in order to give the reader a start.

I present here several Problems.　I shall be very glad to receive, from any reader, who thinks he has solved any one of them (more especially if he has done so *without* using any Method of Symbols), what he conceives to be its completed Conclusion.

It may be well to explain again what I mean by the *complete* Conclusion of a Syllogism or a Sorites.　I distinguish their Terms as being of two kinds—those which *can* be eliminated (e.g., the Middle Term of a Syllogism), which I call the "Eliminands," and those which *cannot*, which I call the "Retinends"; and I do not call the Conclusion *complete*, unless it states *all* the relations, among the Retinends only, which can be deduced from the Premisses.

Chapter II ❧ Problems in Sequences[1]

1. (1) If all *a* are *b*, no *c* are *d*;
   (2) If some *a* are not *b*, some *c* are not *d*.
   Prove that, if all *c* are *d*, no *a* are *b*.

2. (1) If some *a* are *b* and some not, some *c* are not *d*;
   (2) If some *c* are *d*, either some *a* are *b*, or some *e* are not *f*.
   Prove that, if all *c* are *d*, and if all *e* are *f*, all *a* are *b*.

---

[1] These problems in sequences were printed privately by Carroll in his "Eighth Paper on Logic," December, 1892. For his advice on how to approach them, see the excerpts from the "Notes to the Eighth and Ninth Papers on Logic," printed as an addendum to this chapter. Since these problems, like the School-Boys Problem in the next chapter, may be worked by a "Method of Trees" similar to, although not identical to, that presented in the last book, I present here sample solutions to Problems 1 and 3 to indicate one possible way to work these problems. The solution will be contained in the terminal point of those branches that do not lead to contradiction.

TREE FOR PROBLEM 1

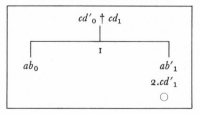

3. (1) If all a are b, no c are d;
   (2) If no a are b, and if some c are not d, some e are not f;
   (3) If some a are b and some not, and if some g are h, no e are f.
        Prove that, if some c are d and some not, and if all e are f, no g are h.

4. (1) If all a are b, and if some e are f and some not, some c are d;
   (2) If all e are f, and if some g are h, some a are not b;
   (3) If some c are d and some not, and if some e are not f, no a are b;
   (4) If some a are not b, and if some e are f, no g are h;
   (5) If some c are d, and if some g are h, some c are not d.
        Prove that, if some a are b, and if all g are h, no e are f.

Commentary on the Tree for Problem 1

We begin by entering the antecedent clause of the final sequence to be proved, "All c are d." In accordance with Carroll's directions, we break this up into the two propositions: $cd'_0 \dagger cd_1$. The information given by cd_1 is the denial of the consequent clause of the first premiss; hence, if cd_1 is given, the antecedent clause of the first premiss must be false. Thus, "Not-all a are b." Thus, either ab_0 or ab'_1. The first of these two possibilities is shown by the left-hand branch, the second by the right-hand branch. The second, or right-hand, possibility leads, by premiss 2, to the conclusion cd'_1. But this contradicts the information given at the outset that cd'_0. This branch thus ends in contradiction, leaving the left-hand branch, which does not lead to contradiction, as the answer, "No a are b."

The editor illustrates the tree for Sequence-Problem 3, but leaves the commentary on it to the reader's ingenuity.

TREE FOR PROBLEM 3

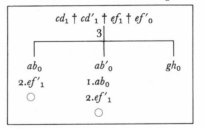

Addendum to Chapter II

Excerpts from the Eighth and Ninth Papers on Logic[2]

Notes

In attempting any of these Problems, the reader is requested to bear in mind the following assumptions, which I have made throughout:

---

[2] The first five sections of these notes are reproduced here. They provide general instructions from Lewis Carroll as to how to deal with problems in sequences.

(1) That the proposition "All *x* are *y*" is the sum total of the *two* propositions "Some *x* are *y*" and "No *x* are not *y*."

(2) That the proposition "No *x* exist" is the sum total of the two propositions "No *x* are *y*" and "No *x* are not *y*."

(3) That, in setting a Problem, I hold myself free to demand proof of a *less* conclusion than might be logically deduced from the premisses: e.g. if the full logical conclusion were "All *x* are *y*," I should hold myself free to set, as the Problem, "Prove that some *x* are *y*"; or, if the full logical conclusion were "No *x* exist," I should hold myself free to set, as the Problem, "Prove that no *x* are *y*." Thus, if it were possible to prove, from the premisses, that "no magistrates exist," I should hold myself free to set, as the Problem, "Prove that no magistrates take snuff."

(4) That, in setting a Problem of the form adopted in the first four of Paper 8, where the premisses and the conclusion assert certain *sequences* among certain sub-propositions, but neither assert nor deny any such sub-proposition taken by itself, I hold myself free to demand proof of a *less* result than might be logically deduced from the premisses; e.g. if the full logical conclusion were "If all *a* are *b*, and if some *c* are *d*, all *x* are *y*," I should hold myself free to set, as the Problem, "Prove that, if all *a* are *b*, and if some *c* are *d*, some *x* are *y*"; or, if the full logical conclusion were "If all *a* are *b*, and if some *c* are *d*, no *x* exist," I should hold myself free to set, as the Problem, "Prove that, if all *a* are *b*, and if some *c* are *d*, no *x* are *y*."

[It may be worthwhile to remark, in reference to the case last mentioned, that it would not be correct to say that the Problem, whose full conclusion is "If all *a* are *b*, and if some *c* are *d*, no *x* exist," is only soluble (i.e., that its conclusion is only true) if one of the terms be non-existent; for this conclusion merely asserts a sequence among the three sub-propositions, "All *a* are *b*," "Some *c* are *d*," "No *x* exist," and the *validity of this sequence* is entirely independent of the truth or falsehood of these sub-propositions taken by themselves. Thus, it would be quite logical, in the case contemplated, to give an additional premiss, viz. "some *x* exist," without making the Problem at all less soluble.

Supposing that this additional premiss were given, the *full* reply to this Problem, if set in the form, "Prove that, if all *a* are *b*, and if some *c* are *d*, no *x* exist," would be, "From the given premisses, omitting the last, we have proved the required sequence, viz. "If all *a* are *b*, and if some *c* are *d*, no *x* exist"; but it is also given that "Some *x* exist": hence, if the two propositions, "All *a* are *b*" and "Some *c* are *d*," were simultaneously true, the two propositions, "No *x* exist" and "Some *x* exist," would be simultaneously true; which is absurd: hence the two propositions, "All *a* are *b*" and "Some *c* are *d*," cannot be simultaneously true.

And the full reply to this same Problem, if set in the form "Prove that, if all *a* are *b*, and if some *c* are *d*, no *x* are *y*," would be from the given premisses, omitting the last, we have proved the sequence "If all *a* are *b*, and if some *c* are *d*, no *x* exist," which contains, as a portion of itself, the required sequence "If all *a* are *b*, and if some *c* are *d*, no *x* are *y*": but it is also given that "Some *x* exist"; hence two results follow: first, combining the two propositions, "No *x* are *y*" and "Some *x* exist," into the single proposition "All *x* are not *y*," we prove the sequence "If all *a* are *b*, and if some *c* are *d*, all *x* are not *y*"; secondly, we see that, if the two propositions, "All *a* are *b*" and "Some *c* are *d*," were simultaneously true, the two propositions "No *x* exist" and "Some *x* exist," would be simultaneously true; which is absurd: hence the two propositions, "All *a* are *b*" and "Some *c* are *d*," cannot be simultaneously true.

To make my meaning yet more clear, let me add a "concrete" illustration.   Supposing I had set a Problem, having, as its premisses, the rules enacted by an eccentric school-master as to the daily dinner, and, as its conclusion, "Prove that, when there is beef and spinach, there are no potatoes"; and supposing it were found that some of the rules led to the conclusion "When there is beef, there are no boiled potatoes," and that the others led to the conclusion "When there is spinach, there are no unboiled potatoes," so that the whole set of rules led to the conclusion "When there is beef and spinach, there are no potatoes": it would not be correct to say that this Problem is only soluble (i.e. that its conclusion is only true) if potatoes never appear on the table: for this conclusion merely asserts a *sequence* among the three propositions, "There is beef," "There is spinach," "There are no potatoes": and, if we were told "There always *are* potatoes on the table," this fact would not in the least affect *the validity of this sequence,* but would merely prove that the dinner never includes both beef and spinach, but that one or the other of them must always be absent.]

(5) That the proposition "*A* is true or *B* is true" is to be regarded as the contradictory of "*A* is false and *B* is false," and that this is the only state of things which it is meant to *exclude.*   Hence it is to be regarded as compatible with any one of the other three possible states of things, viz.:

(a) *A* is true and *B* false;
(b) *A* is false and *B* true;
(c) Both are true.

Chapter III ✕ The Problem of the School-Boys

All the boys, in a certain school, sit together in one large room every evening. They are of no less than *five* nationalities—English, Scotch, Welsh, Irish, and German. One of the Monitors (who is a great reader of Wilkie Collins' novels) is very observant and takes MS. notes of almost everything that happens, with the view of being a good sensational witness, in case any conspiracy to commit a murder should be on foot. The following are some of his notes:

(1) Whenever some of the English boys are singing "Rule, Britannia," and some not, some of the Monitors are wide-awake;

(2) Whenever some of the Scotch are dancing reels, and some of the Irish fighting, some of the Welsh are eating toasted cheese;

(3) Whenever all the Germans are playing chess, some of the Eleven are *not* oiling their bats;

(4) Whenever some of the Monitors are asleep, and some not, some of the Irish are fighting;

(5) Whenever some of the Germans are playing chess, and none of the Scotch are dancing reels, some of the Welsh are *not* eating toasted cheese;

(6) Whenever some of the Scotch are *not* dancing reels, and some of the Irish *not* fighting, some of the Germans are playing chess;

(7) Whenever some of the Monitors are awake, and some of the Welsh are eating toasted cheese, none of the Scotch are dancing reels;

(8) Whenever some of the Germans are *not* playing chess, and some of the Welsh are *not* eating toasted cheese, none of the Irish are fighting;

(9) Whenever all the English are singing "Rule, Britannia," and some of the Scotch are *not* dancing reels, none of the Germans are playing chess;

(10) Whenever some of the English are singing "Rule, Britannia," and some of the Monitors are asleep, some of the Irish are *not* fighting;

(11) Whenever some of the Monitors are awake, and some of the Eleven are *not* oiling their bats, some of the Scotch are dancing reels;

(12) Whenever some of the English are singing "Rule, Britannia," and some of the Scotch are *not* dancing reels, . . .

Here the MS. breaks off suddenly.   The Problem is to complete the sentence, if possible.

Some Answers to the Problem of the School-Boys

The School-Boys Problem was undoubtedly intended by Carroll to be treated as a problem in sequences. Since it is more elaborate than those presented in the preceding chapter, it produces a more complicated tree.

To solve the School-Boys Problem, the reader needs to bear in mind rules that are implicit in Carroll's argument and practice but that he does not state explicitly in this context. *The first rule* is that when the conclusion of a sequence is false, then at least one of the premisses of that sequence must be false. Thus if we are given the statement, "If all a are b, then no c are d," and are also given the information that some c are d, we know that not all a are b. Likewise, if we are given the statement, "If no a are b and if some c are not d, then some e are not f," and also know that no e are not f, then we know that either some a are b or no c are not d.

The second rule permits us to deal with what might appear to some readers to be "dead-ends" in "trees." If one reaches a statement in I and there is no obvious way to combine it with one of the premisses, then one may instead *immediately infer* from it certain information. Thus, for example, when one reaches xy_1, one may immediately infer that either xy'_1 or xy'_0. Similarly, if one reaches xy'_1, one may immediately infer from that that either xy_1 or xy_0. The reasoning here is that if some x exist and are y, then either all the x that exist are y, in which case xy'_0, or else some x are y', in which case xy'_1. The

rule allows the presentation of the two alternatives.

The third rule is that if one has two statements and knows that at least one of them must be false, and also knows that one of them in particular is true, then one may conclude that the other statement is false.

I present three solutions to the problem. The first two would have been acceptable to Carroll. Of these the first is shorter and more elegant, but also requires some thinking to produce it. The second is longer and is repetitive, but has the advantage of requiring little thinking, just a mechanical application of the rules. The two together may convey to the reader how much difference one's *strategy* makes to the solution of these problems.

For the first two solutions I shall use the following dictionary of terms:

$a =$ English boys
$b =$ singing "Rule, Britannia"
$c =$ monitor
$d =$ asleep
$e =$ Scottish boys
$f =$ dancing reels
$g =$ Irish boys
$h =$ fighting
$j =$ Welsh boys
$k =$ eating toasted cheese
$l =$ members of the Eleven
$m =$ oiling their bats
$n =$ German boys
$p =$ playing chess

Applying this dictionary to the wording of Carroll's problem, one obtains the following abstract representation of it:

1. If some a are b and some a are not b, then some c are not d.
2. If some e are f and some g are h, then some j are k.
3. If all n are p, then some l are not m.
4. If some c are d and some c are not d, then some g are h.
5. If some n are p and no e are f, then some j are not k.
6. If some e are not f, and some g are not h, then some n are p.
7. If some c are not d and some j are k, then no e are f.
8. If some n are not p, and some j are not k, then no g are h.
9. If all a are b and some e are not f, then no n are p.
10. If some a are b and some c are d, then some g are not h.
11. If some c are not d and some l are not m, then some e are f.

12. If some a are b and some e are not f. . . .

These may in turn be rendered in subscript form as follows:

1. $ab_1 \dagger ab'_1 \| cd'_1$
2. $ef_1 \dagger gh_1 \| jk_1$
3. $n_1 p'_0 \| lm'_1$
4. $cd_1 \dagger cd'_1 \| gh_1$
5. $np_1 \dagger ef_0 \| jk'_1$
6. $ef'_1 \dagger gh'_1 \| np_1$
7. $cd'_1 \dagger jk_1 \| ef_0$
8. $np'_1 \dagger jk'_1 \| gh_0$
9. $a_1 b'_0 \dagger ef'_1 \| np_0$
10. $ab_1 \dagger cd_1 \| gh'_1$
11. $cd'_1 \dagger lm'_1 \| ef_1$
12. $ab_1 \dagger ef'_1$

The first tree was built as follows. We began with the conditions described in the twelfth premiss, and put these in as the root of our tree. Since these conditions do not combine in any obvious way with any of the premisses, we may take ab_1, and immediately

Our first tree goes as follows:

infer from it ab'_1, as the left-hand branch, and ab'_0 as the right-hand branch. Beginning with the left-hand branch, we find that ab_1 and ab'_1 give us, in accordance with the first premiss, cd'_1. There being no obvious way to work this result into our premisses, we hark back to the root and immediately infer from ef'_1 that either ef_1 or ef_0, and we make another branching to reflect these two possibilities. Turning to ef_1, on the left, we find that that leads us, by the seventh premiss, to the conclusion that jk_0. (To explain: since we know that the conclusion of the seventh premiss is false, and also know that part of the antecedent clause, cd'_1, is given as true, we know that the remainder of the antecedent clause must be false; thus, jk_0.) Taking this result and using the second premiss, we reach gh_0, which in combination with the fourth premiss yields cd_0. We now proceed to the right-hand side of this sub-branch, to ef_0. By the eleventh premiss this yields lm'_0. And this in turn, by the third premiss, gives us the conclusion that not all n are p: in other words, either np_0 or np'_1. Our branching reflects these two possibilities. Taking the left-hand sub-sub-branch, we find that np_0, in combination with premiss 6, yields gh'_0, which in combination with the tenth premiss yields cd_0. Turning back to np'_1, we immediately infer from it that either np_1 or np_0. The first alternative, np_1, combines with premiss 5 to yield jk'_1, which in turn combines with the eighth premiss to yield gh_0. And gh_0 combines with the fourth premiss to yield cd_0. The second alternative in this

lowest sub-branch, np_0, yields gh'_0 by premiss 6, and this yields cd_0 by premiss 10. Returning now all the way to the right, to the original branching, we find that ab'_0, in combination with the ninth premiss, yields np_0. This in turn, in combination with the sixth premiss, yields gh'_0. And this again, in combination with the tenth premiss, yields cd_0.

Everywhere our final step is cd_0. Translating this conclusion, referring back to our original dictionary, it turns out that our result is, "None of the monitors are asleep."

I happen to know that this result is the correct one. For Carroll himself used the dictionary and abstract presentation that I gave above in his paper "A Challenge to Logicians," printed as a private pamphlet in October, 1892, and there his conclusion is shown as cd_0.[1] Again, on the recto of the back cover of one of Lewis Carroll's own copies of the second edition of *Symbolic Logic* (marked: "received June 13/96"), there is written by Carroll, "The end of the sentence must be 'None of the Monitors are asleep,'" This copy is preserved in the Harcourt Amory Collection of Harvard University, Houghton Library.

Our second tree for the School-Boys Problem uses the same dictionary and the same abstract and subscript form as did our first tree. But it makes less use of immediate inference and it grows in a rather repetitive way, some of the strings of sub-branches being identical. In the first tree, the only "end-point" or "fruit" reached was

---

[1] There are minor variations in the version of this problem given in "A Challenge to Logicians": premisses 3, 8, and 9 are rearranged, the problem as a whole being identical in structure to versions Carroll printed in the Appendix to the first three editions of Part I. Example 4 of the "Eighth Paper on Logic" is also similar in structure to this problem.

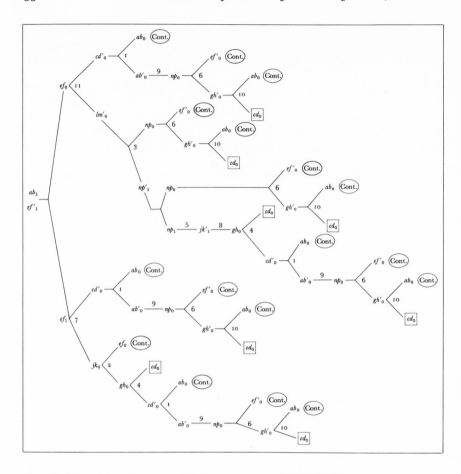

the conclusion cd_0. Here one stops in two ways: by reaching a contradiction, a statement that contradicts something previously given, or else by reaching cd_0.

The third tree for the School-Boy Problem relies on a different dictionary and an entirely different approach. It would not have satisfied Carroll and is added here for the interest of contemporary students of logic.[2]

The dictionary is as follows:

a = some English sing
b = some English sing not
c = some monitors are awake
d = some monitors are not awake
e = some Scotch dance
h = some Scotch dance not
k = some Irish fight
l = some Irish fight not
m = some Welsh eat
n = some Welsh eat not
r = some Germans play
s = some Germans play not
t = some eleven are not oiling

---

[2] This tree was built by Professor T. W. Settle. A resolution of the problem along similar lines was provided by Professor Norman Buder.

In subscript form the premisses are as follows:

1. $ab \mathbin{\P} c$ i.e., abc'_0
2. $ek \mathbin{\P} m$ i.e., ekm'_0
3. $rs' \mathbin{\P} t$ i.e., $rs't'_0$
4. $dc \mathbin{\P} k$ i.e., dck'_0
5. $re' \mathbin{\P} n$ i.e., $re'n'_0$
6. $hl \mathbin{\P} r$ i.e., hlr'_0
7. $cm \mathbin{\P} e'$ i.e., cme_0
8. $sn \mathbin{\P} k'$ i.e., snk_0
9. $ab'h \mathbin{\P} r'$ i.e., $ab'hr_0$
10. $ad \mathbin{\P} l$ i.e., adl'_0
11. $ct \mathbin{\P} e$ i.e., cte'_0

Since the problem is now in the first figure, we can treat it according to the method of Book XII. The register goes as follows:

This gives us ten eliminands, and three retinends. Try adh_0, which is $ah \mathbin{\P} d'$.

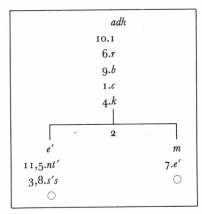

a	b	c	d	e	h	k	l	m	n	r	s	t
1,9,10	1	4,7,11	4,10	2,7	6,9	2,8	6	7	8	3,5,9	8	11
	9	1		5,11		4	10	2	5	6	3	3

Chapter IV ❦ The Pork-Chop Problem[1]

Version I

Problem: To achieve the complete Conclusion.

(1) A logician, who eats pork-chops for supper, will probably lose money;

---

[1] Two versions of this problem exist. The first and best-known version appears in the Appendix to the fourth edition of Part I of *Symbolic Logic*. The second version appeared in the first edition, and was apparently dropped after Cook Wilson showed Carroll that three premisses in Version II were superfluous. See the letter of November 1, 1896, printed below. There may have been yet another version of the Pork-Chop Problem—one consisting of seventeen premisses, for in a letter to Cook Wilson of October 24, 1896, Carroll mentions that he has "repudiated" the seventeen-premiss form of the problem, and asks Wilson to try the *amended* version of fifteen premisses, which is presumably the one first given here.

(2) A gambler, whose appetite is not ravenous, will probably lose money;

(3) A man who is depressed, having lost money and being likely to lose more, always rises at 5 A.M.;

(4) A man, who neither gambles nor eats pork-chops for supper, is sure to have a ravenous appetite;

(5) A lively man, who goes to bed before 4 A.M., had better take to cab-driving;

(6) A man with a ravenous appetite, who has not lost money and does not rise at 5 A.M., always eats pork-chops for supper;

(7) A logician, who is in danger of losing money, had better take to cab-driving;

(8) An earnest gambler, who is depressed though he has not lost money, is in no danger of losing any;

(9) A man, who does not gamble, and whose appetite is not ravenous, is always lively;

(10) A lively logician, who is really in earnest, is in no danger of losing money;

(11) A man with a ravenous appetite has no need to take to cab-driving, if he is really in earnest;

(12) A gambler, who is depressed though in no danger of losing money, sits up till 4 A.M.;

(13) A man, who has lost money and does not eat pork-chops for supper, had better take to cab-driving, unless he gets up at 5 A.M.;

(14) A gambler, who goes to bed before 4 A.M., need not take to cab-driving, unless he has a ravenous appetite;

(15) A man with a ravenous appetite, who is depressed though in no danger of losing money, is a gambler.

Univ. "men"; a = earnest; b = eating pork-chops for supper; c = gamblers; d = getting up at 5 A.M.; e = having lost money; h = having a ravenous appetite; k = likely to lose money; l = lively; m = logicians; n = men who had better take to cab-driving; r = sitting up till 4 A.M.

[N.B.   In this Problem, clauses, beginning with "though," are intended to be treated as *essential* parts of the Propositions in which they occur, just as if they had begun with "and."][2]

---

[2] Carroll's "N.B." here stems from his experience with Cook Wilson, who omitted all clauses beginning with "though" in his first attempt to solve the problem. See Carroll's letter of November 1, 1896, reproduced below.

Version II

Problem: To achieve the *complete* Conclusion.

(1) A logician, who eats pork-chops for supper, will probably lose money;

(2) A young man always gets up at 5 A.M., unless he has lost money;

(3) No earnest man, who does not eat pork-chops for supper, need take to cab-driving, unless he gambles;

(4) A logician, who is in danger of losing money, had better take to cab-driving;

(5) A gambler, whose appetite is not ravenous, will probably lose money;

(6) A man who is depressed, having lost money and being likely to lose more, always rises at 5 A.M.;

(7) A man, who neither gambles nor eats pork-chops for supper, is sure to have a ravenous appetite;

(8) A lively man, who goes to bed before 4 A.M., had better take to cab-driving;

(9) A man with a ravenous appetite, who has not lost money and does not rise at 5 A.M., always eats pork-chops for supper;

(10) An earnest gambler, who is depressed though he has not been losing money, is in no danger of losing any;

(11) A man, who does not gamble, and whose appetite is not ravenous, is always lively;

(12) A lively logician, who is really in earnest, is in no danger of losing money;

(13) A man with a ravenous appetite has no need to take to cab-driving, so long as he is really in earnest;

(14) A gambler, who is depressed though in no danger of losing money, sits up till 4 A.M.

(15) A man, who has lost money and does not eat pork-chops for supper, had better take to cab-driving, unless he gets up at 5 A.M.

(16) A gambler, who goes to bed before 4 A.M., need not take to cab-driving, unless he has a ravenous appetite;

(17) An old man, who does not gamble, and who has not lost money though he is in danger of doing so, always eats pork-chops for supper;

(18) A man with a ravenous appetite, who is depressed though in no danger of losing money, is sure to be a gambler.

Univ. "men"; a = earnest; b = eating pork, &c.; c = gamblers; d = getting up at, &c.; e = had better take, &c.; h = has lost, &c.;

k = has ravenous, &c.; l = lively; m = logicians; n = sitting up till, &c.; r = will probably lose, &c.; s = young.

Solution to the Pork-Chop Problem [3]

2. We are given a head start in solving the Pork-Chop Problem (Version I) by a note in Carroll's hand, dated October 7, 1896, which renders the problem into abstract form as follows:

(1) All mb are k;
(2) All c not-h are k;
(3) All not-lek are d;
(4) All not-c not-b are h;
(5) All l not-r are n;
(6) All h not-e not-d are b;
(7) All mk are n;
(8) All ac not-l not-e are not-k;
(9) All c not-h are l;[3]
(10) All lma are k;[3]
(11) All ha are not-n;
(12) All c not-l not-k are r;
(13) All e not-b not-d are n;
(14) All c not-r not-h are not-n;
(15) All h not-l not-k are c.

Pork-Chop Problem Dictionary

a = earnest
b = eating pork chops
c = gambler
d = getting up at 5 A.M.
e = having lost money
h = having ravenous appetite
k = likely to lose money
l = lively

---

[3] Premisses 9 and 10 above are erroneous.

Nine should be rendered: All not-c not-h are l.

Ten should be rendered: All lma are not-k.

The corrected forms are used in the solution that follows.

m = logicians

n = men who had better take to cab-driving

r = sitting up till 4 A.M.

Pork-Chop Problem in Subscript Form

$$\overset{1}{mb_1k'_0} \dagger \overset{2}{ch'_1k'_0} \dagger \overset{3}{l'ek_1d'_0} \dagger \overset{4}{c'b'_1h'_0} \dagger \overset{5}{lr'_1n'_0} \dagger \overset{6}{he'd'_1b'_0}$$

$$\dagger \overset{7}{mk_1n'_0} \dagger \overset{8}{acl'e'_1k_0} \dagger \overset{9}{c'h'_1l'_0} \dagger \overset{10}{lma_1k_0} \dagger \overset{11}{ha_1n_0} \dagger \overset{12}{cl'k'_1r'_0}$$

$$\dagger \overset{13}{eb'd'_1n'_0} \dagger \overset{14}{cr'h'_1n_0} \dagger \overset{15}{hl'k'_1c'_0}$$

Pork-Chop Problem Register

a	b	c	d	e
8,10,11	1	2,8,12,14		3,13
	4,6,13	4,9,15	3,6,13	6,8

h	k	l	m	n	r
6,11,15	3,7,8,10	5,10	1,7,10	11,14	
2,4,9,14	1,2,12,15	3,8,9,12,15		5,7,13	5,12,14

There are fifteen Premisses, seven Eliminands, and four Retinends; the Retinends being $ad'mr'$.

To solve by the Method of Trees, suppose that $ad'mr'$ is an Entity:

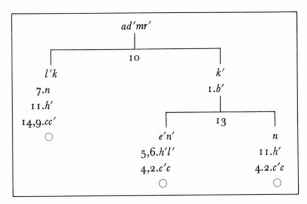

Hence $ad'mr'$ is a Nullity.

Carroll's letters to John Cook Wilson on the
Pork-Chop Problem

–I–

Ch. Ch.

Nov. 12/96

My dear Wilson,

Thanks for your letter. You, say, as to "Pork Chops," "I have no doubt, (humanly speaking), that every Sorites comes out." I think you must have used a *different dictionary* from the printed one, as *your* conclusion is "*MA* is *DN*," whereas *mine* is "*ma* is *dr*." If this is so, would you kindly tell me where the dictionaries differ, & would you give me, in full, one specimen-Sorites (say the 4th), that I may see how you get out your Conclusion. According to your paper, Nos. 10, 6, 4, 13 prove the result "*L′MACHR* is *DN*."

As to the "Jew" Problem,[4] I don't wonder at having utterly failed to understand your "Tree," considering that I was trying to fit it to another Problem! (No. 29 contains all three words "active," "old," & "Jew"; & that misled me.) If you'll kindly let me have it again, I'll compare it with No. 32, & see if I can make out its principle—And please send me the *dictionary* you use for it.

Very truly yours,

C. L. Dodgson.

–II–

Ch. Ch.

Nov. 1/96

My dear Wilson,

We are evidently "at cross purposes" about the Pork Chops"—You say, as to the work you have done on it, "It would be much more useful to *me*, if you had examined it."

I *have* examined the only solution you ever sent me (dated July 26): but, as you ignored all clauses beginning with "though," it wasn't a solution of *my* problem at all.

My reasons for wanting you to try the latest version are (1) I have omitted the three premisses which you showed me were superfluous. (2) I have

---

[4] The Problem of the Active Old Jew is presented in the next book.

worked it out, and believe it is *now* free from mistake: there was, if I remember right, a mistake in the former version.   If you can deduce your Conclusion from the correct version, & would give me the reference-numbers of the Premisses which compose the Soriteses you employ, I should be very grateful.

Ca'n't you get the "M.P." problem into Soriteses?[5]   Unless I have made some mistake, it comes out all right.

Truly yours
C. L. DODGSON

–III–

Ch. Ch.
Nov. 12/96

MY DEAR WILSON,

Many thanks.   I had been working your Soriteses *downwards*.   Trying them *upwards* I have had more success.   Thus, the 2nd, read upwards, is 15, 4, 18, 11, which prove "*LMA* is *C*", & thus dispense with the 1st.   Again, in your 4th, by supplying 16 (apparently omitted by accident), and taking it as 16, 13, 4, 6, I proved your conclusion, "*L'MACHR* is *DN*."   So I've no doubt your solution is a correct one.   I append my own solution.

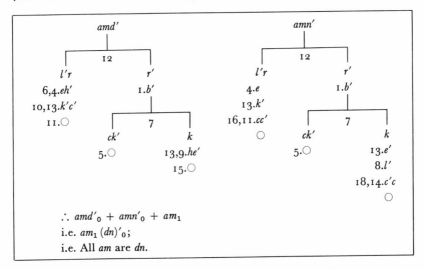

$$\therefore\ amd'_0 + amn'_0 + am_1$$

i.e. $am_1(dn)'_0$;

i.e. All *am* are *dn*.

Truly yours,
C. L. DODGSON.[6]

---

[6] As Carroll confirms in a later letter to Cook Wilson (November 18, 1896), this Tree refers to the original eighteen-Premiss version of the Pork-Chop Problem.

All letters from Carroll to John Cook Wilson are from the collection of Mr. John Sparrow, All Souls College, Oxford.

Chapter V ♘ Froggy's Problem

Problem: To achieve the complete conclusion.[1]

(1) When the day is fine, I tell Froggy "You're quite the dandy, old chap!";

(2) Whenever I let Froggy forget that £10 he owes me, and he begins to

---

[1] Carroll's *Diary* entry for September 5, 1896, records: "Finished, after about two days' work, my Sorites-Problem abt. "Froggy," which contains a beautiful 'trap.'"

strut about like a peacock, his mother declares "He shall *not* go out a-wooing!";

(3) Now that Froggy's hair is out of curl, he has put away his gorgeous waistcoat;

(4) Whenever I go out on the roof to enjoy a quiet cigar, I'm sure to discover that my purse is empty;

(5) When my tailor calls with his little bill, and I remind Froggy of that £10 he owes me, he does *not* grin like a hyæna;

(6) When it is very hot, the thermometer is high;

(7) When the day is fine, and I'm not in the humour for a cigar, and Froggy is grinning like a hyæna, I never venture to hint that he's quite the dandy;

(8) When my tailor calls with his little bill and finds me with an empty purse, I remind Froggy of that £10 he owes me;

(9) My railway-shares are going up like anything!

(10) When my purse is empty, and when, noticing that Froggy has got his gorgeous waistcoat on, I venture to remind him of that £10 he owes me, things are apt to get rather warm;

(11) Now that it looks like rain, and Froggy is grinning like a hyæna, I can do without my cigar;

(12) When the thermometer is high, you need not trouble yourself to take an umbrella;

(13) When Froggy has his gorgeous waistcoat on, but is *not* strutting about like a peacock, I betake myself to a quiet cigar;

(14) When I tell Froggy that he's quite a dandy, he grins like a hyæna;

(15) When my purse is tolerably full, and Froggy's hair is one mass of curls, and when he is *not* strutting about like a peacock, I go out on the roof;

(16) When my railway-shares are going up, and when it is chilly and looks like rain, I have a quiet cigar;

(17) When Froggy's mother lets him go a-wooing, he seems nearly mad with joy, and puts on a waistcoat that is gorgeous beyond words;

(18) When it is going to rain, and I am having a quiet cigar, and Froggy is *not* intending to go a-wooing, you had better take an umbrella.

(19) When my railway-shares are going up, and Froggy seems nearly mad with joy, *that* is the time my tailor always chooses for calling with his little bill;

(20) When the day is cool and the thermometer low, and I say nothing to Froggy about his being quite the dandy, and there's not the ghost of a grin on his face, I haven't the heart for my cigar!

Dictionary for Froggy's Problem[2]

Univ. "Cosmophases"; ε = this; a = Froggy's hair is out of curl; b = Froggy intends to go a-wooing; c = Froggy is grinning like a hyæna; d = Froggy's mother permits him to go a-wooing; e = Froggy seems nearly mad with joy; h = Froggy is strutting about like a peacock; k = Froggy is wearing a waistcoat that is gorgeous beyond words; l = I go out on the roof; m = I remind Froggy of that £10 he owes me; n = I take a quiet cigar; r = I tell Froggy that he's quite the dandy; s = it is going to rain; t = it is very hot; v = my purse is empty; w = my railway-shares are going up; z = my tailor calls with his little bill; A = the thermometer is high; B = you had better take an umbrella.

---

[2] This dictionary is taken from the fragment commentary on Problem 30 given in the next book.

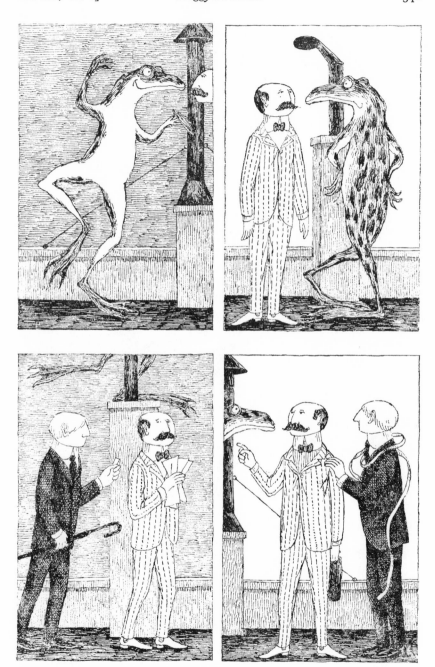

These illustrations were drawn especially by Mr. Edward Gorey to illustrate Froggy's Problem. They were first published in *Antaeus*, Spring/Summer 1974, pp. 401–403. (Edward Gorey)

Carroll was still writing his children's stories, *Sylvie and Bruno*, and *Sylvie and Bruno Concluded*, at the time he began to work on *Symbolic Logic*. Several of the animal characters in the Sylvie and Bruno books—frogs and crocodiles included—found their way into the examples of *Symbolic Logic*.

Chapter VI ⚮ Members of Parliament Problem

Problem: To achieve the complete conclusion:

(1) Any one, fit to be an M.P., who is not always speaking, is a public benefactor;

(2) Clear-headed people, who express themselves well, have had a good education;

(3) A woman, who deserves praise, is one who can keep a secret;

(4) People, who benefit the public, but do not use their influence for good purposes, are not fit to go into Parliament;

(5) People, who are worth their weight in gold and who deserve praise, are always unassuming;

(6) Public benefactors, who use their influence for good objects, deserve praise;

(7) People, who are unpopular and not worth their weight in gold, never can keep a secret;

(8) People, who can talk for ever and are fit to be Members of Parliament, deserve praise;

(9) Any one, who can keep a secret and who is unassuming, is a never-to-be-forgotten public benefactor;

(10) A woman, who benefits the public, is always popular;

(11) People, who are worth their weight in gold, who never leave off talking, and whom it is impossible to forget, are just the people whose photographs are in all the shop-windows;

(12) An ill-educated woman, who is not clear-headed, is not fit to go into Parliament;

(13) Any one, who can keep a secret and is not for ever talking, is sure to be unpopular;

(14) A clear-headed person, who has influence and uses it for good objects, is a public benefactor;

(15) A public benefactor, who is unassuming, is not the sort of person whose photograph is in every shop-window;

(16) People, who can keep a secret and who use their influence for good purposes, are worth their weight in gold;

(17) A person, who has no power of expression and who cannot influence others, is certainly not a *woman*;

343

(18) People, who are popular and worthy of praise, either are public benefactors or else are unassuming.

Univ. "persons"; a = able to keep a secret; b = clear-headed; c = constantly talking; d = deserving praise; e = exhibited in shop-windows; h = expressing oneself well; k = fit to be an M.P.; l = influential; m = never-to-be-forgotten; n = popular; r = public benefactors; s = unassuming; t = using one's influence for good objects; v = well-educated; w = women; z = worth one's weight in gold.

Solution to the Members of Parliament Problem

The Problem in Abstract Form[1]

(1) All k not-c are r;

(2) All bh are v;

(3) All wd are a;

(4) All r not-t are not k;

(5) All zd are s;

(6) All rt are d;

(7) All not-n not-z are not-a;

(8) All ck are d;

(9) All as are mr;

(10) All wr are n;

(11) All zcm are e;

(12) All not-v w not-b are not-k;

(13) All a not-c are not-n;

(14) All not-vlt are r;[2]

(15) All rs are not-e;

(16) All at are z;

(17) All not-h not-l are not-w;

(18) All nd are either r or s.

---

[1] The statement of the problem in abstract form is taken from a note in Carroll's hand dated October 8, 1896. [2] Number 14 should be corrected to read "All blt are r." On this point see Carroll's letter to John Cook Wilson of November 3, 1896 (III), printed on p. 346.

Carroll's Letters to John Cook Wilson concerning the Members of Parliament Problem

–I–

Ch. Ch.
Oct. 29/96

MY DEAR WILSON,

Thanks for your letter.

When next at leisure, would you mind trying the "M.P." Sorites, *before* attending to your series of nine short Problems? The latter are so short, they hardly need any rules at all, for detecting superfluous Premisses.[3] But I am really curious to see how your Method, for detecting them, works on a longer Sorites-Problem, in which I have carefully forborne to tell you whether it has, or has not, superfluous Premisses!

Truly yours,
C. L. DODGSON

–II–

Undated postscript to a letter, probably October 30, 1896

P.S.

The Problem, for which I *most* want to see your solution, is the "M.P." one, No. 6. I hold that, if your method of detecting superfluous Premisses is perfect, it ought to enable you to say either

(1) such & such Premisses are superfluous, or

(2) *none* are superfluous.

I want to see it tested on this Problem.

Don't trouble about No. 5.[4] I have grave doubts as to its correctness.

---

[3] The question whether there exists a rule for detecting superfluous premisses arises frequently in Carroll's letters. Wilson claimed that he *had* such a rule, but apparently was reluctant to reveal it, whereas Carroll doubted both the possibility and the need for such a rule. As he wrote to his sister Louisa on November 13, 1896, "Mr. Cook Wilson says *he* has found a *Rule*: and I'm longing to see him try it on my M.P. Problem.... I have had very little success in devising modes of finding out whether there *are* superfluous Premisses."

[4] There appears a star beside No. 5, and at the bottom of the page, in Wilson's hand, the words: "self-conscious brothers." A corrected version of this problem appears in Book XIV, Example 83.

Whenever you send me your solution of your set of short problems, kindly return *my* solutions, as I have not kept a copy of them.

–III–

Ch. Ch. Nov. 3/96

MY DEAR WILSON,

Forgive my troubling you with that correction of "ill-educated" into "clear-headed": I ought to have remembered that your Solution will be quite as serviceable *without* the correction as it would be *with* it: so please ignore it.

The reason I made the correction was because it occurred to me that the Premiss (with "ill-educated") wd lead to difficulties with a certain Professor, whose criticisms are of great importance to me, & who I felt sure would say "If this is true of an *ill*-educated man, 'a fortiori' it is true of a *well*-educated man: so we may ignore this clause!" And then it would no longer be *my* Problem.

Forgive also my forgetting to answer yr question as to whether your answer to "Pork Chops" is the one I meant to be deduced—It *is* so.

Please don't trouble to copy out the actual *Premisses* which compose your Soriteses, in any Problem of mine. The *reference-numbers* will be amply sufficient.

Truly yours
C. L. DODGSON.

Carroll's Letters to his sister Miss Louisa Dodgson[5]
Concerning the Members of Parliament Problem

–I–

Ch. Ch.
Nov. 16/96

DEAREST LOUI,

Thanks for the 4/6½ in stamps.

You know that the expression $a_1 b'_0$ shows that a Thing, which has the Attribute a is *excluded* from the b'-Class. Hence it is bound to be in the only remaining Class, the b-Class: i.e. "All a are b."

Similarly, $a_1 b' c'_0$ shows that it is *excluded* from the $b'c'$-Class. Hence it is bound to be in one or other of the 3 remaining Classes, bc, bc', and $b'c$.

---

[5] The originals to these letters are in   Princeton University Library.
the Morris L. Parrish Collection,

Ch. Ch.
Nov. 16/96

Dearest Loui,

Thanks for the 4/6½ in stamps.

You know that the expression $a_1b'_0$ shows that a Thing, which has the Attribute 'a', is *excluded* from the 'b'-Class. Hence it is bound to be in the only remaining Class, the b-Class: i.e. "*All* a are b".

Similarly, $a_1b'_0c'_0$ shows that it is *excluded* from the b'c'-Class. Hence it is bound to be in one or other of the 3 remaining

Classes, bc, bc', and b'c. We might, if we liked, translate this into "a is bc; or bc', or *Every* b'c". But this would be clumsy. It is better to *group* these 3 Classes under the 2 headings 'b' and 'c' : & then the Proposition becomes "*Every* a is b or c." (I altered "all" into "every", in order to avoid ambiguity. With "all", it *might* mean "Either all a are bc, or else all a are bc', or else all a are b'c", which would be quite

a different Proposition). Similarly "Every a is b, or c, or d" would be symbolized by $a_1b'_0c'_0d'_0$.

The 3 nieces all came to "Hamlet", in spite of the fog. (Mrs. Wilson said she would take the responsibility of letting Bee go!) We had to walk back in *heavy* rain : however, it was only about 5 minutes' walk : so I don't think they can have got much harm. It was the first play B and G had ever seen : and it really was most creditably acted:

all 3 seemed to enjoy it thoroughly.

After my explanation, I think you might manage the "M.P." Problem.

Yr loving brother,

C.L.D.

They've sent me, from our Common Room, a heap of old "Illustrated" (about 9 inches high) of 1894 and 1895. Would they be of any use to you? Many thanks for review — I think it will help the sale.

The "remisses" was printed right in *my* proof.

We might, if we liked translate this into "Every *a* is *bc*; or *bc'*, or *b'c*."
But this would be clumsy.   It is better to *group* these 3 Classes under the 2
headings *b* and *c*: & then the Proposition becomes "Every *a* is *b* or *c*."
(I altered "all" into "every," in order to avoid ambiguity.   With "all,"
it *might* mean "Either all *a* are *bc*, or else all *a* are *bc'*, or else all *a* are *b'c*,"
which would be quite a different Proposition.)

Similarly, "Every *a* is *b*, or *c*, or *d*" would be symbolized by $a_1b'c'd'_0$.

The 3 nieces all came to "Hamlet," in spite of the fog.   (Mrs. Wilson said
she would take the responsibility of letting Bee go!)   We had to walk back in
heavy rain: however, it was only about 5 minutes' walk: so I don't think they
can have got much harm.   It was the *first* play B and G had ever seen: and it
really was most creditably acted: all 3 seemed to enjoy it thoroughly.

After my explanation, I think you might manage the "M.P." Problem.

Yr loving brother,
CLD

They've sent me, from our Common Room, a heap of old "Illustrated"
(about 9 inches high) of 1894 and 1895.   Would they be of any use to you?

Many thanks for review.   I think it will help the sale.

The "remisses" was printed right in *my* proof.

–II–

Ch. Ch. Nov. 18/96

DEAREST LOUI,

I return your solution of the "M.P." problem, with remarks.

Your representing the 9th Premiss as the aggregate of *three* Nullities is correct
but too lengthy.   The best way, I think, is to write it as $as_1(mr)'_0$, i.e. "All *as*
are *mr*," & to remember that this is equivalent to the *two* Propositions "All *as*
are *m*" & "All *as* are *r*."   Sometimes you may use such a Proposition, all at
once, in a Tree.   Thus, if a Branch ended in *a* & contained *s* higher up, you
might tack on 9. *mr*.   But, if the Branch contained *am'*, then you could only
use one of the *partial* Propositions (viz. $as_1m'_0$).   In that case, I should refer to
it as 9*, and should write underneath 9*.*s'*.

In your Tree, you didn't examine the Register carefully enough.   Your
branchings, 18 and 7, are unnecessary: in each case you might have continued
the single stem.

In verifying your Tree, you shouldn't have included 14 *at all*.   It often
happens, in a Tree, that we tack on Attributes that are of no use further down,
so that the quoted Premiss is, in that place, superfluous.   You may always
know such a Premiss, while verifying, by finding that it wo'n't eliminate

Louisa Dodgson's attempt to solve the "M.P." problem.
(Dodgson Family Collection, Guildford Museum and Muniment Room, Guildford, England)

anything. (You see that your No. 14 has no double score under it.) When this happens, the simple rule is to *ignore* that Premiss, even if it's a Branch-one. Your Branch *really* is

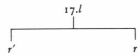

so all you have to do is to run up the left-hand column: then take in the recorded result of the other column: then go upstairs.

I see no harm in letting 3 come in as often as it likes.   It means to be friendly.

My concluding remark will, I expect, be a surprise to you.   *You haven't got the Complete Conclusion*: and *you've used four superfluous Premisses*!   In fact, you've fallen into the trap that I am still hoping Professor Cook Wilson will fall into: but he's taking a tremendous time over it.   I'm afraid he suspects there's something uncanny about it.

Try *kw* as the Root, & ignore 2, 12, 14, 17.

kw_0 is of course a *larger* Conclusion than yours, as it tells you, not only that kwv' is a Nullity, but also that kwv is so.

So the Complete (though unchivalrous) Conclusion is "Women are not fit to be Members of Parliament"!

With 20 Premisses, & only 13 Eliminands, of course there *might* be 6 superfluous Premisses.   So it's worth while, as v' only appears in 2 Premisses, to see if we ca'n't ignore it, by omitting Nos. 2, 12.   Now No. 2 contains, also, b and h.   Its disappearance would *not* prevent the elimination of b: but it *would* prevent that of h.   So No. 17 must also go.   No. 12 contains b', and is the *only* one so doing.   So *its* disappearance spoils b's chance: & all b's Premisses must go.   That means that 14 & 17 must go.   No. 14 contains l: but this does no harm, as 17 goes too.   And 17 does no further harm.   Hence it's worth while to try ignoring 2, 12, 14, 17, which carry with them the Retinend v', and the 3 Eliminands b, h, l.   (I forgot to notice that 14 also contains t: but *there* it does no harm. t can well spare it.)

Yr loving brother
CLD

Chapter VII ✗ The Problem of Six Friends and Their Wives[1]

Version I

Six friends, and their six wives, are staying in the same hotel; and they all walk out daily, in parties of various size and composition.   To ensure a

---

[1] With this problem, compare the so-called Barber-Shop Paradox, in Book XXI, Chapters III and V.

variety in these daily walks, they have agreed to observe the following Rules:

(1) If Acres is with (i.e. is in the same party with) his wife, and Barry with his, and Eden with Mrs. Hall, Cole must be with Mrs. Dix;

(2) If Acres is with his wife, and Hall with his, and Barry with Mrs. Cole, Dix must *not* be with Mrs. Eden;

(3) If Cole and Dix and their wives are all in the same party, and Acres *not* with Mrs. Barry, Eden must *not* be with Mrs. Hall;

(4) If Acres is with his wife, and Dix with his, and Barry *not* with Mrs. Cole, Eden must be with Mrs. Hall.

(5) If Eden is with his wife, and Hall with his, and Cole with Mrs. Dix, Acres must *not* be with Mrs. Barry;

(6) If Barry and Cole and their wives are all in the same party, and Eden *not* with Mrs. Hall, Dix must be with Mrs. Eden.

The Problem is to prove that there must be, every day, at least *one* married couple who are not in the same party.

Version II[2]

(1) Six friends, A, B, C, D, E, F, and their wives, walk out daily, in large or small parties at pleasure;

(2) When A, B, C take their wives, E accompanies (i.e. is in the same party with) F's wife;

(3) When D, E, F take their wives, A accompanies B's wife;

(4) When A, F take their wives, and when B accompanies C's wife, D accompanies E's wife;

(5) When A, D take their wives, and when E accompanies F's wife, B accompanies C's wife;

(6) When C, F take their wives, and when D accompanies E's wife, A does *not* accompany B's wife.

   Prove that there is, every day, at least *one* man who does not take his wife.

---

[2] The second version of the problem of six friends and their wives is taken from "Eighth Paper on Logic," November 1892, where it is the sixth example given.

Chapter VIII ❧ The Problem of the Five Liars. The Salt and Mustard Problem[1]

[1] The two problems presented in this chapter, which are of particular interest, must be read in the context of Carroll's Introduction to the fourth edition, printed above, and of his correspondence with John Cook Wilson, reproduced here. Carroll came to view the Salt and Mustard Problem as a "transformation" of the Problem of the Five Liars that managed to avoid certain difficulties that had arisen in the course of his correspondence with Wilson.

His transformation of the problem is in effect a capitulation to Cook Wilson, incidentally one of only two examples we have of Carroll's having succumbed to Wilson's arguments. Ironically, the contemporary logician would judge Carroll to have been on the right track in the first place and Wilson to have been wrong.

The Problem of the Five Liars concerns five individuals, A, B, C, D, and E, each of whom makes exactly two assertions. For instance, B says "Either A or C tells a Truth and a Lie" and "Either D tells two Lies or E tells two Truths." When an analysis is made of the assertions of the five individuals, *contradictory* conclusions are reached. In effect, the Liar Paradox, as discussed in the Editor's Introduction, is produced. This version of the Liar, "Carroll's Paradox," is particularly amusing and interesting, and his defence of certain kinds of self-reference, in a letter to John Cook Wilson of October 28, 1896, has an almost uncannily modern ring. But the same letter also suggests that

Carroll had not thought the issue through—which is hardly surprising given that it remains controversial today. And so we find him in subsequent letters to Wilson, in the Introduction to the Fourth Edition, and here in the second version of this problem, capitulating in order to avoid self-reference.

In the second version of the problem, known as the "Salt and Mustard Problem," the conversation among A, B, C, D, and E, is replaced by a meal. We learn that E eats salt if and only if either B or A takes both condiments. And we also learn that E eats mustard if and only if C or D takes only one of the two condiments available. The original "telling two Truths" is here translated into "taking both condiments." "Telling two Lies" is translated into "taking neither condiment." And so on.

Carroll's move is quite ingenious. The premises turn out to be inconsistent in the second version, but they no longer lead to contradictory conclusions. Paradox, as well as self-reference, is avoided. *But the original problem remains unsolved.* For it is not at all inconsistent to suppose that five people were to *say* the things attributed to them in the first, Five Liars, version of the problem. (See A. N. Prior's excellent analysis of the two versions, as well as his presentation of yet another variant, in *The Journal of Symbolic Logic*, 22, pp. 309f.)

It is interesting that although Carroll did not modify his lying problem basically until 1896, as shown in the letters to Cook Wilson, he started to work on problems of this general character at least as early as 1894. In his *Diary* entry for May 27, 1894, he writes, "I have worked out in the last few days some curious problems on plan of 'lying' dilemma. e.g. '*A* says *B* lies; *B* says *C* lies; *C* says *A* & *B* lie.' Ans. '*A* & *C* lie; *B* speaks truly.' And today '*A* says *B* says *C* says *D* lies; *D* says two lie & one speaks true.' Ans. '*D* lies; the rest speak truly.'" A later *Diary* entry, for September 24, 1895, goes as follows: "On the 20th I got from Adamson, a 'Liar' Problem in which one says '3 of the others lie, & 3 speak truly.' I have made some of this new kind, viz. 'Liar Problems without personalities.' They seem to need a peculiar kind of Tree."

The Problem of the Five Liars

Version I[2]

There are five friends, *A*, *B*, *C*, *D*, and *E*, each of whom makes two assertions, so that it is possible for him to tell two Truths, or a Truth and a Lie, or two Lies.

(1) *A* says "Either *B* or *D* tells a Truth and a Lie: either *C* or *E* tells two Lies."

(2) *B* says "Either *A* or *C* tells a Truth and a Lie: either *D* tells two Lies or *E* tells two Truths."

(3) *C* says "Either *A* or *D* tells two Truths: either *B* tells a Truth and a Lie or *E* tells two Lies."

(4) *D* says "Either *A* or *E* tells two Lies: either *B* tells two Lies or *C* tells two Truths."

(5) *E* says "Either *A* or *B* tells two Truths: either *C* or *D* tells a Truth and a Lie."

What is the condition, as to truth-telling and lying, of each of these five painfully candid friends?

---

[2] The words "Lies" and "Truths" in the first statements of *D* and *E*, respectively, are sometimes interchanged. The problem has been printed here in accordance with Dodgson's corrigenda slip inserted in the first edition of *Symbolic Logic*.

Version II[3]

After the six friends, named in the previous chapter, had returned from their tour, three of them, Barry, Cole, and Dix, agreed, with two other friends of theirs, Lang and Mill, that the five should meet, every day, at a certain *table-d'hôte*. Remembering how much amusement they had derived from their code of rules for walking-parties, they devised the following rules, to be observed whenever beef appeared on the table:

(1) If Barry takes salt, then either Cole or Lang takes *one* only of the two condiments, salt and mustard: if he takes mustard, then either Dix takes neither condiment, or Mill takes both.

(2) If Cole takes salt, then either Barry takes only *one* condiment, or Mill takes neither: if he takes mustard, then either Dix or Lang takes both.

(3) If Dix takes salt, then either Barry takes neither condiment or Cole takes both: if he takes mustard, then either Lang or Mill takes neither.

(4) If Lang takes salt, then either Barry or Dix takes only *one* condiment: if he takes mustard, then either Cole or Mill takes neither.

(5) If Mill takes salt, then either Barry or Lang takes both condiments: if he takes mustard, then either Cole or Dix takes only *one*.

The Problem is to discover whether these rules are *compatible*; and, if so, what arrangements are possible.

[N.B. In this Problem it is assumed that the phrase "If Barry takes salt" allows of *two* possible cases, viz. (1) "He takes salt *only*"; (2) "He takes *both* condiments." And so with all similar phrases.

It is also assumed that the phrase, "Either Cole or Lang takes *one* only of the two condiments" allows of *three* possible cases, viz. (1) "Cole takes *one* only, Lang takes both or neither"; (2) "Cole takes both or neither, Lang takes *one* only"; (3) "Cole takes *one* only, Lang takes *one* only." And so with all similar phrases.

It is also assumed that every rule is to be understood as implying the words "and *vice versâ*." Thus the first rule would imply the addition "and, if either Cole or Lang takes only *one* condiment, then Barry takes salt."]

---

[3] To understand the relation between the two versions of this problem, note carefully that Carroll has changed the order of the five propositions. Also, whereas *B* stands for *Barry*, *C* for *Cole*, and *D* for *Dix*, *A* stands for *Lang* and *E* for *Mill*. Thus to match the first version with the second, let *B* speak first, *C* second, *D* third, *A* fourth, and *E* fifth.

Carroll's letters to John Cook Wilson concerning the
Five Liars and Salt and Mustard Problems

–I–

Ch. Ch. Oct. 25/96[4]

MY DEAR WILSON,

Pardon my omission to answer your questions about the 5 Liars. They refer
to a now-*discarded* version of that Problem. I was under the impression that

(Collection of Mr. John Sparrow, All Souls College, Oxford)

---

[4] To understand Carroll's note to Wilson here, note that the letter *A* has been changed to *L* (for Lang), and the letter *E* to *M* (for Mill).

I had sent you the *amended* editions of all those Problems.   I now enclose them.
On the other side of this you will find answers to your two questions.   I am sorry
the questions are needed—How can I state the Problem more clearly?   Shall
I say "each of whom makes two assertions, as here given" or "as given below"?

Truly yours,
C. L. DODGSON

Question 1
What are the assertions which *B* makes?
Answer
They are:
(1) Either *C* or *L* tells a Truth & a Lie;
(2) Either *D* tells two Lies or *M* tells two Truths.

Question 2
What are the assertions of *C*, to which *B* refers, when he says "Either *C* or
L tells a Truth & a Lie etc."?
Answer
They are:
(1) Either *B* tells a Truth & a Lie or *M* tells two Lies;
(2) Either *D* or *L* tells two Truths.

–II–

Ch. Ch.
Oct. 28/96

MY DEAR WILSON,

As no shadow of irritation has ever crossed my *mind*, with regard to anything
received from you, it was pure accident that my *language* should have suggested
it: please regard all such language as unwritten.

I fear I ca'n't take your view—that *all* "lying" problems are impossible and
unmeaning: but I haven't yet written *that* chapter in Part II: you shall see it
as soon as I get it into type: meanwhile I will just say that such problems seem
to me to be of *two* kinds—one, where the Premisses *cannot* refer to their subject-
matter: the other, where they *can*.

Your example is of the former kind, viz.

"*A* says that *B* is false (i.e. is speaking falsely): *B* says that *A* is true."

Let *a* = *A* speaks truly; *a'* = *A* speaks falsely.

Then, on hypothesis that these Propositions *can* refer to their subject-matter,
a ¶ *b'*, and *b'* ¶ *a'*; ∴ *a* ¶ *a'*, which is absurd.   Again, *a'* ¶ *b*, and *b* ¶ *a*;
∴ *a'* ¶ *a*, which is absurd.   Hence hypothesis is *false*: i.e. these Propositions
cannot refer to each other.

But, if we take the example "*A* says *B* is false: *B* says *A* is false" we get a
different result.

Viz. on hypothesis that these Props *can* refer to each other, *a* ¶ *b'*, and *b'* ¶ *a*,
which is *possible*.   Again, *a'* ¶ *b*, & *b* ¶ *a'*, which again is *possible*.   Hence these

This letter is a good illustration
of the extraordinary illusions
it gives a leader to, from want of study of anything like real Logic   Ch. Ch.   2
or even real processes of thinking. J.S.W.   Oct. 28/96

My dear Wilson,

   As no shadow of irritation has ever
crossed my mind, with regard to anything
received from you, it was pure accident
that my <u>language</u> should have suggested it:
please regard all such language as <u>unwritten</u>.

   I fear I can't take your view —— that
all "lying" problems are impossible & unmeaning:
but I haven't yet written that chapter in
Part II : you shall see it as soon as I get it
into type: meanwhile I will just say that
such problems seem to me to be of <u>two</u> kinds
—— one, where the Premisses <u>cannot</u> refer to
their subject-matter : the other, where they <u>can</u>.

   <u>Your</u> example is of the <u>former</u> kind, viz.

   "A says that B is false (i.e. is speaking
   falsely): B says that A is true."

Let a = A speaks truly ; a' = A speaks falsely.
Then, on hypothesis that these Propositions
<u>can</u> refer to their subject-matter, $a \, ¶ \, b'$, and
$b' \, ¶ \, a'$; ∴ $a \, ¶ \, a'$, which is absurd. Again,
$a' \, ¶ \, b$, and $b \, ¶ \, a$; ∴ $a' \, ¶ \, a$, which is absurd.
Hence hypothesis is <u>false</u> : i.e. these Propositions
<u>cannot</u> refer to each <u>other</u>.

   But, if we take the example "A says
B is false : B says A is false," we get a different
result, viz. on hypothesis that these Props <u>can</u> refer to
each other, $a \, ¶ \, b'$, and $b' \, ¶ \, a'$, which is possible.
Again, $a' \, ¶ \, b$, & $b \, ¶ \, a'$, which again is possible.
Hence these Propositions <u>can</u> refer to each other,
& the Conclusion is "One of the two lies, & the
other speaks truly : but we have no data to fix
which is which."

   Here is a very pretty example.

   "A says B lies : B says C lies : C says
'you're <u>both</u> of you liars!'."

   My solution of this is as follows:—
Take hypothesis that these Props can refer

The Liar Paradox was the subject of correspondence dated October 28, 1896, between Dodgson and Wilson. At the top of this letter Wilson has scrawled: "This letter is a good illustration of the extraordinary illusions Dodgson is liable to, from want of study of anything like real logic or even real process of thinking. J. C. W." (Collection of Mr. John Sparrow, All Souls College, Oxford)

Propositions *can* refer to each other, & the Conclusion is "One of the two lies, & the other speaks truly: but we have no data to fix which is which."

Here is a very pretty example.

"*A* says *B* lies: *B* says *C* lies: *C* says 'You're *both* of you liars!'"

My solution of this is as follows:

Take hypothesis that these Props *can* refer to each other. Then $a \, \P \, b'$: $b' \, \P \, c$: ∴ $c \, \P \, a'b'$: which is absurd. ∴ *A cannot* be speaking truly. Again, $a' \, \P \, b$: $b \, \P \, c'$: $c' \, \P \, (a \text{ or } b)$: which is *possible*. Hence these Propositions *can* refer to each other, & there is one, & only one, possible state of things, viz. "*A* & *C* lie: *B* speaks truly."

Some of these problems (I've worked out a lot of them) give *several* possibilities. I prefer those that give only *one*. The "Five Liars" problem admits of only *one* possible state of things.

Yours truly,
C. L. DODGSON

–III–

Ch. Ch. Nov. 2/96

MY DEAR WILSON,

I have made a discovery, as to the "Liars" Problems, that has greatly relieved my mind. It is that they can be so transformed as to bring them within the

Ch. Ch. Nov. 2/96

My dear Wilson,

I have made a discovery, as to the "Liars" Problems, that has greatly relieved my mind — It is that they can be so transformed as to bring them within the category of ordinary Problems, & to evade the difficulty of the use of 2 Propositions, each as the Subject of the other.

Take, for example the Problem you declare to be wholly unmeaning, viz. "A says B lies; B says C lies; C says A & B lie." I propose to substitute this form — "Let A, B, C represent 3 such Propositions. The Propositions themselves are *not* specified: but we are told that they are so related to each other that, if A be true B is false, & if A be false B is true; if B be true, C is false, & if B be false, C is true; if C be true, A & B are false, &, if C be false, one at least of the two is true. The question is, are these statements compatible, & is there any possible state of things, as regards the truth or falsity of these 3 Propositions?"

The "5 Liars" can be modified in the same way. Thus :— "B, C, D, L, M represent 5 Pairs of Propositions. We do not know what they are, but merely that they are so related to each other, as to produce the following results :— [let "half-true" mean that *one* of the Pair is true & the *other* false, but it is *not* said which is which.]

If the *first* in the B-Pair be true, then either the C-Pair or the L-Pair is half-true : if false, then this is *not* the case (i.e. neither the C-pair nor the L-Pair, is a "half-true").

If the *second* in the B-Pair be true, then either the D-Pair is all-false or the M-Pair is all-true : if false, then this is *not* the case (i.e. neither is the D-Pair, is (i.e. the D-Pair is *not* all-false, & the M-Pair is *not* all-true)." &c &c —

I greatly hope that you will *now* be willing to try your Method on this *modified* form of the "5 Liars."

Truly yours, C. L. Dodgson.

(Collection of Mr. John Sparrow, All Souls College, Oxford)

category of ordinary Problems, & to evade the difficulty of the use of two Propositions, each as the Subject of the other.

Take, for example the Problem you declare to be wholly unmeaning, viz. "*A* says *B* lies; *B* says *C* lies; *C* says *A* & *B* lie." I propose to substitute this form—"Let *A*, *B*, *C* represent three *Propositions*. The Propositions themselves are *not* specified: but we are told that they are so related to each other that, if *A* be true *B* is false, & if *A* be false *B* is true, if *B* be true, *C* is false, & if *B* be false, *C* is true; if *C* be true, *A* & *B* are false, &, if *C* be false, one at least of the two is true. The question is, are these statements compatible, & is there any possible state of things, as regards the truth or falsity of these three Propositions?

The "Five Liars" can be modified in the same way.

Thus: "*B*, *C*, *D*, *L*, *M* represent five *Pairs of Propositions*. We do not know what they are, but merely that they are so related to each other, as to produce the following results: (let "half-true" mean that *one* of the Pair is true & the *other* false, but it is not said which is which).

If the first in the *B*-Pair be true, then either the *C*-Pair or the *L*-Pair is half-true: if false, then this is *not* the case (i.e. neither the *C*-pair, nor the *L*-Pair, is "half-true").

If the second in the *B*-Pair be true, then either the *D*-Pair is all-false or the *M*-pair is all-true: if false, then this is *not* the case (i.e. the *D*-Pair is *not* all-false, & the *M*-Pair is *not* all-true)." &c. &c.

I greatly hope that you will *now* be willing to try your Method on this *modified* form of the "Five Liars."

Truly yours,
C. L. DODGSON.[5]

–IV[6]**–**

Ch. Ch. Nov. 16/96

MY DEAR WILSON,

I hope you will be pleased to know that I have decided to abandon my "Liar" Problems. The metaphysical* difficulties are too appalling! They can all be utilised, I find, by translating them into other matter, in which these

---

[5] In his *Diary* entry for November 2, 1896, Carroll writes: "It was during my walk yesterday that the idea occurred to me to modify 'Lying' Problems so as to avoid the objection raised to making Propositions serve as Subjects for one another."

[6] At the bottom of the letter Cook Wilson scribbles, "*The difficulties I shewed Dodgson are not metaphysical, they reduce to one which is a matter of quite simple logic.—viz. the absurdity of making a propn *its own* subject. J.C.W."

Ch. Ch. Nov. 16/96

My dear Wilson,
I hope you will be pleased to know that I have decided to abandon my "Liar" Problems. The metaphysical difficulties *are too appalling! They can all be utilised I find, by translating them into other matter, in which these difficulties do not occur—I am having the new version of the "5 Liars" printed, and will send you a copy. Truly yours (CLD).*

I've examined the "Brothers" Problem (which I told you I doubted about) and I believe its all right, & is soluble.
The difficulty I shewed Dodgson was not metaphysical, they reduce to one which is a matter of quite simple logic — by the absurdity of making a proposition its own subject), CW

(Collection of Mr. John Sparrow, All Souls College, Oxford)

difficulties do not occur—I am having the new version of the "Five Liars" printed, and will send you a copy.

Truly yours,
CLD

I've examined the "Brothers" Problem (which, I told you I doubted about) and I believe it's all right, & is soluble.[7]

—V—

Ch. Ch. Dec. 18/96

MY DEAR WILSON,

Many thanks for letter.

I add a copy of what I am inserting in the note to "Salt & Mustard" Problem.

"In this Problem, it is assumed that the phrase 'If Barry takes salt' allows of *two* possible cases—his taking salt *only*, & his taking both condiments."

Very truly yours,
C. L. DODGSON.

---

[7] See the "Problem of the Self-Conscious Brothers", in Book XIV,   Example 83.

Chapter IX ❦ The Great-Grandson Problem[1]

(1) A man can always master his father;

(2) An inferior of a man's uncle owes that man money;

(3) The father of an enemy of a friend of a man owes that man nothing;

(4) A man is always persecuted by his son's creditors;

(5) An inferior of the master of a man's son is senior to that man;

(6) A grandson of a man's junior is not his nephew;

(7) A servant of an inferior of a friend of a man's enemy is never persecuted by that man;

(8) A friend of a superior of the master of a man's victim is that man's enemy;

(9) An enemy of a persecutor of a servant of a man's father is that man's friend.

The Problem is to deduce some fact about great-grandsons.

[N.B.   In this Problem it is assumed that all the men, here referred to, live in the same town, and that every pair of them are either "friends" or "enemies," that every pair are related as "senior and junior," "superior and inferior," and that certain pairs are related as "creditor and debtor," "father and son," "master and servant," "persecutor and victim," "uncle and nephew."]

---

[1] In his *Diary* entry for February 15, 1897, Carroll writes, "Made a splendid Logic-Problem abt. 'great-grandsons' (modeled on one by DeMorgan). My method of solution is quite new, & I greatly doubt if anyone will solve the Problem. I have sent it to Cook Wilson." The original DeMorgan problem, along with an essay on it by Carroll apparently written to his sister Louisa, are printed below in Book XXII, Section 10. Carroll's own problem, printed here together with his letters to Cook Wilson about it, is much more difficult than the original DeMorgan problem.

Solution to the Great-Grandson Problem

Carroll's letters to John Cook Wilson about this problem

–I–

Ch. Ch. Feb. 16/97

MY DEAR WILSON,

I hope, for *your* sake primarily, that you may soon be again up to work—& for *mine*, secondarily, as I shall be much interested to see what you make of this new kind of problem (modeled on one by De Morgan, but far more complicated than his). I have the whole solution written out: it needs only the given nine Premisses.

Yours very truly,
C. L. DODGSON.

P.S.

You can assume, if you like, that a son of a son is a grandson, & that a son of a son of a son is a great-grandson.

–II–

Ch. Ch. May 17/97

MY DEAR WILSON,

I fear I expressed myself very obscurely, in my last, with reference to the conclusion which you deduced from Premisses 7, 8. You say "perhaps you went wrong in thinking it was deduced from 7 only." No: I understood that you had used *8* as well. You also say "you don't dispute the truth of the conclusion." But I *do*. It is clearly wrong, on general grounds, because, whereas 7 asserts a fact as to a set of *five* men, & 8 does the same, & can be made to refer to the *same* five men, any conclusion, drawn from 7 & 8, can only deal with *five* men at the outside. *Your* conclusion deals with *six*.

It will perhaps help you to see your mistake, if I combine 7 & 8, & deduce the only logical conclusion they can give. My symbols will make things shorter.

Let
$\alpha = A$ is servant of B
$\beta = B$ is inferior of C
$\gamma = C, D$ are friends
$\delta = D, E$ are friends $\therefore \delta' =$ they are enemies
$\varepsilon = A$ is victim of E

Now 7 may be written "If A is servant of B, & B inferior of C, & C friend of D, & D enemy of E, then A is *not* victim of E."

i.e., symbolically, $\alpha\beta\gamma\delta'$ proves ε'

Again, 8 may be written "If D is friend of C, & C is superior of B, & B master of A, & A victim of E, then D is enemy of E."   i.e., symbolically, $\gamma\beta\alpha\varepsilon$ proves δ'.

These, stated as Nullities, are

$$\alpha\beta\gamma\delta'\varepsilon_0 \dagger \gamma\beta\alpha\varepsilon\delta_0$$

Eliminating δ, we get $\alpha\beta\gamma\varepsilon_0$, which may be put into concrete form in many ways.   Here is a specimen.

$\alpha\beta\gamma$ proves ε'; i.e. "If A is servant of B, & B inferior of C & C friend of D, then A is not victim of E"; i.e. "A servant of an inferior of a man who has a friend is not victim of anybody (& so is not persecuted *at all*)."

Yours very truly,
CLD

Chapter X ⚹ The Jack Sprat Problem[1]

Jack Sprat could eat no fat;
His wife could eat no lean:
And so, between them both,
They licked the platter clean.

Solve this as a Sorites-Problem, taking lines 3 and 4 as the Conclusion to be proved.   It is permitted to use, as Premisses, not only all that is here *asserted*, but also all that we may reasonably understand to be *implied*.

---

[1] Carroll addresses himself to this problem in a letter (see following) posted to "Loui" on September 28, 1896, mentioning that he intends to put it into the next edition of Part I, as another specimen of the sort of problem to be tackled in Part II.   It appeared in the appendix to the fourth Edition.   The original of the letter to Loui is in the Henry E. Huntington Library.

Carroll's Letter to his Sister, Miss Louisa Dodgson, of September 28, 1896, on the Jack Sprat Problem

2. Bedford Well Road
Eastbourne.
Sep. 28/96

DEAREST LOUI,

However badly the party at the Chestnuts treat me in the way of letter-writing—or rather of letter-*not*-writing—*I* am not in a position to complain about it! But as I am working at Logic—sometimes 8 or 9 hours a day— I think I may be excused for writing few letters.

You don't seem to have got far into the "Jack Sprat" Problem (I'm going to put it into the next edition of Part I, as another of the specimens of Part II), as *yet*. Why, you haven't got even *one* Syllogism drawn out! You have mastered the "Syllogism" & "Sorites" Books in Part I, haven't you? Then do you suppose that the argument

Jack eats no fat;
All the people, who don't eat fat, eat all the lean put upon their plates:
∴ There is no fat left on Jack's plate.

is a *Syllogism*? The Premisses do possess a "middle" term (or, as *I* express it in Part I, a Pair of Eliminands), I grant. But what has become of the Retinends? They ought *both* to appear in the Conclusion; & I ca'n't find *either* of them there! The Problem has puzzled me *much*; but I *think* I've got it out into a good "Sorites" now.... I take "meat" as my "Univ," And I regard the "platter" as the *dish*, not as their *plate*. I *think* they sat facing each other, & had a plate each!

Thanks for telling me so much about the Wilcox party, & of what they have done since dear Clara's death. Some of it is new to me—specially that she left no *Will*. It is getting increasingly difficult, now, to remember *which* of one's friends remain alive, and *which* have gone "into the land of the great departed, Into the silent land." Also, such news comes less & less of a shock: & more & more one realises that it is an experience each of *us* has to face before long. That fact is getting *less* dreamlike to me, now: & I sometimes think what a grand thing it will be to be able to say to oneself "Death is *over*, now: there is not *that* experience to be faced, again!"

I am beginning to realise that, if the *books* I am still hoping to *write*, are to be done *at all*, they must be done *now*, & that I am *meant* thus to utilise the splendid health I have had, unbroken, for the last year & a half, & the working-powers, that are fully as great as, if not greater than, what I have ever had. I brought with me here the MSS, such as it is (very fragmentary and unarranged) for the book about religious difficulties, & I meant, when I came here, to devote myself to *that*; but I have changed my plan. It seems to me that *that* subject is one that hundreds of living men could do, if they would only try, *much* better than I could, whereas there is no living man who could

Has Edwin reached St. Helena yet?

2. Bedford Well Road,
Eastbourne.
Sep. 28/96

Dearest Loui,

However badly, the party
at the Chestnuts treat me
in the way of letter-writing
—— or rather of letter - _not_-
writing, _I_ am not in a position
to complain about it! But
as I am working at Logic
—— sometimes 8 or 9 hours
a day —— I think I may be
excused for writing few letters.

You don't seem to have
got far into the "Jack Sprat"
Problem (I'm going to put
it into the next edition of
Part I, as another of the
specimens of Part II) as yet —
Why, you haven't got even
one Syllogism drawn out! You
have mastered the "Syllogism"
& "Sorites" Books in Part I,

haven't you? Then do you sup-
-pose that the argument
       "Jack eats no fat;
       All the people who don't
eat fat eat all the lean put
upon their plates:
       ∴ There is no fat left
              on Jack's plate"
is a <u>Syllogism</u>? The Premises
do possess a "middle" term (or,
as <u>I</u> express it in Part I, a
Pair of Eliminands), I grant.
But what has become of the
Retinends? They ought both
to appear in the Conclusion;
& I can't find <u>either</u> of
them there! The Problem has
puzzled me <u>much</u>; but I
<u>think</u> I've got it out into a
good "Sorites" now. Would
it be ~~un~~intelligible to you,
if I sent it in the form of
those given from p. 155 to
p. 163? Or must I write it

in words all through? I take
"meat" as my "Univ." And I
regard the "platter" as the dish,
not as their plate. I think
they sat facing each other, &
had a plate each!

Thanks for telling me so
much about the Wilcox party,
& of what they have done since
dear Clara's death. Some of it
is new to me — specially that
she left no will. It is getting
increasingly difficult, now,
to remember which of one's
friends remain alive, and
which have gone "Into the
Land of the great departed,
Into the silent land". Also,
such news comes less & less
of a shock: & more & more
one realises that it is an
experience each of us has
to face before long. That fact
is getting less dreamlike to
me, now: & I sometimes
think what a grand thing
it will be to be able to say

to oneself "Death is over, now:
there is not that experience
to be faced, again!"

I am beginning to realise
that, if the books I am still
hoping to write, are to be done
at all, they must be done now,
& that I am meant thus,
to utilise the splendid health
I have had, unbroken, for
the last year & a half, &
the working-powers, that
are fully as great as, if not
greater than, what I have
ever had. — I brought with
me here the MSS, such as it
is (very fragmentary and
unarranged) for the book
about religious difficulties,
& I meant, when I came
here, to devote myself to
that; but I have changed
my plan. It seems to me
that that subject is one that
hundreds of living men

2

could do, if they would only
try, much better than I could,
whereas there is no living
man who could (or at any
rate who would take the
trouble to) arrange, & finish,
& publish, the 2nd Part of
the Logic — Also I have the
Logic book in my head: it
will only need 3 or 4 months
to write out ; & I have not
got the other book in my
head, & it might take
years to think out — So
I have decided to get Part II
finished first : & I am
working at it day & night.
I have taken to early rising
& sometimes sit down to
my work before 7, & have
1½ hours at it before
breakfast — The book will be
a great novelty, & will help,
I fully believe, to make the

Study of Logic far easier
than it now is: & it will,
I also believe, be a help to
religious thoughts, by giving
clearness of conception &
of expression, which may
enable many people to
face, & conquer, many
religious difficulties for
themselves. So I do really
regard it as work for God.

As to paying another
visit to Guildford, I can do
that at any time, when you
happen to have room. It
need not be lost time, for my
book, as I can easily bring,
in my hand-bag, work enough
to last me for 2 or 3 days.
And *Sundays* of course I can
spare best of all, as I usually
keep the Logic for week-days
only: it is too absorbing a
subject to enter on, on Sundays.
Shall I come next Saturday?
Ever yrs affcetly C.L.Dodgson.

(or at any rate who would take the trouble to) arrange, & finish, & publish, the 2nd Part of the Logic.   Also I *have* the Logic book in my head: it will only need 3 or 4 months to write out; & I have *not* got the other book in my head, & it might take *years* to think out.   So I have decided to get Part II finished *first*: & I am working at it, day & night.   I have taken to early rising, & sometimes sit down to my work before 7, & have 1½ hours at it before breakfast.   The book will be a great novelty, & will help, I fully believe, to make the study of Logic *far* easier than it now is: & it will, I also believe, be a help to religious thoughts, by giving *clearness* of conception & of expression, which may enable many people to face, & conquer, many religious difficulties for themselves.   So I do really regard it as work for *God*.

As to paying another visit to Guildford, I can do that at any time, when you happen to have room.   It need not be lost time for my book as I can easily bring in my hand-bag, work enough to last me for 2 or 3 days.   And *Sundays*, of course I can spare best of all, as I usually keep the Logic for week-days only: it is too absorbing a subject to enter on, on Sundays. Shall I come next Saturday?

Ever yrs afflety
CLDodgson

An Answer to the Jack Sprat Problem[2]

[2] It is important to take Carroll's advice to introduce as premisses not only what is asserted explicitly in the first two lines of the rhyme, but also what is "reasonably implied."

The problem might be worked by forming multiliteral statements conveying the information (e.g., If the meat is lean and the meat is on the platter then Jack eats it, etc.).   This route is, however, precluded by Carroll's advice to Loui that he intended the problem to be done in the form of a biliteral sorites.   This may be done as follows, following a solution by Professor T. W. Settle.

Universe: "meat."
Vocabulary:
a = what Jack could not eat
b = what Jack's wife could not eat
c = eaten by Jack at this meal
d = eaten by Jack's wife at this meal
e = served on Jack's plate at this meal
h = served on Jack's wife's plate at this meal
k = brought to the table on a platter at this meal
l = fat
m = lean

Assume:

1. Jack could eat no fat	la'_0
2. His wife could eat no lean	mb'_0
3. Jack was served with what his wife could not eat	be'_0
4. Jack's wife was served with what Jack could not eat	ah'_0
5. Jack ate all he was served	ec'_0

6. Jack's wife ate all she
was served hd'_0
7. Meat is either lean or
fat $k_1(l'm')_0$
Some meat was served.

Register:

a	b	c	d	e	h	k	l	m
4	3			5	6	7	I	2
I	2	5	6	3	4		7	7

Retinends: $c'd'k$

Assume $c'd'k_1$

$c'd'k$

5. e'
3. b'
2. m'
7. l

1. a
4. h
b. d
  $\bigcirc$

Hence $c'd'k_0$. Inspecting the premisses we see k is affirmed. Hence

$$k_1(c'd')_0$$

Or

All the meat brought to the table on a platter at this meal was eaten either by Jack or by his wife.

There must be any number of ways to solve this problem, which involve rather different "reasonable assumptions." The reader is invited to test his wits on this problem to see whether he can reach a neater solution.

Chapter XI ❧ The Library Problem[1]

What conclusions, if any, can be drawn from these data?
In a certain Library,

(1) All the old books are Greek;
(2) All the quartos are bound;
(3) None of the poets are old quartos.

---

[1] This problem is taken from a letter from Carroll to Cook Wilson dated December 20, 1896. The correspondence that follows, in addition to dealing with a problem of similar structure (see Carroll's letter to Wilson of December 26, 1896), also takes up the question of the nature of a legitimate conclusion and provides a glimpse of Carroll's dispute with Wilson over this issue. Here Carroll is in *apparent* disagreement with contemporary logicians, who would accept the deduction of a portion of the premisses or the aggregate of the premisses as legitimate logical consequences of the premisses in question. To understand the significance of this issue, one must bear in mind the

Let

$a = $ bound

$b = $ Greek

$c = $ old

$d = $ poetry

$e = $ quartos

Carroll's Letters to John Cook Wilson Relevant to the Library Problem[2]

–I–

... Such Problems are easily worked into Soriteses, by assuming, as an Axiom, the beautiful Theorem "The aggregate of the Contradictories of the Classes which constitute an Exhaustive Division is a Nullity."

For example, if a, b, c, d, e be an Exhaustive Division then $a'b'c'd'e'$ is a Nullity. (This is obvious, since anything, which is excluded from *every one* of the Classes, cannot exist at all.) Hence if we are given that a, b, c are Nullities, we proceed thus:

$$a'b'c'd'e'_0 \dagger a_0 \dagger b_0 \dagger c_0 \ \P \ d'e'_0$$

For your No. 9, the Sorites would be

$$(\underline{BC})'(BC')'(B'C)'(\underline{B'C}')'_0 \dagger A\underline{B'C}'_0 \dagger \underline{BC}KD'_0 \ \P \ (BC')'(B'C)'AKD'_0$$

Here is a lovely Problem I've just made, on your pattern. I wonder if you'll find it easy by *your* Method.

(1) A is B or C or D;

(2) AB is C or H;

(3) B is A or C or D;

(4) BCE is D;

"chief problem of logic" as defined by the logical algebraists: "Given any number of universal propositions involving any number of terms, to determine what is all the information that they jointly afford with regard to any given term or combination of terms." (See discussion in Editor's Introduction, Section III.) When one looks further, one sees that the disagreement is only apparent; Carroll does not deny that the statements in question *follow from* the premises given; what he denies is that they can be considered full conclusions answering the demand set forth in the statement of the chief problem of logic just quoted.

[2] The following letter, heavily annotated by Cook Wilson, is dated November 4, 1896. The letter exists only in fragment, beginning on page 2.

(5) *CD* is *A* or *B*;
(6) *E* is *A* or *B* or *D*;
(7) *BD* is *A* or *H*;
(8) *ACK* is *B*;
(9) *DK* is *B* or *C*.

Truly yours,

C. L. DODGSON.

–**II**–

Ch. Ch.

Nov. 11/96

MY DEAR WILSON,

'Re' your Problem No. 9.

You take, as Data, "(1) *AB'* is *C*, (2) *BCK* is *D*" (which I symbolize as "$AB'C'_0 \dagger BCKD'_0$"), and therefrom you deduce "*KA* not (*BC'*) not (*B'C*) is *D*," (which I symbolize as "$KA(BC')'(B'C)'D'_0$"). And you claim that this should be regarded as a genuine "Conclusion."

I maintained, in opposition to this view, that it is only a *Partial* Conclusion, as it contains Eliminands.

I find I was too hasty: further investigation has convinced me that it is not a "Conclusion" *at all*!

I think I can prove this in a very few words.

You will admit, I am sure, that the mere *aggregate* of the Premisses has no claim to be called a "Conclusion." (e.g. if our Data were "All *m* are *x*," "All *y* are *m*," it would be absurd to claim that the Double Proposition "All *m* are *x*, and all *y* are *m*" should be regarded as a "Conclusion.")

And, *a fortiori*, you will admit that the mere *aggregate* of *portions* of the Premisses has no such claim. (e.g. from the above Data, it would be absurd to deduce, as a "Conclusion," "Some *m* are *x*, and some *y* are *m*.")

Now, if we take any Pair of Attributes, any Thing, that has *not* got the Pair, must have either the contradictory of the *one*, or else the contradictory of the *other*. Hence (*BC'*)' is equivalent to (*B'* or *C*); and (*B'C*)' is equivalent to (*B* or *C'*). Hence your (so-called) "Conclusion" is equivalent to *KA* (*B'* or *C*) (*B* or *C'*)*D'_0*; i.e. to *KA* (*B'C* or *BC*)*D'_0*; i.e. to

$$(KAB'C'D'_0 \dagger KABCD'_0)$$

But $KAB'C'D'_0$ is merely a *portion* of $AB'C'_0$; and, similarly, $KABCD'_0$ is merely a *portion* of $BCKD'_0$. Hence your "Conclusion" is merely the *aggregate* of *portions* of the Premisses. Hence it is *not* a "Conclusion" at all.

C.L.D.[3]

---

[3] At the side of this letter Wilson writes,   J.C.W."
"Here Dodgson comes to utter grief.

–III–

My Solution of Problem[4] Given to J. C. W., solved, by him, in *95238* (Carroll's reference number)

$$1 \qquad 2 \qquad 3 \qquad 4 \qquad 5 \qquad 6 \qquad 7 \qquad 8 \qquad 9$$

$$ab'c'd' \dagger abc'h' \dagger ba'c'd' \dagger bced' \dagger cda'b' \dagger ea'b'd' \dagger bda'h' \dagger ackb' \dagger dkb'c'$$

a	b	c	d	e	h	k
1,2,8	2,3,4,7	4,5,8	5,7,9	4,6		8,9
3,5,6,7	1,5,6,8,9	1,2,3,9	1,3,4,6		2,7	

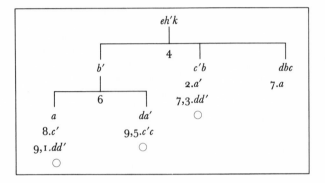

Hence we cannot prove $eh'k_0$. It *may* possibly exist, with Attributes *abcd*.

–IV–

The Chestnuts, Guildford
Dec. 26/96

MY DEAR WILSON,

Thanks for your interesting letter.

You say "You ca'n't really know that 'Some *S* is P,' without knowing *what* *S* is P. If any one used such a Proposition in argument, you would at once ask him 'What *S* is P?,' &, if he couldn't answer, you would exclude his premiss as nonsense."

I fear I cannot agree with you in limiting the application of Logic to exact Science. In my view, it is of very great use in ordinary life, where *Particular*

---

[4] This solution was enclosed with a letter to Cook Wilson of November 18, 1896, on which Cook Wilson scrawled, "This is a complete breakdown of Dodgson's Method which cannot touch problems of this sort." The solution is for the problem given at the very end of Carroll's letter to Wilson of November 4, 1896 (Item I above).

Conclusions are often the best we can get.   Suppose you, as Judge, heard a
Counsel say "We can prove that the Prisoner's employer never signed more
than twenty cheques on that bank: we can also prove that the Prisoner
presented more than thirty such cheques: hence *some* of these cheques must be
forgeries," would you say "You must point out *which* cheques are forgeries:
&, if you ca'n't do this, I shall tell the Jury to set aside your conclusion as
nonsense"?

As you seem to think my "Library" Sorites is not "scientific," I will
translate it into other matter:

(1) All animals that have claws are carnivorous;
(2) All animals that have hoofs are graminivorous;
(3) No quadrupeds have both claws & hoofs.

Univ. "animals"; A = carnivorous; B = graminivorous; C = having claws;
D = having hoofs; E = quadrupeds.

Your solution would, I suppose, be as follows:

(1) C is A;
(2) D is B;
(3) No E is CD.

By 1, 2, CD is AB.

I.   Categorical Conclusion. CD is ABE', i.e. "All animals, that have claws
& hoofs, are carnivorous & graminivorous & are not quadrupeds."
II.   Disjunctive Conclusion. E is $C'D'$ or BC' or AD', i.e. "A quadruped is
either without claws or hoofs, or is graminivorous & without claws, or
carnivorous & without hoofs."

I venture to think that, even from a *scientific* point of view, Conclusion I is
valueless, *unless* we have evidence that animals, with claws & hoofs, *really exist.*

I also regard Conclusion II as of doubtful value, though I admit its truth.

My reason is that I think a Proposition, which gives the *choice* of *three*
Predicates, & cannot tell us *which* is the true one, is not worth stating *unless it is
the only one attainable.*   If it *were* the only one, I would accept it as worth
stating: many of the Sorites-Problems in Part II are of this form.

The two Categorical Conclusions, which you have missed, are *certainties*, &
not (like your No. I) dependent for their value on the wild chance that some
animal may be found with claws & hoofs.   But they are both *Particular*:
so I fear you will set them aside as "ridiculous."   They are $A(DE)'_1$ and
$B(CE)'_1$ i.e. "Some carnivorous animals are not hoofed quadrupeds;

"Some graminivorous animals are not quadrupeds with claws."

You say "I imagined you were committed to the view that from 'A is B,
C is D, BD is E' might be concluded 'AC is E.'"

As I found you always stated my Nullities ("No A is B'," etc.) in the form
of Universal Affirmatives ("A is B," etc), I accepted your form, but always
with the mental addition "if existent."

You say "Your remark that my Conclusion (b) '*D* is *C'E'* or *B* or *A*' is contained in (a) '*D* is *C'E'* or *BE'* or *AC'*,' is very unfortunate.... You are unconsciously attacking your patron saint *Barbara*. From '*S* is *M*, *M* is *P*,' we get '*S* is *MP*' (a). Now, as you put it, the Conclusion '*S* is *P*' (b) is contained in (a)."

All this I accept: &, if any one offered me these *two* Conclusions, I should say "If your (a) were a genuine Conclusion, then your (b) would be superfluous. But your (a) is *not* a genuine Conclusion: it is merely the *aggregate* of the true Conclusion '*S* is *P*' & the Premiss '*S* is *M*.'"

Very truly yours,
C.L.D.

Chapter XII ⚜ The Pigs and Balloons Problem[1]

(1) All, who neither dance on tight ropes nor eat penny-buns, are old.

(2) Pigs, that are liable to giddiness, are treated with respect.

(3) A wise balloonist takes an umbrella with him.

---

[1] The original to this problem is preserved in the Morris L. Parrish Collection, Princeton University Library. The nine premisses, and the conclusion, but not Carroll's working out of the problem, have been published in Philip C. Blackburn and Lionel White (Eds.) *Logical Nonsense* (New York: Putnam, 1934), where the editors write, "The author then analyses the series of propositions according to a complicated system of his own devising (baffling even mathematicians), and reaches his conclusion."

We see from this problem that Carroll had another way, in addition to the Method of Trees, for treating multiliteral soriteses in the first figure.

The method is closely related to the method of underscoring presented in Part I, but also introduces the technique of "barring" and "barred premisses" to which Carroll alluded earlier, in Book XII, Chapter III. To find out which premisses are "barred," one inspects the register, attending to eliminands. Some of the terms involved appear in one premiss, whereas their complements appear in two or more premisses. Thus in the Pigs and Balloons Problem, "dancing on tight ropes" appears in premiss 7, whereas "not-dancing on tight ropes" appears in premisses 1, 6, and 9. In Carroll's terminology, premiss 7 is thus *barred* by premisses 1, 6, and 9. His rule is that a

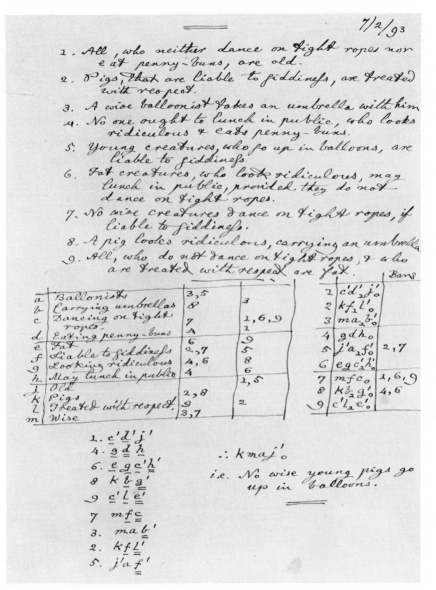

(Morris L. Parrish Collection, Princeton University Library)

barred premiss may not be used in a sorites until the premisses that are barring it have first been used. Thus in his solution premiss 7 is introduced only after premisses 1, 6, and 9 have been used; premiss 5 is not introduced until premisses 2 and 7 have been used; and premiss 8 is not introduced until after premisses 4 and 6 have been used.

(4) No one ought to lunch in public, who looks ridiculous and eats penny-buns.

(5) Young creatures, who go up in balloons, are liable to giddiness.

(6) Fat creatures, who look ridiculous, may lunch in public, provided they do not dance on tight ropes.

(7) No wise creatures dance on tight ropes, if liable to giddiness.

(8) A pig looks ridiculous, carrying an umbrella.

(9) All, who do not dance on tight ropes, and who are treated *with respect* are fat.

Bars

a	Balloonists	3,5		1	$c'd'_1j'_0$	
b	Carrying umbrellas	8	3	2	$kf_1l'_0$	
c	Dancing on tight ropes	7	1,6,9	3	$ma_1b'_0$	
d	Eating penny-buns	4	1	4	gdh_0	
e	Fat	6	9	5	$j'a_1f'_0$	2,7
f	Liable to giddiness	2,7	5	6	$egc'_1h'_0$	
g	Looking ridiculous	4,6	8	7	mfc_0	1,6,9
h	May lunch in public	4	6	8	$kb_1g'_0$	4,6
				9	$c'l_1e'_0$	
j	Old		1,5			
k	Pigs	2,8				
l	Treated with respect	9	2			
m	Wise	3,7				

1. $c'd'j'$

4. gdh

6. $e\ gc'h'$

8. kbg'

9. $c'le'$

7. mfc

3. mab'

2. kfl'

5. $j'af'$

∴ $kmaj'_0$

i.e. No wise young pigs go up in balloons.

Chapter XIII ❧ The Problem of Grocers on Bicycles[1]

(1) All honest industrious men are healthy;

(2) No grocers are healthy;

(3) All industrious grocers are honest;

(4) All cyclists are industrious;

(5) All unhealthy cyclists are dishonest.

∴ Grocers do not (never) ride cycle.

One premiss is superfluous. Which is it?

---

[1] John Cook Wilson, in a memorandum dated August 5, 1896, works this problem as follows:

SOLUTION

Let H = honest, I = industrious, X = healthy, G = grocer, C = cyclist. The premisses are

1. HI is X;
2. G is not X;
3. IG is H;
4. C is I;
5. C not X is not H.

Conclusion G is not C.

(i) (4) C is I;
　　∴ CG is I thus CG is GI;
　　∴ by (3) CG is HI;
　　∴ by (1) CG is X.

But by (2) CG is not X

∴ CG is impossible;

∴ G is not C.

In this proof premiss (5) is superfluous.

(ii) (2) G is not X;
　　∴ CG is C not X;
　　∴ by (5) CG is not H;
(4) C is I;
　　∴ CG is GI;
　　∴ by (3) CG is H;
　　hence CG is H and not H.

∴ G is not C.

In this proof premiss (1) is superfluous.

Hence the problem is *wrongly stated*. It should be "There are two premisses such that either makes the other superfluous. Which are they?"

381

Chapter XIV ❧ The Pets Problem[1]

Problem: To achieve the complete conclusion:

(1) All old monkeys are docile;
(2) All affectionate cats purr;
(3) All healthy dogs bark;
(4) All my fat pets are in this basket;
(5) No small pigs are affectionate;
(6) Black cats can be easily carried about;
(7) No cross active creatures jump, except monkeys;
(8) I make pets of all affectionate docile creatures;
(9) A healthy monkey, if electrified, becomes a pig;
(10) The large creatures in this basket are all cats;
(11) Old dogs are always cross;
(12) No fat creatures bark, except when electrified;
(13) All affectionate old creatures jump;
(14) All the creatures in this basket, that purr, are black;
(15) Large dogs cannot be easily carried about;
(16) Creatures, that are cross and destitute of affection, are always lazy;
(17) Unhealthy creatures are either large or thin.

Chapter XV ❧ The Winds and Windows Problem[2]

From the following Premisses, prove that, when the wind is in the East, I keep my window shut:

(1) There is always sunshine when the wind is in the East;
(2) When it is cold and foggy, my neighbour practises the flute;
(3) When my fire smokes, I set the door open;

---

[1] This problem appears as number three of "Sixth Paper on Logic," June 1887.

[2] This problem is given as example one in the "Ninth Paper on Logic," November 1892.

(4) When it is cold and I feel rheumatic, I light my fire;

(5) When the wind is in the East and comes in gusts, my fire smokes;

(6) When I keep the door open, I am free from headache;

(7) Even when the sun is shining and it is not cold, I keep my window
shut if it is foggy;

(8) When the wind does not come in gusts, and when I have a fire and
keep the door shut, I do not feel rheumatic;

(9) Sunshine always brings on fog;

(10) When my neighbour practises the flute, I shut the door, even if I
have no headache;

(11) When there is a fog and the wind is in the East, I feel rheumatic.

BOOK XIV
SOME FURTHER
PROBLEMS TO BE
SOLVED BY THE
METHODS OF PART II[1]

[1] This book contains nearly seventy logical problems that will be unfamiliar to most readers. It is drawn from twenty-one galley sheets marked "Symbolic Logic, Part 2. Examples." Here no solutions are given, and I know of no surviving correspondence related to them. A number of the exercises produced here were, however, circulated by Carroll in his various "Papers on Logic" that he had privately printed for his friends during the preparation of this manuscript. Usually differences of detail exist between the exercises given in the "Papers" and those given here. My footnotes indicate the source of variant versions.

These new problems are numbered from 1 to 83, and I have retained Carroll's numbering even though some of the problems and exercises are missing. Numbers 4, 6, 11, and 14–26 are missing entirely. Only the dictionary for Number 30 survives, but we can tell from that that this is "Froggy's Problem," produced in the preceding book.

If we assume that Carroll intended the other thirteen problems (apart from the elementary sequences problems) which were presented in Book XIII to be incorporated eventually into this book, and that the problems missing from the galleys include these problems, then only one problem is missing. Otherwise sixteen problems are missing. The overlap of Problem 30 with Book XIII argues for the former supposition, but there is no way to know.

Carroll's correspondence numbers on these galley sheets indicate that they were set up in this form in 1896.

Evidently they were not all received at once, for several bear Richard Clay printers' stamps with dates, one being dated August 24, 1896; another, September 21, 1896. Carroll apparently had them to hand a few days later, for on September 25, 1896 he wrote to Cook Wilson, "I have now got in type more than 80 Sorites-Problems for Part II (one with 50 Premisses!). Would you care to see them?" The correspondence shows that Cook Wilson had the galleys in hand prior to November 6 of that year.

Problems and Exercises 1–83

–1–

(1) I don't like walking with any London-friend of mine, unless he wears a tall hat;

(2) The Colonel is ready to play billiards with any man who is not the subject of general conversation, unless he happens to be fat;

(3) A man, who knows what o'clock it is and who never yields to me in argument, is unattractive;

(4) No old tight-rope-dancer ever rouses me to enthusiasm;

(5) Any novelist, whom I take pleasure in cutting, always cuts me dead;

(6) A man, who goes about in kid-gloves, but without his coat, is a humbug;

(7) All my intimate friends in London are young men;

(8) No man, who is the subject of general conversation, ever rouses me to enthusiasm, unless he is a horsey man;

(9) A man, who has his wits about him and does not choose his own wines, is always "at home" when I call;

(10) A man, who is a good shot and never tells pointless anecdotes, is sure to have a good temper;

(11) All humbugs, who write novels, are intimate friends of mine;

(12) I like to walk with a good-tempered man, unless he goes about in his shirt-sleeves;

(13) A man, who never loses his umbrella, and is not easily taken in, is sure to be an early riser;

(14) Fat men, who do not dance on the tight-rope, are universally respected;

(15) I regard with contemptuous pity a man who fails in life, and who runs across the street;

(16) A man, who does not stick to business, is not likely to be elected Mayor, unless he has bushy whiskers;

(17) An elephant hunter always rouses me to enthusiasm, unless he happens to be a farmer;

(18) Any London friend of mine, who tells pointless anecdotes, is a humbug;

(19) I never invite an old man to dinner, unless he has lent me money;

(20) A man, who does not stick to business, does not run across the street, and has bushy hair, is in no danger of getting a bad fall;

(21) A man, who gets up late and sometimes loses his umbrella, has little chance of marrying an heiress;

(22) An old man, who cares for appearances, always wears kid-gloves;

(23) A good-tempered man never cuts me dead, unless he is a humbug;

(24) A man, who never tells pointless anecdotes and has never lent me money, has his wits about him;

(25) A man, who chooses his own wines and always yields to me in argument, is the sort that I invite to dine with me;

(26) I always try to be civil to a man who fails in life, unless he has bushy whiskers;

(27) All farmers are horsey men;

(28) A novelist is a dull companion, unless he rouses me to enthusiasm;

(29) All men, who get up early, and stick to business and win universal respect, are rich;

(30) Any London friend of mine, to whom I try to be civil, will probably be elected Mayor;

(31) Any good-tempered man, who has lent me money and does not care for appearances, is willing to shake hands with me when I am in rags;

(32) The only men, with whom the Colonel will play billiards, are either horsey men or farmers;

(33) I always invite an attractive man to dine with me, provided he is rich;

(34) A man, who is apt to walk on tip-toe and whom I regard with contemptuous pity, is sure to be one who sticks to business;

(35) The only men, who are always "at home" to me, but whom I never invite to dinner, are magistrates;

(36) I always make an intimate friend of a man who will shake hands

with me when I am in rags and will give up his umbrella to me when it is raining;

(37) Any London friend of mine, who understands horses, is universally respected;

(38) An unattractive man, who chooses his own wines, is easily taken in;

(39) I have sufficient courage to insult any novelist, unless he happens to be a good shot;

(40) An old man, who is apt to walk on tip-toe, will probably get a bad fall;

(41) A man, who never knows what o'clock it is, and who has never lent me money, will probably marry an heiress;

(42) No London-friend of mine, who has his wits about him, is easily taken in;

(43) I never forget any old man who is willing to shake hands with me when I am in rags;

(44) A novelist, who does not stick to business, is sure to fail in life;

(45) I do not dare to insult an ill-tempered man, unless he happens to be an intimate friend of mine;

(46) Those magistrates, who will not shake hands with me when I am in rags, always choose their own wine;

(47) All dull companions are either horsey men or elephant-hunters;

(48) Men, who wear tall hats and kid gloves, always cut me dead;

(49) A man, who has bushy whiskers and is universally respected, is apt to walk on tip-toe;

(50) I delight in cutting a man, whom I perfectly remember, but who will not give up his umbrella to me when it is raining.

Univ. "men"; a = apt to tell pointless anecdotes; b = apt to walk on tip-toe; c = "at home" to me; d = attractive; e = caring for appearances; f = choosing his own wines; g = dull companions; h = early risers; j = easily taken in; k = elephant-hunters; l = farmers; m = fat; n = good shots; p = good-tempered; q = having bushy whiskers; r = having his wits about him; s = horsey; t = humbugs; u = intimate friends of mine; v = invited to dine with me; w = knowing what o'clock it is; x = likely to be elected Mayor; y = likely to get a bad fall; z = likely to marry an heiress; A = London-friends of mine; B = magistrates; C = men to whom I try to be civil; D = men who cut me; E = men who have lent me money; F = men whom I dare insult; G = men whom I delight to cut; H = men with whom I like to walk; $\mathcal{J}$ = men with whom the Colonel is willing to play billiards; K = novelists; L = old; M = regarded by me with contemptuous pity; N = remembered by me; P = rich; Q = rousing me to enthusiasm; R = running across a street; S = sometimes losing his umbrella; T = sticking to business; U = subjects of general conversation; V = successful in life; W = tight-rope dancers; X = universally respected; Υ = wearing a coat; Z = wearing a tall hat; β = wearing kid gloves; δ = willing to give up his umbrella to me when it is raining; ζ = willing to shake hands with me when I am in rags; λ = yielding to me in argument.

—2[2]—

(1) A man, who is neither a speculator nor bad to lend money to, is no curmudgeon;

(2) All my friends, who are members of this Club, are would-be celebrities;

(3) A wise man demands a receipt when he pays a bill;

(4) No handsome man, outside this town, is sure to be well spoken of;

(5) No dancing-master is sought after, if very fat;

(6) No passionate man is popular, unless he is generous;

(7) A foolish speculator is on the road to ruin;

(8) A generous man gets testimonials, if he blows his own trumpet;

(9) All wise enthusiasts are poetical;

(10) A man, who dresses in sheepskins and lives on whale-blubber is an Arctic voyager;

(11) A generous man, who is not a dandy, retails other people's jokes;

(12) A passionate man, who is not above taking advice, is sure to be well spoken of;

(13) An ugly man, who gets on badly, is not an eligible suitor;

(14) All foolish dandies are old;

(15) All British merchants are economical;

(16) A man, who has not dreamy eyes, is despised by ladies, unless he is intimate with the Royal Family;

(17) A man, who blows his own trumpet, gets noticed by Society;

(18) All wise noblemen are rich;

(19) A man does not demand receipts when he pays bills, unless he is getting on badly;

---

[2] A similar problem appears as Example 5 of "Ninth Paper on Logic," November 1892.

(20) All the firemen in this town are ugly;

(21) All men, who are neither curmudgeons, nor would-be celebrities, are members of this Club;

(22) A man, who is noticed by Society and gets testimonials, is no fool;

(23) No economical man is bad to lend money to, unless he lives on whale-blubber;

(24) No influential man is sought after, unless he is a dancing-master;

(25) Commoners, who are intimate with the Royal Family, are eligible suitors;

(26) All wise dreamy-eyed men are fond of barley-sugar;

(27) A man without enthusiasm loves walking by moonlight;

(28) A passionate overbearing man is influential if he is generous;

(29) Arctic voyagers, who dress in sheepskin, are wise;

(30) An overbearing man, who is not a merchant, is above taking advice;

(31) All would-be celebrities, who retail other people's jokes, blow their own trumpets;

(32) All the wise men in this town are firemen;

(33) A man, who is despised by ladies, is sought after, provided he loves walking by moonlight;

(34) Old dandies retail other people's jokes;

(35) All foreign merchants are wise;

(36) All foolish members of the Club are friends of mine;

(37) No overbearing man has influence, if he is above taking advice;

(38) A speculator, who is on the road to ruin, is a bad person to lend money to;

(39) Men with dreamy eyes, who are fond of barley-sugar, are despised by ladies;

(40) All wise dancing-masters are very fat;

(41) Rich noblemen are eligible suitors;

(42) All men, who live on whale-blubber and are not above taking advice dress in sheep-skins;

(43) All poetical enthusiasts love walking by moonlight;

Univ. "men"; a = above taking advice; b = Arctic voyagers; c = bad to lend money to; d = blowing one's own trumpet; e = British; h = curmudgeons; k = dancing-masters; l = dandies; m = demanding a receipt when paying a bill; n = despised by ladies; r = dressed in sheepskins; s = economical; t = eligible suitors; u = enthusiastic; v = firemen; w = fond of barley-sugar; x = generous; z = getting on badly; A = getting testimonials; B = handsome; C = having dreamy eyes;

D = influential; E = intimate with the Royal Family; F = in this town; G = living on whale-blubber; H = loving to walk by moonlight; J = members of this Club; L = merchants; M = my friends; N = noblemen; P = noticed by Society; Q = old; R = on the road to ruin; T = overbearing; V = passionate; W = poetical; X = popular; Y = retailing other people's jokes; α = rich; β = sought after; δ = speculators; ε = sure to be well spoken of; ζ = very fat; θ = wise; λ = would-be celebrities.

$$-3^3-$$

(1) All whom I have taught, except my own sons, know something;
(2) A contented barber is a welcome visitor;
(3) All, except those who are in this house, are good scholars;
(4) All the dandies, who have been plucked, are grinning;
(5) Any one, who admires a bald head, is either a brother of mine or is in good spirits;
(6) Those, who do not think intensely, know nothing;
(7) Nobody with a headache likes beating a gong;
(8) Any one in this house, who makes foolish remarks, is a son of mine;
(9) None who value health like toffy;
(10) All barbers wear white aprons;
(11) A fanciful man, who does not read hard, is always complaining;
(12) Peter is a candidate for Matriculation;
(13) All, who do little, except my sons, are contented;
(14) The candidates for Responsions, who have not been plucked, are all in good spirits;
(15) No son of mine, who is in good health, is a dandy;
(16) Good scholars, who think intensely but have no self-respect, are boastful;
(17) My brothers are all barbers;
(18) Any one, who wears a white apron and can endure a hurdy-gurdy, is worthy of honour;
(19) Nobody, who respects himself, dances jigs while at lessons;
(20) Those of my sons, who are always complaining, are ambitious men;
(21) All the hard-reading men, who have been plucked, are dandies;

---

[3] A similar problem appears as Example 4 in "Ninth Paper on Logic," November 1892.

(22) All barbers, who are worthy of honour, dance jigs;

(23) Any one, who has a headache, either thinks intensely or is one of my old pupils;

(24) Boasters do little;

(25) Those, who do not value their health, like beating a gong when they are not at lessons;

(26) All, except good scholars, make foolish remarks;

(27) Those, who respect themselves, are mild in manner;

(28) All my sons, except Peter, are candidates for Responsions;

(29) Barbers, who grin, are in good health;

(30) Any one in good spirits, who does not like beating a gong, cannot endure a hurdy-gurdy;

(31) All ambitious men read hard;

(32) All candidates for Matriculation have been plucked;

(33) No boaster is a welcome visitor;

(34) All persons, who are mild in manner, except my sons, like toffy;

(35) Any one, who does not admire a bald head, is a barber;

(36) All, who indulge in reverie, are fanciful men.

Univ. "persons"; a = able to endure a hurdy-gurdy; b = admiring a bald head; c = ambitious men; d = at lessons; e = barbers; h = boasters; k = candidates for Matriculation; l = candidates for Responsions; m = complaining; n = contented; r = dancing jigs; s = dandies; t = doing little; u = fanciful men; v = good scholars; w = grinning; x = hard-reading men; z = having a headache; A = healthy; B = indulging in reverie; C = in good spirits; D = in this house; E = knowing something; F = liking to beat a gong; G = liking toffy; H = making foolish remarks; J = mild in manner; L = my brothers; M = my sons; N = Peter; P = plucked; Q = self-respecting; R = taught by me; T = thinking intensely; V = valuing health; W = wearing a white apron; X = welcome visitors; Y = worthy of honour.

–5[4]–

(1) All Jews wear beards;

(2) No learned traveler cares for pitch-and-toss;

---

[4] A version of this problem appears as Number 6 of "Sixth Paper on Logic," June 1887.

(3) All Frenchmen walk fast;

(4) A good-humoured cab-driver is always graceful;

(5) The house is empty, unless Ebenezer is in it;

(6) No discontented person is interesting, unless he has traveled a good deal;

(7) Those who can see always avoid pigs;

(8) People with heads on their shoulders are not irritating, so long as they do not talk too much;

(9) A Gentile, who is easily taken in, ought not to buy a horse;

(10) Any one, who is willing to be painted green, is a discontented idiot;

(11) No one of learning, if very remarkable, travels much;

(12) Any one, who has not been educated by a pig, will take to smoking, unless he is threatened with a blunderbuss;

(13) All, who are not in the house, have heads on their shoulders;

(14) Nothing but a pig can be made into bacon;

(15) The learned are always interesting;

(16) No squinting Jew is fond of pigs;

(17) Those, who wear beards and look shy, are in failing health;

(18) Any one, who looks anxious, is an irritating bore;

(19) All idiots are fretful and troublesome;

(20) When a cab-driver retires from business, he is always threatened with a blunderbuss;

(21) None but Frenchmen are fat and yet graceful;

(22) Those, who wear beards, always retire from business when their health fails;

(23) Gentiles are easily taken in;

(24) Any fretful creature, that grunts, can be made into bacon;

(25) Those who are dull are not troublesome, so long as they have some sense in their heads;

(26) Those, who are fat and wish to ride, are always good-humoured;

(27) Those, who are unlearned, but still avoid pigs, have some sense in their heads;

(28) Any one, who is willing to be painted green and does not care for pitch-and-toss, is very remarkable;

(29) A talkative cab-driver is never a bore;

(30) All bearded Frenchmen, who squint, are fond of pigs;

(31) A Jewish cab-driver always looks shy;

(32) Ebenezer will never take to smoking, unless he is threatened with a blunderbuss;

(33) No fat pigs walk fast;

(34) The unlearned are always dull;

(35) Creatures, that are not pigs, but have been educated by pigs, always grunt;

(36) Those, who have heads on their shoulders, always look anxious;

(37) Any one, who is blind and easily taken in, may buy a horse, provided he does not wish to ride;

(38) All pigs are fat.

[N.B. Two of these Premisses are superfluous. Which are they?]

Univ. "creatures"; a = able to see; b = avoiding pigs; c = bearded; d = bores; e = cab-drivers; f = capable of being made into bacon; h = caring for pitch-and-toss; j = contented; k = creatures who may buy a horse; l = dull; m = easily taken; n = Ebenezer; p = educated by a pig; q = failing in health; r = fat; s = fond of pigs; t = Frenchmen; v = fretful; w = good-humoured; y = graceful; z = grunting; A = having a head on his shoulders; B = having some sense in his head; C = idiots; D = interesting; E = in the house; G = irritating; H = Jews; J = learned; L = looking anxious; M = looking shy; N = pigs; P = retiring from business; Q = smokers; R = squinting; T = talkative; X = threatened with a blunderbuss; β = travellers; δ = troublesome; ζ = very remarkable; θ = walking fast; λ = willing to be painted green; μ = wishing to ride.

—7[5]—

(1) Fortunate men, who are lawyers' clerks, are always hungry;

(2) All the basket-makers are out of work;

(3) A man without self-restraint is helped five times to plum-pudding;

(4) No one but Whittington ever heard bells speak;

(5) A poor man, who has self-restraint, never wears slippers;

(6) No lean and slippered pantaloon is respected;

(7) A man, who is helped five times to plum-pudding, is a glutton;

(8) Those who complain always get listened to;

(9) A rich man, who has never heard bells speak, is always lean;

(10) None but lawyers' clerks have self-restraint;

(11) A pantomime actor, who wears slippers, is a pantaloon;

---

[5] This problem appears as Number 5 of "Sixth Paper on Logic," June 1887.

(12) A man, who talks without cessation when any one will listen to him, is a bore;

(13) The famous Whittington was elected Lord Mayor;

(14) All lean persons, who are self-restrained, act in pantomimes;

(15) Those who never complain get underpaid;

(16) Egoists are intolerable;

(17) Any one, who has heard bells speak, is fortunate;

(18) No hungry lawyer's clerk was ever elected Lord Mayor;

(19) All letter-carriers, who do not live in this village, complain if underpaid;

(20) Any one, who is listened to, will talk without cessation;

(21) Pantaloons, employed in pantomimes, are respected if rich;

(22) All, who have not heard bells speak, are egoists;

(23) A bore is endurable, provided he does not wear slippers;

(24) Hungry men, who have failed to become famous, never complain;

(25) The people in this village are all basket-makers.

Univ. is "men"; a = basket-makers; b = bores; c = complaining; d = egoists; e = famous; h = fat; k = fortunate; l = gluttons; m = having heard bells speak; n = helped five times to plum-pudding; r = hungry; s = in this village; t = lawyers' clerks; u = letter-carriers; v = listened to; w = Lord Mayor; x = out of work; z = pantaloons; A = pantomimists; B = respected; C = rich; D = self-restraining; E = slippered; F = talking without cessation; G = tolerable; H = underpaid; J = Whittington.

–8⁶–

(1) A quarrelsome man does not deserve blame if he is not in his right mind;

(2) Men, who are objects of terror, are always avoided;

(3) The popular candidates in this election are Liberals;

(4) Captains always tell long yarns;

(5) A man of slim figure, who is constantly quoted as a model-citizen, is always conceited;

---

⁶ This problem appears in the "Sixth Paper on Logic," June 1887, as No. 4.

(6) Any man of genial manners may safely go through the town today, except Mr. Brown;

(7) No good man of business, who is cautious as to what he states, ever says he has seen the sea-serpent;

(8) A thoughtless man is a constant cause of mischief;

(9) A popular man, who is fat, is always out of breath;

(10) A man, who tells long yarns and has no geniality of manner, is an object of terror;

(11) Mr. Brown is a candidate in this election;

(12) A man, who is ready to make amends for any harm he has done, is always a humble man;

(13) No man, who tells long yarns without giving names or dates, is readily believed;

(14) No quarrelsome man would be safe in the streets today, unless he were a candidate in this election;

(15) A good business-man, who is not quarrelsome, is cautious as to everything he states;

(16) No man ever tells long yarns, when running to catch a train and out of breath;

(17) A man, who is a constant cause of mischief and is not ready to make amends for the harm he has done, cannot be in his right mind;

(18) No man, who gives names and dates, is avoided, unless he is in his second childhood;

(19) The Liberal candidates in this election are all running to catch the train;

(20) Any man, who gives names and dates, is a good man of business;

(21) No quarrelsome man is an object of terror if he is in his second childhood;

(22) A man deserves blame if he is not ready to make amends for any harm he has done;

(23) A man who tells long yarns is always popular;

(24) A man of genial manners, who is ready to make amends for any harm he has done, is constantly quoted as a model-citizen.

Univ. "men"; a = avoided; b = Brown; c = candidates in this election; d = captains; e = cautious in making statements; h = conceited; k = constantly causing mischief; l = constantly quoted as a model-citizen; m = deserving blame; n = fat; r = genial; s = giving names and dates; t = good men of business; v = in his second childhood; w = Liberals; z = objects of terror; A = out of breath; B = popular; C = quarrelsome;

D = readily believed; E = ready to make amends for any harm he has done; F = running to catch a train; G = safe in the streets to-day; H = sane; J = saying that he has seen the sea-serpent; L = telling long yarns; M = thoughtful.

–9–

(1) Tall men, who drive about in carriages, are cheered by the little boys;

(2) Men with blue eyes, who like running across a ploughed field, are worth looking at;

(3) All the grocers in the street have grey hair;

(4) A man, who is listened to with respect, can influence others;

(5) Men with long beards, who look like patriarchs, are all Jews;

(6) A tall man, who has sprained his ankle, walks lame;

(7) Rheumatic men, who are fond of arm-chairs, are fretful;

(8) All men, who are over ninety years old, are wrinkled;

(9) No influential man, who is cheered by little boys, is an object of scorn;

(10) Men, who hold up their heads, are fascinating, provided that they have blue eyes;

(11) All the men in this street, who have long beards, look like goats;

(12) All short wise-looking men are grocers;

(13) A wrinkled grey-haired man is always fond of an arm-chair;

(14) A man, who is fit to be a judge and is cheered by the little boys, is always conceited;

(15) All grocers have blue eyes and long beards;

(16) Wise-looking men are always listened to with respect;

(17) All men, who are Jews, and who look like goats, suffer from rheumatism;

(18) All the tall men in this street are fit to be judges;

(19) No grey-haired man is fascinating if he is fretful;

(20) Conceited men, who drive in carriages, are objects of scorn;

(21) No man in this street is worth looking at unless he holds up his head;

(22) All wrinkled men look wise;

(23) A man, who looks like a goat, is not listened to with respect, unless he also looks like a patriarch;

(24) A man, who is fit to be a judge and who can influence others, drives about in a carriage if he happens to walk lame.

Univ. "men"; a = blue-eyed; b = cheered by the little boys; c = conceited; d = driving about in a carriage; e = fascinating; h = fit to be a judge; k = fond of arm-chairs; l = fretful; m = grey-haired; n = grocers; r = having a long beard; s = having sprained his ankle; t = holding up his head; v = influential; w = in this street; z = Jews; A = liking to run across a ploughed field; B = listened to with respect; C = looking like a goat; D = looking like a patriarch; E = looking wise; F = objects of scorn; G = over ninety; H = rheumatic; L = tall; M = walking lame; N = worth looking at; P = wrinkled.

—10—

(1) I take snuff;

(2) No uncourteous snuff-taker is popular;

(3) Publicans, who drink toast-and-water, are wise;

(4) Those who read Tupper go to bed early;

(5) A really humble man, who is a bad violinist, is unhappy;

(6) All who do not go to plays are readers of Tupper;

(7) Old people, who cannot easily be excited, never get front seats;

(8) My brothers think that pigs can fly;

(9) A man, who goes to bed early, and lies there till noon, is an utter villain;

(10) Unhappy men always drink toast-and-water;

(11) The only contented man in the world is myself;

(12) No wise man thinks that pigs can fly;

(13) No one is an utter villain, if he reads Tupper;

(14) Snuff-takers, who have a right to sneeze, should be forebearing;

(15) An inattentive play-goer is difficult to excite;

(16) No man, who does not think that pigs can fly, need be forbearing;

(17) No conceited man is happy;

(18) Poor old saddlers have a right to sneeze;

(19) No toast-and-water drinker reads Tupper, unless he lies in bed till noon;

(20) Saddlers are never good violinists;

(21) None but publicans think that pigs can fly;

(22) Play-goers, who do not get front seats, have no right to sneeze;

(23) All courteous men, except my brothers, are inattentive.

Univ. "men"; a = attentive; b = conceited; c = contented; d = courteous; e = drinking toast-and-water; h = excitable; k = getting front seats; l = going to bed early; m = good violinists; n = happy; r = having right to sneeze; s = I; t = lying in bed till noon; v = men who should be forebearing; w = men who think that pigs can fly; z = my brothers; A = old; B = play-goers; C = popular; D = publicans; E = readers of Tupper; F = rich; G = saddlers; H = snuff-takers; J = utter villains; L = wise.

–12–

(1) A grown-up man, who doubts that we are a free nation, is a simpleton;

(2) Any student of Modern History has heard of Magna Charta;

(3) Wilson is a thoughtful man;

(4) A student of Ancient History, who does not know many attornies, will have to push his own way in life;

(5) All rich men are worth knowing;

(6) A simpleton who, not understanding Politics, talks about himself, is not a remarkable man;

(7) Wilson doubts whether we are a free nation;

(8) A student of Law is remarkable, if he never heard of Magna Charta;

(9) A grown-up man, who does not study Modern History, cannot understand Politics;

(10) A simpleton is likely to succeed at the Bar, if he knows many attornies;

(11) Wilson is not a cricketer;

(12) A minor, who doubts if we are a free nation, is not worth knowing;

(13) All, who are likely to succeed at the Bar, study Law or Modern History;

(14) A thoughtful man, who doubts if we are a free nation, is a dreamer who never reads the papers;

(15) No clever man, who is grown up, talks about himself;

(16) Dreamers, who are not cricketers, believe that cricket is extinct;

(17) A simpleton, who is worth knowing, need not push his own way in life;

(18) No one, who has heard of Magna Charta doubts that we are a free nation;

(19) A man, who walks rather than take a cab, who believes that cricket is extinct, and who never reads the paper, is worth knowing;

(20) Wilson is studying History;

(21) A poor man will walk rather than take a cab.

Univ. "men"; a = believing that cricket is extinct; b = clever; c = cricketers; d = doubting whether we are a free nation; e = dreamers; h = grown-up; k = having heard of Magna Charta; l = knowing many attornies; m = likely to succeed at the Bar; n = needing to push his own way in life; r = reading the papers; s = remarkable; t = rich; v = simpletons; w = studying Ancient History; z = studying Modern History; A = studying Law; B = talking about himself; C = thoughtful; D = understanding Politics; E = willing to walk rather than take a cab; F = Wilson; G = worth knowing.

[N.B. No. (20) is to be understood to mean that Wilson is either studying Modern History only; or Ancient only; or both together.]

–13–

Write an account of *Wilson*, the hero of the previous Example, stating all that is known with *certainty* about him.

–27–

(1) No old men are active;

(2) All who hunt tigers are brave;

(3) No husbands are really free men;

(4) An old man is always selfish;

(5) No miser is sane;

(6) All savage fat men like fighting;

(7) All old tiger-hunters are egoists;

(8) No brave soldiers are slaves;

(9) All inactive lunatics are fat;

(10) No selfish egoist likes fighting;

(11) Fat civilians are always savage.

Univ. "men"; a = active; b = brave; c = egoists; d = fat; e = husbands; h = liking to fight; k = lunatics; l = misers; m = old; n = savage; r = selfish; s = slaves; t = soldiers; v = tiger-hunters.

–28[7]–

(1) All inactive babies get fat;

(2) Civilians are liable to toothache;

(3) Those, who are always contented and happy, are well-fed;

(4) A fat glutton is always happy;

(5) Active soldiers have plenty of common sense;

(6) No English alderman is badly fed;

(7) Babies, except those in my family, are not always happy;

(8) A glutton, if he has common sense, never goes into the army;

(9) Well-fed people are liable to toothache, unless they are active;

(10) All fat members of my family are aldermen;

(11) Discontented foreigners are sometimes unhappy;

(12) The only gluttons without any common sense are babies.

Univ. "persons"; a = active; b = aldermen; c = always contented; d = always happy; e = babies; h = English; k = fat; l = gluttons; m = in my family; n = liable to toothache; r = sensible; s = soldiers; t = well-fed.

–29–

(1) All prize-fighters are active;

(2) Burglars, when taken up, are sent to prison;

(3) All old Jews are poor;

(4) No prize-fighter, who is admired, is unpopular;

(5) Paupers, when sent to prison, cease to be violent;

(6) Ugly old people get taken up;

(7) No one, who is awkward and violent, can be anything but a burglar;

(8) No young detectives are ugly;

(9) An active Gentile is always admired;

---

[7] A similar problem appears as Problem 30 in "Fifth Paper on Logic," May 1887.

(10) No awkward prize-fighter is beautiful;
(11) No violent detective is popular.

Univ. "men"; a = active; b = admired; c = awkward; d = beautiful; e = burglars; h = detectives; k = Jews; l = old; m = poor; n = popular; r = prize-fighters; s = sent to prison; t = taken up; u = violent.

-30[8]-

Univ. "Cosmophases"; ε = this; a = Froggy's hair is out of curl; b = Froggy intends to go a-wooing; c = Froggy is grinning like a hyæna; d = Froggy's mother permits him to go a-wooing; e = Froggy seems nearly mad with joy; h = Froggy is strutting about like a peacock; k = Froggy is wearing a waistcoat that is gorgeous beyond words; l = I go out on the roof; m = I remind Froggy of the £10 he owes me; n = I take a quiet cigar; r = I tell Froggy that he's quite the dandy; s = it is going to rain; t = it is very hot; v = my purse is empty; w = my railway-shares are going up; z = my tailor calls with his little bill; A = the thermometer is high; B = you had better take an umbrella.

-31-

(1) None of the ripe rosy apples, that I have bought from you, are of good flavour;
(2) There are no small ripe apples, in this box, that are not rosy;
(3) All the small apples of good flavour, that are unripe, are unfit for the table;
(4) The small rosy apples, that are wanting in good flavour, were not bought from you;
(5) There are no apples, in this box, that are neither ripe nor rosy nor of good flavour;
(6) The large ripe apples, belonging to me, that are wanting in good flavour, are not in this box;

---

[8] Only this fragment of Example 30 remains. It goes with Chapter V (Froggy) in Book XIII.

(7) No large rosy apples are fit for the table, unless they are ripe;

(8) None of the large apples, that are of good flavour but not rosy, were bought from you;

Univ. "my apples"; a = bought from you; b = fit for the table; c = in this box; d = large; e = of good flavour; h = ripe; k = rosy.

−32[9]−

(1) All active old Jews are healthy;

(2) All indolent magistrates are unpopular;

(3) All rich snuff-takers are unhealthy;

(4) All sarcastic magistrates are Jews;

(5) All young snuff-takers are pale;

(6) All rich, old men, who are unhealthy, are sarcastic;

(7) All magistrates, who are not poets, are studious;

(8) All rosy magistrates are talented men;

(9) All talented and popular students are rich;

(10) All pale snuff-takers are unpopular;

(11) All unpopular magistrates abstain from snuff;

(12) All talented poets, who are active, are rich.

Univ. "persons"; a = active; b = healthy; c = Jews; d = magistrates; e = men; h = old; k = poets; l = popular; m = rich; n = rosy; r = sarcastic; s = snuff-takers; t = studious; v = talented.

−33−

A certain Railway Company has a Standing Committee of Share-holders constituted under the following conditions:

(1) Directors are *ex-officio* members of it;

(2) Bond-holders are eligible;

(3) All others are ineligible.

---

[9] This problem resembles Problem 7 of "Eighth Paper on Logic," November 1892, and December 1892.

It is known that

    (4) All elderly Bond-holders, who are not Directors, are lame;

    (5) All short-sighted members of the Committee live in town;

    (6) All eligible Share-holders, who are lame, are young;

    (7) All Share-holders living out of town, who are not Bond-holders, are members of the Committee;

    (8) All elderly Directors are short-sighted.

Univ. "Shareholders"; a = bond-holders; b = directors; c = elderly; d = eligible; e = lame; h = living in town; k = members of the Committee; l = short-sighted.

$-33a^{10}-$

A certain Railway-Company has appointed a Committee of Shareholders, under the following conditions: Directors are *ex-officio* members of it; Bondholders also are admissible; all others are inadmissible.

    It is given that:

    (1) All admissible Shareholders, who are on the Committee and are lame Directors, live in town;

    (2) All short-sighted elderly Shareholders, who are admissible but are not Directors, are on the Committee;

    (3) All elderly Shareholders, living out of town, who are neither Directors nor Members of the Committee, are admissible.

    (4) All lame short-sighted Shareholders, who are admissible and are on the Committee, are Directors.

    Prove that no lame elderly Shareholders, who live out of town, are short-sighted.

$-34-$

    (1) No pitiless swindlers deserve help;

    (2) No one, who is sought after for a noble purpose, can be worthless;

    (3) No undetected conspirators are otherwise than dangerous;

    (4) No pitiful man is heartless;

---

[10] This version of Exercise 33 appeared in the "Ninth Paper on Logic," November 1892.

(5) Useless persons have no value;

(6) There are no dangerous people in this town, except my friends;

(7) No unreformed person is a desirable acquaintance;

(8) No detected swindlers are otherwise than contemptible;

(9) Those who are reformed deserve help;

(10) No useful person is contemptible;

(11) All my friends are heartless.

Univ. "persons"; a = conspirators; b = contemptible; c = dangerous; d = deserving help; e = desirable acquaintances; h = detected; k = heartless; l = in this town; m = my friends; n = pitiful; r = reformed; s = sought after for a noble purpose; t = swindlers; v = useful; w = worthless.

−35−

(1) Sleepy old misers are easily robbed;

(2) No Jews in this street are hunch-backed;

(3) All bald misers are old;

(4) Old people, who are easily robbed, are poor;

(5) No bald smoker can keep awake;

(6) No one can be a Jew, unless he is either hunch-backed or a miser.

Univ. "persons"; a = bald; b = easily robbed; c = hunch-backed; d = in this street; e = Jews; h = misers; k = old; l = rich; m = sleepy; n = smokers.

−36−

(1) A just man is always respected;

(2) No fat kings are active and merry;

(3) A man who is hated or respected is no longer young;

(4) None but kings and queens wear crowns;

(5) No man who is lean or indolent is much admired;

(6) An unjust queen is hated.

Univ. "persons"; a = active; b = fat; c = hated; d = just; e = kings; h = men; k = merry; l = much admired; m = old; n = queens; r = respected; s = wearing a crown.

–**37**[11]–

(1) No happy old friends of mine are wise;
(2) No wise old friends of mine are honest;
(3) No rich young friends of mine are unhealthy;
(4) No honest old friends of mine are happy, unless they are wise;
(5) No rich friends of mine are talkative, unless they are old;
(6) No poor young friends of mine are healthy;
(7) No foolish old friends of mine are unhappy;
(8) No rich healthy young friends of mine are silent;
(9) No dishonest old friends of mine are talkative, unless they are happy;
(10) No young friends of mine are poor, unless they are talkative;
(11) No old friends of mine are foolish and dishonest;
(12) No talkative young friends of mine are unhealthy, unless they are rich;
(13) No silent friends of mine are dishonest, unless they are foolish.

Univ. "friends of mine"; a = happy; b = healthy; c = honest; d = old; e = rich; h = talkative; k = wise.

–**38**–

(1) A simpleton, who is not always shouting, is sure to be a crab;
(2) None but spiders are good-humoured;
(3) No unsuccessful frog is despised, so long as it is healthy;
(4) All oysters are good-humoured;
(5) All spiders are healthy, except the green ones;
(6) Unsuccessful crabs, if good-humoured, are popular;
(7) Green crabs are always singing;
(8) The only simpletons, that are popular, are frogs;
(9) Rash young oysters are always unsuccessful;
(10) None but simpletons are good-humoured and yet despised;
(11) No old crabs are healthy;
(12) A rash spider is always despised.

Univ. "creatures"; a = always shouting; b = always singing; c = crabs; d = despised; e = frogs; h = good-humoured; k = green; l = healthy;

---

[11] This is a much more elaborate version of Problem 2 in "Sixth Paper on Logic," June 1887.

m = old; n = oysters; r = popular; s = rash; t = simpletons; u = spiders; v = successful.

—39—

(1) No insignificant ponies in Shetland are wanting in liveliness;
(2) My only delight is in conversation;
(3) Nothing but a shrimp is at once lively and insignificant;
(4) My conversation is made up of your jokes;
(5) Nothing, that I can take no delight in, is of any importance;
(6) I can remember all puns but my own;
(7) No shrimp is remarkable for sagacity;
(8) I can remember anything that is not a pun;
(9) All your jokes are insignificant.

Univ. "things"; a = conversation; b = delightful to me; c = insignificant; d = lively; e = my; h = puns; k = remarkable for sagacity; l = remembered by me; m = Shetland-ponies; n = shrimps; r = your jokes.

—40[12]—

(1) All the young and hopeful like toffy;
(2) All old gorilla-keepers are good-tempered;
(3) All gay cyclists ought to take snuff;
(4) Young people never despair;
(5) Good-tempered people need not take snuff;
(6) Young people, who like toffy, are inexperienced;
(7) All good-tempered captains ride bicycles;
(8) People of experience, who suffer from low spirits, do not keep gorillas.

Univ. "persons"; a = captains; b = cyclists; c = experienced; d = gay; e = good-tempered; h = hopeful; k = keeping gorillas; l = liking toffy; m = needing to take snuff; n = old.

---

[12] A version of this problem appears as Number 28 of "Fifth Paper on Logic," May 1887.

–**41**–

(1) All cunning savage animals are destructive;
(2) No fat lazy animals climb trees;
(3) All poisonous animals with claws wriggle;
(4) No lizards are destructive unless they climb trees;
(5) All animals, that have claws but no scales, are fat;
(6) All grinning animals, that are dreaded, have claws;
(7) No active destructive animal is fat;
(8) All animals with scales, that are dreaded, are poisonous;
(9) All grinning animals with claws are cunning;
(10) No savage lizard is viewed without dread;
(11) A savage lizard is an object of dread.

Univ. "animals"; a = active; b = climbing trees; c = cunning; d = destructive; e = dreaded; h = fat; k = grinning; l = having claws; m = lizards; n = poisonous; r = savage; s = scaly; t = wriggling.

–**42**[13]–

(1) There are no savage animals that I can trust;
(2) Sheep-dogs are domesticated wolves;
(3) All warm-blooded domesticated carnivora have claws;
(4) All quadrupeds are warm-blooded;
(5) My property consists of savage quadrupeds;
(6) No wolf with claws inspires me with distrust, provided that it wags its tail when it sees me;
(7) There are no animals in this house except my dogs;
(8) All dogs are carnivorous;
(9) No animals ever wag their tails when they see me, except what are in this house.

Univ. "animals"; a = carnivorous; b = dogs; c = domesticated; d = having claws; e = in this house; h = my; k = quadrupeds; l = savage; m = sheep-dogs; n = trusted by me; r = wagging its tail when it sees me; s = warm-blooded; t = wolves.

---

[13] This problem is similar to Problem 27 of "Fifth Paper on Logic," May 1887.

–43–

(1) I do not care for any visitor who breaks my windows;

(2) No old visitors, who help themselves to my cigars, are good-tempered;

(3) All who visit me before 5 A.M., except kittens, are interesting;

(4) I consider a visitor to be good-tempered, if he does not break my windows;

(5) All, who visit me after 5 A.M., help themselves to my cigars;

(6) When kittens come to see me, they break my windows.

Univ. "my visitors"; a = breaking my windows; b = cared for by me; c = coming before 5 A.M.; d = good-tempered; e = helping themselves to my cigars; h = interesting; k = kittens; l = old.

–44[14]–

(1) All novels are exciting;

(2) I have no books but novels;

(3) Nothing exciting belongs to me.

a = books; b = exciting; c = my; d = novels.

–45[15]–

(1) All eels wriggle;

(2) No eel wears boots;

(3) Nothing that wriggles and wears no boots can act Shakespeare.

a = can act, &c.; b = eels; c = wearing boots; d = wriggling.

–46[16]–

(1) All pencils are made of lead;

(2) No rubbish is useful;

(3) All lead-pencils are useful.

a = containing lead; b = pencils; c = rubbish; d = useful.

---

[14] This appears as Problem 4 of "Fifth Paper on Logic," May 1887.

[15] This appears as Problem 8 of "Fifth Paper on Logic," May 1887.

[16] This appears as Problem 5 of "Fifth Paper on Logic," May 1887.

$-47^{17}-$

(1) No hoofed animal has scales;
(2) No pigs are destitute of hoofs;
(3) No pigs without scales have wings.

Univ. "animals"; a = hoofed; b = pigs; c = scaly; d = winged.

$-48^{18}-$

(1) No cats sing well;
(2) None of my visitors get any cream, unless they sing well;
(3) No cats fail to get cream.

Univ. "creatures"; a = cats; b = getting cream; c = my visitors; d = singing well.

$-49^{19}-$

(1) No fat old men are active;
(2) All wise men are old;
(3) No unwise lawyers are fat.

Univ. "men"; a = active; b = fat; c = lawyers; d = old; e = wise.

$-50^{20}-$

(1) No pins of mine, that will bend, are useful;
(2) Nothing made of steel will bend;
(3) All my useless pins are made of steel.

Univ. "things"; a = flexible; b = made of steel; c = my; d = pins; e = useful.

---

[17] This appears as Problem 13 of "Fifth Paper on Logic," May 1887.
[18] Similar problems are Problem 10 of "Fifth Paper on Logic," May 1887, and Problem 15 of "Symbolic Logic: Specimen-Syllogisms," February 1894.

[19] This appears as Problem 3 of "Fifth Paper on Logic," and as Problem 17 of "Symbolic Logic: Specimen Syllogisms," February 1894.
[20] This appears as Problem 19 of "Fifth Paper on Logic."

–51²¹–

(1) No frogs are dignified;
(2) All fat creatures in this garden eat greedily;
(3) Nothing that eats greedily is fat, except a frog.

Univ. "creatures"; a = dignified; b = eating greedily; c = fat; d = frogs; e = in this garden.

–52–

(1) All old English magistrates are crabbed;
(2) No foreign magistrates are just;
(3) All crabbed old hermits are foreigners.

Univ. "men"; a = crabbed; b = English; c = hermits; d = just; e = magistrates; h = old.

–53²²–

(1) Nothing, that is meant to hold fluids, is worth taking care of when broken;
(2) Nothing that is useful is unworthy of care;
(3) Jugs are meant to hold fluids.

Univ. "things"; a = broken; b = jugs; c = meant to hold fluids; d = worthy of care; e = useful.

–54–

(1) Every book in my library is either all in verse or all in prose;
(2) All poetry-books, except those edited by Brown, have notes in prose;
(3) All prose-books, except those published by Jones, contain poetical quotations.

Univ. "books"; a = containing poetry; b = containing prose; c = edited by Brown; d = in my library; e = published by Jones.

---

[21] This appears as Problem 17 of "Fifth Paper on Logic."

[22] A similar problem appears as Number 14 of "Fifth Paper on Logic."

–55–

(1) All old men admire John;
(2) John admires all old men;
(3) Any man, who admires all old men, is wise;
(4) The only wise men, who do not admire themselves, are old.

Univ. "men"; a = admiring all old men; b = admiring John; c = admiring oneself; d = John; e = old; h = wise.

–56–

(1) No members of this Committee, except the bishops, are healthy;
(2) No active men, who are younger than I am, are unhealthy;
(3) No bishops are bankers;
(4) None of my brothers, who are not bankers, are healthy.

Univ. "persons"; a = active; b = bankers; c = members of this Committee; d = healthy; e = bishops; h = men; k = my brothers; l = younger than I am.

–57[23]–

(1) All rolling stones are restless;
(2) No stones are light;
(3) No restless things, that gather moss, are heavy.

Univ. "things"; a = gathering moss; b = heavy; c = restless; d = rolling; e = stones.

–58–

(1) All my guests are unmusical;
(2) All these birds are musical;
(3) These are the only birds that are good-tempered when hungry.

---

[23] A similar problem is printed as Number 20 of "Fifth Paper on Logic," and as Number 18 of "Symbolic Logic: Specimen Syllogisms," February 1894.

Univ. "creatures"; a = birds; b = good-tempered when hungry; c = musical; d = my guests; e = these.

−59−

(1) All my friends look discontented;
(2) All earnest thinkers are happy;
(3) A rich man, who never thinks, does not look discontented;
(4) All my friends are in earnest;
(5) Those who are happy never look discontented.

Univ. "persons"; a = earnest; b = happy; c = looking discontented; d = my friends; e = rich men; h = thinkers.

−60[24]−

(1) Ungraceful creatures, that are left alone, are thoughtful;
(2) No elephants are graceful;
(3) When one is disliked, one is left alone;
(4) Thoughtful elephants are universally liked;
(5) No ungraceful creatures, that are not fond of apples, are liked.

Univ. "creatures"; a = elephants; b = fond of apples; c = graceful; d = left alone; e = liked; h = thoughtful.

−61−

(1) All gouty aldermen are boisterous;
(2) All beadles, who are not gouty, are teetotalers;
(3) No gouty old folk are boisterous;
(4) All retired aldermen are beadles;
(5) All boisterous beadles are old.

Univ. "persons"; a = aldermen; b = beadles; c = boisterous; d = gouty; e = old; h = retired; k = teetotalers.

---

[24] This appears as Problem 23 of "Fifth Paper on Logic," and as Problem 19 of "Symbolic Logic: Specimen-Syllogisms," February 1894.

–62–

(1) Tight shoes are always uncomfortable;
(2) Whatever *I* wear is comfortable;
(3) The cheap things that I wear are always tight.

Univ. "articles of clothing"; a = cheap; b = comfortable; c = shoes; d = tight; e = worn by me.

–63[25]–

(1) No unkind advice is welcome;
(2) No welcome letters, that I have had to-day, remain unanswered;
(3) None of to-day's letters, that I have answered, are kind.

a = advice; b = answered; c = received to-day; d = letters; e = to-day's; h = welcome.

–64–

(1) No pretty children are unkindly treated;
(2) Ugly persons are unhealthy, unless they are kindly treated;
(3) Any one, who has good looks and is kindly treated, is healthy;
(4) No healthy person is sulky, if kindly treated;
(5) No one is agreeable who is both ugly and unhealthy.

Univ. "persons"; a = agreeable; b = beautiful; c = children; d = healthy; e = kindly treated; h = sulky.

–65–

(1) All the poetry-books in this house are octavo;
(2) Some of the bound English books are mine, and some are not mine;
(3) None of the new octavos are bound;
(4) The books in this box are either all mine, or all not mine;
(5) All the old octavos are foreign.

---

[25] This appears as Problem 9 of "Fifth Paper on Logic."

Univ. "books in this house"; a = bound; b = English; c = in this box; d = my; e = octavos; h = old; k = poetry.

–66–

(1) None of my new English poets are unbound;
(2) All my old illustrated octavos are prose;
(3) All my new bound octavos are foreign;
(4) All my illustrated English books, that are not octavos, are unbound;
(5) None of my unbound poetry-books are old, except the octavos.

Univ. "my books"; a = bound; b = English; c = illustrated; d = octavo; e = old; h = poetry.

–67²⁶–

(1) All boots are leathern;
(2) Nothing, that is made of buttered toast, is unfit to eat;
(3) No leather boots are fit to eat.

Univ. "things"; a = boots; b = fit to eat; c = leathern; d = made of buttered toast.

–68–

(1) None but goblins are tidy;
(2) No fat pets of mine are noisy;
(3) All lobsters are pets of mine;
(4) All goblins are fat and noisy.

Univ. "things"; a = fat; b = goblins; c = lobsters; d = my pets; e = noisy; h = tidy.

---

²⁶ Problem 11 of "Fifth Paper on Logic" goes as follows:

    All boots are leather;

Anything made of buttered toast is good to eat;

No leather boots are good to eat.

–**69**[27]–

(1) All, who have lost their way and have not learned to dance, are unfriendly;

(2) No gypsies, who have learned to dance, are wild;

(3) No wild people are civil, unless they happen to have lost their way;

(4) All my nephews have lost their way;

(5) All uncivil people, who are not nephews of mine, have learned to dance.

Univ. "persons"; a = civil; b = friendly; c = gypsies; d = having lost their way; e = having learned to dance; h = my nephews; k = wild.

–**70**–

(1) A Jew is always obsequious unless he is very young;

(2) All policemen are strong and fierce;

(3) No one is fierce, unless he is elderly or arrogant;

(4) A weak Gentile is always arrogant.

Univ. "persons"; a = arrogant; b = elderly; c = fierce; d = Jews; e = obsequious; h = policemen; k = strong.

–**71**–

(1) The beadles in this town are all simpletons who are friends of mine;

(2) Uneducated birds, who lunch on cayenne peppers, are easily provoked;

(3) No beadles in this town are bad-tempered;

(4) All my friends lunch on cayenne pepper;

(5) All easily-provoked simpletons are bad-tempered.

Univ. "men"; a = bad-tempered; b = beadles; c = easily provoked; d = educated; e = in this town; k = lunching on cayenne pepper; k = my friends; l = simpletons.

---

[27] This problem is similar to Problem 24 of "Fifth Paper on Logic." It also appeared in an earlier set of seventy-six soriteses sent to John Cook Wilson in 1895. In a letter dated September 13, 1895, Carroll asks Wilson to correct it, and the corrected version appears here.

$$-72^{28}-$$

(1) Despised and silent gluttons are quarrelsome and discontented;

(2) An idiot is always shy, silent, and sulky;

(3) No discontented quarrelsome creatures are hated if they are shy;

(4) Crocodiles are lazy gluttons;

(5) All lazy and sulky creatures are hated and despised.

Univ. "creatures"; a = contented; b = crocodiles; c = despised; d = gluttons; e = hated; h = idiots; k = lazy; l = quarrelsome; m = shy; n = silent; r = sulky.

$$-73-$$

(1) An interesting book, about the upper ten thousand, always sells well;

(2) No libelous book, of *your* writing, has any wit in it;

(3) An interesting book, that is unfavourably reviewed in the *Times*, is no doubt libelous;

(4) You have written some biographies of the upper ten thousand;

(5) A witty book, not libelous, that is favourably reviewed in the *Times* and sells well, is certainly not written by *you*;

(6) An instructive book, that sells well, is sure to be witty.

Univ. "books"; a = about the upper ten thousand; b = biographical; c = favourably reviewed in the *Times*; d = instructive; e = interesting; h = libelous; k = selling well; l = witty; m = written by you.

$$-74-$$

(1) All old grocers are unhealthy;

(2) No one who wears a tarpaulin-cape is young;

(3) All rich healthy people are householders;

(4) All greedy old coxcombs are grocers;

(5) There is no doctor who is not both healthy and greedy;

(6) All rich old householders are coxcombs.

Univ. "persons"; a = doctors; b = coxcombs; c = greedy; d = grocers; e = healthy; h = householders; k = old; l = rich; m = wearing a tarpaulin-cape.

---

[28] A version of this problem appears as   Logic," June 1887.
the first problem of "Sixth Paper on

-75-

(1) All who are wise are just and kind;
(2) All who are considerate, except Magistrates, are liked;
(3) No grinning policemen are kind;
(4) All who are not tyrants are considerate;
(5) All wise magistrates grin;
(6) All tyrants are unjust.

Univ. "persons"; a = considerate; b = grinning; c = just; d = kind; e = liked; h = magistrates; k = policemen; l = tyrants; m = wise.

-76-

(1) All the boys under ten in this School, who worry the Teacher of Hebrew, are full of mischief;
(2) All the melancholy boys, who study Hebrew, worry their Teacher;
(3) None of the boys, who have good health but do no mischief, have high spirits;
(4) All the boys under ten, who are studying Hebrew, either do no mischief, or practise it on their Teacher;
(5) All the boys, who are melancholy but mischievous, are fully ten years old;
(6) The high-spirited boys, who worry the Teacher of Hebrew, are not studying that language.

Univ. "boys in this school"; a = healthy; b = high-spirited; c = mischievous; d = studying Hebrew; e = under ten; h = worrying the Teacher of Hebrew.

-77[29]-

(1) All short-hand writers are fit to be printers;
(2) No rifleman, who can read small print, has bad eyesight;
(3) No young folk need be pitied, unless they are short-hand writers;
(4) Those who have good eyesight do not wear spectacles;

---

[29] A similar problem appears as Number 26 of "Fifth Paper on Logic."

(5) No young folk, who have bad eyesight and cannot read small print, are fit to be printers;

(6) Those who cannot read small print are to be pitied.

Univ. "persons"; a = able to read small print; b = fit to be printers; c = having good eyesight; d = needing pity; e = riflemen; h = short-hand writers; k = wearing spectacles; l = young.

$-78\ ^{30}-$

(1) All my sons, over 6 feet high, who are in the wine-trade, are dishonest;

(2) None of my sons, who are slender and unhealthy, are dishonest;

(3) All my sons, who are over 6 feet high and healthy, are either honest or active;

(4) None of my sons, who are healthy and active, are in the wine-trade;

(5) All my indolent sons are either fat or else over 6 feet high;

(6) All my sons, who are active and not over 6 feet high, are either dishonest or healthy.

Univ. "my sons"; a = active; b = fat; c = in the wine-trade; d = honest; e = in trade; h = over 6 feet high.

$-79-$

(1) No ill-tempered hungry auctioneers are bland and courteous;

(2) All young schoolmasters are impatient;

(3) Mayors are always wise and courteous;

(4) No ill-tempered schoolmaster is dignified;

(5) Graham is an ill-tempered schoolmaster, and is Mayor;

(6) No courteous old man is undignified, unless he is hungry;

(7) All wise schoolmasters are bland and patient.

Univ. "men"; a = auctioneers; b = bland; c = courteous; d = dignified; e = Graham; h = hungry; k = ill-tempered; l = Mayors; m = old; n = patient; r = schoolmasters; s = wise.

---

[30] Carroll asked Cook Wilson to work this sorites, referring to it in his letter to him of September 13, 1895.

–80–

(1) No conceited beauties are attractive, unless they are dreamy;
(2) Unattractive people, if geniuses, are idolized;
(3) My governess is conceited, but not dreamy;
(4) Brown's daughters are beautiful young ladies, but are not idolized;
(5) Every young lady is a genius;
(6) All the bridesmaids are daughters of Brown.

Univ. "persons"; a = attractive; b = beauties; c = bridesmaids; d = Brown's daughters; e = conceited; h = dreamy; k = geniuses; l = idolized; m = my governess; n = young ladies.

–81 [31]–

(1) No invalids are unromantic civilians;
(2) All architects are dreamy enthusiasts;
(3) No lovers are unpoetical;
(4) No military men are dreamy;
(5) All romantic enthusiasts are in love;
(6) None live on muffins except unpoetical invalids.

Univ. "persons"; a = architects; b = dreamy; c = enthusiasts; d = invalids; e = living on, &c.; h = lovers; k = military; l = poetical; m = romantic.

–82 [32]–

(1) No young crabs are melancholy;
(2) All healthy policemen are sane;
(3) No discontented judges are chickens;
(4) All rich bakers are fat;
(5) Some rich healthy young judges are unmarried.

Univ. "creatures"; a = bakers; b = chickens; c = contented; d = crabs; e = fat; h = healthy; k = judges; l = married; m = melancholy; n = policemen; r = rich; s = sane; t = young.

---

[31] A similar problem appears as Number 25 of "Fifth Paper on Logic," and as Number 20 of "Symbolic Logic: Specimen-Syllogisms," February 1894. [32] This problem appears as Number 22 of "Fifth Paper on Logic."

–83–

(1) Brothers, who are much admired, are apt to be self-conscious;

(2) When two men of the same height are on opposite sides in Politics, if one of them has his admirers, so also has the other;

(3) Brothers, who avoid general Society, look well when walking together;

(4) Whenever you find two men, who differ in Politics and in their views of Society, and who are not both of them handsome, you may be sure that neither of them is *John*;

(5) Ugly men, who look well when walking together, are not both of them free from self-consciousness;

(6) Brothers, who differ in Politics, and are not both of them handsome, never give themselves airs;

(7) John declines to go into Society, but never gives himself airs;

(8) Brothers, who are apt to be self-conscious, and who do not look well when walking together, though not *both* of them ugly, usually dislike Society;

(9) Men of the same height, who do not give themselves airs, are free from self-consciousness;

(10) Men, who agree on questions of Art, though they differ in Politics, and who are not both of them ugly, are always admired;

(11) Men, who hold opposite views about Art and are not admired, always give themselves airs;

(12) Brothers of the same height always differ in Politics;

(13) Two handsome men, who are neither both of them admired nor both of them self-conscious, are no doubt of different heights;

(14) Brothers, who are self-conscious and do not both of them like Society, never look well when walking together.

Univ. "Pairs of men"; A = containing one who is admired; a = containing one who is *not* admired; B, b = ditto as to "apt to be self-conscious"; C, c = ditto as to "giving oneself airs"; D, d = ditto as to "handsome"; E, e = ditto as to "John"; F, f = ditto as to "liking Society"; G = agreeing in Art; H = agreeing in Politics; J = brothers; K = looking well when walking together; L = of the same height.

BOOK XXI
LOGICAL PUZZLES

Chapter I ❧ Introductory

Under this general heading I shall discuss various arguments, which are variously described by Logical writers. Some have been classified as "Sophisms," that is, according to etymology, "cunning arguments," whose characteristic Attribute seems to be that they are intended to *confuse*: others as "Paradoxes," that is, according to etymology, "things contrary to expectation," whose characteristic Attribute seems to be that they seem to prove what we know to be false: but all may be described by the general name "Puzzles."

Galley proofs discovered by the editor at Christ Church, Oxford, in 1959 (shown above and on page 424) were the first clue that major portions of Dodgson's missing second book on symbolic logic might still exist. The number in the upper left corner was penned by Dodgson, who kept a register of all his correspondence. A fold in the galley proof partially obscures a line of type (Library of Christ Church, Oxford)

contrary to expectation", whose characteristic Attribute seems to be that they seem to prove what we know to be false : but all may be described by the general name "Puzzles."

CHAPTER II.
CLASSICAL PUZZLES.

§ 1.
Introductory.

I SHALL here enunciate five certain well-known Puzzles, which have come down to us from ancient times, and which the Reader will no doubt like to know by their classical titles.

§ 2.
Pseudomenos.

This may also be described as "*Mentiens*", or "*The Liar*". In its simplest form it runs thus :——

"If a man says 'I am telling a lie', and speaks truly, he *is* telling a lie, and therefore speaks falsely : but, if he speaks falsely, he is *not* telling a lie, and therefore speaks truly".

§ 3.
Crocodilus.

That is, "*The Crocodile*". This tragical story runs as follows :——

"A Crocodile had stolen a Baby off the banks of the Nile. The Mother implored him to restore her darling. 'Well', said the Crocodile, 'if you say truly what I shall do, I will restore it : if not, I will devour it". "You will devour it!" cried the distracted Mother. "Now", said the wily Crocodile, "I *cannot* restore your Baby : for, if I do, I shall make you speak falsely : and I warned you that, if you spoke falsely, I would devour it". "On the contrary", said the yet wilier Mother, "you cannot *devour* my Baby : for, if you do, you will make me speak *truly*, and you promised me that, if I spoke *truly*, you would *restore* it !" (We assume, of course, that he was a Crocodile of his word ; and that his sense of honour outweighed his love of Babies.)

§ 4.
Antistrephon.

That is "The Retort". This is a tale of the law-courts.

"Protagoras had agreed to train Euathius for the profession of a barrister, on the condition that half his fee should be paid at once, and that the other half should be paid, or not paid, according as Euathius should win, or lose, his first case in Court. After a time, Protagoras, becoming impatient, brought an action against his pupil, to recover the second half of his fee. It seems that Euathius decided to plead his own cause. "Now, if I *win* this action", said Protagoras, "you will have to pay the money by the decision of the Court : if I *lose* it, you will have to pay by our agreement. Therefore, in any case, you must pay it ". "On the contrary", retorted Euathius, "if you *win* this action, I shall be released from payment by our agreement : if you *lose* it, I shall be released by the decision of the Court. Therefore, in any case, I need not pay the money".

§ 5.
Achilles.

This may be described, more fully, as "*Achilles and the Tortoise*". The legend runs as

Chapter II ⚔ Classical Puzzles

[§1] Introductory

I shall here enunciate five certain well-known Puzzles, which have come down to us from ancient times, and which the Reader will no doubt like to know by their classical titles.

[§2] Pseudomenos

This may also be described as *Mentiens,* or *The Liar.* In its simplest form it runs thus:

If a man says "I am telling a lie," and speaks truly, he *is* telling a lie, and therefore speaks falsely: but if he speaks falsely, he is *not* telling a lie, and therefore speaks truly.

[§3] Crocodilus

That is, "*The Crocodile.*" This tragical story runs as follows:

A Crocodile had stolen a Baby off the banks of the Nile. The Mother implored him to restore her darling. "Well," said the Crocodile, "if you say truly what I shall do I will restore it: if not, I will devour it." "You will devour it!" cried the distracted Mother. "Now," said the wily Crocodile, "I *cannot* restore your Baby: for if I do, I shall make you speak *falsely*: and I warned you that, if you spoke *falsely*, I would *devour* it." "On the contrary," said the yet wilier Mother, "you cannot *devour* my Baby: for if you do, you will make me speak *truly*, and you promised me that, if I spoke *truly*, you would *restore* it!" (We assume, of course, that he was a Crocodile of his word; and that his sense of honour outweighed his love of Babies.)[1]

---

[1] In his *Diary* entry for June 1, 1894, Carroll records an amusing variant of the Crocodile: "I have worked out some pretty varieties of the 'Crocodile' Dilemma: e.g. *two* thieves, each saying to a person he has robbed: 'If you say truly whether my friend will keep his word, I will restore: if not, not.'"

[§4] **Antistrephon**

That is, *The Retort.* This is a tale of the law-courts.

Protagoras had agreed to train Euathius for the profession of a barrister, on the condition that half his fee should be paid at once, and that the other half should be paid, or not paid, according as Euathius should win, or lose, his first case in Court. After a time, Protagoras, becoming impatient, brought an action against his pupil, to recover the second half of his fee. It seems that Euathius decided to plead his own cause. "Now, if I *win* this action," said Protagoras, "you will have to pay the money by the decision of the Court: if I *lose* it, you will have to pay by our agreement. Therefore, in any case, you must pay it." "On the contrary," retorted Euathius, "if you *win* this action, I shall be released from payment by our agreement: if you *lose* it, I shall be released by the decision of the Court. Therefore, in any case, I need not pay the money."

[§5] **Achilles**

This may be described, more fully, as *Achilles and the Tortoise.* The legend runs as follows:

Achilles and the Tortoise were to run a race on a circular course; and, as it was known that Achilles could run ten times as fast as the Tortoise, the latter was allowed 100 yards' start. There was no winning-post, but the race was to go on until Achilles either overtook the Tortoise or resigned the contest. Now it is evident that, by the time Achilles had run the 100 yards, the Tortoise would have got 10 yards further; and, by the time he had run those 10 yards, it would have got a yard further; and so on for ever. Hence, in order to overtake the Tortoise, he must pass over an *infinite* number of successive distances. Hence, Achilles can never overtake the Tortoise.

[§6] **Raw Meat**

The meat that I eat at dinner is meat that I buy in the market;
The meat that I buy in the market is raw meat.

Therefore, the meat that I eat at dinner is raw meat.

Chapter III ❦ Other Puzzles

(§1) About Less

He, who says that 5 is less than 10, speaks truly;
He, who says that 5 is less than 10 and more than 6, says that 5 is less than 10.

> Therefore, he who says that 5 is less than 10 and more than 6, speaks truly.

(§2) Men Tall and Numerous

Men over 5 feet high are numerous;
Men over 10 feet high are not numerous.

> Therefore, men over 10 feet high are not over 5 feet high.

(§3) The Socialist Orator and the Irish Mob

"Isn't one man as good as another?" demanded a Socialist orator, addressing an Irish mob. "Av *coorse* he is," was the eager response, "*and a great deal betther!*"

(§4) Death at Any Moment

"You *may* die at any moment, and probably *will*." (See *The Mystery of Mr. E. Drood*, by Orpheus C. Kerr, p. 136/217.)

The *first* part of this statement seems reasonable enough: the *second* is obviously absurd. Yet how can it be absurd to assert that you *will* do what it is quite reasonable to assert that you *may* do?

(§5) The Small Girl and Her Sympathetic Friend [1]

Small Girl: I'm *so* glad I don't like asparagus!
Sympathetic Friend: Why, my dear?

---

[1] I do not know the origin of this puzzle. It has been used by several persons who could have had no access to Carroll's manuscripts. I have in mind the comedienne Gracie Allen, who used it over the radio in the 1930s, and Jean-Paul Belmondo, the French actor, who used it in the film *Pierrot le Fou*.

Small Girl: Because, if I did, I should have to eat it—and I ca'n't bear it!

Examine the reasoning process, if any, which has taken place in the mind of the Small Girl.

(§6) A Notice at the Seaside

The blue ensign denotes that all boats, licensed to carry from two to four persons, are prohibited from putting off, and no other boat must put to sea without a licensed boatman.

The red ensign denotes that only large rowing-boats carrying from five to seven persons, and sailing boats, can put to sea with boatmen.

[N.B.   The above Notice is exhibited at a certain seaside-place not 100 miles from the Needles.]

What boats, if any, *can* put to sea when one of these two ensigns is hoisted, but *cannot* when the other is *hoisted*?

(§7) On the Way to the Barber-Shop[2]

"What, *nothing* to do?" said Uncle Jim.   "Then come along with me down to Allen's.   And you can just take a turn while I get myself shaved."

"All right," said Uncle Joe.   "And the Cub had better come too, I suppose?"

The "Cub" was *me*, as the reader will perhaps have guessed for himself. I'm turned *fifteen*—more than three months ago; but there's no sort of use in mentioning *that* to Uncle Joe: he'd only say "Go to your cubbicle, little boy!" or "Then I suppose you can do cubbic equations?" or some equally vile pun.   He asked me yesterday to give him an instance of a Proposition in *A*.   And I said, "All uncles make vile puns."   And I don't think he liked it.   However, that's neither here nor there.   I was glad enough to go.   I *do* love hearing those uncles of mine "chop logic," as they call it; and they're desperate hands at it, *I* can tell you!

"That is not a logical inference from my remark," said Uncle Jim.

"Never said it was," said Uncle Joe; "it's a *Reductio ad Absurdum*."

"An *Illicit Process of the Minor*!" chuckled Uncle Jim.

---

[2] This is the famous Barber-Shop   for a discussion, and Appendix B for
Paradox. See Appendix A to Book XXI   variant versions.

That's the sort of way they always go on, whenever *I'm* with them. As if there was any fun in calling me a minor!

After a bit, Uncle Jim began again, just as we came in sight of the barber's. "I only hope *Carr* will be at home," he said. "Brown's so clumsy. And Allen's hand has been shaky ever since he had that fever."

"Carr's *certain* to be in," said Uncle Joe.

"I'll bet you sixpence he *isn't*!" said I.

"Keep your bets for your betters," said Uncle Joe. "I mean"—he hurried on, seeing by the grin on my face what a slip he'd made—"I mean that I can *prove* it logically. It isn't a matter of *chance*."

"Prove it *logically*!" sneered Uncle Jim. "Fire away, then! I defy you to do it!"

"For the sake of argument," Uncle Joe began, "let us assume Carr to be *out*. And let us see what that assumption would lead to. I'm going to do this by *Reductio ad Absurdum*."

"Of course you are!" growled Uncle Jim. "Never knew any argument of *yours* that didn't end in some absurdity or other!"

"Unprovoked by your unmanly taunts," said Uncle Joe in a lofty tone, "I proceed. Carr being out, you will grant that, if Allen is *also* out, *Brown* must be at home?"

"What's the good of *his* being at home?" said Uncle Jim. "I don't want *Brown* to shave me! He's too clumsy."

"Patience is one of those inestimable qualities—" Uncle Joe was beginning; but Uncle Jim cut him short.

"*Argue*!" he said. "Don't *moralise*!"

"Well, but *do* you grant it?" Uncle Joe persisted. "Do you grant me that, if Carr is out, it follows that if Allen is out Brown *must* be in?"

"Of course he must," said Uncle Jim; "or there'd be nobody to mind the shop."

"We see, then, that the absence of Carr brings into play a certain Hypothetical, whose *protasis* is 'Allen is out,' and whose *apodosis* is 'Brown is in.' And we see that, so long as Carr remains out, this Hypothetical remains in force?"

"Well, suppose it does. What then?" said Uncle Jim.

"You will also grant me that the truth of a Hypothetical—I mean its *validity* as a logical *sequence*—does not in the least depend on its *protasis* being actually *true*, nor even on its being *possible*. The Hypothetical 'If you were to run from here to London in five minutes you would surprise people,' remains true as a *sequence*, whether you can do it or not."

"I *ca'n't* do it," said Uncle Jim.

"We have now to consider *another* Hypothetical. What was that you told me yesterday about Allen?"

"I told you," said Uncle Jim, "that ever since he had that fever he's been so nervous about going out alone, he always takes Brown with him."

"Just so," said Uncle Joe. "Then the Hypothetical 'if Allen is out, Brown is out' is *always* in force, isn't it?"

"I suppose so," said Uncle Jim. (He seemed to be getting a little nervous, himself, now.)

"Then, if Carr is out, we have *two* Hypotheticals, 'if Allen is out, Brown is *in*' and 'if Allen is out, Brown is *out*,' in force at once. And two *incompatible* Hypotheticals, mark you! They ca'n't *possibly* be true together!"

"*Ca'n't* they?" said Uncle Jim.

"How *can* they?" said Uncle Joe. "How *can* one and the same *protasis* prove two contradictory *apodoses*? You grant that the two *apodoses*, 'Brown is *in*,' and 'Brown is *out*,' are contradictory, I suppose?"

"Yes, I grant *that*," said Uncle Jim.

"Then I may sum up," said Uncle Joe. "If Carr is out, these two Hypotheticals are true together. And we know that they *cannot* be true together. Which is absurd. Therefore Carr *cannot* be out. There's a nice *Reductio ad Absurdum* for you!"

Uncle Jim looked thoroughly puzzled; but after a bit he plucked up courage, and began again. "I don't feel at all clear about that *incompatibility*. Why shouldn't those two Hypotheticals be true together? It would seem to me that would simply prove '*Allen* is in.' Of course it's clear that the *apodoses* of those two Hypotheticals are incompatible— 'Brown is in' and 'Brown is out.' But why shouldn't we put it like this? If Allen is out, Brown is *out*. If Carr and Allen are *both* out, Brown is *in*. Which is absurd. Therefore Carr and Allen ca'n't be *both* of them out. But, so long as Allen is *in*, I don't see what's to hinder Carr from going *out*."

"My dear, but most illogical, brother!" said Uncle Joe. (Whenever Uncle Joe begins to "dear" you, you may make pretty sure he's got you in a cleft stick!) "Don't you see that you are wrong by dividing the *protasis* and the *apodosis* of that Hypothetical? Its *protasis* is simply 'Carr is out'; and its *apodosis* is a sort of sub-Hypothetical, 'If Allen is out, Brown is *in*.' And a most absurd apodosis it is, being hopelessly incompatible with that other Hypothetical, that we know is *always* true, 'If Allen is out, Brown is *out*.' And it's simply the assumption 'Carr is out' that has caused this absurdity. So there's only *one* possible conclusion. *Carr is in*!"

How long this argument *might* have lasted, I haven't the least idea. I believe *either* of them could argue for six hours at a stretch. But, just at this moment, we arrived at the barber's shop; and, on going inside, we found—

(§8) What the Tortoise said to Achilles[3]

Achilles had overtaken the Tortoise, and had seated himself comfortably on its back.

"So you've got to the end of our race-course?" said the Tortoise. "Even though it *does* consist of an infinite series of distances? I thought some wiseacre or other had proved that the thing couldn't be done?"

"It *can* be done," said Achilles. "It *has* been done! *Solvitur ambulando.* You see the distances were constantly *diminishing*; and so—"

"But if they had been constantly *increasing*?" the Tortoise interrupted. "How then?"

"Then I shouldn't be *here*," Achilles modestly replied; "and *you* would have got several times round the world, by this time!"

"You flatter me—*flatten*, I mean," said the Tortoise; "for you *are* a heavy weight, and *no* mistake! Well now, would you like to hear of a race-course, that most people fancy they can get to the end of in two or three steps, while it *really* consists of an infinite number of distances, each one longer than the previous one?"

"Very much indeed!" said the Grecian warrior, as he drew from his helmet (few Grecian warriors possessed *pockets* in those days) an enormous note-book and a pencil. "Proceed! And speak *slowly*, please! *Short-hand* isn't invented yet!"

"That beautiful First Proposition of Euclid!" the Tortoise murmured dreamily. "You admire Euclid?"

"Passionately! So far, at least, as one *can* admire a treatise that wo'n't be published for some centuries to come!"

"Well, now, let's take a little bit of the argument in that First Proposition—just *two* steps, and the conclusion drawn from them. Kindly enter them in your note-book. And, in order to refer to them conveniently, let's call them *A*, *B*, and *Z*:

"(*A*) Things that are equal to the same are equal to each other.

---

[3] This section Carroll published in *Mind* in 1895. See Appendix C to Book XXI　　for an account of some of the debate concerning it.

"(*B*) The two sides of this Triangle are things that are equal to the same.

"(*Z*) The two sides of this Triangle are equal to each other.

"Readers of Euclid will grant, I suppose, that *Z* follows logically from *A* and *B*, so that any one who accepts *A* and *B* as true, *must* accept *Z* as true?"

"Undoubtedly! The youngest child in a High School—as soon as High Schools are invented, which will not be till some two thousand years later—will grant *that*."

"And if some reader had *not* yet accepted *A* and *B* as true, he might still accept the *Sequence* as a *valid* one, I suppose?"

"No doubt such a reader might exist. He might say 'I accept as true the Hypothetical Proposition that, *if A* and *B* be true, *Z* must be true; but I *don't* accept *A* and *B* as true.' Such a reader would do wisely in abandoning Euclid, and taking to football."

"And might there not *also* be some reader who would say 'I accept *A* and *B* as true, but I *don't* accept the Hypothetical'?"

"Certainly there might. *He*, also, had better take to football."

"And *neither* of these readers," the Tortoise continued, "is *as yet* under any logical necessity to accept *Z* as true?"

"Quite so," Achilles assented.

"Well, now, I want you to consider *me* as a reader of the *second* kind, and to force me, logically, to accept *Z* as true."

"A Tortoise playing football would be—" Achilles was beginning.

"—an anomaly, of course," the Tortoise hastily interrupted. "Don't wander from the point. Let's have *Z* first, and football afterwards!"

"I'm to force you to accept *Z*, am I?" Achilles said musingly. "And your present position is that you accept *A* and *B*, but you *don't* accept the Hypothetical—"

"Let's call it *C*," said the Tortoise.

"—but you *don't* accept."

"(*C*) If *A* and *B* are true, *Z* must be true."

"That is my present position," said the Tortoise.

"Then I must ask you to accept *C*."

"I'll do so," said the Tortoise, "as soon as you've entered it in that note-book of yours. What else have you got in it?"

"Only a few memoranda," said Achilles, nervously fluttering the leaves; "a few memoranda of—of the battles in which I have distinguished myself!"

"Plenty of blank leaves, I see!" the Tortoise cheerily remarked.

"We shall need them *all*!" (Achilles shuddered.) "Now write as I dictate:

"(*A*) Things that are equal to the same are equal to each other.

"(*B*) The two sides of this Triangle are things that are equal to the same.

"(*C*) If *A* and *B* are true, *Z* must be true.

"(*Z*) The two sides of this Triangle are equal to each other."

"You should call it *D*, not *Z*," said Achilles. "It comes *next* to the other three. If you accept *A* and *B* and *C*, you *must* accept *Z*."

"And why *must* I?"

"Because it follows *logically* from them. If *A* and *B* and *C* are true, *Z* *must* be true. You don't dispute *that*, I imagine?"

"If *A* and *B* and *C* are true, *Z must* be true," the Tortoise thoughtfully repeated. "That's *another* Hypothetical, isn't it? And, if I failed to see its truth, I might accept *A* and *B* and *C*, and *still* not accept *Z*, mightn't I?"

"You might," the candid hero admitted; "though such obtuseness would certainly be phenomenal. Still, the event is *possible*. So I might ask you to grant one more Hypothetical!"

"Very good. I'm quite willing to grant it, as soon as you've written it down. We will call it

"(*D*) If *A* and *B* and *C* are true, *Z* must be true.

"Have you entered that in your note-book?"

"I *have*!" Achilles joyfully exclaimed, as he ran the pencil into its sheath. "And at last we've got to the end of this ideal race-course! Now that you accept *A* and *B* and *C* and *D*, *of course* you accept *Z*."

"Do I?" said the Tortoise innocently. "Let's make that quite clear. I accept *A* and *B* and *C* and *D*. Suppose I *still* refused to accept *Z*?"

"Then Logic would take you by the throat, and *force* you to do it!" Achilles triumphantly replied. "Logic would tell you 'You ca'n't help yourself. Now that you've accepted *A* and *B* and *C* and *D*, you *must* accept *Z*!' So you've no choice, you see."

"Whatever *Logic* is good enough to tell me is worth *writing down*," said the Tortoise. "So enter it in your book, please. We will call it

"(*E*) If *A* and *B* and *C* and *D* are true, *Z* must be true.

"Until I've granted *that*, of course I needn't grant *Z*. So it's quite a *necessary* step, you see?"

"I see," said Achilles; and there was a touch of sadness in his tone.

Here the narrator, having pressing business at the Bank, was obliged to leave the happy pair, and did not again pass the spot until some months afterwards. When he did so, Achilles was still seated on the back of the much-enduring Tortoise, and was writing in his note-book, which appeared to be nearly full. The Tortoise was saying, "Have you got that last step written down? Unless I've lost count, that makes a thousand and one. There are several millions more to come. And *would* you mind, as a personal favour—considering what a lot of instruction this colloquy of ours will provide for the Logicians of the Nineteenth Century— *would* you mind adopting a pun that my cousin the Mock-Turtle will then make, and allowing yourself to be re-named *Taught-Us*?"

"As you please!" replied the weary warrior, in the hollow tones of despair, as he buried his face in his hands. "Provided that *you*, for *your* part, will adopt a pun the Mock-Turtle never made, and allow yourself to be re-named *A Kill-Ease*!"

Chapter IV ⚔ Solutions of Classical Puzzles

[§1] Introductory

The following Solutions have *not* come down to us from ancient times, but are merely modern speculations, which the Reader can take or reject "at his own sweet will."

[§2] Pseudomenos

This Puzzle might be described as a "Paradox," since it seems to prove that the man in question is speaking both truly and falsely at the same moment.

The best way out of the difficulty seems to be to raise the question whether the Proposition "I am telling a lie" can reasonably be supposed to refer to *itself* as its own subject-matter: to which the answer seems to be that it can *not*, since its doing so would lead to an absurdity.

Symbolically, it may be solved as follows:

Let Univ. be "Cosmophases"; a = the man speaks truly; b = the Proposition, stated by the man, can be its own subject-matter.

Then we have a ¶ $a'b$, and $a'b$ ¶ a; i.e. aba_0 † $a'ba'_0$; i.e. ab_0 † $a'b_0$, which together prove b_0; i.e. the Proposition can *not* be its own subject-matter.

Let us now consider what result would have followed if the man's statement had been "I am telling the truth" instead of "I am telling a lie."

Here, if we assume that the Proposition can be its own subject-matter, it evidently follows that, if he speaks truly, he *is* telling the truth, and that, if he speaks falsely, he is *not* telling the truth.   In either case, the supposition does *not* lead to any absurdity.

Symbolically, it would run as follows, using the same Dictionary as before: ab ¶ a, and $a'b$ ¶ a'; i.e. aba'_0 † $a'ba_0$; each of which Nullities is a truism, and proves nothing as to the existence, or non-existence, of b. Hence there is nothing in the *Data* to prevent the Proposition from being its own subject-matter, and nothing to tell us whether the man is speaking truly or falsely.

In short, such Data lead to no result at all, and it is not worth while to discuss them.

This Puzzle is sometimes given in a more complex form, viz.

Epimenides the Cretan asserted that Cretans were *always* liars.   If he spoke truly, they *were* always liars, and therefore he, being a Cretan, was lying at that moment, and therefore spoke falsely.   Hence he did *not* speak truly; that is, he *must* have been lying.

Here we cannot show that, if he spoke falsely, he also spoke truly. Hence no absurdity follows from the supposition that the Proposition can be its own subject-matter; and the conclusion, however unwelcome to Epimenides, is correct.

Symbolically, it runs thus:

Let Univ. be "Cosmophases"; a = Epimenides speaks truly; b = the Proposition, stated by him, can be its own subject-matter.

Then we have ab ¶ a'; i.e. aba_0; i.e. ab_0; i.e. b ¶ a'; i.e. On the supposition that the Proposition, stated by Epimenides, *could* be its own subject-matter, he was certainly lying.

If the statement made by Epimenides had been "The Cretans always speak the truth," there would have been nothing in the *Data* to prevent the Proposition from being its own subject-matter, and nothing to tell us whether Epimenides was speaking truly or falsely.

(From *Sylvie and Bruno*)

(§3) **Crocodilus**

On this Sophism Lotze makes the discouraging remark, "There is no way out of this dilemma." I think, however, that we shall find the machinery of Symbolic Logic sufficient for its solution.

Let Univ. be "Cosmophases"; a = the Mother speaks truly; b = the Crocodile keeps his word; c = the Crocodile devours the Baby.

(From *Sylvie and Bruno*)

Then we have, as *Data*,

$$\overset{\text{I}}{ab_1c_0} \dagger \overset{2}{ab'_1c'_0} \dagger \overset{3}{a'b_1c'_0} \dagger \overset{4}{a'b'_1c_0} \dagger \overset{5}{c_1a'_0} \dagger \overset{6}{c'_1a_0}$$

Here we may ignore 2, 4, as being contained in 6, 5;[1] and we see, by inspection, that b is the only Retinend.

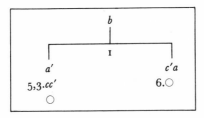

∴ b_0; i.e. Whatever the Crocodile does, he *breaks* his word.

Thus, if he devours the Baby, he makes her speak truly, and so *breaks* his word; and if he restores it, he makes her speak falsely, and so *breaks* his word. His sense of honour being thus hopeless of satisfaction, we cannot doubt that he would act in accordance with his *second* ruling passion, his love of *Babies*!

[The Reader will find it an interesting exercise to work out for himself the result which would have followed if the Mother's first statement had been "You will *restore* the Baby."[2] He will find that, in that case, whatever

---

[1] Carroll's statement here that 6 and 5 contain 2 and 4 is, strictly speaking, on his own terms, mistaken; 6 and 5 contain 2 and 4 only if we neglect existential import. Thus $6^*(c'a_0)$ contains $2^*(ab'c'_0)$; and $5^*(ca'_0)$ contains $4^*(a'b'c_0)$. Of course, when our letters denote propositions rather than terms, as they do here, existential import is indeed irrelevant, and the subscript 1 serves no purpose other than to demarcate antecedent and consequent clauses.

[2] This version of the problem is easily worked out as follows. If the Mother says, "You will restore the Baby," datum 5 becomes c_1a_0 (all c are not-a), and datum 6 becomes $c'_1a'_0$ (all not-c are a). That is, "If the Crocodile devours the Baby, then the Mother speaks falsely," and "If the Crocodile restores the Baby, the Mother speaks truly." Here data 1 and 3 can be disregarded because they are derivable

from data 5 and 6. The relevant data are then 2, 4, 5, and 6. The conclusion is b'_0, "Whatever the Crocodile does he keeps his word." To test the argument by Dodgson's logic-tree method, assume that b'_0 is false and test whether or not this leads to absurdity. If b'_0 is false, then b'_1 is true, and this together with the second premiss (datum) allows for two possibilities.

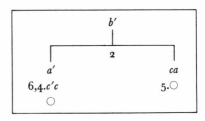

The first (the left branch of the tree) is a' (the Mother speaks falsely), but $a'b'_1$ by the fourth premiss leads to c' and by the sixth premiss to c. Having c' and c together is absurd. The

the Crocodile does, he *keeps his* word. Hence his sense of honour is entirely satisfied, whatever he does: so that, again, his only guide is his *second* ruling passion—and the result to the Baby would, I fear, be much the same as before.]

[§4] Antistrephon

The best way out of this Paradox must seem to be to demand an answer to the question "*Which* of the two things, the agreement and the decision of the Court, is to over-rule the other, in case they should come into collision?"

(1) Let us suppose that the *agreement* is to be supreme. In this case, if Protagoras *wins* his action, he *loses* the money; and, if he *loses* his action, he *wins* the money.

(2) Let us suppose the *decision of the Court* to be supreme. In this case, if Protagoras *wins* his action, he *wins* the money; and, if he *loses* his action, he *loses* the money.

The *Data* do not enable us to answer this question. Protagoras naturally makes one, or the other, supreme, as best suits his purpose: and his docile pupil follows his example.

The right decision of the Court would obviously be *against* Protagoras, seeing that the terms of the agreement were still unfulfilled. And, when that decision had been pronounced, the practical result would be that, if the *agreement* was to be supreme, Euathius would have to pay the money: if the *decision of the Court* was to be supreme, he would be released from payment.

[§5] Achilles

This is a *mathematical* Fallacy, and involves the false assumption that a series of distances, infinite as to *number*, is also infinite as to *total length*.

---

second possibility is ca_1 (the right branch), which contradicts the fifth premiss and so is absurd. Thus b'_0 must be true and whatever the crocodile does, he keeps his word.

Although the crocodile dilemma was not originated by Carroll (it goes back at least to the Stoic logic of ancient Greece and appears twice in Diogenes Laertius), I have never seen its full implications so precisely—and movingly—set out. Still, a lingering doubt remains: Carroll maintains in his text that he had solved the dilemma. What dilemma, if any, did he solve (as opposed to analyzing)? Indeed, precisely what is the dilemma of the crocodile? I leave that problem with you: the proof of the spoof is in the putting.

Here the assumption is that

$$\left(111 + \frac{1}{10} + \frac{1}{10^2} + \frac{1}{10^3} + \&c.\right)$$

of a mile, where the number of terms can be made greater than any assigned *number*, can be made greater than any assigned *length*. But the above series is the circulating decimal $111.\dot{1}$ which as the Reader probably knows, can never reach the limit $111\frac{1}{9}$. Hence, by the time Achilles has run $111\frac{1}{9}$ yards, he must necessarily have overtaken the Tortoise.[3]

[§6] Raw Meat

The best way of escaping from this savage Paradox seems to be to introduce the Dated Copula.[4]   *Two* epochs have to be taken into consideration, viz.

(a) The time (say 10 A.M.) at which I purchased the meat;

(b) The time (say 7 P.M.) at which I dine.

At epoch (a), the *second* Premiss is true; and the piece of meat in question possesses, at that moment, the Pair of Attributes, "bought by me in the market" and "raw."

At epoch (b), the *first* Premiss becomes true, and the second ceases to be true.   That is to say, the piece of meat possesses, at that moment, the Pair of Attributes, "eaten by me at dinner" and "bought by me in the market," but it has ceased to possess the Attribute "raw."

Hence, we cannot assert that the two Premisses are true *at the same moment*.

Hence there is no Conclusion.

[Professor DeMorgan (in his *Formal Logic*, p. 251/336) says that this Puzzle involves the Fallacy *a dicto simpliciter ad dictum secundum quid*, which consists, he tells us, "in inferring of the subject with an accident that which was premised of the subject only."

Mr. J. Welton (in his *Manual of Logic*, Vol. II, p. 244/292) takes the same view, and adds that "the fallacy lies in not making clear that the

---

[3] An earlier manuscript treatment of the paradox of Achilles and the Tortoise exists among Carroll's papers in the Christ Church Library. In dialogue form, it is titled "An Inconceiv- able Conversation between S. and D. on Indivisibility of Time and Space," and is dated November 22, 1874.

[4] This is never discussed in the remains of Part II.

'rawness' is not regarded in the second Premiss as a relevant circum-
stance, and then assuming it to be relevant in the Conclusion."]

Chapter V ❧ Solutions of Other Puzzles

(§1) About Less

This (apparently valid) Syllogism belongs to the Class "Paradoxes," since
it seems to prove that 5 *is* less than 10 and more than 6.

The first thing to be said about it is that its second Premiss is mere
tautology, being of the form "All *xy* are *x*." Hence, if the Conclusion
follows at all, it must follow as an *Immediate Inference* from the first Premiss.

But such an Inference would involve the Fallacy of *Vox Ambigua*, since
the phrase "speaks truly" is capable of *two* interpretations, viz.

(a) Says what is wholly true;

(b) Says what contains a truth.

With (a), the first Premiss cannot be accepted as true, unless we are
assured that the speaker *says no more*.

With (b), the Inference is a valid one, and the Conclusion true.

[Professor DeMorgan (in his *Formal Logic*, p. 242/336) explains this Puzzle
as follows. (He treats of another example: so, in quoting him, I have had
to make some verbal alterations.) "The middle term is 'He who says
that 5 is *one* among all numbers less than 10.' He speaks truth; and he,
who says that 5 is less than 10 and more than 6, certainly says that 5 is
one among all numbers less than 10. The equivocation is in the two
different uses of the word 'one': in the first Premiss, it is an entirely
indefinite 'one'; in the second it is a less indefinite 'one.' The 'one' is
not attached to the quantity of the middle term, which is universal in the
first Premiss, and particular in the second; but it is part of the middle
term itself."]

(§2) Men Tall and Numerous

This involves the Fallacy of *Vox Ambigua*. The phrase "men over 5 feet
high" may be taken to mean, either "*every* man over 5 feet high," or "the

Class composed of men over 5 feet high" regarded as *one single Thing.*
(See Part I, Book I, Chapter II.)

With the *first* interpretation, the Premisses are not true: the Attribute
"numerous" cannot be applied to an individual man.

With the *second* interpretation, the Subject of each Premiss is a *single
Thing*; and what the Conclusion asserts is that one of these two single
Things is *not* the other. In this case, the Syllogism is valid, and the
Conclusion true.

(§3) The Socialist Orator and the Irish Mob

At first sight, this reply might be thought to *support* the position taken by
the orator: but, on further examination, it is seen to *contradict* it. The
Paradox, here involved, may be logically stated as follows:

The orator's implied assertion is that, in *every* Pair of men, *each* is *not less
good* than the other; from which it may easily be proved that *every* Pair of
men possesses the Attribute "*equal* in merit."

Pat's ready reply asserts that, in *every* Pair of men, *each* is better than the
other; i.e. that *every* Pair of men possesses the Attribute "*unequal* in merit."
This not only contradicts the previous assertion, but also contradicts
itself, since it may easily be shown to involve the assertion that *each* is at
once *better*, and *worse*, than the other. But *self-contradiction*, in a Proposition, is not an Attribute that would for a moment discredit it in the
Emerald Isle!

(§4) Death at Any Moment

The best explanation I can find, for this bewildering Paradox, does not
altogether satisfy me; and I shall be grateful to any Reader who will
suggest a better. My solution is as follows:

This is a *mathematical* Paradox. The first clause of it asserts that, at any
given moment during a certain period (say the next ten years), the death
of Mr. E. Drood *possibly may* occur: Now, if we take n to represent the
number of moments in the period, and assume that the event is equally
likely at each moment, the probability of its occurrence is $1/n$th of certainty, and therefore is *not* (what the word "probable" usually implies)
greater than one-half of certainty. Hence the Proposition is necessarily
false, even if we assign to n its *minimum* possible value, viz. 2. If, however,
we re-word the Proposition thus, "At any given moment, during the next

period of *n* moments, your death possibly *may* occur, and there is a probability, amounting to 1/*n*th of certainty, that it *will* occur," we make it logically correct.   But it is to be feared that it has lost, during the corrective process, all the sparkle and humour with which it came from the pen of its ingenious author!

(§7) On the Way to the Barber-Shop[1]

The Paradox, of which this story is an ornamental presentment, seems to be a very real difficulty in the Theory of Hypotheticals.   The disputed point has been for some years under discussion by several practised Logicians, to whom I have submitted it, and the various conflicting opinions, which my correspondence with them has elicited, convince me that the subject needs further consideration, in order that logical teachers and writers may come to some agreement as to what Hypotheticals are, and how they ought to be treated.

The original controversy, which arose, about the year 1893, between two students of Logic, may be symbolically represented as follows:

Let there be three Propositions, represented by *A*, *B*, *C*.

Let it be given that
  (1) If *C* is true, then, if *A* is true, *B* is not true;
  (2) If *A* is true, *B* is true.   Can *C* be true?

The Reader will see that, if, in these two Propositions, we replace the letters *A*, *B*, *C*, by the names "Allen," "Brown," "Carr," and the words "true" and "not true" by the words "out" and "in," we get

  (1) If Carr is out, then, if Allen is out, Brown is in;
  (2) If Allen is out, Brown is out.

These are the very two Propositions on which "Uncle Joe" builds his argument.

In connection with this matter, several very interesting questions suggest themselves, such as

  (1) Can a Hypothetical, whose Protasis is false, be regarded as legitimate?

---

[1] A *version* of this commentary appeared in *Mind* as a note to "A Disputed Point in Logic" in 1894.   In the version printed in *Mind* Carroll introduces only two propositions, *A* and *B*, at the outset.

Ch. Ch.
Oxford

Dear Sir,
    I am anxious to collect the opinions of Students of Logic on the enclosed paper, & shall be greatly obliged if you will favour me with yours, as briefly as possible.
    The paper need not be returned to me.
        Believe me,
            faithfully yours,
                C. L. Dodgson.
J. Welton, Esq.

Carroll sent out copies of his puzzles to many persons, "to all my logical friends," as he put it.   He carefully inventoried their replies and errors and sometimes assigned them points for scores.   This letter was sent to the logician J. Welton and concerns the Barber-Shop puzzle. (Morris L. Parrish Collection, Princeton University)

(2) Are two Hypotheticals, of the form "If A, then B" and "If A, then not-B," compatible?

(3) What difference in meaning, if any, exists between the following Propositions?

    (a) A, B, C cannot be all true at the same time;

    (b) If C and A are true, B is not true;

    (c) If C is true, then, if A is true, B is not true;

    (d) If A is true, then, if C is true, B is not true.

The following concrete form of the Paradox may perhaps, as embodying *necessary* truth, throw light on the subject.

Let there be three Lines, KL, LM, MN, making, at L and M, equal angles on the same side of LM.

Let Univ. be "Cosmophases"; and let $A =$ the Points K, N coincide, so that three Lines form a Triangle; $B =$ the angles at L and M are equal; $C =$ the Lines KL and MN are unequal.

Then we have

(1) If C is true, then, if A is true, B is not true;

(2) If A is true, B is true.

The first of these two Propositions is proved in Euclid I.6: the second needs no proof.

Appendix A ❧ Editor's Note on Carroll's Barber-Shop Paradox

What is known as Lewis Carroll's "Barber-Shop Paradox" is one of the more curious anomalies of logical controversy during the past eighty years.

Eight versions of the puzzle exist: One was printed above as Sections 7 to Chapters III and IV of Book XXI; seven other versions are reproduced in Appendix B, immediately following the present note.

Since its origin, the puzzle has been a subject of controversy. It arose in a disagreement carried on, largely by correspondence, between Carroll and John Cook Wilson, Professor of Logic at Oxford. Their duel began around December, 1892, and was pursued for nearly two years. The issues still exercised Wilson seven years after Carroll's death, and in 1905 he published in *Mind* a brief note in which he finally accepted Carroll's original solution. A minor scandal is connected with Cook Wilson's change of mind, and I shall go into that briefly below.

Disagreement has not been confined to Carroll and Cook Wilson. Immediately after Carroll's first publication of the paradox in 1894, philosophers and logicians began to write about it. John Venn published a solution to it in the 1894 edition of his *Symbolic Logic*. Alfred Sidgwick published two papers on it in *Mind* in 1894 and 1895—as did W. E. Johnson. Bertrand Russell discussed the paradox in *The Principles of Mathematics* in 1903, and referred to it admiringly throughout his life. *Mind* also published two essays by E. E. C. Jones concerning the puzzle in 1905—in which Jones described it, even then, as "this now ancient puzzle." In 1950 two distinguished American logicians, Irving Copi and Arthur W. Burks, took the matter up again in *Mind*, and it has since then been widely discussed in connection with controversies about material implication and modal logic.

In the course of the past eighty years, the *original* issue between Cook Wilson and Carroll has been obscured, and many different controversies concerning a number of different subjects have been *read into* Carroll's "ornamental presentation" of the plight of the three barbers. One of the main purposes of this note is therefore to clarify what is or might be at stake.

First of all, despite the use of the word "paradox" from the very beginning of the discussion, the Barber-Shop puzzle is not a genuine *logical paradox*—such as the Liar Paradox, or the paradoxes of Russell, Burali-Forti, Richard, or Grelling. On this point there is no controversy.

In fact, if we stick to the original disagreement between Cook Wilson and Carroll, *the Barber-Shop is not even much of a puzzle*. It is an almost trivially easy exercise of a sort that was very common in the logical textbooks of the late nineteenth century. Since the character of the exercises set in logic textbooks has changed radically since the late nineteenth century, my claim here may puzzle some readers, including logicians, and therefore has to be explained and defended.

The provision of a general method for dealing with exercises of the sort exemplified by the Barber-Shop was described repeatedly by Boole, Jevons, Venn, John Neville Keynes, and others as "the central problem of symbolic logic." Each of these writers believed that he had in his logical writings attained such a general method.

The kind of problem encountered in the Barber-Shop was characterised by Boole. "Boole," so Jevons reports, "first put forth the problem of Logical Science in its complete generality: *Given certain logical premises or conditions, to determine the description of any class of objects under those conditions.*"[1] Keynes puts a similar point, "The great majority of direct problems involving

---

[1] See W. Stanley Jevons, *Philosophical Transactions* (1870), and *Principles of Science* (London: Macmillan, 1874), 6, §5. See also John N. Keynes, *Studies and Exercises in Formal Logic* (London: Macmillan, 1906), p. 506.

complex propositions may be brought under the general form, *Given any number of universal propositions involving any number of terms, to determine what is all the information that they jointly afford with regard to any given term or combination of terms.* If the student turns to Boole, Jevons, or Venn, he will find that this problem is treated by them as the central problem of symbolic logic."

The "algebraic" character of this formulation of the central problem of logic is obvious, and is connected with the origin of its formulation by Boole in the course of developing his logical algebra. Given any particular term whatever—*A*, *B*, *C*, etc.—that occurs once or more in a set of propositions, the problem is to determine the total amount of combined information about the given term contained in the whole set of propositions.

The Barber-Shop problem is not the only example of such an exercise in Part II of Carroll's *Symbolic Logic.* Several are produced in Book XXII. One of these, Problem 9 of Book XXII, borrowed by Carroll from Venn, goes as follows: "There are four girls at school, Anna, Bertha, Cora, and Dora. It has been observed that (1) when Anna or Bertha (or both) stopped at home, Cora stopped at home; (2) when Bertha went out, Anna went out; (3) when Cora stopped at home, Anna stopped at home. What information is here conveyed concerning Dora?"

In Exercise 23 of the same book of *Symbolic Logic*, Carroll produces another such problem—one that had earlier been discussed both by Keynes and by Mrs. Ladd-Franklin. Its similarity to the Barber-Shop problem is particularly obvious:

"Six children, *A*, *B*, *C*, *D*, *E*, *F*, are required to obey the following rules:

"(1) On Monday and Tuesday no four can go out;

"(2) On Thursday, Friday, and Saturday, no three can stay in;

"(3) On Tuesday, Wednesday, and Saturday, if *B* and *C* are together (i.e., if both go out, or both stay in), then *A*, *B*, *E*, and *F* must be together;

"(4) On Monday and Saturday, *B* cannot go out, unless either *D* stays in or *A*, *C*, and *E* stay in.

"*A* and *B* are first to decide what they will do; and *C* makes his decision before the other three. Find: (1) When *C* must go out, (2) When he must stay in, (3) When he may do as he pleases."

This problem is worked out by Keynes, and references to his treatment are given in the notes to Book XXII of Carroll's *Symbolic Logic.*

Once the Barber-Shop problem is set in this historical context, it is obvious how it must have struck persons like Venn, Johnson, and Carroll himself—all of whom were thoroughly familiar with the kind of problem represented here, and with the routine methods of solution provided by the writers named above. By comparison to the rather tricky problem of the four schoolgirls, and the rather complicated problem of the six children, the problem of the three barbers must have seemed trivially easy.

Recall that two rules govern the movements of the three barbers, Allen, Brown, and Carr, in and out of their shop:

(1) When Carr goes out, then if Allen goes out, Brown stays in;

(2) When Allen goes out, Brown goes out.

The problem set is to determine what information these two rules provide concerning the possible movements of Carr. Cook Wilson claimed that under these conditions Carr could never leave the shop; and Carroll claimed that he could leave the shop.

I shall not rehearse Carroll's solution, which has been given above, and which is set out in great detail by his spokesmen, Outis and Uncle Jim, in the versions of the exercise which follow in Appendix B.

Outis and Uncle Jim (Carroll), and Venn, Johnson, and Bertrand Russell used virtually identical arguments to show that Carr could leave the shop. Their arguments on this point, *just as their solutions to the problems of the four girls and the six children*, happened to use a particular "model" of the "if ... then ..." or "Hypothetical" relationship which is known as "material implication." When one uses material implication, the truth of the hypothetical in which it is used is judged *entirely* by determining the truth values of the antecedent (protasis) and consequent (apodosis) involved, regardless of the *meaning* or content of the antecedent and consequent, and regardless of any causal or logical connexion between antecedent and consequent. The fact that almost all developments of symbolic logic at Carroll's time— and indeed even today—are based on material implication is due to what has been called the "unfortunate historical accident" of their having been built up on Boole's foundation—that is, on a calculus devised to deal with the relations of classes.[2]

Many contemporary logicians argue that material implication provides a weak and totally inadequate model of the "if..., then..." relationship, and have developed other stronger models, such as "strict" or logical implication, and "causal implication" to deal with hypotheticals in which there exists some causal or logical connexion between antecedent and consequent. Such logicians—Burks and Copi, for instance—have used the Barber-Shop example in illustration of their arguments; and have proceeded to fault Venn's Johnson's and Russell's use of material implication to deal with the example.

Without for a moment taking issue with efforts to achieve a more adequate understanding of implication or entailment—or of "hypotheticals"—I should like to enter certain *caveats*. First, these controversies over material implication do not affect the *original issue* between Carroll and Cook Wilson. Even under causal implication as developed by Burks and Copi, Carr may leave the shop! Far from its being the case that Wilson was striving for a more adequate model of implication, it *appears* that he did not, at least in 1892 and 1893, even understand material implication—let alone have any glimmerings of strict and causal implication. We no longer, unfortunately, have Cook Wilson's letters to Carroll (they appear, as discussed in Appendix B, to have been stolen from Christ Church in the 1920s). But it is a matter of record that he staunchly opposed mathematical logic, dismissed Boole's work as "trivial," and regarded Bertrand Russell's work as unworthy of publication. Wilson earned whatever scholarly reputation he enjoyed not as a logician but as a classical scholar.

---

[2] See C. I. Lewis and C. H. Langford, *Symbolic Logic* (New York: Dover, 1959), pp. 88–89.

On the other hand, despite the quite evident fact that Carroll used material implication in order to argue Carr out of the Barber Shop, there is evidence that he at least came to feel uneasy about the treatment of hypotheticals that this involved. He always referred to hypothetical statements as "very puzzling," and some months after the controversy with Cook Wilson had ended, he recorded the following in his *Diary* (entry for December 21, 1894): "My night's thinking over the very puzzling subject of 'Hypotheticals' seems to have evolved a new idea— that there are *two* kinds, (1) where the Protasis is *in*dependent of the Hypothetical, (2) where it is dependent on it." There is, alas, no evidence that Carroll developed this notion further; but this brief diary remark, together with the "Note" appended to the *Mind* article and the comments printed above as Chapter V, Section 7, sounds like a foretaste of what was to come a few years later and from other logicians as strict and causal implication.

If we may return from the interpretation of the disagreement between Carroll and Cook Wilson, as well as from its broader ramifications, to the historical details of the disagreement itself, I shall refer back to the "scandal" that I alluded to briefly at the beginning of this note.

It was Carroll's practice to send out versions of his puzzles to "all my logical friends," as he called them; and he carefully inventoried and compared their replies and errors, and assigned them points for scores. As he wrote to the logician J. Welton concerning the Barber-Shop puzzle, "I am in correspondence with about a dozen logicians on this curious point; &, so far, opinions seem equally divided as to C's freedom." No doubt his correspondence

afforded Carroll immense pleasure and amusement: he mentioned to his sister Loui various "traps" that he had set for Cook Wilson, and exclaimed in his *Diary*, "Now I have got him!" In order to avoid tipping his hand, and allowing his colleagues to know how *he* would solve a problem, Carroll kept his own solution to himself as long as possible. In the case of the Barber-Shop puzzle, he did not announce publicly whether he was Nemo or Outis.

Since Carroll's death, all writers on the subject have nonetheless attributed Nemo's position to Carroll, and Outis's to Cook Wilson; and this attribution is accepted in *The Lewis Carroll Handbook*. This was only reasonable, for after Carroll's death, Cook Wilson published the article in *Mind* mentioned above, in which he took up the cause of Outis and Uncle Jim, and agreed that Carr could indeed leave his shop.

Wilson evidently was cheating. Despite his pompous and self-assured note of 1905, it is obvious from Carroll's correspondence with Wilson and the successive versions of the puzzle (see my note to Version I) that Carroll had been Outis all along, and that Cook Wilson had originally, in 1892 and 1893, been Nemo.

What seems to have happened, in sum, is something like this. Carroll had originally sent along his puzzle to Wilson without any expectation that it would cause any difficulty for him, and had then found to his surprise that Wilson could not handle material implication. In a letter to Cook Wilson, now lost, written in November or December, 1892, Carroll writes, "I am charmed with your letter just received and regard it as a real 'feather in my cap' that I have caught the Professor tripping. So you would really have the courage to assert that the two Rules: (i) When I go out, I wear my hat: (ii) When I stay in, I do not wear my hat: are 'contradictory.' Yet may I venture to assure you that I own an unbroken allegiance to both and never disobey either of them."[3] In his *Diary* entry of January 21, 1893, Carroll records: "... am still unsuccessfully trying to convince the Professor of Logic [J. Cook Wilson] that he has committed a fallacy!" During the controversy itself, both parties appear to have stuck to their positions; in the months that followed, however, *both* appear to have had second thoughts— although there is some doubt that either would have conveyed these to the other. Cook Wilson gradually learned material implication, and even came to accept it, as shown by his *Mind* article of 1905. Carroll, on the other hand, began to wonder about the adequacy of material implication to express hypothetical statements.

Appendix B ✥ Versions of the Barber-Shop Paradox

There exist at least eight versions of what has come to be known as the "Barber-Shop Paradox." These are as follows.

1. "A Disputed Point in Logic." Privately printed, April 1894. Original copy in Morris L. Parrish Collection, Princeton University Library.

2. "A Disputed Point in Logic. A Concrete Example." Manuscript enclosed in letter to J. Welton, April 11, 1894. Original in Morris L. Parrish Collection, Princeton University Library.

3. "A Disputed Point in Logic. A Concrete Example." Manuscript dated April 16, 1894. Original in Christ Church Oxford Library.

4. "A Disputed Point in Logic." Privately printed, May 1, 1894. Original copy in Morris L. Parrish Collection, Princeton University Library.

5. "A Theorem in Logic." Privately printed, presumably in June 1894. Original and only known copy in Morris L. Parrish Collection, Princeton University Library. (This item is incorrectly described in *The Lewis Carroll Handbook*, p. 176, as a version of the Liar Paradox.)

6. "A Logical Paradox." Published in *Mind*, July 1894.

---

[3] Quoted in John Cook Wilson's posthumous *Statement and Inference* (Oxford University Press, 1926), p. xlii. The position attributed to Wilson here is identical to that taken by J. Welton in his *Manual of Logic*, p. 457, where it is claimed that "Either *C* or *D*" and "Either not *C* or not *D*" are incompatible. Dodgson wrote to Welton about this error on April 30, 1894. This formulation, however, differs from Nemo's eventual contention, which is that the two statements, "When I go out, I wear my hat," and "When I go out, I don't wear my hat," are incompatible.

7. "A Logical Puzzle." Privately printed, September 1894. Original copies in Morris L. Parrish Collection, Princeton University Library, and in Christ Church Oxford Library.

8. "A Logical Paradox." Printed in galley proof as Sections 7 to Chapters III and IV of Book XXI of *Symbolic Logic*, Part II. A very slightly amended version of Item 6 above. Original in Christ Church Oxford Library.

In this series we find a gradually developing presentation. The first version introduces the two disputants, Nemo (John Cook Wilson) and Outis (Carroll), and devolves about the truth of two hypothetical statements involving three propositions, *A*, *B*, and *C*.

The second and third versions, never before published, contain Carroll's first attempt to put the puzzle in concrete form. The second speaks of the movements of three men, *A*, *B*, and *C*, in and out of a house. The third devolves around a real-estate sale between two persons, one of whom is named Brown. Once again two hypotheticals and three propositions, *A*, *B*, *C*, are under examination; this time with a view to ascertaining whether *C*, "The sale is completed," can be true.

The fourth version reintroduces the disputants Nemo and Outis, and introduces for the first time Allen, Brown, and Carr. At this point Allen, Brown, and Carr have not yet taken on the occupation of barbers, but are merely three men living in a house. The issue remains whether Carr can ever go out of the house given the two hypothetical statements that govern his movements.

The fifth version, "A Theorem in Logic," puts Nemo's argument in abstract form, considering the truth of the propositions *A*, *B*, and *C* under the conditions specified by two hypotheticals—the argument being conducted algebraically.

In the sixth version, we find the familiar Barber-Shop version of the puzzle, as presented in *Mind*. Here Allen, Brown, and Carr have become barbers, and the question is whether Carr, the preferred barber, may leave the shop. The disputants are Uncle Jim (Carroll) and Uncle Joe (Cook Wilson).

In the seventh version, Allen, Brown, Carr, Uncle Joe, and Uncle Jim all disappear; and Nemo and Outis return to consider the two hypothetical statements containing *A*, *B*, and *C*. The argument here is at its most elaborate with most of the paper devoted to "Outis's Second Reply," fourfold in character. First Outis (Carroll) argues, in terms of a trio of hypotheticals, that Nemo's argument is self-destructive. Second, he offers a proof that Nemo's algebraic example fails correctly to represent the data. Third, he argues that when the algebraic example is corrected, it illustrates Outis's contention and not Nemo's. Finally, Outis offers what is described as "a simple proof of the *true* outcome of these two Hypotheticals" in terms of a truth table, showing that under certain conditions *C* can be true (or Carr can be out).

The eighth version contains only slight alterations in the *Mind* presentation.

Throughout, Carroll presses the point, against Wilson's apparently strong resistance, that a conditional (hypothetical) is false only when the antecedent is true and the conclusion false.

One's ability to interpret the exact

terms of reference of the Barber-Shop debate between Carroll and Cook Wilson would be greatly enhanced if their correspondence on this subject were preserved. In the mid-twenties it evidently still was in existence, for the editor of Cook Wilson's posthumous work, *Statement and Inference*,[1] writes that Cook Wilson's letters to Carroll, "dated from 11.xi.92 to Christmas Eve 92... were preserved by Dodgson and may be seen in the Christ Church Library."

The Librarian of Christ Church has, however, informed me that these letters are no longer preserved at Christ Church, and that there is no evidence that they were ever there. The late Deputy Librarian of Christ Church, Mr. W. G. Hiscock, recorded that the letters in question were "Never here in my time 1928–62." It is possible that they disappeared in the late 1920s at the same time that the Library of Christ Church was robbed of its copy of the 1865 *Alice*.

Version 8 has been printed in the immediately preceding chapter. The other seven versions are reproduced here.

I. A Disputed Point in Logic

There are two Propositions, A and B.

Let it be granted that

If A is true, B is true. (i)

Let there be another Proposition C, such that

If C is true, then if A is true, B is not true. (ii)

Nemo and Outis differ about the truth of C.
Nemo says C cannot be true: Outis says it may be.

Nemo's Argument

Number (ii) amounts to this:

If C is true, then (i) is not true.

But, *ex hypothesi*, (i) is true.
∴ C cannot be true; for the assumption of C involves an absurdity.

---

[1] John Cook Wilson, *Statement and Inference* (Oxford: Oxford University Press, 1926), p. xli, footnote 3.

Outis's Reply

Nemo's two assertions, "If C is true, then (i) is not true" and "the assumption of C involves an absurdity," are erroneous.

The assumption of C does *not* involve any absurdity; since the two propositions, "If A is true, B is true" and "If A is true, B is not true," are *compatible*.

But the assumption of C and A together *does* involve an absurdity; since the two propositions, "B is true" and "B is not true," are *incompatible*.[2]

Hence it follows, not that C is untrue, but that C and A cannot be true together.

Nemo's Rejoinder

Outis has wrongly divided protasis and apodosis in (ii).

The absurdity is not the last clause of (ii), "B is not true," but *all* that follows the word "then," i.e. the Hypothetical "If A is true, B is not true";
and, by (ii), it is the assumption of C only which causes this absurdity.

In fact, Outis has made (ii) equivalent to "If C is true [and if A is true], then if A is true B is not true."

This is erroneous: the words in the brackets in the compound protasis are superfluous, and the remainder is the true protasis which conditions the absurd apodosis, as is evident from the form of (ii) originally given.

[April 1894][3]

---

[2] In the printed version, "compatible" appears as "*not* contradictories," and "incompatible" appears as "contradictories." The printed version is, however, corrected in Carroll's hand; and a separate note of instruction, also in Carroll's hand, instructs the change. The paper is printed here as corrected.
[3] In his *Diary* entry for March 31, 1894 Carroll writes, "Have just got printed, as a leaflet, 'A Disputed Point in Logic' —the point Professor Wilson and I have been arguing so long. This paper is wholly in his own words, and puts the point very clearly. I think of submitting it to all my logical friends." The reference is to the version reproduced here. This version of Nemo's position may have been in Carroll's hands as early as February 1, 1884, for on that date he records in his *Diary*, "I got from Cook Wilson, what I have been so long trying for, an *accepted* transcript of the fallacious argument over which we have had an (apparently) endless fight. I think the end is near, *now*."

II. A Disputed Point in Logic[4]

A Concrete Example

Three men, *A, B, C,* are in a house, bound by two rules, which must never be violated:

(1) If *A* goes out, *B* must go out.
(2) If *C* goes out, then, if *A* goes out, *B* must stay in.
   Can *C* ever go out?

What are the various possible plans for the day?

[April 11, 1894]

III. A Disputed Point in Logic

A Concrete Example

This island consists of a Northern and a Southern Division; but I am not sure where the boundary-line is.

The Northern Division is Brown's estate: the Southern is mine.

Brown is selling his estate to me; but I do not know whether the sale is completed.

The following propositions are true:

I. If this field is Brown's, it must be in the Northern Division (for otherwise it would be part of *my* estate).

II. If the sale is completed, then, if this field is Brown's, it cannot be in the Northern Division (for otherwise it would be *mine* by purchase).

Now let

A is true = this field is Brown's
B is true = this field is in the Northern Division
C is true = the sale is completed

Then Propositions I, II, are equivalent to (i), (ii), and the question "Can *C* be true?" is equivalent to "Is it possible that the sale is completed?"

---

[4] This brief version of the puzzle is enclosed as a "concrete example" in a letter from Carroll to J. Welton dated April 11, 1894. The original is in the Morris L. Parrish Collection, Princeton University Library.

Here the two Propositions, "If A is true, B is true" and "If A is true, B is not true," both of them contain a logical sequence. Also they are *compatible*; their combined effect being "A is not true."

Hence, if C is true, A is not true: and, *vice versa*, if A is true, C is not true; i.e. A and C cannot be true together.

But there is nothing to prevent C *alone* being true; i.e. it is possible, consistently with I and II, that the sale *may* have been completed.

[April 16, 1894]

IV. A Disputed Point in Logic

There are three men in a house, Allen, Brown, and Carr, who may go in and out, provided that (1) they never go out all at once, and that (2) Allen never goes out without Brown.

Can Carr ever go out?

Nemo and Outis differ on this point.
Nemo says he cannot: Outis says he can.

The rules, by which the men are bound, may be expressed thus:
(1) If Carr goes out, then if Allen goes out, Brown does not go out.
(2) If Allen goes out, Brown goes out.

Nemo's Argument

Number (1) amounts to this:
If Carr goes out, then (2) is not true.
But, *ex hypothesi*, (2) is true.
∴ Carr cannot go out; for the assumption that he goes out involves an absurdity.

Outis's Reply

Nemo's two assertions, "If Carr goes out, then (2) is not true" and "The assumption that Carr goes out involves an absurdity," are erroneous.

The assumption, that Carr goes out, does *not* involve any absurdity; since the two propositions, "If Allen goes out, Brown does not go out" and "If Allen goes out, Brown goes out," are *compatible*.

But the assumption, that Carr and Allen go out both at once, *does* involve an absurdity; since the two propositions, "Brown does not go out" and "Brown goes out," are *incompatible*.

Hence it follows, not that Carr cannot go out, but that Carr and Allen cannot go out both at once.

Nemo's Rejoinder

Outis has wrongly divided protasis and apodosis in (1).

The absurdity is not the last clause of (1), "Brown does not go out," but *all* that follows the word "then," i.e. the Hypothetical "If Allen goes out, Brown does not go out"; and, by (1), it is the assumption, that Carr goes out, which causes this absurdity.

In fact, Outis has made (1) equivalent to "If Carr goes out [and if Allen goes out], then if Allen goes out, Brown does not go out." This is erroneous: the words in the brackets in the compound protasis are superfluous, and the remainder is the true protasis which conditions the absurd apodosis, as is evident from the form of (1) originally given.

[May 1, 1894]

V. A Theorem in Logic [5]

There are three Propositions, *A*, *B*, and *C*.

It is given that

  If *A* is true, *B* is true;   (i)

  If *C* is true, then if *A* is true *B* is not true.   (ii)

Number (ii) amounts to this:

  If *C* is true, then (i) is not true.

But, *ex hypothesi*, (i) is true.

   ∴ *C* cannot be true; for the assumption of *C* involves an absurdity.

This Theorem in Hypotheticals—that the Propositions, numbered (i)

---

[5] This item bears Carroll's correspon- June 1894.
dence number 87515, placing it in

and (ii), together prove that C cannot be true—may be illustrated by the following algebraical example:

Let

$$ax + (a - b)y + z = 5; \qquad (1)$$
$$bx + z = 6 \qquad (2)$$

Equation (1) may be stated as a Hypothetical, thus:

If ax, $(a - b)y$, and z be added together, the number 5 is obtained.
Let

A mean ax, $(a - b)y$, and z are added together;

B mean the number 5 is obtained;

C mean $a = b$.

Then we have

If A is true, B is true.

Assume that C is true; i.e. that $a = b$.

Then $(ax + (a - b)y + z)$ becomes $(bx + z)$, which, by Equation (2), must *always* $= 6$.

Hence

If C is true, then if A is true B is not true.

Therefore C cannot be true; i.e. a cannot $= b$.

[June 1894]

VI. A Logical Paradox

"What, *nothing* to do?" said Uncle Jim. "Then come along with me down to Allen's. And you can just take a turn while I get myself shaved."

"All right," said Uncle Joe. "And the Cub had better come too, I suppose?"

The "Cub" was *me*, as the reader will perhaps have guessed for himself. I'm turned *fifteen*—more than three months ago; but there's no sort of use in mentioning *that* to Uncle Joe: he'd only say "Go to your cubbicle, little boy!" or "Then I suppose you can do cubbic equations?" or some equally vile pun. He asked me yesterday to give him an instance of a Proposition in A. And I said "All uncles make vile puns." And I don't think he liked it. However, that's neither here nor there. I was glad enough to go. I *do* love hearing those uncles of mine "chop logic," as they call it; and they're desperate hands at it, *I* can tell you!

"That is not a logical inference from my remark," said Uncle Jim.

"Never said it was," said Uncle Joe: "it's a *Reductio ad Absurdum.*"

"An *Illicit Process of the Minor!*" chuckled Uncle Jim.

That's the sort of way they always go on, whenever *I'm* with them. As if there was any fun in calling me a Minor!

After a bit, Uncle Jim began again, just as we came in sight of the barber's. "I only hope *Carr* will be at home," he said. "Brown's so clumsy. And Allen's hand has been shaky ever since he had that fever.'

"Carr's *certain* to be in," said Uncle Joe.

"I'll bet you sixpence he *isn't!*" said I.

"Keep your bets for your betters," said Uncle Joe. "I mean"—he hurried on, seeing by the grin on my face what a slip he'd made—"I mean that I can *prove* it, logically. It isn't a matter of *chance.*"

"Prove it *logically!*" sneered Uncle Jim. "Fire away, then! I defy you to do it!"

"For the sake of argument," Uncle Joe began, "let us assume Carr to be *out.* And let us see what that assumption would lead to. I'm going to do this by *Reductio ad Absurdum.*"

"Of course you are!" growled Uncle Jim. "Never knew any argument of *yours* that didn't end in some absurdity or other!"

"Unprovoked by your unmanly taunts," said Uncle Joe in a lofty tone, "I proceed. Carr being out, you will grant that, if Allen is *also* out, *Brown* must be at home?"

"What's the use of *his* being at home?" said Uncle Jim. "I don't want *Brown* to shave me! He's too clumsy."

"Patience is one of those inestimable qualities—" Uncle Joe was beginning; but Uncle Jim cut him off short.

"*Argue!*" he said. "Don't *moralise!*"

"Well, but *do* you grant it?" Uncle Joe persisted. "Do you grant me that, if Carr is out, it follows that if Allen is out, Brown *must* be in?"

"Of course he must," said Uncle Jim; "or there'd be nobody to mind the shop."

"We see, then, that the absence of Carr brings into play a certain Hypothetical, whose *protasis* is 'Allen is out,' and whose *apodosis* is 'Brown is in.' And we see that, so long as Carr remains out, this Hypothetical remains in force?"

"Well, suppose it does. What then?" said Uncle Jim.

"You will also grant me that the truth of a Hypothetical—I mean its *validity* as a logical *sequence*—does not in the least depend on its *protasis* being actually true, nor even on its being *possible.* The Hypothetical

'If you were to run from here to London in five minutes you would surprise people,' remains true as a *sequence*, whether you can do it or not."

"I *ca'n't* do it," said Uncle Jim.

"We have now to consider *another* Hypothetical. What was that you
told me yesterday about Allen?"

"I told you," said Uncle Jim, "that ever since he had that fever he's
been so nervous about going out alone, he always takes Brown with him."

"Just so," said Uncle Joe. "Then the Hypothetical 'If Allen is out,
Brown is out' is *always* in force, isn't it?"

"I suppose so," said Uncle Jim. (He seemed to be getting a little
nervous, himself, now.)

"Then, if Carr is out, we have *two* Hypotheticals. 'If Allen is out,
Brown is *in*' and 'If Allen is out, Brown is *out*,' in force at once. And two
incompatible Hypotheticals, mark you! They ca'n't *possibly* be true
together!"

"*Ca'n't* they?" said Uncle Jim.

"How *can* they?" said Uncle Joe. "How *can* one and the same
protasis prove two contradictory *apodoses*? You grant that the two
apodoses, 'Brown is *in*' and 'Brown is *out*,' *are* contradictory, I suppose?"

"Yes, I grant *that*," said Uncle Jim.

"Then I may sum up," said Uncle Joe. "If Carr is out, these two
Hypotheticals are true together. And we know that they *cannot* be true
together. Which is absurd. Therefore Carr *cannot* be out. There's a
nice *Reductio ad Absurdum* for you!"

Uncle Jim looked thoroughly puzzled: but after a bit he plucked up
courage, and began again. "I don't feel at all clear about that *incompatibility*. Why shouldn't those two Hypotheticals be true together?
It seems to me that would simply prove '*Allen* is in.' Of course it's clear
that the *apodoses* of those two Hypotheticals are incompatible—'Brown
is in' and 'Brown is out.' But why shouldn't we put it like this? If
Allen is out, Brown is *out*. If Carr and Allen are *both* out, Brown is *in*.
Which is absurd. Therefore Carr and Allen ca'n't be *both* of them out.
But, so long as Allen is *in*, I don't see what's to hinder Carr from going
out."

"My dear, but most illogical, brother!" said Uncle Joe. (Whenever
Uncle Joe begins to "dear" you, you may make pretty sure he's got you
in a cleft stick!) "Don't you see that you are wrongly dividing the
protasis and the *apodosis* of that Hypothetical? Its *protasis* is simply 'Carr
is out': and its *apodosis* is a sort of sub-Hypothetical, 'If Allen is out,
Brown is *in*.' And a most absurd apodosis it is, being hopelessly incom-

patible with that other Hypothetical, that we know is *always* true, 'If Allen is out, Brown is *out*.' And it's simply the assumption 'Carr is out' that has caused this absurdity. So there's only *one* possible conclusion. *Carr is in*!"

How long this argument *might* have lasted, I haven't the least idea. I believe *either* of them could argue for six hours at a stretch. But, just at this moment, we arrived at the barber's shop; and, on going inside, we found—

Note

The paradox, of which the foregoing paper is an ornamental presentment, is, I have reason to believe, a very real difficulty in the Theory of Hypotheticals. The disputed point has been for some time under discussion by several practised logicians, to whom I have submitted it; and the various and conflicting opinions, which my correspondence with them has elicited, convince me that the subject needs further consideration, in order that logical teachers and writers may come to some agreement as to what Hypotheticals *are*, and how they ought to be treated.

The original dispute, which arose, more than a year ago, between two students of Logic, may be symbolically represented as follows:

There are two Propositions, A and B.
It is given that

(1) If C is true, then if A is true, B is not true;
(2) If A is true, B is true.

The question is, can C be true?

The reader will see that if, in these two Propositions, we replace the letters A, B, C by the names Allen, Brown, Carr, and the words "true" and "not true" by the words "out" and "in" we get

(1) If Carr is out, then if Allen is out, Brown is in;
(2) If Allen is out, Brown is out.

These are the very two Propositions on which "Uncle Joe" builds his argument.

Several very interesting questions suggest themselves in connexion with this point, such as

Can a Hypothetical, whose protasis is false, be regarded as legitimate?

Are two Hypotheticals, of the forms "If A, then B" and "If A, then not-B," compatible?

What difference in meaning, if any, exists between the following Propositions?

(1) A, B, C, cannot be all true at once;

(2) If C and A are true, B is not true;

(3) If C is true, then if A is true, B is not true;

(4) If A is true, then if C is true, B is not true.

The following concrete form of the paradox has just been sent me, and may perhaps, as embodying *necessary* truth, throw fresh light on the question.

Let there be three lines, KL, LM, MN, forming, at L and M, equal acute angles on the same side of LM.

Let A mean "The points K and N coincide, so that the three lines form a triangle."

Let B mean "The triangle has equal base-angles."

Let C mean "The lines KL and MN are unequal."

Then we have

(1) If C is true, then if A is true, B is not true;

(2) If A is true, B is true.

The second of these Propositions needs no proof; and the first is proved in Euc., i, 6, though of course it may be questioned whether it fairly represents Euclid's meaning.

I greatly hope that some of the readers of *Mind* who take an interest in logic will assist in clearing up these curious difficulties.

[July 1894]

VII. A Logical Puzzle

There are three Propositions, A, B, and C.

It is given that

If A is true, B is true; . . . . (i)

If C is true, then if A is true, B is not true . . . . (ii)

Nemo and Outis differ about the truth of C.

Nemo says C cannot be true; Outis says it can.

Nemo's Argument

Number (ii) amounts to this:

If *C* is true, then (i) is not true.

But, *ex hypothesi*, (i) *is* true.

∴ *C* cannot be true; for the assumption of *C* involves an absurdity.

Outis's Reply

Nemo's two assertions, "If *C* is true, then (i) is not true" and "The assumption of *C* involves an absurdity," are erroneous.

The assumption of *C* *alone* does *not* involve any absurdity, since the two Hypotheticals, "If *A* is true, *B* is true" and "If *A* is true, *B* is not true," are *compatible*; i.e. they can be true together, in which case *A* cannot be true.

But the assumption of *C* and *A* *together does* involve an absurdity; since the two Propositions, "*B* is true" and "*B* is not true," are *incompatible*.

Hence it follows, not that *C*, *taken by itself*, cannot be true, but that *C* and *A* cannot be true *together*.

Nemo's Rejoinder

Outis has wrongly divided Protasis and Apodosis in (ii).

The absurdity is not the last clause of (ii), "*B* is not true," but *all* that follows that word "then," i.e. the Hypothetical "If *A* is true, *B* is not true"; and, by (ii), it is the assumption of *C* only which causes this absurdity.

In fact, Outis has made (ii) equivalent to "If *C* is true [and if *A* is true], then if *A* is true, *B* is not true." This is erroneous: the words in the brackets in the compound Protasis are superfluous, and the remainder is the true Protasis which conditions the absurd Apodosis, as is evident from the form of (ii) originally given.

This Theorem in Hypotheticals—that the Propositions, numbered (i) and (ii), together prove that *C* cannot be true—may be illustrated by the following algebraical example:

Let

$$ax + (a - b)y + z = 5; \tag{1}$$
$$bx + z = 6 \tag{2}$$

Equation (1) may be stated as a Hypothetical, thus:

If ax, $(a - b)y$, and z be added together, the number 5 is obtained.
Let

A mean ax, $(a - b)y$, and z are added together;
B mean the number 5 is obtained;
C mean $a = b$.

Then we have

If A is true, B is true.

Assume that C is true; i.e. that $a = b$.

Then $(ax + (a - b)y + z)$ becomes $(bx + z)$, which, by Equation (2), must *always* = 6.

Hence

If C is true, then if A is true B is not true.

Therefore C cannot be true; i.e. a cannot $= b$.

Outis's Second Reply

This reply will include (α) a proof that "Nemo's Argument" is self-destructive; (β) a proof that his algebraical example fails, owing to its not correctly representing the data; (γ) a proof that, when corrected, it illustrates Outis's contention, viz. that Hypotheticals (i) and (ii) prove, not that C, *taken by itself*, cannot be true, but that C and A cannot be true *together*; (δ) a simple proof of the *true* outcome of these two Hypotheticals.

(α)

Let us consider the Trio of Hypotheticals (which we will call (K), (L), and (M))

(K) If X is true, Y is not true.
(L) If X is true, Y is true.
(M) If X is not true, Y is true.

It will not be disputed that (*L*) and (*M*), taken together, are equivalent to the Categorical (which we will call *N*) "*Y* is true." Hence the above Trio of Hypotheticals is equivalent to the Hypothetical and Categorical

(*K*) If *X* is true, *Y* is not true.

(*N*) *Y* is true.

For this Trio (or its equivalent Pair) two different interpretations might be proposed, viz.

(*K*) and (*L*) cannot be true together.   Hence, (*K*), (*L*), and (*M*) cannot be true together.

(*K*) and (*N*) can be true together; that is, (*K*), (*L*), and (*M*) can be true together.

These interpretations are *incompatible*.

Now, when Nemo says "The assumption of *C* involves an absurdity," the absurdity to which he alludes is the *simultaneous truth* of the two Propositions "If *A* is true *B* is true" and "If *A* is true *B* is not true."

These two Propositions are Hypotheticals of the forms (*L*) and (*K*): and, in declaring that the assumption of their simultaneous truth involves an absurdity, Nemo virtually declares that they *cannot be true together*.

Here, then, he adopts the *first* interpretation of the Trio of Hypotheticals, (*K*), (*L*), and (*M*).

Again, when he says " ∴ *C* cannot be true," the premisses, from which he deduces this conclusion, are the two Propositions "If *C* is true, then (i) is not true.   But, *ex hypothesi*, (i) *is* true."

These two Propositions are a Hypothetical and a Categorical of the forms (*K*) and (*N*): and, in deducing a conclusion from them, regarded as premisses, Nemo virtually declares that they *can be true together*.

Here, then, he adopts the *second* interpretation of the Trio of Hypotheticals, (*K*), (*L*), and (*M*).

Thus he has adopted, in the course of one and the same argument, *two incompatible* interpretations of this Trio.

Hence "Nemo's Argument" is self-destructive.

(*β*)

Let us now examine Nemo's algebraical example.

He gives us Equations (1) and (2) as *always true*.

Hence Equation (1) remains true, even when $a = b$.

Hence, his second Hypothetical is incomplete: it ought to be "If C is true, then if A is true, B is (by Equation 1) true, but (by Equation 2) not true."

Hence his algebraical example fails, owing to its not correctly representing the data.

(γ)

The two Hypotheticals, when fully stated, run thus:

If A is true, B is (by Equation 1) true;
If C is true, then if A is true, B is (by Equation 1) true, but (by Equation 2) not true.

These two may be stated as *three* Hypotheticals, viz.

If A is true, B is (by Equation 1) true;
If C is true, then if A is true, B is (by Equation 1) true;
If C is true, then if A is true, B is (by Equation 2) not true.

The second of these we omit, as it leads to no result. The other two may be more briefly stated thus:

If A and (1) are true, B is true;
If C and A and (2) are true, B is not true.

And the correct conclusion is, not that C, *taken by itself*, cannot be true, but that C, A, (1), and (2) cannot all be true *together*.

But A is *always possible*; so that we may, if we like, assume it as *always true*, and not mention it.

The two Hypotheticals may now be written thus:

If (1) is true, B is true;
If C and (2) are true, B is not true.

Therefore C and (1) and (2) cannot all be true *together*, though any *two* of them may be true *by themselves*.

Thus, if C and (1) are true, then (2) cannot be true; that is, if $a = b$ (so that Equation 1 becomes $bx + z = 5$), and if Equation (1) is true, then it cannot be true that $bx + z = 6$.

Secondly, if C and (2) are true, then (1) cannot be true: that is, if $a = b$, and if $bx + z = 6$, then it cannot be true that $ax + (a - b)y + z = 5$.

Thirdly, if (1) and (2) are true, then C cannot be true: that is, if *both* the given Equations are true, then a cannot $= b$.

This algebraical example might easily mislead an unwary reader, from the fact that its Conclusion, "C cannot be true," is (on the assumption that Equations 1 and 2 are always true) a true one.   The fallacy lies in prefixing the word "therefore," and thereby asserting that this Conclusion *follows from the two Hypotheticals*.   This is *not* the case: the *real* reason, why C cannot be true, is that *it is incompatible with Equations (1) and (2)* (by subtraction we get $(a - b)(x + y) = -1$, whence it follows that $(a - b)$ cannot $= 0$; i.e. that a cannot $= b$): the two Hypotheticals, by themselves, do *not* prove it.

(δ)

The *true* outcome, of the original Hypotheticals numbered (i) and (ii), may be very simply exhibited as follows:

Let t stand for "true," and f for "false."

There are eight conceivable combinations of A, B, and C, with regard to truth and falsity: these are as follows:

	1	2	3	4	5	6	7	8
A	t	t	t	t	f	f	f	f
B	t	t	f	f	t	t	f	f
C	t	f	t	f	t	f	t	f

Of these, Nos. 3 and 4 are forbidden by (i), and No. 1 is forbidden by (ii).

The other five combinations are *possible*; and *two* of them, viz. Nos 5 and 7, contain the condition "C is true," which Nemo believes to be *impossible* [6]

[September 1894]

---

[6] The table is not a *complete* truth table in the strictest sense in which a truth table specifies the truth value of the *compound* for each assignment of truth values to the components.   The matrix is used by Carroll for the components; but the analysis and assignment of truth values to the compounds are conducted in prose commentary on the table.

Appendix C ✧ Editor's Note on Carroll's "What the Tortoise Said to Achilles"

Carroll's story, published in *Mind*, on "What the Tortoise Said to Achilles," has remained a source of great interest to contemporary philosophers. In recent decades philosophers have repeatedly appealed to it in order to justify certain ideas about scientific explanation, and to attack the widely accepted "hypothetico-deductive model" of scientific explanation.

In his article "If, So and Because,"[1] Gilbert Ryle, of Oxford University, has denied one of the most important features of this model: its requirement that universal hypotheses or natural laws be included in the premises of explanatory arguments. Moreover, he warned that the attempt to use them as premises was not only mistaken, but led to the logical absurdity of infinite regress. If universal hypotheses do not act as premises in our explanatory arguments, what role then do they play? Ryle states that they are "inference licenses" in accordance with which one argues from, say, p to q. Instead of deducing q from the conjunction of p and some laws, we deduce q from p "in accordance with" laws. Ryle maintains that in this respect natural laws are analogous to logical rules: These too—the principle of the syllogism, for instance—cannot be incorporated as premises into arguments without leading to an infinite regress.

Although Ryle's view has been widely accepted, I know of no attempt to explain what it involves and how it is to be understood, nor of any effort to provide the view with some argumentative support. Rather, Carroll's essay on "What the Tortoise Said to Achilles" is regularly appealed to as if it were an authoritative and lucid demonstration of the view's correctness.

What actually takes place in the story? At the end of their famous race, Achilles and the Tortoise pause for a philosophical chat. At once, the indefatigable Tortoise dictates the following three statements to the dutiful Achilles, who writes them down in a notebook:

(*A*) Things that are equal to the same are equal to each other.

(*B*) The two sides of this Triangle are things that are equal to the same.

(*Z*) The two sides of this Triangle are equal to each other.

The Tortoise points out to Achilles that a person might refuse to accept the conclusion (*Z*) on two different grounds: He might deny the *truth of the premises*; or, accepting the premises as true, he might deny the *validity of the inference* from premises to conclusion. The Tortoise then asks Achilles to

---

[1] Printed in Max Black (Ed.), *Philosophical Analysis* (Ithaca: Cornell, 1950).

imagine that he (the Tortoise) is a person of the second kind, and challenges Achilles to force him logically to accept Z as true. In short, the Tortoise is to be imagined as a person who accepts A and B as true but who denies the "hypothetical" proposition:

(C) If A and B are true, Z must be true.

Through his spokesmen, Carroll indicates that even if the Tortoise can be induced to accept C as true and to incorporate it as a premiss into a new argument in which A, B, and C are premisses and Z the conclusion, the doubting Tortoise still could refuse to accept Z. For he might not accept a further hypothetical:

(D) If A and B and C are true, Z must be true.

And so on, *ad infinitum*.

Without any hesitation, Ryle extracted the following lesson from Carroll's story: "... as the Tortoise proved to Achilles... [the] principle of an inference cannot be one of its premisses or part of its premiss. Conclusions are drawn from premisses in accordance with principles, not from premisses that embody those principles.... It is not merely that the officially recognized Rules of Inference cannot be given the role of premiss components in all the specific inferences that are made in accordance with them. The same thing is true of the most 'meaty' and determinate

hypothetical statements.... In saying 'q, because p,' we are not just asserting but *using* what is expressed by 'if p, then q'; we are putting it to work or applying it... just as the inference 'p, so q' does not embody 'if p, then q' as a component of its premiss, but rather applies it in being an operation with p and q executed in conformity with it, so 'q, because p' does not embody 'if p, then q' as a component of its 'because' clause but applies it in another way."

Professor Stephen E. Toulmin has endorsed Ryle's "inference license" theory with equal assurance as follows: "Lewis Carroll showed in his paper, *What the Tortoise said to Achilles*, what impossible conclusions one is led into if one treats the Principle of the Syllogism as a super-major premise, instead of as an inference-license;... It is the same with laws of nature. The conclusions about the world which scientists derive from laws of nature are not deduced from those laws, but rather drawn in accordance with them or inferred as applications of them.... Certainly they act hardly more as premises in physical arguments than the Principle of the Syllogism does in syllogistic ones."[2]

The interpretation of Carroll's story given by Ryle and Toulmin is plainly wrong—as is the belief that the story is relevant to the problems of scientific explanation. As for the story itself, I do not share the view that there is one clear interpretation of it and its intended moral.[3] It seems most plausible to understand it as an attempt on

---

[2] S. E. Toulmin, *Introduction to the Philosophy of Science* (London: Hutchinson, 1953), p. 102. A similar argument which also refers to Lewis Carroll appears in R. Harré, *An Introduction to the Logic of the Sciences* (London: Macmillan, 1960), p. 80.
[3] Discussion and interpretation of Carroll's puzzle have been rather curious. For example, in her book *Lewis Carroll* (New York: Dover, 1972), p. 328, F. B. Lennon manages to identify it with two other problems: the Zeno problem of infinitesimals

Carroll's part to express some difficulties he felt but could not adequately explain; his failure in turn being largely due to the inadequacy of the logical theory available to him—lacking as it did the modern distinction due to Alfred Tarski between object language and metalanguage.

On the basis of contemporary discussions of the ways in which the validity of an inference may be questioned and defended, we might illustrate the following possible lesson with the Achilles story: *Given a challenge to the validity of an argument, we give no defence by simply adding in, as another premiss, a version of the logical rule in accordance with which the argument proceeds.* The validity of an argument, as opposed to the truth of the conclusion, must be defended metalinguistically. In order to defend a derivation, one would have to show metalinguistically that no counterexample exists for any interpretation of the inference which is form-preserving and whose premisses are true.[4]

Such a defence may, of course, be anything but a straightforward affair. Indeed, a number of extremely important further problems and difficulties arise in connection with the evaluation and defence of the validity of arguments. Controversy may begin over the admission of proposed counterexamples: For example, is the Cheshire Cat a counterexample to the King's rule that "anything that had a head could be beheaded"?[5] Argument may continue over which signs are to be interpreted as descriptive and which as formative. And that demarcation may in turn become controversial—as Carroll himself well knew.[6]

Moreover, if such argument is conducted in the context of what I have elsewhere called a "justification philosophy,"[7] which makes the rationality of an argument dependent on its positive justifiability, a vicious infinite regress may readily be generated in the metalanguage. It can indeed be shown through the device of the infinite regress that certain views about the possibilities of demonstrative argument

---

and the old problem of presuppositions, or of the defence of our "ultimate presuppositions," or criteria, which was implicit in Aristotle and perhaps first fully presented by the Sceptics, especially by Carneades and Agrippa (see his second, fourth, and fifth tropes). For the latter, consult Sextus Empiricus, *Outlines of Pyrrhonism*, Trans., R. G. Bury (London: Heinemann, 1933), Book I. These three problems do indeed have at least one common feature—i.e., a potential infinite regress causes the trouble in each; moreover, the first is indeed connected indirectly with the third. Still, they are distinct problems. For an attempted solution to the problem of presuppositions, see Chapters IV and V of W. W. Bartley, III, *The Retreat to Commitment* (New York: A. A. Knopf, 1962, and London: Chatto & Windus, 1964) and W. W. Bartley, III, "Rationality versus the Theory of Rationality," printed in *The Critical Approach to Science and Philosophy* (New York: Basic Books, 1964).

[4] See Alfred Tarski, "On the Concept of Logical Consequence," and "The Concept of Truth in Formalised Languages," in *Logic, Semantics, Metamathematics* (Oxford: Oxford University Press, 1956), and K. R. Popper, "Logic Without Assumptions," *Proceedings of the Aristotelian Society* (London: Harrison and Sons, 1947), pp. 251–292, especially note 21.

[5] *Alice in Wonderland* (London: Macmillan, 1965), Chapter VIII.

[6] See Carroll's remarks on the copula, in *Symbolic Logic*, Book X.

[7] See Bartley, *The Retreat to Commitment* and "Rationality versus the Theory of Rationality."

and "being forced to a conclusion" are incorrect. But as I have tried to show in the place cited, such a justificational concept of argument can be avoided; and in any case an infinite regress so generated would be quite different in character from that illustrated in Carroll's story, in which the distinction between object language and meta-language is not yet made.

Yet even if Carroll's story *were* a perfect illustration of some important logical dilemma it is difficult to see how such problems about *valid inference* and *proof* bear in any direct way upon the concept of *satisfactory explanation*—or how they support at all the comments made by Ryle and Toulmin about the role of universal hypotheses in arguments. For the explanation model is not a picture of a standard of proof or demonstration. When one explains *q* by citing *p*, one is not faced with the task of finally proving that *q* happened or forcing a doubting Tortoise to accept *q*. Rather, the assumption is that *q* happened; what is required is a highly testable set of premisses from which *q* may be *derived* (not *demonstrated*).

Once this has been understood, it is easy to see that the mere addition of some further premisses—including natural hypotheses of universal form—cannot in itself lead to any infinite regress. For the existing argument is either valid or invalid. Suppose it is valid. In accordance with the logical rule of augmentation of premisses, we can add *any* premiss we like to a valid argument without affecting that validity. The rule of augmentation of premisses may be expressed thus:

$$a_1, \ldots, a_n/b \rightarrow a_1, \ldots, a_{n+1}/b$$

To explain in ordinary English: If the conclusion "Socrates is mortal" can be derived from the two premisses "Socrates is a man," and "All men are mortal," then "Socrates is mortal" may also be derived from the augmented set of three premisses: "Socrates is a man," and "All men are mortal," and "Socrates is a philosopher." To take another example, "Socrates is mortal" may be validly derived from the set of premisses: "Socrates is a man," and "All men are mortal," and "The moon is made of green cheese." It is interesting to note in this connection that the first three statements dictated by the Tortoise, i.e. *A*, *B*, and *Z*, did constitute a valid argument from Euclidean geometry.

But what if the original argument is not valid? Could the addition of a natural law premiss to an *invalid* argument lead to logical paradox? Provided the added premiss is consistent, the answer to this question is also negative. At best, the addition of the law statements to the existing argument will render it valid; i.e., the conjunction of the law premisses and the others will logically entail the conclusion. At worst, the altered argument will remain invalid.

What leads to an infinite regress is not the use of any particular statement, be it logical rule or natural law, to strengthen or to defend an argument, whether valid or invalid, but the claim that one can thereby finally establish or prove the truth of a conclusion or the validity of an argument.

One final explanatory comment and question may be raised here. Behind the arguments of Ryle and Toulmin, and their belief that the Achilles story is relevant here, is a familiar instrumentalist view of science. On such a view, scientific hypotheses are usually regarded not as true or false statements but rather as "transformation rules" for getting one empirical observation statement out of another. This is not the place to discuss the advantages and disadvantages of instrumentalism. But even if we were to assume the instrumentalist view as correct—i.e., even if scientific laws were *no more* than rules of inference—it might be asked whether it follows that scientific laws, so interpreted, would be sufficiently analogous to *logical* rules of inference to support the contention that a logical difficulty that is supposed to apply to one will also apply to the other?[8]

I reproduce here two letters in the Parrish Collection at Princeton between Carroll and G. F. Stout, editor of *Mind*, concerning "What the Tortoise Said to Achilles." The letter from Dodgson to Stout appears from the marking at the top of the page to have been a first draft of his reply to Stout's question and the final version may have differed somewhat. Carroll's reply to Stout's specific question, as given here, is quite in order: The point of the puzzle does not turn on any claimed difference between "affirming *A*" and "affirming the truth of *A*."

I also produce a copy of a letter from Carroll to Cook Wilson which suggests that the question of the difference between a premiss and a rule of inference was at issue between them in 1896. The original of this letter is to be found in the John Sparrow Collection, All Souls College, Oxford.

---

[8] On the more general problem involved here, see W. W. Bartley III, "Achilles, the Tortoise and Explanation in Science and in History," in *British Journal for the Philosophy of Science*, May 1962.

> St John's College,
> Cambridge.
> August 24 1894
>
> Dear Sir,
>
> Is there any difference between affirming <u>A</u> and affirming the <u>truth</u> of <u>A</u>? If there is <u>no</u> difference, there would appear to be no point in your puzzle; if there <u>is</u> a difference, ought you not to bring it out? What do you say?
>
> Yours very truly,
> G. F. Stout.
>
> Jevons states as a primary law of Logical Symbolism :— A . A = A .

An exchange of letters between G. F. Stout, editor of *Mind,* and Carroll concerning "What the Tortoise Said to Achilles." (Morris L. Parrish Collection, Princeton University)

[Reproduce
all this,
as 87845]

7. *Lushington Road,*
Eastbourne.
Aug. 25/94

Dear Sir,

Of course affirming a Proposition, & affirming
that the Proposition is _true_, are the same thing: but
if 'A' represents a long enunciation, it is very convenient
to be allowed to say 'A is true', instead of quoting it
at full length. My paradox does _not_ attempt to draw
any distinction between these 2 proofs: it turns on
the fact that, in a Hypothetical, the _truth_ of the
Protasis, the _truth_ of the Apodosis, & the _validity of_
the sequence, are 3 distinct Propositions.

For instance, if I grant

(1) All men are mortal, & Socrates is a man.

but _not_ (2) The sequence "A# of all men are mortal
and if Socrates is a man, then Socrates is mortal"
is valid.

then I do _not_ grant

(3) Socrates is mortal.

Again, if I grant (2), but _not_ (1), I still fail
to grant (3).

Hence, _before_ granting (3), I must grant (1) & (2)
We may call this write this assertion viz.

(4) "Before granting (3), I must grant (1) & (2)")

in the form

(4) "If (1) and (2) be true, then (3) is true".

Now suppose I _deny_ this last sequence to be
a valid one? Suppose I say "I grant (1) & (2), but
I do _not_ grant that I am thereby obliged to grant (3)"

Surely, my granting (3) must wait until I
have been made to see the validity of this sequence:
i.e. in order to grant (3), I must grant (1), (2), & (4)!

And so on.

I think you will find that it goes on like
"the house that Jack built."

Very truly yours,
C. L. Dodgson

[T. O.]

P. S.

To make my meaning clear, I will write out, in full, some of the series of Propositions, whose truth is needed to prove "Socrates is mortal."

(1). All men are mortal and Socrates is a man.

(2) If "all men are mortal and Socrates is a man", ~~then~~ "Socrates is mortal."

(3) If (1)" all men are mortal and Socrates is a man" and if the Hypothetical (2)" if "all men are mortal and Socrates is a man, then Socrates is mortal" be a valid sequence, then Socrates is mortal.

(4) If (1)" all men are mortal & Socrates is a man", and if the Hypothetical (2)" if all men are mortal & Socrates is a man, then Socrates is mortal" be a valid Sequence, and if the Hypothetical (3)" if the Proposition (1)" all men are mortal & Socrates is a man" be true and ~~also~~ if the Hypothetical (2)" if all men are mortal & Socrates is a man, then Socrates is mortal" be a valid Sequence, ~~and if the Hypothetical (3)" if (1) all men are mortal & Socrates is a man, & if the Hypothetical (2)" if all men are mortal & Socrates is a man, then Socrates is mortal" be a valid sequence, then Socrates is mortal~~

then Socrates is mortal

Propositions which must
be true, to prove "Socrates
is mortal".   25/8/94

(1) All men are mortal & Socrates is a man.

(2) If (1) All men are mortal & Socrates is a man,
then Socrates is mortal.

(3) If (1) All men are mortal & Socrates is a man,
and if (2) " If (1) All men are mortal and
Socrates is a man,
then Socrates is mortal "
then Socrates is mortal.

(4) If (1) All men are mortal & Socrates is a man,
and if (2) " If (1) All men are mortal & Socrates
is a man,
then Socrates is mortal "
and if (3) " If (1) All men are mortal & Socrates
is a man,
and if (2) " If (1) All men are mortal
& Socrates is a man,
then Socrates is mortal "
then Socrates is mortal "
then Socrates is mortal.

Ch. Ch. Oxford
Dec. 14/96

My dear Wilson,

I feel very guilty in causing you to write so many long letters, & in proving myself so heretical on points where we differ. But they are not matters which will appear in Part II: so I don't think they are worth your further consideration.

What you say about "Conclusions" is most interesting. One passage is I think worth troubling you about, as I don't accept the position you assign to me. You say

"In your view it seems that to conclude, from 'S is M' and 'P' is M',' that 'SP' is MM',' is merely to give, as Conclusion, the sum of the Premisses."

To this I agree. You proceed

"Yet 'SP' is MM'' yields SP' is impossible."

To this I demur—if you mean, by the word "yields," that it yields it as an *immediate inference*, i.e. that it *contains* it. In my view, it does *not* contain it, & cannot be made to prove it, without the help of *another* Proposition, viz. "MM' is impossible."

Yours very truly,
C. L. Dodgson.[9]

---

[9] At the bottom of this letter Cook Wilson scribbles: "In reply I proved to Dodgson that inferences which he considered *immediate* also involved the very principle of Contradiction & then he was conquered. Further I shewed that it is a fallacy to treat the principle of Contradiction as a premiss. It's a rule of thinking not a premiss, a rule for manipulating material not part of the material manipulation."

BOOK XXII[1]

SOLUTIONS OF PROBLEMS SET BY OTHER WRITERS

Chapter I ☙ Problems

The books, from which the following twenty-five Problems are quoted, are as follows:

[A] *An Investigation of the Laws of Thought.* By George Boole, LL.D. London, 1854, Demy 8vo.

[B] *Formal Logic.* By Augustus DeMorgan. London, 1847, Demy 8vo.

[C] *Memoir of Augustus DeMorgan.* London, 1882, Demy 8vo.

[D] Article, by Augustus DeMorgan, published in *Notes and Queries*, 2nd Series, Vol. IX, p. 25. London, 1860.

[E] Articles, by W. B. Grove, B.A., published in *The Educational Times*. London, 1881.

---

[1] Carroll's correspondence number 96409 appears on the galley proofs for this book, placing the printed version in April 1897. Only Chapter I survives. Presumably Chapter II, following the pattern of the preceding book, would have contained solutions to the problems set in Chapter I. Some of Carroll's solutions to these problems are given in draft in his logic workbook, preserved in the Princeton Library. Samples are given in the illustrations to this book.

[F] *The Principles of Science.* By W. Stanley Jevons, M.A., F.R.S. London, 1874, Demy 8vo.

[G] *Studies and Exercises in Formal Logic.* By John Neville Keynes, M.A., Sc.D. Second Edition, London, 1887, Crown 8vo.

[H] The same. Third Edition, London, 1894, Demy 8vo.[2]

[J] *Symbolic Logic.* By John Venn, Sc.D., F.R.S. Second Edition, London, 1894, Crown 8vo.

[K] *Studies in Logic.* By Members of the John [sic] Hopkins University. Boston, 1883, Demy 12vo.

1. [F] Vol. I, p. 77

All planets are subject to gravity;
Fixed stars are not planets.

Let a = planets; b = fixed stars; c = subject to gravity. The Reader will try in vain to produce from these Premises, by legitimate substitution, any relation between b and c.

[Nevertheless I recommend him to try!]

2. [B] p. 124.   Quoted in [H] p. 432[3]

Every A is one only of the two B or C. Every D is both B and C, except when B is E; and then it is neither.

[The Problem is to prove that no A is D.]

3. [J] p. 342[4]

If x that is not-a is the same as b, and a that is not-x is the same as c, what is x in terms of a, b, and c?

---

[2] The sale of Carroll's effects in 1898 included a copy of the third edition of Keynes's work inscribed, "Rev. C. L. Dodgson, with the author's kind regards."

[3] Problem 2 is partly worked in Carroll's copybook, preserved in the Princeton University Library.

[4] Venn takes this from Lambert's *Logische Abhandlung*, I. 14.

4. [J] p. 340

At a certain town where an examination is held, it is known that
- (1) Every candidate is either a junior who does not take Latin, or a senior who takes Composition;
- (2) Every junior candidate takes either Latin or Composition;
- (3) Every candidate, who takes Composition, also takes Latin, and is a junior.

Show that, if this be so, there can be no candidates.

5. [F] Vol. I, p. 191

For every man in the house there is a person who is aged: some of the men are not aged.

[The Problem is to prove that some persons in the house are not men.]

6. [J] p. 336.   Quoted in [H] p. 433

There is a certain Class of Things, from which A picks out all the x that are z and all the y that are not-z; and B picks out from the remainder the z which are y and the x that are not-y.   It is then found that what is left exactly comprises the Class of z that are not-x.   What can be determined as to the original Class?

7. [J] p. 350.   Quoted in [H] p. 437, and [K] p. 53

Given $xy = a, yz = c$: find xz in terms of a and c.

8. [C] p. 209

- (1) For every Z there is an X which is not Y;
- (2) Some Y's are Z's.
    - Required the inference.

9. [J] p. 345

There are four girls at school, Anna, Bertha, Cora, and Dora.   It has been observed that
>   (1) When Anna or Bertha (or both) stopped at home, Cora stopped at home;
>   (2) When Bertha went out, Anna went out;
>   (3) When Cora stopped at home, Anna stopped at home.

What information is here conveyed concerning Dora?

10. [D] p. 25

A Question in Logic.   A great many persons think that without any systematic study it is in their power to see at once all the relations of Propositions to one another.   With some persons this is nearer the truth than with others: with some it is all but the truth; that is, as to all such relations as frequently occur.   I propose a case which does not frequently occur; and I shall be curious to see whether you receive more than one answer; for I am satisfied, by private trial, that you will not receive many.

Take the three following assertions:
>   (1) A master of a person is a superior;
>   (2) A servant of an inferior is not a parent;
>   (3) An inferior of a child is not a master.

It is to be understood that *absolute* equality between two persons is supposed impossible; so that, any two persons being named, one of them is the superior of the other.   Is either of these Propositions a consequence of another?   Is either a contradiction of another?   Are any two of them indifferent?

[The wording of these Propositions is a little confusing.   The writer's meaning may, I think, be more clearly expressed as follows:
>   (1) The master of a man's father is that man's superior;
>   (2) A man-servant of a man's inferior is not that man's father;
>   (3) An inferior of a man's son is not that man's master.

It is evident, from the writer's own solution of this Problem, that he does not regard these Premises as asserting the *existence* of their Subjects.]

Carroll's Essay on DeMorgan's Problem[5]

[Your solution is *nearly* right.   You have made the Propositions identical, in asserting xy'_0, but you make them differ in that (1) asserts x_1, while (2) and

---

[5] Carroll was intrigued by the problem just presented, and created a difficult problem modelled on it that has been printed above as Chapter IX of Book XIII. Appended here is a short essay on DeMorgan's problem showing Carroll's own

(3) assert y'_1. You have a right to assert x_1 in No. (1): i.e. you have a right to say "*B* possesses a parent's master: for I do not mean to apply the name *B* to any one that hasn't: such men are not concerned in Prop. (1)." Similarly, in No. (2), you have a right to call the man *C*, and to say "I only apply this name to men who *have an inferior*." But you have no right to use *B* in both cases: for *this* is as much as to say "I only apply Prop. (1) to men who have a parent's master *and also* have an inferior: no other men are concerned in it": and this is not true: any man is concerned in it who *has a parent's master*: he need not be known to *have an inferior*. No doubt the Proposition *asserts* that he has an inferior: but that does not require him to *have* one: for the Proposition may be false.

Also you say "the third is *contained* in the second." This is incorrect. They are, in your solution, *identical*.

The best way of solving it is, I think, the "Method of Cosmophases." A "Cosmophase" is the state of the Universe at some particular moment: and I regard any Proposition, which is true at that moment, as an *Attribute* of that Cosmophase. Thus, if x and y represent Propositions, the assertion "x proves y" is equivalent to "All x-Cosmophases, if any exist, are y-Cosmophases." But this must not be written $x_1 y'_0$, since *this* would assert that x-Cosmophases *do* exist; i.e. that x is *sometimes true*: which we have no right to assert. All we mean to assert is that, *if* any x-Cosmophases *did* exist, they *would* be y-Cosmophases. And this is fully expressed by xy'_0.

The solution is

(1) A master of a man's parent is that man's superior;
(2) A servant of a man's inferior is not that man's parent;
(3) An inferior of a man's child is not that man's master.

Univ. "Cosmophases"; $a = X$ is parent of Y; $b = Z$ is master of X; $c = Z$ is superior of Y; hence $c' = Y$ is superior of Z.

(1) If X is parent of Y, and if Z is master of X, then Z is superior of Y;
(2) If Z is inferior of Y, and if X is servant of Z, then X is not parent of Y;
(3) If Y is child of X, and if Z is inferior of Y, then Z is not master of X.

i.e. (1) $ab \, ¶ \, c$; (2) $c'b \, ¶ \, a'$; (3) $ac' \, ¶ \, b'$.

$$\overset{1}{} \quad \overset{2}{} \quad \overset{3}{}$$
i.e. $abc'_0 \dagger c'ba_0 \dagger ac'b_0$

Hence the three Propositions are *identical*.

You should get Miss Puckle to cure herself of her morbid love of *truth*. In Logic, we are *not* concerned with the question: "Are the Premisses *true*?" but merely with the question, "*If* they *were* true, would the Conclusion be necessarily *also* true?"]

---

solution. Since the original essay (dated March 15, 1897), which bears no address or heading, is preserved in the Dodgson Family Collection at Guildford, it was probably addressed to Louisa.

11. [C] p. 209

"To say nothing of those who succeeded by effort, there were some who owed all to fortune, for they gained the end without any attempt whatever, if indeed it be not more correct to say that the end gained them.   But for every one who was successful with or without effort, at least one could be pointed out who began, but abandoned the trial before the result was declared.   And yet, so strangely is desert rewarded in this world, there was none of these faint-hearted men but was as fortunate as any of those who used their best endeavours."

I will answer for it that, if this were presented to any writer on Logic without warning, he would pass it over as not self-contradictory at least. But, for all that, it contains the same error as the following: "All men are animals and some are not."

12. [J] p. 343

If every xy is zw, does it follow that the Class, in which every z is x, is the same as that in which every y is w?

13. [G] p. 418

At a certain examination it was observed that (i) All candidates, who took Greek, took Latin also; (ii) All, who did not take Greek, took English and French, and, if they took Latin, they took German also; (iii) All, who took Latin and Greek but not English, did not take French; (iv) All, who took Latin and Greek but not French, did not take German.

Shew that (1) All took either English or else both Latin and Greek; (2) All took either Latin or else both English and French; (3) All, who took French, took English also; (4) All, who took German, also took both English and French; (5) All, who did not take English, did not take either French or German, but took both Latin and Greek; (6) All, who did not take French, took Latin and Greek but not German; (7) All, who took Latin, and also either took German or did not take Greek, took English, French, and German; (8) All, who took both Greek and German, took English, Latin, and French; (9) All, who took neither Greek nor German, took English and French but not Latin; (10) Every candidate took at least two languages, and no candidate, who took only two, took German.

14. [G] p. 408

A given Class is made up of those who are not either male guardians, or female rate-payers, or lodgers who are neither guardians nor rate-payers.

How can we simplify the description of this Class, if we know that all
guardians are rate-payers, that every person who is not a lodger is either a
guardian or a rate-payer, and that all male rate-payers are guardians?

15. [G] p. 410

If thriftlessness and poverty are inseparable, and virtue and misery are
incompatible, and if thrift be a virtue, can any relation be proved to exist
between misery and poverty? If moreover all thriftless people are either
virtuous or not miserable, what follows?

[The writer evidently means the phrase "thrift is a virtue" to be regarded
as equivalent to "all thrifty people are virtuous."]

16. [G] p. 380, and [H] p. 413

Given that whatever is hk or ah is $b'cd$ or $a'b'd'e$ or $a'bcd'e$ or $ab'c'd'$, shew
that (1) All $a'b'h$ is cd or $d'e$ or k; (2) All dh is $b'c$ or $a'k'$; (3) All b or cd' or
$c'd$ is a' or h'; (4) All b is c or h' or $a'k'$; (5) All cd' is a' or h'; (6) All ab
is h'; (7) All $a'e'$, that is c' or d', is h' or k'; (8) All bh, that is c' or d, is
$a'k'$.

17. [A] p. 146.   Quoted in [H] p. 434, [J] p. 351, and [K] p. 82

Let the observation of a class of natural productions be supposed to have
led to the following general results.
   First, that, in whichsoever of these productions the properties A and C
are missing, the property E is found, together with one of the properties
B and D, but not with both.
   Second, that, wherever the properties A and D are found, while E is
missing, the properties B and C will either both be found or both be
missing.
   Third, that, wherever the property A is found in conjunction with either
B or E or both of them, there either the property C or the property D
will be found, but not both of them. And conversely, wherever the
property C or D is found singly, there the property A will be found in
conjunction with either B or E or both of them.

[The inferences which Mr. Boole proposes, to be proved from these *Data*,
are as follows:]

In whatever substances the property A is found, there will also be found
either the property C, or the property D, but not both, or else the
properties B, C, and D will all be missing. And conversely, wherever

either the property C or the property D is found singly, or the properties B, C, and D are together missing, there the property A will be found.

Wherever the Property A is absent and C present, the property D is present.

Wherever the property B is present, either the properties A, C, and D are all absent, or else some one alone of them is absent. And conversely, wherever they are all absent, the property B is present.

Wherever the properties A and C are both present or both absent, the property D is absent.

[Mr. Venn says, in reference to the above Problem, that it is, he thinks, "the most intricate of any given by Boole."][6]

18. [K] p. 52

What are the precise points of agreement and difference between two disputants, A and B, if A asserts that "space = three-way spread with points as elements," while B asserts that "space = three-way spread," and at the same time admits that "space has points as elements"?

19. [K] p. 53.   Quoted in [H] p. 438

From the Premisses, (1) ax' is not $c'(d'$ or $y')$; (2) bx is not $c'(d'$ or $y')e'$; (3) $a'b'$ is not $x'(d'$ or $e)c'$; (4) a or b or c is not $x'y'$, deduce a Proposition containing neither x nor y.

20. [A] p. 134

(1) Virtue is either a passion or a faculty or a habit;

(2) Passions are neither things according to which we are praised or blamed, nor things in which we exercise deliberate preference;

(3) Faculties are not things according to which we are praised or blamed, and which are accompanied by deliberate preference;

---

[6] John Cook Wilson has scribbled and signed the following comment on the galley proof here: "This most 'intricate' prob. is very simply settled by my method which shews four super-fluous premisses." Part of Wilson's continuing script is illegible, but it contains the words "in fact Boole case is both clumsy & inadequate to a degree."

(4) Virtue is something according to which we are praised or blamed, and which is accompanied by deliberate preference;

(5) Whatever art or science makes its work to be in a good state avoids extremes, and keeps the mean in view relative to human nature;

(6) Virtue is more exact and excellent than any art or science.

[What can be inferred concerning virtue? The writer evidently regards Premisses (5) and (6) as equivalent to "Every thing human, which makes its work to be in a good state, keeps the mean in view relative to human nature" and "Virtue makes its work to be in a good state."]

21. [E] Feb. 1, 1881.   Quoted in [H] p. 439, and [K] p. 54

The Members of a scientific Society are divided into three sections, which are denoted by *a, b, c*.   Every Member must join one, at least, of these sections, subject to the following conditions:

(1) Any one, who is a member of *a* but not of *b*, of *b* but not of *c*, or of *c* but not of *a*, may deliver a lecture to the other members, if he has paid his subscription, but otherwise not;

(2) Any one, who is a member of *a* but not of *c*, of *c* but not of *a*, or of *b* but not of *a*, may exhibit an experiment to the other members, if he has paid his subscription, but otherwise not;

(3) Every Member of the Society must either deliver a lecture or exhibit an experiment every year.

Find the least possible addition to these rules which will compel every Member of the Society to pay his subscription or forfeit his Membership.

22. [E] Ap. 1, 1881.   Quoted in [A] p. 237

A number of pieces of cloth, striped with different colours, were submitted to inspection, and the following two observations were made upon them:

(1) Every piece, striped with white and green, was also striped with black and yellow; and *vice versâ*.

(2) Every piece, striped with red and orange, was also striped with blue and yellow; and *vice versâ*.

It is required to eliminate yellow, and to express the conclusions in terms of green.[7]

---

[7] This problem is worked by Carroll in   commentary, p. 486–487.
his notebook. See illustration and

Studies in Logic

p. 55.

$$wg_1(by)'_0$$
$$by_1(wg)'_0$$
$$dr_1(uy)'_0$$
$$uy_1(dr)'_0$$

eliminate y, & express result in terms of

(1)	wgb'_0	3,4		b	3,4	1
(2)	wgy'_0			d	5,6	7
(3)	byw'_0	1,2		g	1,2	4
(4)	$bg g'_0$	1,2		r	5,6	8
(5)	dru'_0	7,8		u	7,8	5
(6)	dry'_0			y	3,4,7,8	2,6
(7)	uyd'_0	5,6		w	1,2	3
(8)	uyr'_0	5,6				

$$\left.\begin{array}{l}(2)\ wgy'\\(6)\ dry'\end{array}\right\}\ y'\{(wg)'(dr)'\}'_0$$

$$\left.\begin{array}{l}(3)\ byw'\\(4)\ bg g'\\(7)\ uyd'\\(8)\ uyr'\end{array}\right\}\ y\{(bw')'(bg')'(ud')'(ur')'\}$$

$$\therefore\ \{(wg)'(dr)'\}\{(bw')'(bg')'(ud')'(ur')'\}_0$$

On these two pages reproduced from Carroll's workbook, preserved in the Princeton Library, we see him working out his answer to Problem 22 of this book.

23. [K] p. 58. Quoted in [G] p. 423, and [H] p. 440[8]

Six children, *A, B, C, D, E, F*, are required to obey the following rules:

   (1) On Monday and Tuesday no four can go out;

---

[8] In the fourth edition of Keynes's work *Studies and Exercises in Formal Logic* (London: Macmillan, 1906), which is more widely available, this problem appears on p. 520. Carroll here follows Keynes's lettering, which differs from that of Mrs. Ladd-Franklin in the original paper in the Johns Hopkins

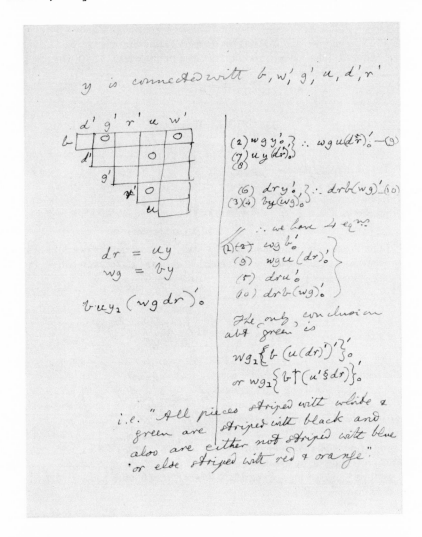

(2) On Thursday, Friday, and Saturday, no three can stay in;

(3) On Tuesday, Wednesday, and Saturday, if *B* and *C* are together (i.e. if both go out, or both stay in), then the other four must be together;

(4) On Monday and Saturday, *B* cannot go out, unless either *D* stays

---

Studies. Carroll has changed Keynes's wording slightly; for example he drops the word "together" from the phrases "go out together" and "stay in together"—an allowable move, since the question of whether those who go out or stay in remain together does not enter into the argument or the conclusion in the Johns Hopkins Studies or in those of Keynes.

in or *A*, *C*, and *E* stay in.   *A* and *B* are first to decide what they will do; and *C* makes his decision before the other three.

Find (1) when *C* must go out, (2) when he must stay in, (3) when he may do as he pleases.

24. [F] Vol. II, p. 368[9]

Let us suppose that eight objects are presented to us, which exhibit the following combinations of the five properties *a*, *b*, *c*, *d*, *e*.

1. *abcd'e*	5. *a'bcd'e*
2. *abc'd'e*	6. *a'bc'd'e'*
3. *ab'cde*	7. *a'b'cde*
4. *ab'c'de'*	8. *a'b'c'de'*

[The Problem is to discover certain "laws of correlation"[10] which must be as few and as simple as possible, which shall make these combinations the *only possible ones*.]

25. [F] Vol. II, p. 369[11]

If the reader entertains any doubt as to the difficulty of classifying combinations so as to disclose their relations, let him test the matter practically upon the following series of combinations.   They involve only six properties, which are subject to four laws of correlation of no great complexity.

1. *abcdeh*	7. *abc'de'h'*
2. *abcde'h*	8. *ab'c'd'eh'*
3. *abcde'h'*	9. *a'bc'deh*
4. *abcd'eh'*	10. *a'bc'de'h*
5. *abc'deh*	11. *a'bc'de'h'*
6. *abc'de'h*	12. *a'b'c'd'eh'*

I shall be happy to receive the solution of this problem from any reader who thinks he has solved it.

[See preceding Problem.]

---

[9] Carroll works this problem in the workbook preserved at Princeton.

[10] The "laws of correlation" Jevons requires are those of correlation between the letters yielding the above combinations.

[11] Carroll attempts this problem in the workbook at Princeton.   His solution covers many pages, and employs a two-valued tabular matrix, for which see the illustration.

This page, one of many in Carroll's logic notebook devoted to the last problem in Book XXII, uses a tabular matrix.

INDEX

"About Less" Puzzle   427, 440
Abstract Proposition   109
Achilles and the Tortoise Problems
   3, 7, 7fn, 8, 29, 426, 431–34, 438–39,
   439fn., 466–75
Adjective   64
Adjunct   59
Affirmative Proposition   68
Agrippa   468fn.
Aldrich, Henry   16, 236, 236fn.
Alice in Wonderland   3, 4, 5, 11, 33,
   468fn.
All Souls College, Oxford   10, 37,
   279fn.
Alternation   256
Anderson, Alan Ross   33
Angell, Richard B.   34fn.
Antistrephon Puzzle   426, 438
Aristotle   15, 16, 468fn.
Artis Logicae Compendium   16, 236fn.
Assertion   232–37
Attribute   59

Barbara (Aristotelian Syllogism)   378
Barber-Shop Paradox   15, 22, 23, 24,
   29, 350fn., 428–31, 442–65
Barred Premisses   279fn., 287, 287fn.,
   378fn.
Bayne, Thomas Vere   7, 8
Bell, Eric Temple   29
Beth, Evert W.   19fn., 32, 32fn.
Biliteral Diagram   79
Biliteral Proposition   83
Bishop of Oxford.   *See* Strong, Thomas
   Banks
Bishop of Peterborough.   *See* Blagden,
   Claude M.

Blagden, Claude M.   14, 14fn.
Boole, George   15, 19, 21, 22, 24, 27,
   28, 31, 34, 34fn., 445, 446, 447, 477,
   484, 484fn.
Bosanquet, Bernard   31
Bradley, F. H.   30, 31
Braithwaite, R. B.   30, 33, 33fn.
British Museum Library   37
Buder, Norman   25fn., 330fn.
Burks, Arthur W.   445, 447

Cambridge University   30, 31, 35, 36
Carneades   468fn.
Carroll, Lewis (pseud.)
   Academic career   19, 30
   Birth   19
   Children and   4, 5, 6
   Correspondence.   *See* Correspon-
      dence by Lewis Carroll
   Fame of   4
   General   3–16, 19, 21, 22, 24,
      28–36
   Nephew of.   *See* Collingwood,
      Stuart Dodgson
   Poems by   33
   Professional interests
      as logician   4, 7, 16, 28–36
      as mathematician   4, 19
      as photographer   4, 4fn.
      as writer   4, 24, 29
   Pseudonym   5, 6
   Religion and   4, 365–72
   Sister of.   *See* Dodgson, Louisa
Lewis Carroll Handbook   263fn., 448,
   449
Categorical propositions   17, 18, 34,
   256

Causal implication 447, 448

Cell 79–82

"A Challenge to Logicians" 329, 329fn.

Christ Church, Oxford 5, 7, 8, 11, 12, 14, 19, 37, 131fn., 204fn., 257, 260fn., 423, 439fn., 447, 449, 450, 451

Church, Alonzo 19fn.

Class 55, 60

Class-inclusion inference 19

Classes, arbitrary limits of 62
subdivision of 63

Classification 60

Clay, Richard (Messrs.), printers 9, 12, 386

Codivisional classes 62

Cohen, Morton N. 10, 10fn., 37

Collingwood, Stuart Dodgson 4fn., 6, 6fn

Collins, Wilkie 24

Compartment. *See* Cell

Complete Conclusion (of a Sorites) 133, 322

Conclusion(s) 16, 18, 107, 133

Conclusion of a Sorites. *See* Complete Conclusion (of a Sorites)

Conclusion of a Syllogism 107

Concrete Proposition 109

Conjunction 255, 274

Consequent in a Sorites 133

Consequent in a Syllogism 107

Contradiction 62

Contradictory of a Pair of Attributes 285, 286, 286fn.

Converse Propositions 86

Conversion (Converting) of a Proposition 86

Copi, Irving 445, 447

Copula of a Proposition 68, 232, 468fn.

Correspondence by Lewis Carroll 4, 5, 9, 10, 11, 12, 14, 15, 30, 35, 36, 238, 305fn., 310fn., 331fn., 336, 337, 338, 345–50, 355–61, 363, 364, 365–72, 373fn., 374–78, 386, 423, 448, 451, 453fn., 470–75

Counter 82

Counterexample 16, 17

Crocodile Puzzle 3, 425, 425fn., 436–38

Darapti 235

Datisi 236

"Death at any Moment" Puzzle 427, 441–42

Definition 65

DeMorgan, Augustus 19, 22, 27, 28, 30, 31, 362fn., 363, 439, 440, 480, 480fn.

DeMorgan's Laws 256, 286fn.

Derivability 256

Diaries of Lewis Carroll 9, 12, 19, 35, 338fn., 353, 360fn., 362fn., 425fn., 448, 449, 452fn.

Dichotomy 62
by contradiction 239

Differentia 60

Diogenes Laertius 438fn.

Disamis 236

Disjunction 274

"A Disputed Point in Logic" 442fn., 449, 451–55

Division 61

Dodgson, Louisa 4, 14, 36, 310fn., 346–50, 364–72, 448, 481fn.

Dodgson, The Rev. Charles Lutwidge. *See* Carroll, Lewis

Dodgson Family Collection 256, 285fn., 348fn., 481fn.

Donagan, Alan 27fn.

Double Proposition 56, 74, 75

Doyle, Sir Arthur Conan 24

Eliminand 57
of a Sorites 133
of a Syllogism 107

Entity 119

Epimenides the Cretan. *See* Liar Paradox.

Equivalence, of propositions 68, 75, 256

Euclid and His Modern Rivals 30, 35, 119fn., 134fn., 257

Euler, Leonhard 30, 240, 249

Euler's method of diagrams 231, 240–42

Examination papers 140–42

Existence 17, 55, 56, 232–8

Existential Import, of propositions 17, 34, 35, 231, 232–38, 242fn., 252, 257
Explanation 27, 466, 469

Fallacy 129, 131fn., 260–63, 260fn.
Farquharson, A. S. L. 10
Felapton 236
Ferio 247
Figures (Formulae for Syllogisms) 126, 250, 257–60, 260fn.
Five Liars Problem 3, 55, 56, 57, 352–61
Form of inference 16, 17
Formalization 18
Forms. *See* Figures
Foster, Michael 7
Four Schoolgirls Problem 446, 480
Fowler, T. 238, 238fn.
Frege, Gottlob 15, 28, 31
Fresison 236, 247
Froggy's Problem 338–42, 385fn., 402fn.

Game of Logic 5, 19, 47, 57
Gardner, Martin 19fn., 232fn.
Genealogical Method. *See* Method of Trees
Genus 60
Gernsheim, Helmut 4fn.
Gilbert, J. 31
Gilman, B. I. 31
Goclenius 250
Gorey, Edward 340
Great-Grandson Problem 362–64
Green, Roger Lancelyn 9, 9fn., 10fn.
Grocers on Bicycles Problem 381
Grove, W. B. 477
Guildford Museum and Muniment Room 37, 285fn.

Hamilton, Sir William 16, 31
Hartley, Brig.-General Sir Harold 10
Harvard University 9, 10, 37
    Harcourt Amory Collection 37, 329
Horniman, Michael 37
Hunting of the Snark 5, 7
Henry E. Huntington Library 9, 10, 11, 37, 146fn., 153fn., 158fn., 201fn., 204fn., 207fn., 364fn.

Hypothetical Propositions 256, 429–30, 442, 444, 447–50, 456–65
Hypothetical Statements 29
Hypothetico-deductive theory of scientific explanation 26, 466

Idealism 30
Implication 255–56, 447–49
In Terms of 83
Individual 61, 68
Infinite regress 468, 468fn., 469
Instrumentalism 469, 470

Jack Sprat Problem 364–73
Jacques, Philip D. 37
Jeffrey, Richard C. 32, 32fn.
Jevons, William Stanley 22, 25, 28, 31, 238fn., 445, 445fn., 446, 478
Johnson, William Ernest 30, 445, 446, 447 ·
Jones, E. E. C. 445
Jørgenson, Jørgen 15

Kanger, Stig 32, 32fn.
Keynes, John Neville 19, 22, 23, 25, 28, 30, 31, 235, 445, 445fn., 446, 478, 478fn., 486fn.

Ladd-Franklin, Christine 23, 31, 446, 486fn.
Langford, Cooper Harold 447fn.
Lattice 245
Lennon, Florence Becker 29fn., 30fn., 467fn.
Lewis, Clarence Irving 447fn.
Liar Paradox 32, 33, 352, 358, 425, 434–46, 445, 449
Library Problem 373–78
Like. *See* Like Signs of Terms
Like Signs of Terms 120
Logic
    Algebraic 15, 16, 19, 21–29, 31, 34
    Aristotelian 15–19, 19fn., 21, 24, 28, 30, 34, 255
    Central problem of 22, 23, 374fn., 445
    Continuity in the history of 24–29
    General 15–36, 46, 47, 57

Mathematical   14, 15, 16, 25–34
 Psychologistic   30
Logical Charts   263–78
 Interpretations of   269–74
"A Logical Paradox"   450, 456–60
"A Logical Puzzle"   450, 460–65
Logical Symbols. *See* Symbols, logical
Lotze, R. H.   31, 436
"Loui." *See* Dodgson, Louisa
Łucasiewicz, Jan   31

Macmillan and Company, Ltd.   9
Macmillan, Frederick O.   5, 9, 12, 30
Mansel, Henry   236fn.
Marquand, Allan   31
Material implication   256, 445, 447,
 449
Mathematics   24, 25, 27, 30, 35
Meaning   26
Members of Parliament Problem   343–
 50
"Men Tall and Numerous" Puzzle
 427, 440–41
Mentiens Paradox. *See* Liar Paradox
Metalanguage   255, 468, 469
Metaphysics   26, 360
Method of Diagrams (Carroll's)   231,
 244–46
Method of Subscripts—Table   126
Method of treating syllogisms and
 sorites   231, 250–51
Method of Trees   31, 32, 279–319,
 321fn.
Methods of Solution of Soriteses   135,
 250–51
  Method of Separate Syllogisms
   135
  Method of Trees. *See separate
   heading*
  Method of Underscoring   138–40
Methods of Solution of Syllogisms
 109ff., 231, 246–47, 250–51
  Carroll's Method of Diagrams
   249
  Euler's Method of Diagrams
   247–49
  Method of Subscripts   119ff, 249
  Ordinary Method   246–47
  Symbolic Representation   247
  Venn's Method of Diagrams   249
Mill, John Stuart   21, 31

Mind (journal)   7, 445, 466, 471
Mitchell, O. H.   31
Modal logic   445
Modes of argumentation   21
Modes of reasoning   19

Name   15, 63
National Portrait Gallery, London   37
Negation   255
Negative Copula   231, 238–39
Negative Proposition   68
Normal Form of a Proposition   55, 67,
 68
  of Existence   69
  of Relation   71
Not   62
Notation   29, 34, 35, 107, 122, 255–57
"Notice at the Seaside" Puzzle   428
Nullity   119
Numerical and Geometrical Problems
 230

Object language   256, 468, 469
Octoliteral Diagram   245
"On the Way to the Barber-Shop."
 See Barber-Shop Paradox
Ornamental presentations   29
Oxford University   4, 5, 9, 11, 14, 19,
 30, 31, 236fn.
Oxford University Press   9

Paradox   26, 423, 445
Partial Conclusion of a Sorites   133
Particular Proposition. *See* Proposition
 in (form) I
Passmore, John   24, 24fn.
Peculiar Attributes   60
Peirce, Charles Sanders   6, 6fn., 23, 30
 31
Pets Problem   382
Philosophy, contemporary   25–27
Pigs and Balloons Problem   378–80
Popper, Sir Karl Raimund   26fn.,
 468fn.
Pork-chop Problem   331–38
Port-Royal Logic   15
Predicate of a Proposition   18, 55, 67
  of Proposition of Existence   69
  of Proposition of Relation   70
Premiss(es)   16, 18, 107, 133, 470,
 475, 475fn.

of a Sorites 133
of a Syllogism 107
Presuppositions, Problem of 468fn.
Princeton University Library 5, 9, 10, 13, 37, 478fn., 486
  Morris L. Parrish Collection 13, 37, 238fn., 274, 278, 346fn., 347fn., 378fn., 379, 443, 449, 450, 453fn., 470, 471
Prior, Arthur N. 34fn., 352
Probability theory 27
Proof 469
Proposition
  General 67
  in Form A 34, 35, 56, 68, 232–37, 242fn., 251–52, 256
  in Form E 68, 232–37, 251–52, 256
  in Form I 68, 232–37, 251–52, 256
Proposition of Existence 69, 83, 96
Proposition of Relation 56, 69, 70, 85, 97, 102
Pseudomenos Paradox. *See* Liar Paradox
Puzzles (logical) 423–75

Queen Victoria 11
Quine, Willard Van Orman 7

Ramus, Peter 15
Rationality 468
Raw Meat Puzzle 426, 439
Real Class 60, 69, 76
Real Name 64
Reductio ad absurdum 31, 281
Reichenbach, Hans 27, 27fn.
Relations 18
Remainder 62
Retinend 57
  of a Sorites 133
  of a Syllogism 107
Retort Puzzle. *See* Antistrephon Puzzle
Rosenbach (Philip H., and A. S. W.) Foundation Museum 37
Rule(s) of Inference 17, 18, 470, 475, 475fn.
Rules of valid argument 16
Russell, Bertrand 15, 26, 27, 28, 29, 30, 445, 447
Ryle, Gilbert 7, 466, 467, 469

Salt and Mustard Problem. *See* Five Liars Problem
Schoolboys Problem 24, 25, 326–31
Schütte, Kurt 32, 32fn.
Self-reference 26, 32, 33, 352, 435
Semantic Tableaux 32, 32fn.
Set of Things 55
Settle, Thomas 25fn., 330fn., 372fn.
Sextus Empiricus 468fn.
Sidgwick, Alfred 445
Sign of Quantity in a Proposition 68, 69, 70
Sitting on the fence 82
Six Children Problem 23, 446, 486
Six Friends and their Wives Problem 350–51
"Small Girl and her Sympathetic Friend" Puzzle 3, 427
"Socialist Orator and Irish Mob" Puzzle 427, 441
"Some," technical meaning of 67
Sophism 423
Sorites 18, 19, 57, 133, 250–51
  Aristotelian 250
  Goclenian 250
Sparrow, John 10, 37, 279fn., 338, 358, 359, 361, 470
Species 60
Stout, George Frederick 470, 471–74
Strict implication 447, 448
Strong, Thomas Banks 14, 31
Subject of a Proposition 18, 55, 56, 67
  of Existence 69
  of Relation 70
Subscripts of Terms 119
Substantive 64
Superfluous Premisses 331fn., 345, 345fn., 349
Syllogism 16, 17, 18, 19, 21, 22, 30, 107, 122, 246–49, 250–51
Sylvie and Bruno 3, 5, 29, 29fn., 33, 225, 341, 436
Sylvie and Bruno Concluded 3, 33
Symbolic Logic (by Lewis Carroll)
  Part I 3, 4, 5, 8, 11, 12, 29, 30, 33, 35, 45–57, 76, 146fn., 153fn., 158fn., 201fn., 204fn., 207fn., 229fn., 244, 255, 256, 257, 321fn., 331fn., 365
  Part II 3, 4, 5, 7, 8, 9, 11, 12–23, 28, 29, 35, 70, 70fn., 229,

229fn., 230, 255, 256, 264, 321fn., 365, 372, 446
Part III 5, 12, 229, 229fn
Symbolic Method 231
Symbols, logical
    Subscripts 119, 256
    ∴ 107
    † 122, 255–57
    ⫪ 122, 255–57
    ′ 255–57
    § 256

Tarski, Alfred 32, 468, 468fn.
Teachers, appendix addressed to 229fn., 321fn.
Term of a Proposition 68
Texas, University of
    Humanities Research Center 37
    Helmut Gernsheim Collection 20
    Warren Weaver Collection 11, 257
Textbooks 27, 28
"A Theorem in Logic" 449, 450, 455–56
Thing 59, 64
Through the Looking-Glass 3, 4, 5, 33
Todhunter, Isaac 30, 35, 36, 36fn.
Toulmin, Stephen E. 26fn., 467, 467fn., 469
Translation of a Proposition
    from "abstract" to "subscript" 121
    from "concrete" to "abstract" 109
Triliteral Diagram 93
Truth 134fn.
Truth Table 31, 465fn.
Two Negative Premisses 231, 240

Underscoring of Letters 138
Uniliteral Proposition 83
Univ. *See* Universe of Discourse

Universal Affirmative. *See* Proposition in Form A
Universal Hypotheses 466, 469
Universal Negative. *See* Proposition in Form E
Universal Proposition 68
Universe 59, 60
Universe of Discourse 70, 107, 133
Unlike. *See* Unlike Signs of Terms
Unlike Signs of Terms 120
Unreal Class 60, 69
Unreal Name 64

Validity 16, 17, 134fn., 468, 469
Venn, John 19, 22, 25, 28, 30, 31, 34, 242, 242fn., 243, 243fn., 249, 445, 446, 447, 478, 478fn., 484
Venn's Method of Diagrams 231, 242–43, 249
Vox Ambigua Fallacy 440

Warner, William 7
Weaver, Warren 9, 10, 11
Welton, J. 439, 443, 448, 449fn., 453fn.
"What the Tortoise Said to Achilles" 431–44, 466–75
Whately, Richard 16, 16fn., 21, 21fn., 28
Whewell, William 31
Whitehead, Alfred North 28, 29, 30
Wilson, John Cook 4, 10, 14, 23, 31, 33, 35, 36, 279fn., 286fn., 305fn., 321fn., 331fn., 332fn., 336, 345, 345fn., 346, 350, 352, 353, 355–61, 362fn., 363, 373fn., 374–78, 381fn., 386, 416fn., 419fn., 445, 447, 448, 449, 450, 451, 451fn., 452fn., 470, 475, 475fn., 484fn.
Winds and Windows Problem 382–83
Wittgenstein, Ludwig 26fn., 31

Zeno's Paradox 467fn.

A NOTE ON THE EDITOR

WILLIAM WARREN BARTLEY III, is Professor of Philosophy at
California State University, Hayward.   From 1967–1973 he
taught at the University of Pittsburgh, where he held the
titles of Professor of Philosophy and of History and Philosophy
of Science, and Associate Director of the Center for the
Philosophy of Science.   Previous appointments include the
University of London, the University of California, and
Cambridge University.   Born in Pittsburgh, he graduated
from Harvard College, and received his doctorate in Logic
and Scientific Method at the London School of Economics.
He is the author of four books and many scholarly articles in
various branches of philosophy.   He has held research
fellowships from The United States Educational Commission
in the United Kingdom, the American Council of Learned
Societies, the University of California Institute for the
Humanities, the Danforth Foundation and other bodies.

A NOTE ON THE TYPE

The text of this book was set in Monotype Baskerville.
While Caslon had been influenced by the Dutch letter,
John Baskerville (1706–1775) broke with tradition and
reflected in his types the rounder, more sharply-cut letter of
eighteenth-century stone inscriptions and copy books.   His
types foreshadow the "modern" cut in such novel charac-
teristics as the increase in contrast between thick and thin
strokes and the shifting of the stress from the diagonal to the
vertical.   He realized that his new style of letter would be
most effective *if cleanly printed on smooth paper with really black
ink.*   He built his own presses, experimented with special ink
and evolved a method of hot-pressing the printed sheet to a
smooth and glossy finish.   His types never entered into
general commercial use in England until the cutting of
"Monotype" Baskerville in 1923.

This book was composed by William Clowes & Sons,
Limited, edited by Joan Lee, and designed by Hermann
Strohbach.